SERMONS AND DISCOURSES

(1839-57)

John Henry Cardinal Newman

SERMONS

AND

DISCOURSES

(1839-57)

NEW EDITION, EDITED WITH A PREFACE AND INTRODUCTION BY

CHARLES FREDERICK HARROLD

1949

LONGMANS, GREEN AND CO.

NEW YORK · LONDON · TORONTO

LONGMANS, GREEN AND CO., INC.
55 FIFTH AVENUE, NEW YORK 3

LONGMANS, GREEN AND CO. LTD.
6 & 7 CLIFFORD STREET, LONDON W I

LONGMANS, GREEN AND CO.
215 VICTORIA STREET, TORONTO I

SERMONS AND DISCOURSES (1839-57)

PUBLISHED SIMULTANEOUSLY IN THE DOMINION OF CANADA
BY LONGMANS, GREEN AND CO., TORONTO

NEW EDITION

DESIGNED BY ROBERT JOSEPHY

Printed in the United States of America

VAN REES PRESS • NEW YORK

PREFACE

O F THE SERMONS in the present volume, five are from
Newman's *Parochial and Plain Sermons*, four from
Sermons Bearing on Subjects of the Day, one from
the *Oxford University Sermons*, nine from *Discourses to Mixed
Congregations*, and four from *Sermons Preached on Various
Occasions*. The text of the first five sermons reprinted here is
that of Newman's final version, 1870-73. Sermons numbers 6,
8, 9, and 10 are presented here in the text edited, at Newman's
request, by W. J. Copeland in 1869. Newman's discourse,
number 7, on "The Theory of Developments in Religious Doctrine," the fifteenth Oxford University sermon, is here given as
it appears in the edition of 1872 (new edition, 1892). The
sermons from the *Discourses to Mixed Congregations*, numbers 11-19, which came out originally in 1849, are taken from
the seventh edition, 1891. The last four sermons in the present
volume are given in the edition of 1892. *The Sermons Preached
on Various Occasions* (1857) originally contained the eight
sermons which Newman preached before the Catholic University of Ireland, in 1856-57, during the first year of the opening of its Church; from these eight sermons, that on "Omnipotence in Bonds" is here reprinted. As this volume passed
through succeeding editions (in 1870, 1881, 1892, to mention
only a few), the author added some earlier and some later
addresses, spanning a period from the date of "Christ Upon the
Waters" (1850) to "In the World, but not of the World" (1873).
Of these, the present volume contains three sermons.

The reader may wonder why no sermon after 1857 appears

in the present collection. The answer is that in point of relevancy and content and literary quality they do not compare favorably with the sermons here presented. The sermon preached at the funeral of James R. Hope Scott, on May 5, 1873, while readable enough—when is Newman unreadable?—does not rank in any way with that preached twenty-one years before, at St. Mary's, Oscott, in the first Provincial Synod of Westminster, namely, "The Second Spring." Both sermons are the product of an occasion, but the latter sermon, as a work of art, still commands admiration; the former has lost its vitality, or, more properly, never had the vitality which the occasion of the Provincial Synod caused Newman to impart to his famous sermon on "The Second Spring."

The dates of the sermons in the present volume are those on which the sermons were first written or first preached, and are based on the chronological tables to be found in the back of Copeland's edition of *Sermons Bearing on Subjects of the Day*. The exceptions to this statement are the sermons from *Discourses to Mixed Congregations*, which are simply dated 1849, when they were first published; they were delivered, of course, in Newman's first Catholic years, probably between his ordination on May 30, 1847, and the Feast of St. Charles, 1849, which latter date Newman affixed to the dedication of the volume to Bishop (later Cardinal) Wiseman. Except for these sermons, the twenty-three sermons in the present collection are presented in exact chronological order. No alterations have been made, except in the very few cases of misprint. Newman's spelling, punctuation, capitalization, and use of italics have been left as in the original text.

Charles Frederick Harrold

The Ohio State University
Columbus, Ohio
January 19, 1948

CONTENTS

vii

INTRODUCTION

As is pointed out in the Introduction to the companion volume of this edition of Newman's sermons, the "life-expectancy" of the printed sermon has never been very high. Yet Newman's sermons and discourses continue to be read. The fame of his contemporaries in the pulpit—Robertson, Maurice, Kingsley, Thomas Arnold—has long since vanished with their spoken word. When published, their sermons provided a faint, short-lived afterglow to their memory. Newman alone, of all the great Victorian sermon-writers, survives, still as moving and eloquent in print as he was quietly stirring in the pulpit. This is not true, of course, of *all* of his sermons. A considerable number of the *Parochial and Plain Sermons* no longer have any vitality or any striking relevance to our own time. On the other hand, a sufficient number of them indicate the nature and the development of Newman's mind to make it advisable to turn to them if one is a student of his work; thus in the present two-volume selected edition of his sermons there are twenty-seven from the eight-volume set of *Parochial and Plain Sermons*. Five of these twenty-seven are the productions of Newman's mind when he was undergoing one of the most critical trials of his life.

When we turn to these sermons, numbers 1 through 5, and notice their date-span, and then observe their content, we are surprised by the fact that they reflect so little of the stormy years between 1839 and 1842. By August of 1839 Newman had become convinced that the "shadow of the fifth century was on the sixteenth,"—that the spirit of the early heresies, e.g. Monophysitism, had reappeared in the Reformation and had tainted the life of his Church. Later in the same year, he read Wiseman's article in the *Dublin Review,* and saw a parallel between the Anglican Church and the Donatist heresy of the fourth century. His theory of the English Church as occupying the *via media* between the "corruptions" of Romanism and the "errors" of popular Protestantism, was, as he later said in his *Apologia,* "absolutely pulverized." Yet in this same year he preached such quiet, uncontroversial sermons as "Present Blessings" and "Peace in Believing." Of course, it is possible to see in these gentle sermons Newman's power, in the midst of struggle, to fall back on his inner resources, just as it is possible to read 'The Thought of God, the Stay of the Soul" in terms of his consciousness of being always in the presence of God.

The background of the next sermon in our list, "The Cross of Christ the Measure of the World," is even more striking. Tract XC had appeared in February, 1841, and was condemned in March. All England was aroused over its publication and its condemnation; Newman himself was shocked at discovering how Protestant was the Church of England. Yet in the midst of this tumult, he took the opportunity of writing a series of letters to *The Times,* in highly idiomatic and sardonic style, objecting to the secularization of educational theory as seen in a recent speech of Sir Robert Peel; these letters became known later as *The Tamworth Reading Room.* While they were being read and discussed, Tract XC was being condemned, and Newman's integrity as a tutor and as an Anglican was being widely questioned. Yet a month after the condemnation, he preached "The Cross of Christ the Measure of the World," in which there is not the slightest hint that the speaker had been through a most gruelling ordeal. By the time he delivered the sermon on "The Crucifixion" Newman had begun to withdraw from his activities in Oxford, and to retire into semi-monastic seclusion at Littlemore. In all of these five selections from the *Parochial and Plain Sermons,* we see the author's growing aloofness from the world, his increasingly dogmatic, institutional, and Catholic interpretation of Christianity. It is noteworthy that all of these High-Anglican sermons could have been delivered in a Roman Catholic pulpit.

Only one of the *Oxford University Sermons* is reproduced in the present volume: "The Theory of Developments in Religious Doctrine," preached on the morning of February 2, 1843. By its very title, one can see that it treats, in sermon form, of some of the ideas to be set forth formally, with great learning and eloquence, two years later, in his *Essay on the Development of Christian Doctrine.* The ideas in Newman's sermon had a long background: in his labors on *The Arians of the Fourth Century,* in several of his contributions to the *Tracts for the Times,* and in his deep and probing study of the early Fathers which he had begun as far back as 1828. As for Newman's method and style in this sermon, one is struck by the degree in which it differs from the style and approach observed in the selections from the *Parochial and Plain Sermons.* Here we notice Newman's characteristic habit of adjusting his sermon to his hearers. He is addressing, for the most part, university students and some of the faculty, together with a number of people who have been drawn by the fame of these Oxford sermons. The manner is therefore more intellectual, expository, and academic than the one we notice in the earlier Anglican sermons. It is a reasoning, argumentative manner. Yet, characteristically, Newman in the end puts reason in her place; the sermon closes with a reminder that "reason can but ascertain the profound difficulties of our condition, it cannot remove them; it has no work, it makes no beginning, it does but continually fall back, till it is content to be a child, to follow where Faith guides it." Readers of the *Essay on Development* and of the *Grammar of Assent* should always remember these words from Newman's sermon; it may be said that he never addressed unbelievers, that he was always concerned with clarifying and substantiating the faith of those who already believed but who needed the light of reason and rhetoric to reinforce their position. According to Ward, when Newman preached his sermon on developments of doctrine, he was practically certain that "the Roman Catholic Church was the Church of the Apostles," that "England was in schism," and that "such graces as were apparent in the Anglican Communion were 'extraordinary and from the overflowing of the Divine dispensation.'" [1]

The next group of sermons, numbers 6, 8, 9, and 10, is from the extremely interesting volume, *Sermons Bearing on Subjects of the Day* (1843). It is the product of that period when, as he tells us in the *Apologia,* he was on his "Anglican deathbed." He had led the Tractarian party for years in the utmost confidence that he was strengthening his Church against Rome; he had in fact denounced Rome in many of his writings. Now that Anglicanism no longer seemed Catholic, his sermons betray a kind of ambiguity; those preached on the Church are not really about the Anglican Communion, but about an ideal Church, which had found its historical approximation in the Church of Rome. His listeners hardly believed that he was discussing the English Church when he preached such sermons as those on "The Christian Church as an Imperial Power," "Sanctity the Token of the Christian Empire," and "Condition of the Members of the Christian Empire." Nor could they believe that he was considering ordinary Victorian Anglicans when he preached on "The Apostolical Christian," in which he maintained, to the horror of Charles Kingsley, that "the humble monk and the holy nun" are "but Christians after the very pattern given us in Scripture."

Newman, who had spoken and written so much against the Roman Church, was now evidently making his way toward that Church. His position was becoming impossible. "His parochial sermons," writes Shairp, "assumed an uneasy tone which perplexed his followers." But besides being "uneasy," they were also dogmatic, audacious, severe. No doubt it was the sermon on "Wisdom and Innocence" which was the most perplexing. This was the sermon which provided Charles Kingsley with his charge of duplicity against the Roman clergy, which in turn

[1] Ward, *Life of Newman,* I, 76.

led to the controversy that ended in one of Newman's master-pieces, the *Apologia*. Of course, a reasonably careful reading of this sermon shows that there was no foundation for Kingsley's charge; but there is, in fact, the old emphasis on the primitive severity of Apostolical Christianity which Newman demanded of his congregation. And this was a demand most awkward for many of Newman's complacent, prosperous, well-educated hearers.

The final sermon in the volume is in some ways Newman's supreme triumph in the art of the sermon. A week before, on September 18, he had resigned the vicarage of St. Mary's in Oxford. In the *Conservative Journal* he had also, about this time, retracted all of his attacks on the Church of Rome. Every-one knew the inevitable sequel—the parting from all the Oxford friends and disciples who had for so many years followed him loyally and believed in his religious wisdom. Now on September 25, 1843, he preached his last Anglican sermon, on "The Parting of Friends." Not only as a preacher but also as a man, Newman here takes farewell of his parish and of his friends. He chooses the same text he had used on preaching his first sermon nineteen years before: "Man goeth forth to his work and to his labor until the evening" (Psalm CIV:23). His sermon-fabric is biblical quotation and paraphrase, biblical character, and biblical symbol. Thus, hardly once speaking out in his own words, Newman can use biblical language both as a means of expression and as a screen from which he can eloquently suggest the shortcomings of his Church, his own anguish at leaving it, and the thoughts and feelings of his congregation, which by the end is in tears. According to one tradition, "his voice broke and his words were interrupted by the sobs of his hearers as he said his last words of farewell." With consummate skill he parallels Christ's parting from His disciples "at a feast" with his own farewell at Littlemore. Carrying the theme of farewell through the Old and New Testaments, he shows how similar partings took place in the lives of Jacob, Ishmael, Naomi, David, and St. Paul. As he approaches his closing paragraphs, his hearers' minds are full of biblical image and thought; they have been spellbound by Newman's wonderful manipulation of biblical texts to dramatize his departure. Suddenly they hear him cry: "O Jerusalem, Jerusalem, which killest the prophets!" All know to what he is referring. The final paragraph is a feat of reticence and personal entreaty.

We now come to the sermons selected from those he preached shortly after his entrance into the Roman Catholic Church, published under the unprepossessing title of *Discourses to Mixed Congregations*. Here we find a Newman strikingly different from the Newman of the parochial sermons of his Anglican days. The old simple, cool, reserved manner is displaced by a new manner: that of a man who feels the enthusiasm of the convert, and of a man who enjoys the freedom of his newly found and proper sphere. Newman is no longer the anxious and troubled Anglican; he is now the son of St. Philip Neri. He no longer feels obliged to attempt a reconciliation between apparent irreconcilables; he can speak out boldly, passionately, rhetorically. He exults, as it were, in his mature self-confidence as a Roman Catholic. He permits himself greater range in effects; these new sermons have a sharper irony, a more unrelenting pursuit of his hearers' worldliness, a more exquisite pathos, greater sublimity, a deeper scorn, and more daring imaginative flights (as in "The Mental Sufferings of Our Lord in His Passion"). His psychological probings are more direct and merciless than ever (as in "Nature and Grace," and "Faith and Private Judgment"). Yet he is still able on occasion to employ his old tightly wrought style, colorless but incisive, superb in definitions and distinctions (as in the sermons just cited, and also in "Purity and Love," "Faith and Doubt," and "God's Will the End of Life").

What has given the *Discourses to Mixed Congregations* its particular fame, however, is the remarkably colorful, highly imaginative style in such sermons as the "Mental Sufferings of Our Lord," "The Glories of Mary," and the "Fitness of the Glories of Mary." Here Newman is giving free rein to those pious mental re-creations with which the Catholic Fathers had supplied him as interpreting and illustrating the theology of the Church. These sermons are a great trouble to the Protestant mind, which cannot easily appreciate their artistry because of their content. "I know of no passage in Newman," says Hutton about the "Death of the Mother of Christ," "which so thoroughly bewilders the Protestant imagination." Yet these vivid, highly Catholic sermons are still admired by readers interested in the power of rhetoric, and are of course a peculiar treasure to Newman's Catholic followers.

The last four sermons in the present volume represent Newman in his final Roman Catholic manner as a sermon-writer and as a preacher. Here he has returned somewhat to his earlier Anglican formality. These sermons have none of the passionate rhetoric of those in the *Discourses to Mixed Congregations.* Newman has been in the Roman Catholic Church for about five years when he preaches his sermon on "The Mission of St. Philip Neri." He feels at home in English Catholicism. Even though there is less intensity than in the preceding volume, the sermons drawn from *Sermons Preached on Various Occasions* show considerable variety of effect: the memorable contrast between St. Philip Neri and Savonarola in "The Mission of St. Philip"; the quiet, history-tinged atmosphere of "Christ Upon the Waters"; the controlled biblical eloquence of "The Second Spring," which, to some readers, has a peculiar rhetorical affinity with "The Parting of Friends"; and the intellectual and argumentative effects in "Omnipotence in Bonds," with its unforgettable passage on the nature of God. Newman tells us in his "Advertisement" that "Christ Upon the Waters" and "The Mission of St. Philip" were "composed from the original notes, the former of them immediately after delivery, the latter at this date [1857]." "The Second Spring" and "Omnipotence in Bonds," he says, "were preached in High Mass, and written before delivery."

It is noteworthy that Newman also declares in his "Advertisement," that both the *Discourses to Mixed Congregations* and the *Sermons Preached on Various Occasions* are largely "polemical and hortatory, after all, rather than dogmatic, and addressed to those who are external to the [Catholic] Church." This explains much in the tone, the severity, and the general treatment in the sermons from those two volumes.

We may add now, in conclusion, that all of the sermons reprinted in the present volume exhibit Newman's characteristic traits as a preacher: his penetrating insight, his variety of literary effects, his constant hope to make his hearers *realize* concretely what he is saying, his irony and pathos and occasional epigrammatical utterance. Except in the sermons from *Discourses to Mixed Congregations,* there is little effort to stir one's emotions; even here the emotional tone of such a sermon as the "Mental Sufferings of Our Lord" is refined into subtle realization of the imagery Newman is evoking, notably in the famous passage in which Christ takes upon Himself all the sins of the world, past, present, and future.

In reading any of these sermons, we should never forget that Newman was addressing a highly religious Victorian audience, which spoke his language, understood his images, and had accepted all the basic tenets of his belief. It was willing to accompany him on his flights of eloquence without asking how literally his words were to be taken. Very few in his congregation, for example, thought Newman was engaged in a factually historical description when, in "Christ Upon the Waters," he pictured the rise and spread of Christianity among the Anglo-Saxons; in his silvery voice he intoned: "The fair form of Christianity rose up and grew and expanded like a beautiful pageant from north to south; it was majestic, it was solemn, it was bright, it was beautiful and pleasant, it was soothing to the griefs, it was indulgent to the hopes of man.... A brotherhood of holy pastors, with mitre and crosier and uplifted hand, walked forth and blessed and ruled a joyful people ... and sweet chants resounded, and the holy Latin tongue was heard, and boys came forth in white, swinging censers...." Newman was fully aware of the brutality of the Middle Ages and of the shortcomings of the medieval Church. That he fully realized the extent to which the Church was touched with corruption in the Renaissance is to be seen in his sermon on St. Philip Neri. His sermons are to be read as sermons, and their eloquence to be accepted on the level of poetry, of symbol, of spiritual intimation. Read thus, his sermons rank high in the world's religious literature.

—C.F.H.

I

PRESENT BLESSINGS[1]

"I have all, and abound: I am full."—Phil. iv. 18.

SUCH IS ST. PAUL'S CONFESSION concerning his temporal
condition, even in the midst of his trials. Those trials
brought with them spiritual benefits; but, even as regarded this world, he felt he had cause for joy and thankfulness, in spite of sorrows, pains, labours, and self-denials. He
did not look on this life with bitterness, complain of it
morosely, or refuse to enjoy it; he was not soured, as the children of men often are, by his trials; but he felt, that if he had
troubles in this world, he had blessings also; and he did not
reject these, but made much of them. "I have all, and abound:
I am full," he says. And, elsewhere, he tells us, that "every creature of God is good," and that "godliness is profitable unto
all things, having the promise of the life that now is, and of
that which is to come."[2]

Gloom is no Christian temper; that repentance is not real,
which has not love in it; that self-chastisement is not acceptable, which is not sweetened by faith and cheerfulness. We
must live in sunshine, even when we sorrow; we must live in
God's presence, we must not shut ourselves up in our own
hearts, even when we are reckoning up our past sins.

These thoughts are suitable on this day, when we first catch
a sight, as it were, of the Forty Days of Lent. If God then gives
us grace to repent, it is well; if He enables us to chasten heart

[1] Preached on Septuagesima Sunday. From *Parochial and Plain Sermons*, V, No. 19. [Ed.]
[2] 1 Tim. iv. 4, 8.

1

and body, to Him be praise; and for that very reason, while we do so, we must not cease rejoicing in Him. All through Lent we must rejoice, while we afflict ourselves. Though "many be called, but few chosen;" though all run in the race, but "one receiveth the prize;" though we must "so run that we may obtain;" though we must be "temperate in all things," and "keep under our body and bring it into subjection, lest we be castaways;" yet through God alone we can do this; and while He is with us, we cannot but be joyful; for His absence only is a cause for sorrow. The Three Holy Children are said to have stood up in the midst of the fire, and to have called on all the works of God to rejoice with them; on sun and moon, stars of heaven, nights and days, showers and dew, frost and cold, lightnings and clouds, mountains and hills, green things upon the earth, seas and floods, fowls of the air, beasts and cattle, and children of men,—to praise and bless the Lord, and magnify Him for ever. We have no such trial as theirs; we have no such awful suspense as theirs, when they entered the burning fiery furnace; we attempt for the most part what we know, we begin what we think we can go through. We can neither instance their faith nor equal their rejoicing; yet we can imitate them so far, as to look abroad into this fair world, which God made "very good," while we mourn over the evil which Adam brought into it; to hold communion with what we see there, while we seek Him who is invisible; to admire it, while we abstain from it; to acknowledge God's love, while we deprecate His wrath; to confess that, many as are our sins, His grace is greater. Our sins are more in number than the hairs of our head; yet even the hairs of our head are all numbered by Him. He counts our sins, and, as He counts, so can He forgive; for that reckoning, great though it be, comes to an end; but His mercies fail not, and His Son's merits are infinite.

Let us, then, on this day, dwell upon a thought, which it will be a duty to carry with us through Lent, the thought of the blessings and mercies of which our present life is made up. St. Paul said that he had all, and abounded, and was full; and this, in a day of persecution. Surely, if we have but religious hearts and eyes, we too must confess that our daily and hourly blessings in this life are not less than his. Let us recount some of them.

1. First, then, we ought to bless and praise God that we have the gift of life. By this I mean, not merely that we live, but for those blessings which are included in the notion of our living. He has made life in its very nature to imply the existence of certain blessings which are themselves a happiness, and which bring it to pass that, in spite of all evils, life in itself, except in rare cases, cannot be otherwise than desirable. We cannot live without the means of life; without the means of life we should die; and the means of life are means of pleasure. It might have so been ordered that life could not have been sustained without the use of such means as were indifferent, neither pleasurable nor painful,—or of means which were even painful; as in the case of illness or disease, when we actually find that we cannot preserve it without painful remedies. Now, supposing the ordinary ways of preserving it had been what are now but extraordinary: supposing food were medicine; supposing wounds or blows imparted health and strength. But it is not so. On the contrary, life consists in things pleasant; it is sustained by blessings. And, moreover, the Gospel, by a solemn grant, guarantees these things to us. After the Flood, God Almighty condescended to promise that there never should be such a flood again; that seed-time and harvest should not fail. He ratified the stability of nature by His own Word, and by that Word it is upheld. And in like manner He has, in a special way, guaranteed to us in the Gospel that law of nature whereby good and pleasant gifts are included in our idea of life, and life becomes a blessing. Did He so will, He might sustain us Christians, not by bread only, but by every word that proceedeth out of His mouth. But He has not done so. He has pledged to us those ordinary means of sustenance which we naturally like: "bread shall be given us; our water shall be sure;" "all these things shall be added unto us." He has not

indeed promised us what the world calls its great prizes; He
has not promised us those goods, so called, of which the goodness depends on the imagination; He has not promised us large
estates, magnificent domains, houses like palaces, sumptuous
furniture, retainers and servants, chariots and horses, rank,
name, credit, popularity, power, the deference of others, the
indulgence of our wills, luxuries, sensual enjoyments. These,
on the contrary, He denies us; and, withal, He declares, that
specious and inviting as they are, really they are evil. But
still He has promised that this shall be His rule,—that thus
shall it be fulfilled to us as His ordinary providence, viz.—that
life shall not be a burden to us, but a blessing, and shall contain more to comfort than to afflict. And giving us as much as
this, He bids us be satisfied with it; He bids us confess that we
"have all" when we have so much: that we "abound" when we
have enough; He promises us food, raiment, and lodging; and
He bids us, "having food and raiment, therewith to be content." [3] He bids us be content with those gifts, and withal un-
solicitous about them; tranquil, secure, and confident, because
He has promised them; He bids us be sure that we shall have
so much, and not be disappointed that it is no more. Such is
His merciful consideration of us; He does not separate us from
this world, though He calls us out of it; He does not reject our
old nature when He gives us a new one; He does but redeem
it from the curse, and purify it from the infection which came
through Adam, and is none of His. He especially blesses the
creation to our use, though we be regenerate. "Every creature
of God," says the Apostle, "is good, and nothing to be refused,
if it be received with thanksgiving, for it is sanctified by the
word of God and prayer." [4] He does not bid us renounce the
creation, but associates us with the most beautiful portions of
it. He likens us to the flowers with which He has ornamented
the earth, and to the birds that live solitary under heaven, and
makes them the type of a Christian. He denies us Solomon's

[3] 1 Tim. vi. 8.
[4] 1 Tim. iv. 4, 5.

regal magnificence, to unite us to the lilies of the field and the fowls of the air. "Take no thought for your life, what ye shall eat or what ye shall drink; nor yet for your body, what ye shall put on. Is not the life more than meat, and the body than raiment? Behold the fowls of the air, for they sow not, neither do they reap, nor gather into barns; yet your heavenly Father feedeth them. Are ye not much better than they? . . . And why take ye thought for raiment? Consider the lilies of the field, how they grow; they toil not, neither do they spin; and yet I say unto you, that even Solomon in all his glory was not arrayed like one of these." [5]

Here then, surely, is a matter for joy and thankfulness at all seasons, and not the least at times when, with a religious forbearance, and according to the will of the Giver, not from thanklessness but from prudence, we, for a while, more or less withhold from ourselves His good gifts. Then, of all times, when we think it right to suspend our use of the means of life, so far as may not hurt that life, His gift, and to prove how pleasant is the using them by the pain of abstaining from them, —now especially, my brethren, in the weeks in prospect, when we shall be called on to try ourselves, as far as may be, by hunger, or cold, or watching, or seclusion, that we may be brought nearer to God,—let us now thank God that He has not put us into an evil world, or subjected us to a cruel master, but has given us a continual record of His own perfections in all that lies around us. Alas! it will be otherwise hereafter with those whom God puts out of His sight for ever. Their world will be evil; their life will be death; their rulers will be the devil and his angels; flames of fire and the lake of brimstone will be their meat and drink; the heaven above them will be brass; their earth will be dust and ashes; the blood in their veins will be as molten lead. Fearful thought! which it is not right to do more than glance at. Let us utter it, and pass by. Rather it is for us to rejoice that we are still in the light of His countenance, on His good earth, and under His warm sun. Let us

[5] Matt. vi. 25–29.

thank Him that He gives us the fruits of the earth in their season; that He gives us "food out of the earth, and wine that maketh glad the heart of man, and oil to make him a cheerful countenance, and bread to strengthen man's heart." [6] Thus was it with our fathers of old time; thus is it with us now. After Abraham had fought with the kings, Melchizedek brought forth bread and wine to refresh him. The Angels who visited him made themselves men, and ate of the calf which he dressed for them. Isaac blessed Jacob after the savoury meat. Joseph's brethren ate and drank, and were merry with him. The seventy elders went up Mount Sinai with Moses, Aaron, Nadab, and Abihu, and they saw God, and moreover "did eat and drink." David, after his repentance, had "bread set before him, and he did eat." When Elijah went for his life, and requested that he might die, "an Angel touched him, and said unto him, Arise and eat;" and he did eat and drink, once and twice, and lay down to sleep between his meals; and when he arose, he "went in the strength of that meat forty days and forty nights unto Horeb the mount of God." St. Paul also, after his conversion and baptism, "received meat and was strengthened." [7]

2. Again, what a great blessing is that gift, of which I have just spoken in Elijah's case, the gift of sleep! Almighty God does not suffer us to be miserable for a long while together, even when He afflicts us; but He breaks our trial into portions; takes us out of this world ever and anon, and gives us a holy-day time, like children at school, in an unknown and mysterious country.

All this then must be borne in mind, in reflecting on those solemn and sobering truths concerning the Christian's calling, which it is necessary often to insist upon. It is often said, and truly, that the Christian is born to trouble,—that sorrow is the rule with him, and pleasure the exception. But when this is said, it is with reference to seasons, circumstances, events, such

[6] Ps. civ. 14, 15.

[7] Gen. xiv. 18; xviii. 8; xxvii. 25; xliii. 34. Exod. xxiv. 11. 2 Sam. xii. 20. 1 Kings xix. 5–8. Acts ix. 19.

things as are adventitious and additional to the gift of life itself. The Christian's *lot* is one of sorrow, but, as the regenerate *life* with him is happiness, so is the gift of natural life also. We live, therefore we are happy; *upon* this life of ours come joys and sorrows; and in proportion as we are favourites of God, it is sorrow that comes, not joy. Still after all considered in ourselves, that we live; that God breathes in us; that we exist in Him; that we think and act; that we have the means of life; that we have food, and sleep, and raiment, and lodging; and that we are not lonely, but in God's Church, and are sure of brethren by the very token of our having a Father which is in heaven; so far, rejoicing is the very condition of our being, and all pain is little more than external, not reaching to our inmost heart. So far all men almost are on a level, seasons of sickness excepted. Even delicate health and feebleness of life does not preclude these pleasures. And as to seasons of sickness, or even long and habitual pain or disease, the good Lord can compensate for them in His own way by extraordinary supplies of grace, as in early times He made even the torments of Christians in persecution literally pleasant to them. He who so ordered it, that even the red-hot iron did feel pleasant to the Martyrs after a while, cannot fail of means to support His servants when life becomes a burden. But, generally speaking, it is a happiness, and that to all ranks. High and low, rich and poor, have the same refreshment in their pilgrimage. Hunger is as pleasantly appeased by the low as by the high, on coarse fare as on delicate. Sleep is equally the comfort and recruiting of rich and poor. We eat, drink, and sleep, whether we are in sorrow or in joy, in anxiety or in hope. Our natural life is the type of our spiritual life, and thus, in a literal as well as higher sense, we may bless Him "who saveth our life from destruction, and crowneth us with mercy and loving-kindness; who satisfieth our mouth with good things, making us young and lusty as an eagle." [8]

3. Now, again, consider the blessings which we have in

[8] Ps. ciii. 4, 5.

Christian brotherhood. In the beginning, woman was made, that man might not be alone, but might have a help meet for him; and our Lord promised that all who gave up this world and this world's kindred for Him, should "receive manifold more in this present time, houses, and brethren, and sisters, and mothers, and children, and lands, with persecutions." [9] You see He mentions the troubles of Christians, which were their lot *as* Christians; but still these did not interfere with the prior law of their very nature, that they should not be friendless. As food and raiment are necessary conditions of life, society is an inseparable adjunct of it. God does not take away food and raiment when He gives grace, nor does He take away brotherhood. He removes from the world to put into the Church. Religion without a Church is as unnatural as life without food and raiment. He began our life anew, but He built it up upon the same foundations; and as He did not strip us of our body, when He made us Christians, neither did He of social ties. Christ finds us in the double tabernacle, of a house of flesh and a house of brethren, and He sanctifies both, not pulls them down. Our first life is in ourselves; our second in our friends. They whom God forces to part with their near of kin, for His sake, find brethren in the spirit at their side. They who remain solitary, for His sake, have children in the spirit raised up to them. How should we thank God for this great benefit! Now especially, when we are soon to retire, more or less, into ourselves, and to refrain from our ordinary intercourse with one another, let us acknowledge the blessing, whether of the holy marriage bond, or of family affection, or of the love of friends, which He so bounteously bestows. He gives, He takes away; blessed be His Name. But He takes away to give again, and He withdraws one blessing, to restore fourfold. Abraham offered his only son, and received Him back again at the Angel's voice. Isaac "took Rebekah, and she became his wife, and he loved her; and Isaac was comforted after his mother's death." Jacob lost Joseph, and found him governor

[9] Mark x. 30.

of Egypt. Job lost all his children, yet his end was more blessed than his beginning. We too, through God's mercy, whether we be young or old, whether we have many friends or few, if we be Christ's, shall all along our pilgrimage find those in whom we may live, who will love us and whom we may love, who will aid us and help us forward, and comfort us, and close our eyes. For His love is a secret gift, which, unseen by the world, binds together those in whom it lives, and makes them live and sympathise in one another.

4. Again, let us bless and praise God for the present peace of the Church, and the freedom of speech and action which He has vouchsafed to us. There have been times when, to be a Christian, was to be an outcast and a criminal, when to profess the faith of the Saints would have subjected us to bonds and imprisonment. Let us thank God that at present we have nothing to fear, but may serve Him zealously, "no man forbidding" us. No thanks indeed to the world, which has given us this peace, not from any love to the Church or the Truth, but from selfish and ungodly principles of its own; but great thanks to God, who has made use of the world, and has overruled its course of opinion to our benefit. We have large and noble Churches to worship in; we may go freely to worship when we will; we may enjoy the advice of those who know better than ourselves; we may speak our mind one to another; we may move about freely; we may hold intercourse with whom we will; we may write what we will, explaining, defending, recommending, spreading the truth, without suffering or inconvenience. This is the blessing which we pray for in our Collects; and wonderfully has God granted it for very many years past. We pray daily that God would "give peace in our time." We pray three times a week that "those evils, which the craft and subtilty of the devil or man worketh against us, be brought to nought;" and "that, being hurt by no persecutions, we may evermore give thanks unto God in His Holy Church." We pray yearly that "the course of this world may be so peaceably ordered by His governance, that His Church may joyfully

serve Him in all godly quietness;" and that He may "keep His
household, the Church, in continual godliness, that through His
protection it may be free from all adversities, and devoutly
given to serve Him, in good works, to the glory of His Name."
Now all this is most wonderfully fulfilled to us at this day,—
praised be His great mercy! You will ask, perhaps, whether too
much prosperity is not undesirable for the Church?—It is so;
but I am speaking, not of the Church, but of ourselves as individuals: what is dangerous to the body, may be a blessing
to the separate members. As to ourselves, one by one, God has
His own secret chastisements for us, which, if He loves us, He
will apply when we need them; but, if we know how to use
the blessing duly, it is, I say, a great gift, that we are allowed
to serve God with such freedom and in such peace as are now
vouchsafed us. Great mercy indeed, which we forget because
we are used to it; which many prophets and righteous men in
the first ages of the Gospel had not, yet which we have had
from our youth up. We from our youth up have lived in peace;
with no persecution, no terror, no hindrance in serving God.
The utmost we have had to endure, is what is almost too trifling
for a Christian to mention,—cold looks, or contempt, or ridicule,
from those who have not the heart themselves to attempt the
narrow way.

5. Lastly, and very briefly, my brethren, let us remind ourselves of our own privileges here in this place. How great is
our privilege, my brethren!—every one of us enjoys the great
privilege of daily Worship and weekly Communion. This great
privilege God has given to me and to you,—let us enjoy it while
we have it. Not any one of us knows how long it may be his
own. Perhaps there is no one among us all who can reckon
upon it for a continuance. Perhaps, or rather probably, it is
a bright spot in our lives. Perhaps we shall look upon these
days or years, time hence; and then reflect, when all is over,
how pleasant they were; how pleasant to come, day after day,
quietly and calmly, to kneel before our Maker,—week after
week, to meet our Lord and Saviour. How soothing will then

be the remembrance of His past gifts! we shall remember how we got up early in the morning, and how all things, light or darkness, sun or air, cold or freshness, breathed of Him,—of Him, the Lord of glory, who stood over us, and came down upon us, and gave Himself to us, and poured forth milk and honey for our sustenance, though we saw Him not. Surely we have all, and abound: we are full.

[*March 10, 1839.*]

II

PEACE IN BELIEVING [1]

"And one cried unto another, and said, Holy, Holy, Holy, is the Lord of Hosts."—Isaiah vi. 3.

EVERY LORD'S DAY IS A DAY OF REST, but this, perhaps, more than any. It commemorates, not an act of God, however gracious and glorious, but His own unspeakable perfections and adorable mysteriousness. It is a day especially sacred to peace. Our Lord left His peace with us when He went away; "Peace I leave with you; My peace I give unto you: not as the world giveth, give I unto you;" [2] and He said He would send them a Comforter, who should give them peace. Last week we commemorated that Comforter's coming; and to-day, we commemorate in an especial way the gift He brought with Him, in that great doctrine which is its emblem and its means. "These things have I spoken unto you, that in Me ye might have peace: in the world ye shall have tribulation." [3] Christ here says, that instead of this world's troubles, He gives His disciples peace; and, accordingly, in to-day's Collect, we pray that we may be kept in the faith of the Eternal Trinity in Unity, *and* be "defended from all adversities," for in keeping that faith we are kept from trouble.

Hence, too, in the blessing which Moses told the priests to pronounce over the children of Israel, God's Name is put upon them, and that three times, in order to bless and keep them,

[1] Preached on Trinity Sunday. From *Parochial and Plain Sermons*, VI, No. 25. [Ed.]
[2] John xiv. 27.
[3] John xvi. 33.

to make His face shine on them, and to give them peace. And hence again, in our own solemn form of blessing, with which we end our public service, we impart to the people "the peace of God, which passeth all understanding," and "the blessing of the Father, the Son, and the Holy Ghost."

God is the God of peace, and in giving us peace He does but give Himself, He does but manifest Himself to us; for His presence is peace. Hence our Lord, in the same discourse in which He promised His disciples peace, promised also, that "He would come and manifest Himself unto them," that "He and His Father would come to them, and make Their abode with them." [4] Peace is His everlasting state; in this world of space and time He has wrought and acted; but from everlasting it was not so. For six days He wrought, and then He rested according to that rest which was His eternal state; yet not so rested, as not in one sense to "work hitherto," in mercy and in judgment, towards that world which He had created. And more especially, when He sent His Only-begotten Son into the world, and that most Gracious and All-pitiful Son, our Lord, condescended to come to us, both He and His Father wrought with a mighty hand; and They vouchsafed the Holy Ghost, the Comforter, and He also wrought wonderfully, and works hitherto. Certainly the whole economy of redemption is a series of great and continued works; but still they all tend to rest and peace, as at the first. They began out of rest, and they end in rest. They end in that eternal state out of which they began. The Son was from eternity in the bosom of the Father, as His dearly-beloved and Only-begotten. He loved Him before the foundation of the world. He had glory with Him before the world was. He was in the Father, and the Father in Him. None knew the Son but the Father, nor the Father but the Son. "In the beginning was the Word, and the Word was with God, and the Word was God." He was "the Brightness of God's glory and the express Image of His Person;" and in this unspeakable Unity of Father and Son, was the Spirit also, as

[4] John xiv. 21, 23.

being the Spirit of the Father, and the Spirit of the Son; the Spirit of Both at once, not separate from them, yet distinct, so that they were Three Persons, One God, from everlasting.

Thus was it, we are told, from everlasting;—before the heavens and the earth were made, before man fell or Angels rebelled, before the sons of God were formed in the morning of creation, yea, before there were Seraphim to veil their faces before Him and cry "Holy," He existed without ministers, without attendants, without court and kingdom, without manifested glory, without any thing but Himself; He His own Temple, His own infinite rest, His own supreme bliss, from eternity. O wonderful mystery! O the depth of His majesty! O deep things which the Spirit only knoweth! Wonderful and strange to creatures who grovel on this earth, as we, that He, the All-powerful, the All-wise, the All-good, the All-glorious, should for an eternity, for years without end, or rather, apart from time, which is but one of His creatures, that He should have dwelt without those through whom He might be powerful, in whom He might be wise, towards whom He might be good, by whom He might be glorified. O wonderful, that all His deep and infinite attributes should have been without manifestation! O wonderful thought! and withal, O thought comfortable to us worms of the earth, as often as we feel in ourselves and see in others gifts which have no exercise, and powers which are quiescent! He, the All-powerful God, rested from eternity, and did not work; and yet, why *not* rest, wonderful though it be, seeing He was so blessed in Himself? why should *He* seek external objects to know, to love, and to commune with, who was all-sufficient in Himself? How could He need fellows, as though He were a man, when He was not solitary, but had ever with Him His Only-begotten Word in whom He delighted, whom He loved ineffably, and the Eternal Spirit, the very bond of love and peace, dwelling in and dwelt in by Father and Son? Rather how was it that He ever began to create, who had a Son without beginning and without imperfection, whom He could love with a perfect love? What exceeding exuberance of goodness was it that *He* should deign at length to surround Himself with creation, who had need of nothing, and to change His everlasting silence for the course of Providence and the conflict of good and evil! I say nothing of the apostasies against Him, the rebellions and blasphemies which men and devils have committed. I say nothing of that unutterable region of woe, the prison of the impenitent, which is to last for eternity, coeval with Himself henceforth, as if in rivalry of His blissful heaven. I say nothing of this, for God cannot be touched with evil; and all the sins of those reprobate souls cannot impair His everlasting felicity. But, I ask, how was it that He who needed nothing, who was all in all, who had infinite Equals in the Son and the Spirit, who were One with Him, how was it that He created His Saints, but from simple love of them from eternity? Why should He make man in the Image of God, whose Image already was the Son, All-perfect, All-exact, without variableness, without defect, by a natural propriety and unity of substance? And when man fell, why did He not abandon or annihilate the whole race, and create others? why did He go so far as to begin a fresh and more wonderful dispensation towards us, and, as He had wrought marvellously in Providence, work marvellously also in grace, even sending His Eternal Son to take on Him our fallen nature, and to purify and renew it by His union with it, but that, infinite as was His own blessedness, and the Son's perfection, and man's unprofitableness, yet, in His loving-kindness, He determined that unprofitable man should be a partaker of the Son's perfection and His own blessedness?

And thus it was that, as He had made man in the beginning, so also He redeemed him; and the history of this redemption we have been tracing for the last six months in our sacred Services. We have gone through in our memory the whole course of that Dispensation of active providences, which God, in order to our redemption, has superinduced upon His eternal and infinite repose. First, we commemorated the approach of Christ, in the weeks of Advent; then His birth, of the Blessed

Mary, after a miraculous conception, at Christmas; then His circumcision; His manifestation to the wise men; His baptism and beginning of miracles; His presentation in the Temple; His fasting and temptation in the wilderness, in Lent; His agony in the garden; His betrayal; His mocking and scourging; His cross and passion; His burial; His resurrection; His forty days' converse with His disciples after it; then His Ascension; and, lastly, the coming of the Holy Ghost in His stead to remain with the Church unto the end,—unto the end of the world; for so long is the Almighty Comforter to remain with us. And thus, in commemorating the Spirit's gracious office during the past week, we were brought, in our series of representations, to the end of all things; and now what is left but to commemorate what will follow after the end?—the return of the everlasting reign of God, the infinite peace and blissful perfection of the Father, the Son, and the Holy Ghost, differing indeed from what it once was by the fruits of creation and redemption, but not differing in the supreme blessedness, the ineffable mutual love, the abyss of holiness in which the Three Persons of the Eternal Trinity dwell. He, then, is the subject of this day's celebration,—the God of love, of holiness, of blessedness; in whose presence is fulness of joy and pleasures for evermore; who is what He ever was, and has brought us sinners to that which He ever was. He did not bring into being peace and love as part of His creation, but He was Himself peace and love from eternity, and He blesses us by making us partakers of Himself, through the Son, by the Spirit, and He so works in His temporal dispensations that He may bring us to that which is eternal.

And hence, in Scripture, the promises of eternity and security go together; for where time is not, there vicissitude also is away. "The Eternal God is thy refuge," says Moses, before his death, "and underneath are the everlasting arms: and He shall thrust out the enemy from before thee, and shall say, Destroy them; Israel then shall dwell in safety alone." And again, "Thou wilt keep him in perfect peace, whose mind is stayed on Thee, because he trusteth in Thee. Trust ye in the Lord for ever; for in the Lord Jehovah is everlasting strength." And again, "Thus saith the High and Lofty One that inhabiteth eternity. . . . I dwell in the high and holy place, with him also that is of a contrite and humble spirit, to revive the spirit of the humble, and to revive the heart of the contrite ones. . . . I create the fruit of the lips; peace, peace to him that is afar off, and to him that is near." And, in like manner, our Lord and Saviour is prophesied of as being "the *Everlasting* Father, the Prince of *peace*." And again, speaking more especially of what He has done for us, "The work of righteousness shall be *peace*; and the effect of righteousness, quietness and *assurance for ever*." [5]

As then we have for many weeks commemorated the economy by which righteousness was restored to us, which took place in time, so from this day forth do we bring before our minds the infinite perfections of Almighty God, and our hope hereafter of seeing and enjoying them. Hitherto we have celebrated His great works; henceforth we magnify Himself. Now, for twenty-five weeks we represent in figure what is to be hereafter. We enter into our rest, by entering in with Him who, having wrought and suffered, has opened the kingdom of heaven to all believers. For half a year we stand still, as if occupied solely in adoring Him, and, with the Seraphim in the text, crying, "Holy, Holy, Holy," continually. All God's providences, all God's dealings with us, all His judgments, mercies, warnings, deliverances, tend to peace and repose as their ultimate issue. All our troubles and pleasures here, all our anxieties, fears, doubts, difficulties, hopes, encouragements, afflictions, losses, attainments, tend this one way. After Christmas, Easter, and Whitsuntide, comes Trinity Sunday, and the weeks that follow; and in like manner, after our soul's anxious travail; after the birth of the Spirit; after trial and temptation; after sorrow and pain; after daily dyings to the world; after daily risings unto holiness; at length comes that "rest which remain-

[5] Deut. xxxiii. 27, 28. Isa. xxvi. 3, 4; lvii. 15, 19; ix. 6; xxxii. 17.

eth unto the people of God." After the fever of life; after weari-
nesses and sicknesses; fightings and despondings; languor and
fretfulness; struggling and failing, struggling and succeeding;
after all the changes and chances of this troubled unhealthy
state, at length comes death, at length the White Throne of
God, at length the Beatific Vision. After restlessness comes rest,
peace, joy;—our eternal portion, if we be worthy;—the sight
of the Blessed Three, the Holy One; the Three that bear witness in heaven; in light unapproachable; in glory without spot
or blemish; in power without "variableness, or shadow of turning." The Father God, the Son God, and the Holy Ghost God;
the Father Lord, the Son Lord, and the Holy Ghost Lord; the
Father uncreate, the Son uncreate, and the Holy Ghost uncreate; the Father incomprehensible, the Son incomprehensible, and the Holy Ghost incomprehensible. For there is one
Person of the Father, another of the Son, and another of the
Holy Ghost; and such as the Father is, such is the Son, and
such is the Holy Ghost; and yet there are not three Gods, nor
three Lords, nor three incomprehensibles, nor three uncreated;
but one God, one Lord, one uncreated, and one incomprehensible.

Let us, then, use with thankfulness the subject of this day's
Festival, and the Creed of St. Athanasius, as a means of peace,
till it is given us, if we attain thereto, to see the face of God
in heaven. What the Beatific Vision will then impart, the contemplation of revealed mysteries gives us as in a figure. The
doctrine of the Blessed Trinity has been made the subject of
especial contention among the professed followers of Christ.
It has brought a sword upon earth, but it was intended to
bring peace. And it does bring peace to those who humbly receive it in faith. Let us beg of God to bless it to us to its right
uses, that it may not be an occasion of strife, but of worship; not
of division, but of unity; not of jealousy, but of love. Let us devoutly approach Him of whom it speaks, with the confession of
our lips and of our hearts. Let us look forward to the time when
this world will have passed away and all its delusions; and when

we, when every one born of woman, must either be in heaven or in hell. Let us desire to hide ourselves under the shadow of His wings. Let us beg Him to give us an understanding heart, and that love of Him which is the instinct of the new creature, and the breath of spiritual life. Let us pray Him to give us the spirit of obedience, of true dutifulness; an honest spirit, earnestly set to do His will, with no secret ends, no selfish designs of our own, no preferences of the creature to the Creator, but open, clear, conscientious, and loyal. So will He vouchsafe, as time goes on, to take up His abode in us; the Spirit of Truth, whom the world cannot receive, will dwell in us, and be in us, and Christ "will love us, and will manifest Himself to us," and "the Father will love us, and They will come unto us, and make Their abode with us." And when at length the inevitable hour comes, we shall be able meekly to surrender our souls, our sinful yet redeemed souls, in much weakness and trembling, with much self-reproach and deep confession, yet in firm faith, and in cheerful hope, and in calm love, to God the Father, God the Son, God the Holy Ghost; the Blessed Three, the Holy One; Three Persons, One God; our Creator, our Redeemer, our Sanctifier, our Judge.

[*May 26, 1839.*]

III

THE THOUGHT OF GOD, THE STAY
OF THE SOUL [1]

"Ye have not received the spirit of bondage again to fear, but ye have received the Spirit of adoption, whereby we cry, Abba, Father."—Rom. viii. 15.

WHEN ADAM FELL, his soul lost its true strength; he forfeited the inward light of God's presence, and became the wayward, fretful, excitable, and miserable being which his history has shown him to be ever since; with alternate strength and feebleness, nobleness and meanness, energy in the beginning and failure in the end. Such was the state of his soul in itself, not to speak of the Divine wrath upon it, which followed, or was involved in the Divine withdrawal. It lost its spiritual life and health, which was necessary to complete its nature, and to enable it to fulfill the ends for which it was created,—which was necessary both for its moral integrity and its happiness; and as if faint, hungry, or sick, it could no longer stand upright, but sank on the ground. Such is the state in which every one of us lies as born into the world; and Christ has come to reverse this state, and restore us the great gift which Adam lost in the beginning. Adam fell from his Creator's favour to be a bond-servant; and Christ has come to set us free again, to impart to us the Spirit of adoption, whereby we become God's children, and again approach Him as our Father.

I say, by birth we are in a state of defect and want; we have

[1] Preached on Quinquagesima Sunday. From *Parochial and Plain Sermons*, V, No. 22. [Ed.]

not all that is necessary for the perfection of our nature. As the body is not complete in itself, but requires the soul to give it a meaning, so again the soul till God is present with it and manifested in it, has faculties and affections without a ruling principle, object, or purpose. Such it is by birth, and this Scripture signifies to us by many figures; sometimes calling human nature blind, sometimes hungry, sometimes unclothed, and calling the gift of the Spirit light, health, food, warmth, and raiment; all by way of teaching us what our first state is, and what our gratitude should be to Him who has brought us into a new state. For instance, "Because thou sayest, I am rich, and increased in goods, and have need of nothing; and knowest not that thou art wretched, and miserable, and poor, and blind, and naked: I counsel thee to buy of Me gold tried in the fire, that thou mayest be rich; and white raiment, that thou mayest be clothed, . . . and anoint thine eyes with eye-salve, that thou mayest see." Again, "God, who commanded the light to shine out of darkness, hath shined in our hearts, to give the light of the knowledge of the glory of God, in the face of Jesus Christ." Again, "Awake, thou that sleepest, and arise from the dead, and Christ shall give thee light." Again, "Whosoever drinketh of the water that I shall give him, shall never thirst; but the water that I shall give him shall be in him a well of water springing up into everlasting life." And in the Book of Psalms, "They shall be satisfied with the plenteousness of Thy house; and Thou shalt give them drink of Thy pleasures as out of the river. For with Thee is the well of life, and in Thy Light shall we see light." And in another Psalm, "My soul shall be satisfied, even as it were with marrow and fatness, when my mouth praiseth Thee with joyful lips." And so again, in the Prophet Jeremiah, "I will satiate the souls of the priests with fatness; and My people shall be satisfied with My goodness. . . . I have satiated the weary soul, and I have replenished every sorrowful soul." [2]

Now the doctrine which these passages contain is often truly

[2] Rev. iii. 17, 18. 2 Cor. iv. 6. Ephes. v. 14. John iv. 14. Ps. xxxvi. 8, 9; lxiii. 5. Jer. xxxi. 14, 25.

expressed thus: that the soul of man is made for the contemplation of its Maker; and that nothing short of that high contemplation is its happiness; that, whatever it may possess besides, it is unsatisfied till it is vouchsafed God's presence, and lives in the light of it. There are many aspects in which the same solemn truth may be viewed; there are many ways in which it may be signified. I will now dwell upon it as I have been stating it.

I say, then, that the happiness of the soul consists in the exercise of the affections; not in sensual pleasures, not in activity, not in excitement, not in self esteem, not in the consciousness of power, not in knowledge; in none of these things lies our happiness, but in our affections being elicited, employed, supplied. As hunger and thirst, as taste, sound, and smell, are the channels through which this bodily frame receives pleasure, so the affections are the instruments by which the soul has pleasure. When they are exercised duly, it is happy; when they are undeveloped, restrained, or thwarted, it is not happy. This is our real and true bliss, not to know, or to affect, or to pursue; but to love, to hope, to joy, to admire, to revere, to adore. Our real and true bliss lies in the possession of those objects on which our hearts may rest and be satisfied.

Now, if this be so, here is at once a reason for saying that the thought of God, and nothing short of it, is the happiness of man; for though there is much besides to serve as subject of knowledge, or motive for action, or means of excitement, yet the affections require a something more vast and more enduring than anything created. What is novel and sudden excites, but does not influence; what is pleasurable or useful raises no awe; self moves no reverence, and mere knowledge kindles no love. He alone is sufficient for the heart who made it. I do not say, of course, that nothing short of the Almighty Creator can awaken and answer to our love, reverence, and trust; man can do this for man. Man doubtless is an object to rouse his brother's love, and repays it in his measure. Nay, it is a great duty, one of the two chief duties of religion, thus to be minded towards our neighbour. But I am not speaking here of what we can do, or ought to do, but what it is our happiness to do; and surely it may be said that though the love of the brethren, the love of all men, be one half of our obedience, yet exercised by itself, were that possible, which it is not, it would be no part of our reward. And for this reason, if for no other, that our hearts require something more permanent and uniform than man can be. We gain much for a time from fellowship with each other. It is a relief to us, as fresh air to the fainting, or meat and drink to the hungry, or a flood of tears to the heavy in mind. It is a soothing comfort to have those whom we may make our confidants; a comfort to have those to whom we may confess our faults; a comfort to have those to whom we may look for sympathy. Love of home and family in these and other ways is sufficient to make this life tolerable to the multitude of men, which otherwise it would not be; but still, after all, our affections exceed such exercise of them, and demand what is more stable. Do not all men die? are they not taken from us? are they not as uncertain as the grass of the field? We do not give our hearts to things irrational, because these have no permanence in them. We do not place our affections in sun, moon, and stars, or this rich and fair earth, because all things material come to nought, and vanish like day and night. Man, too, though he has an intelligence within him, yet in his best estate he is altogether vanity. If our happiness consists in our affections being employed and recompensed, "man that is born of a woman" cannot be our happiness; for how can he stay another, who "continueth not in one stay" himself?

But there is another reason why God alone is the happiness of our souls, to which I wish rather to direct attention:—the contemplation of Him, and nothing but it, is able fully to open and relieve the mind, to unlock, occupy, and fix our affections. We may indeed love things created with great intenseness, but such affection, when disjoined from the love of the Creator, is like a stream running in a narrow channel, impetuous, vehement, turbid. The heart runs out, as it were, only at one door;

it is not an expanding of the whole man. Created natures cannot open us, or elicit the ten thousand mental senses which belong to us, and through which we really live. None but the presence of our Maker can enter us; for to none besides can the whole heart in all its thoughts and feelings be unlocked and subjected. "Behold," He says, "I stand at the door and knock; if any man hear My voice and open the door, I will come in to him, and will sup with him, and he with Me." "My Father will love him, and We will come unto him, and make Our abode with him." "God hath sent forth the Spirit of His Son into your hearts." "God is greater than our heart, and knoweth all things." [3] It is this feeling of simple and absolute confidence and communion, which soothes and satisfies those to whom it is vouchsafed. We know that even our nearest friends enter into us but partially, and hold intercourse with us only at times; whereas the consciousness of a perfect and enduring Presence, and it alone, keeps the heart open. Withdraw the Object on which it rests, and it will relapse again into its state of confinement and constraint; and in proportion as it is limited, either to certain seasons or to certain affections, the heart is straitened and distressed. If it be not over bold to say it, He who is infinite can alone be its measure; He alone can answer to the mysterious assemblage of feelings and thoughts which it has within it. "There is no creature that is not manifest in His sight, but all things are naked and opened unto the eyes of Him with whom we have to do." [4]

This is what is meant by the peace of a good conscience; it is the habitual consciousness that our hearts are open to God, with a desire that they should be open. It is a confidence in God, from a feeling that there is nothing in us which we need be ashamed or afraid of. You will say that no man on earth is in such a state; for we are all sinners, and that daily. It is so; certainly we are quite unfitted to endure God's all-searching Eye, to come into direct contact (if I may so speak) with His

[3] Rev. iii. 20.   John xiv. 23.   Gal. iv. 6.   1 John iii. 20.
[4] Heb. iv. 13.

glorious Presence, without any medium of intercourse between Him and us. But, first, there may be degrees of this confidence in different men, though the perfection of it be in none. And again, God in His great mercy, as we all well know, has revealed to us that there is a Mediator between the sinful soul and Himself. And as His merits most wonderfully intervene between our sins and God's judgment, so the thought of those merits, when present with the Christian, enables him, in spite of his sins, to lift up his heart to God; and believing, as he does, that he is (to use Scripture language) in Christ, or, in other words, that he addresses Almighty God, not simply face to face, but in and through Christ, he can bear to submit and open his heart to God, and to wish it open. For while he is very conscious both of original and actual sin, yet still a feeling of his own sincerity and earnestness is possible; and in proportion as he gains as much as this, he will be able to walk unreservedly with Christ his God and Saviour, and desire His continual presence with him, though he be a sinner, and will wish to be allowed to make Him the one Object of his heart. Perhaps, under somewhat of this feeling, Hagar said, "Thou, God, seest me." It is under this feeling that holy David may be supposed to say, "Examine me, O Lord, and prove me; try out my reins and my heart." "Try me, O God, and seek the ground of my heart; prove me, and examine my thoughts. Look well, if there be any way of wickedness in me; and lead me in the way everlasting." [5] And especially is it instanced in St. Paul, who seems to delight in the continual laying open of his heart to God, and submitting it to His scrutiny, and waiting for His Presence upon it; or, in other words, in the joy of a good conscience. For instance, "I have lived in all good conscience before God until this day." "Herein do I exercise myself, to have always a conscience void of offence toward God, and toward men." "I say the truth in Christ, I lie not; my conscience also bearing me witness in the Holy Ghost." "Our rejoicing is this, the testimony of our conscience, that in sim-

[5] Ps. xxvi. 2; cxxxix. 23, 24.

plicity and godly sincerity, not with fleshly wisdom, but by the grace of God, we have had our conversation in the world, and more abundantly to you-ward." [6] It is, I say, the characteristic of St. Paul, as manifested to us in his Epistles, to live in the sight of Him who "searcheth the reins and the heart," to love to place himself before Him, and, while contemplating God, to dwell on the thought of God's contemplating him.

And, it may be, this is something of the Apostle's meaning, when he speaks of the witness of the Spirit. Perhaps he is speaking of that satisfaction and rest which the soul experiences in proportion as it is able to surrender itself wholly to God, and to have no desire, no aim, but to please Him. When we are awake, we are conscious we are awake, in a sense in which we cannot fancy we are, when we are asleep. When we have discovered the solution of some difficult problem in science, we have a conviction about it which is distinct from that which accompanies fancied discoveries or guesses. When we realize a truth we have a feeling which they have not, who take words for things. And so, in like manner, if we are allowed to find that real and most sacred Object on which our heart may fix itself, a fulness of peace will follow, which nothing but it can give. In proportion as we have given up the love of the world, and are dead to the creature, and, on the other hand, are born of the Spirit unto love of our Maker and Lord, this love carries with it its own evidence whence it comes. Hence the Apostle says, "The Spirit itself beareth witness with our spirit, that we are the children of God." Again, he speaks of Him "who hath sealed us, and given the earnest of the Spirit in our hearts." [7]

I have been saying that our happiness consists in the contemplation of God;—(such a contemplation is alone capable of accompanying the mind always and everywhere, for God alone can be always and everywhere present;)—and that what is commonly said about the happiness of a good conscience,

[6] Acts xxiii. 1; xxiv. 16.   Rom. ix. 1.   2 Cor. i. 12.
[7] Rom. viii. 16.   2 Cor. i. 22.

confirms this; for what is it to have a good conscience, when
we examine the force of our words, but to be ever reminded
of God by our own hearts, to have our hearts in such a state
as to be led thereby to look up to Him, and to desire His eye
to be upon us through the day? It is in the case of holy men
the feeling attendant on the contemplation of Almighty God.

But, again, this sense of God's presence is not only the
ground of the peace of a good conscience, but of the peace of
repentance also. At first sight it might seem strange how repentance can have in it anything of comfort and peace. The
Gospel, indeed, promises to turn all sorrow into joy. It makes
us take pleasure in desolateness, weakness, and contempt. "We
glory in tribulations also," says the Apostle, "because the love
of God is shed abroad in our hearts by the Holy Ghost which
is given unto us." It destroys anxiety: "Take no thought for
the morrow, for the morrow shall take thought for the things
of itself." It bids us take comfort under bereavement: "I would
not have you ignorant, brethren, concerning them which are
asleep, that ye sorrow not, even as others which have no
hope." [8] But if there be one sorrow, which might seem to be
unmixed misery, if there be one misery left under the Gospel,
the awakened sense of having abused the Gospel might have
been considered that one. And, again, if there be a time when
the presence of the Most High would at first sight seem to be
intolerable, it would be then, when first the consciousness
vividly bursts upon us that we have ungratefully rebelled
against Him. Yet so it is that true repentance cannot be without the thought of God; it has the thought of God, for it seeks
Him; and it seeks Him, because it is quickened with love; and
even sorrow must have a sweetness, if love be in it. For what is
to repent but to surrender ourselves to God for pardon or punishment; as loving His presence for its own sake, and account-
ing chastisement from Him better than rest and peace from
the world? While the prodigal son remained among the swine,
he had sorrow enough, but no repentance; remorse only; but

[8] Rom. v. 3, 5.   Matt. vi. 34.   1 Thess. iv. 13.

repentance led him to rise and go to his Father, and to confess his sins. Thus he relieved his heart of its misery, which before was like some hard and fretful tumour weighing upon it. Or, again, consider St. Paul's account of the repentance of the Corinthians; there is sorrow in abundance, nay, anguish, but no gloom, no dryness of spirit, no sternness. The penitents afflict themselves, but it is from the fulness of their hearts, from love, gratitude, devotion, horror of the past, desire to escape from their present selves into some state holier and more heavenly. St. Paul speaks of their "earnest desire, their mourning, their fervent mind towards him." He rejoices, "not that they were made sorry, but that they sorrowed to repentance." "For ye were made sorry," he proceeds, "after a godly manner that ye might receive damage by us in nothing." And he describes this "sorrowing after a godly sort," to consist in "carefulness, which it wrought in them," "clearing of themselves,"—"indignation,"—"fear,"—"vehement desire,"— "zeal,"—"revenge," [9]—feelings, all of them, which open the heart, yet, without relaxing it, in that they terminate in acts or works.

On the other hand, remorse, or what the Apostle calls "the sorrow of the world," worketh death. Instead of coming to the Fount of Life, to the God of all consolation, remorseful men feed on their own thoughts, without any confidant of their sorrow. They disburden themselves to no one: to God they will not, to the world they cannot confess. The world will not attend to their confession; it is a good associate, but it cannot be an intimate. It cannot approach us or stand by us in trouble; it is no Paraclete; it leaves all our feelings buried within us, either tumultuous, or, at best, dead: it leaves us gloomy or obdurate. Such is our state, while we live to the world, whether we be in sorrow or in joy. We are pent up within ourselves, and are therefore miserable. Perhaps we may not be able to analyse our misery, or even to realize it, as persons oftentimes who are in bodily sicknesses. We do not know, perhaps, what or where

[9] 2 Cor. vii. 7, 9, 11.

our pain is; we are so used to it that we do not call it pain. Still so it is; we need a relief to our hearts, that they may be dark and sullen no longer, or that they may not go on feeding upon themselves; we need to escape from ourselves to something beyond; and much as we may wish it otherwise, and may try to make idols to ourselves, nothing short of God's presence is our true refuge; everything else is either a mockery, or but an expedient useful for its season or in its measure.

How miserable then is he, who does not practically know this great truth! Year after year he will be a more unhappy man, or, at least, he will emerge into a maturity of misery at once, when he passes out of this world of shadows into that kingdom where all is real. He is at present attempting to satisfy his soul with that which is not bread; or he thinks the soul can thrive without nourishment. He fancies he can live without an object. He fancies that he is sufficient for himself; or he supposes that knowledge is sufficient for his happiness; or that exertion, or that the good opinion of others, or (what is called) fame, or that the comforts and luxuries of wealth, are sufficient for him. What a truly wretched state is that coldness and dryness of soul, in which so many live and die, high and low, learned and unlearned. Many a great man, many a peasant, many a busy man, lives and dies with closed heart, with affections undeveloped, unexercised. You see the poor man, passing day after day, Sunday after Sunday, year after year, without a thought in his mind, to appearance almost like a stone. You see the educated man, full of thought, full of intelligence, full of action, but still with a stone heart, as cold and dead as regards his affections, as if he were the poor ignorant countryman. You see others, with warm affections, perhaps, for their families, with benevolent feelings towards their fellow-men, yet stopping there; centring their hearts on what is sure to fail them, as being perishable. Life passes, riches fly away, popularity is fickle, the senses decay, the world changes, friends die. One alone is constant; One alone is true to us; One alone can be true; One alone can be all things to us;

One alone can supply our needs; One alone can train us up to our full perfection; One alone can give a meaning to our complex and intricate nature; One alone can give us tune and harmony; One alone can form and possess us. Are we allowed to put ourselves under His guidance? this surely is the only question. Has He really made us His children, and taken possession of us by His Holy Spirit? Are we still in His kingdom of grace, in spite of our sins? The question is not whether we should go, but whether He will receive. And we trust, that, in spite of our sins, He will receive us still, every one of us, if we seek His face in love unfeigned, and holy fear. Let us then do our part, as He has done His, and much more. Let us say with the Psalmist, "Whom have I in heaven but Thee? and there is none upon earth I desire in comparison of Thee. My flesh and my heart faileth; but God is the strength of my heart, and my portion for ever." [10]

[*June 9, 1839.*]

[10] Ps. lxxiii. 25, 26.

THE CROSS OF CHRIST THE MEASURE
OF THE WORLD [1]

"And I, if I be lifted up from the earth, will draw all men unto Me."—John xii. 32.

A GREAT NUMBER OF MEN live and die without reflecting at all upon the state of things in which they find themselves. They take things as they come, and follow their inclinations as far as they have the opportunity. They are guided mainly by pleasure and pain, not by reason, principle, or conscience; and they do not attempt to *interpret* this world, to determine what it means, or to reduce what they see and feel to system. But when persons, either from thoughtfulness of mind, or from intellectual activity, begin to contemplate the visible state of things into which they are born, then forthwith they find it a maze and a perplexity. It is a riddle which they cannot solve. It seems full of contradictions and without a drift. Why it is, and what it is to issue in, and how it is what it is, and how we come to be introduced into it, and what is our destiny, are all mysteries.

In this difficulty, some have formed one philosophy of life, and others another. Men have thought they had found the key, by means of which they might read what is so obscure. Ten thousand things come before us one after another in the course of life, and what are we to think of them? what colour are we to give them? Are we to look at all things in a gay and mirthful way? or in a melancholy way? in a desponding or a hopeful

[1] Preached on the Sixth Sunday in Lent. From *Parochial and Plain Sermons*, VI, No. 7. [Ed.]

way? Are we to make light of life altogether, or to treat the whole subject seriously? Are we to make greatest things of little consequence, or least things of great consequence? Are we to keep in mind what is past and gone, or are we to look on to the future, or are we to be absorbed in what is present? *How* are we to look at things? this is the question which all persons of observation ask themselves, and answer each in his own way. They wish to think by rule; by something within them, which may harmonise and adjust what is without them. Such is the need felt by reflective minds. Now, let me ask, what *is* the real key, what is the Christian interpretation of this world? What is given us by revelation to estimate and measure this world by? The event of this season,—the Crucifixion of the Son of God.

It is the death of the Eternal Word of God made flesh, which is our great lesson how to think and how to speak of this world. His Cross has put its due value upon every thing which we see, upon all fortunes, all advantages, all ranks, all dignities, all pleasures; upon the lust of the flesh, and the lust of the eyes, and the pride of life. It has set a price upon the excitements, the rivalries, the hopes, the fears, the desires, the efforts, the triumphs of mortal man. It has given a meaning to the various, shifting course, the trials, the temptations, the sufferings, of his earthly state. It has brought together and made consistent all that seemed discordant and aimless. It has taught us how to live, how to use this world, what to expect, what to desire, what to hope. It is the tone into which all the strains of this world's music are ultimately to be resolved.

Look around, and see what the world presents of high and low. Go to the court of princes. See the treasure and skill of all nations brought together to honour a child of man. Observe the prostration of the many before the few. Consider the form and ceremonial, the pomp, the state, the circumstance; and the vain-glory. Do you wish to know the worth of it all? look at the Cross of Christ.

Go to the political world: see nation jealous of nation, trade rivalling trade, armies and fleets matched against each other. Survey the various ranks of the community, its parties and their contests, the strivings of the ambitious, the intrigues of the crafty. What is the end of all this turmoil? the grave. What is the measure? the Cross.

Go, again, to the world of intellect and science: consider the wonderful discoveries which the human mind is making, the variety of arts to which its discoveries give rise, the all but miracles by which it shows its power; and next, the pride and confidence of reason, and the absorbing devotion of thought to transitory objects, which is the consequence. Would you form a right judgment of all this? look at the Cross.

Again: look at misery, look at poverty and destitution, look at oppression and captivity; go where food is scanty, and lodging unhealthy. Consider pain and suffering, diseases long or violent, all that is frightful and revolting. Would you know how to rate all these? gaze upon the Cross.

Thus in the Cross, and Him who hung upon it, all things meet; all things subserve it, all things need it. It is their centre and their interpretation. For He was lifted up upon it, that He might draw all men and all things unto Him.

But it will be said, that the view which the Cross of Christ imparts to us of human life and of the world, is not that which we should take, if left to ourselves; that it is not an obvious view; that if we look at things on their surface, they are far more bright and sunny than they appear when viewed in the light which this season casts upon them. The world seems made for the enjoyment of just such a being as man, and man is put into it. He has the *capacity* of enjoyment, and the world supplies the *means*. How natural this, what a simple as well as pleasant philosophy, yet how different from that of the Cross! The doctrine of the Cross, it may be said, disarranges two parts of a system which seem made for each other; it severs the fruit from the eater, the enjoyment from the enjoyer. How does this solve a problem? does it not rather itself create one?

I answer, first, that whatever force this objection may have, surely it is merely a repetition of that which Eve felt and Satan urged in Eden; for did not the woman see that the forbidden tree was "good for food," and "a tree to be *desired*"? Well, then, is it wonderful that we too, the descendants of the first pair, should still be in a world where there is a forbidden fruit, and that our trials should lie in being within reach of it, and our happiness in abstaining from it? The world, at first sight, appears *made* for pleasure, and the vision of Christ's Cross is a solemn and sorrowful sight interfering with this appearance. Be it so; but why may it not be our duty to abstain from enjoyment notwithstanding, if it was a duty even in Eden?

But again; it is but a superficial view of things to say that this life is made for pleasure and happiness. To those who look under the surface, it tells a very different tale. The doctrine of the Cross does but teach, though infinitely more forcibly, still after all it does but teach the very same lesson which this world teaches to those who live long in it, who have much experience in it, who know it. The world is sweet to the lips, but bitter to the taste. It pleases at first, but not at last. It looks gay on the outside, but evil and misery lie concealed within. When a man has passed a certain number of years in it, he cries out with the Preacher, "Vanity of vanities, all is vanity." Nay, if he has not religion for his guide, he will be forced to go further, and say, "All is vanity and vexation of spirit;" all is disappointment; all is sorrow; all is pain. The sore judgments of God upon sin are concealed within it, and force a man to grieve whether he will or no. Therefore the doctrine of the Cross of Christ does but antipicate for us our experience of the world. It is true, it bids us grieve for our sins in the midst of all that smiles and glitters around us; but if we will not heed it, we shall at length be forced to grieve for them from undergoing their fearful punishment. If we will not acknowledge that this world has been made miserable by sin, from the sight of Him on whom our sins were laid, we shall experience it to be miserable by the recoil of those sins upon ourselves.

It may be granted, then, that the doctrine of the Cross is not on the surface of the world. The surface of things is bright only, and the Cross is sorrowful; it is a hidden doctrine; it lies under a veil; it at first sight startles us, and we are tempted to revolt from it. Like St. Peter, we cry out, "Be it far from Thee, Lord; this shall not be unto Thee." [2] And yet it is a true doctrine; for truth is not on the surface of things, but in the depths.

And as the doctrine of the Cross, though it be the true interpretation of this world, is not prominently manifested in it, upon its surface, but is concealed; so again, when received into the faithful heart, there it abides as a living principle, but deep, and hidden from observation. Religious men, in the words of Scripture, "live by the faith of the Son of God, who loved them and gave Himself for them:" [3] but they do not tell this to all men; they leave others to find it out as they may. Our Lord's own command to His disciples was, that when they fast, they should "anoint their head and wash their face." [4] Thus they are bound not to make a display, but ever to be content to look outwardly different from what they are really inwardly. They are to carry a cheerful countenance with them, and to control and regulate their feelings, that those feelings, by not being expended on the surface, may retire deep into their hearts and there live. And thus "Jesus Christ and He crucified" is, as the Apostle tells us, "a hidden wisdom;"—hidden in the world, which seems at first sight to speak a far other doctrine,—and hidden in the faithful soul, which to persons at a distance, or to chance beholders, seems to be living but an ordinary life, while really it is in secret holding communion with Him who was "manifested in the flesh," "crucified through weakness,"

[2] Matt. xvi. 22.
[3] Gal. ii. 20.
[4] Matt. vi. 17.

"justified in the Spirit, seen of Angels, and received up into glory."

This being the case, the great and awful doctrine of the Cross of Christ, which we now commemorate, may fitly be called, in the language of figure, the *heart* of religion. The heart may be considered as the seat of life; it is the principle of motion, heat, and activity; from it the blood goes to and fro to the extreme parts of the body. It sustains the man in his powers and faculties; it enables the brain to think; and when it is touched, man dies. And in like manner the sacred doctrine of Christ's Atoning Sacrifice is the vital principle on which the Christian lives, and without which Christianity is not. Without it no other doctrine is held profitably; to believe in Christ's Divinity, or in His manhood, or in the Holy Trinity, or in a judgment to come, or in the resurrection of the dead, is an untrue belief, not Christian faith, unless we receive also the doctrine of Christ's sacrifice. On the other hand, to receive it presupposes the reception of other high truths of the Gospel besides; it involves the belief in Christ's true divinity, in His true incarnation, and in man's sinful state by nature; and it prepares the way to belief in the sacred Eucharistic feast, in which He who was once crucified is ever given to our souls and bodies, verily and indeed, in His Body and in His Blood. But again, the heart is hidden from view; it is carefully and securely guarded; it is not like the eye set in the forehead, commanding all, and seen of all: and so in like manner the sacred doctrine of the Atoning Sacrifice is not one to be talked of, but to be lived upon; not to be put forth irreverently, but to be adored secretly; not to be used as a necessary instrument in the conversion of the ungodly, or for the satisfaction of reasoners of this world, but to be unfolded to the docile and obedient; to young children, whom the world has not corrupted; to the sorrowful, who need comfort; to the sincere and earnest, who need a rule of life; to the innocent, who need warning; and to the established, who have earned the knowledge of it.

One more remark I shall make, and then conclude. It must

not be supposed, because the doctrine of the Cross makes us sad, that therefore the Gospel is a sad religion. The Psalmist says, "They that sow in tears shall reap in joy;" and our Lord says, "They that mourn shall be comforted." Let no one go away with the impression that the Gospel makes us take a gloomy view of the world and of life. It hinders us indeed from taking a superficial view, and finding a vain transitory joy in what we see; but it forbids our immediate enjoyment, only to grant enjoyment in truth and fulness afterwards. It only forbids us to *begin* with enjoyment. It only says, If you begin with pleasure, you will end with pain. It bids us begin with the Cross of Christ, and in that Cross we shall at first find sorrow, but in a while peace and comfort will rise out of that sorrow. That Cross will lead us to mourning, repentance, humiliation, prayer, fasting; we shall sorrow for our sins, we shall sorrow with Christ's sufferings; but all this sorrow will only issue, nay, will be undergone in a happiness far greater than the enjoyment which the world gives,—though careless worldly minds indeed will not believe this, ridicule the notion of it, because they never have tasted it, and consider it a mere matter of words, which religious persons think it decent and proper to use, and try to believe themselves, and to get others to believe, but which no one really feels. This is what they think; but our Saviour said to His disciples, "Ye now therefore have sorrow, but I will see you again, and your heart shall rejoice, and your joy no man taketh from you." . . . "Peace I leave with you; My peace I give unto you; not as the world giveth, give I unto you." And St. Paul says, "The natural man receiveth not the things of the Spirit of God; for they are foolishness unto him; neither can he know them, because they are spiritually discerned." "Eye hath not seen, nor ear heard, neither have entered into the heart of man, the things which God hath prepared for them that love Him." [5] And thus the Cross of Christ, as telling us of our redemption as well as of His sufferings, wounds us indeed, but so wounds as to heal also.

[5] John xvi. 22; xiv. 27.   1 Cor. ii. 9, 14.

And thus, too, all that is bright and beautiful, even on the surface of this world, though it has no substance, and may not suitably be enjoyed for its own sake, yet is a figure and promise of that true joy which issues out of the Atonement. It is a promise beforehand of what is to be: it is a shadow, raising hope because the substance is to follow, but not to be rashly taken instead of the substance. And it is God's usual mode of dealing with us, in mercy to send the shadow before the substance, that we may take comfort in what is to be, before it comes. Thus our Lord before His Passion rode into Jerusalem in triumph, with the multitudes crying Hosanna, and strewing His road with palm branches and their garments. This was but a vain and hollow pageant, nor did our Lord take pleasure in it. It was a shadow which stayed not, but flitted away. It could not be more than a shadow, for the Passion had not been undergone by which His true triumph was wrought out. He could not enter into His glory before He had first suffered. He could not take pleasure in this semblance of it, knowing that it was unreal. Yet that first shadowy triumph was the omen and presage of the true victory to come, when He had overcome the sharpness of death. And we commemorate this figurative triumph on the last Sunday in Lent, to cheer us in the sorrow of the week that follows, and to remind us of the true joy which comes with Easter-Day.

And so, too, as regards this world, with all its enjoyments, yet disappointments. Let us not trust it; let us not give our hearts to it; let us not begin with it. Let us begin with faith; let us begin with Christ; let us begin with His Cross and the humiliation to which it leads. Let us first be drawn to Him who is lifted up, that so He may, with Himself, freely give us all things. Let us "seek first the Kingdom of God and His righteousness," and then all those things of this world "will be added to us." They alone are able truly to enjoy this world, who begin with the world unseen. They alone enjoy it, who have first abstained from it. They alone can truly feast, who have first fasted; they alone are able to use the world, who have learned not to abuse it; they alone inherit it, who take it as a shadow of the world to come, and who for that world to come relinquish it.

[*April 9, 1841.*]

V

THE CRUCIFIXION[1]

"He was oppressed, and He was afflicted, yet He opened not His mouth; He is brought as a lamb to the slaughter, and as a sheep before her shearers is dumb, so He openeth not His mouth."— Isaiah liii. 7.

ST. PETER MAKES IT almost a description of a Christian, that he loves Him whom he has not seen; speaking of Christ, he says, "whom having not seen, ye love; in whom, though now ye see Him not, yet believing, ye rejoice with joy unspeakable and full of glory." Again he speaks of "tasting that the Lord is gracious." [2] Unless we have a true love of Christ, we are not His true disciples; and we cannot love Him unless we have heartfelt gratitude to Him; and we cannot duly feel gratitude, unless we feel keenly what He suffered for us. I say it seems to us impossible, under the circumstances of the case, that any one can have attained to the love of Christ, who feels no distress, no misery, at the thought of His bitter pains, and no self-reproach at having through his own sins had a share in causing them.

I know quite well, and wish you, my brethren, never to forget, that feeling is not enough; that it is not enough merely to feel and nothing more; that to feel grief for Christ's sufferings, and yet not to go on to obey Him, is not true love, but a mockery. True love both feels right, and acts right; but at the same time as warm feelings without religious conduct are a kind of hypocrisy, so, on the other hand, right conduct, when

[1] From *Parochial and Plain Sermons*, VII, No. 10. [Ed.]
[2] 1 Pet. i. 8; ii. 3.

40

unattended with deep feelings, is at best a very imperfect sort
of religion. And at this time of year [3] especially are we called
upon to raise our hearts to Christ, and to have keen feelings
and piercing thoughts of sorrow and shame, of compunction
and of gratitude, of love and tender affection and horror and
anguish, at the review of those awful sufferings whereby our
salvation has been purchased.

Let us pray God to give us *all* graces; and while, in the first
place, we pray that He would make us holy, really holy, let us
also pray Him to give us the *beauty* of holiness, which consists
in tender and eager affection towards our Lord and Saviour:
which is, in the case of the Christian, what beauty of person
is to the outward man, so that through God's mercy our souls
may have, not strength and health only, but a sort of bloom
and comeliness; and that as we grow older in body, we may,
year by year, grow more youthful in spirit.

You will ask, *how* are we to learn to feel pain and anguish
at the thought of Christ's sufferings? I answer, *by* thinking of
them, that is, by *dwelling* on the thought. This, through God's
mercy, is in the power of every one. No one who will but
solemnly think over the history of those sufferings, as drawn
out for us in the Gospels, but will gradually gain, through
God's grace, a sense of them, will in a measure realize them,
will in a measure be as if he saw them, will feel towards them
as being not merely a tale written in a book, but as a true
history, as a series of events which took place. It is indeed a
great mercy that this duty which I speak of, though so high,
is notwithstanding so level with the powers of all classes of
persons, learned and unlearned, if they wish to perform it. Any
one can think of Christ's sufferings, if he will; and knows well
what to think about. "It is not in heaven that thou shouldst
say, Who shall go up for us to heaven and bring it to us, that
we may hear it and do it? Neither is it beyond the sea that
thou shouldst say, Who shall go over the sea for us? . . . but
the word is very nigh unto thee;" very nigh, for it is in the

[3] Passion-tide.

four Gospels, which, at this day at least, are open to all men. All men may read or hear the Gospels, and in knowing them, they will know all that is necessary to be known in order to feel aright; they will know all that any one knows, all that has been told us, all that the greatest saints have ever had to make them full of love and sacred fear.

Now, then, let me make one or two reflections by way of stirring up your hearts and making you mourn over Christ's sufferings, as you are called to do at this season.

1. First, as to these sufferings you will observe that our Lord is called a lamb in the text; that is, He was as defenceless, and as innocent, as a lamb is. Since then Scripture compares Him to this inoffensive and unprotected animal, we may without presumption or irreverence take the image as a means of conveying to our minds those feelings which our Lord's sufferings should excite in us. I mean, consider how very horrible it is to read the accounts which sometimes meet us of cruelties exercised on brute animals. Does it not sometimes make us shudder to hear tell of them, or to read them in some chance publication which we take up? At one time it is the wanton deed of barbarous and angry owners who ill-treat their cattle, or beasts of burden; and at another, it is the cold-blooded and calculating act of men of science, who make experiments on brute animals, perhaps merely from a sort of curiosity. I do not like to go into particulars, for many reasons; but one of those instances which we read of as happening in this day, and which seems more shocking than the rest, is, when the poor dumb victim is fastened against a wall, pierced, gashed, and so left to linger out its life. Now do you not see that I have a reason for saying this, and am not using these distressing words for nothing? For what was this but the very cruelty inflicted upon our Lord? He was gashed with the scourge, pierced through hands and feet, and so fastened to the Cross, and there left, and that as a spectacle. Now what is it moves our very hearts, and sickens us so much at cruelty shown to

poor brutes? I suppose this first, that they have done no harm; next, that they have no power whatever of resistance; it is the cowardice and tyranny of which they are the victims which makes their sufferings so especially touching. For instance, if they were dangerous animals, take the case of wild beasts at large, able not only to defend themselves, but even to attack us; much as we might dislike to hear of their wounds and agony, yet our feelings would be of a very different kind; but there is something so very dreadful, so satanic in tormenting those who never have harmed us, and who cannot defend themselves, who are utterly in our power, who have weapons neither of offence nor defence, that none but very hardened persons can endure the thought of it. Now this was just our Saviour's case: He had laid aside His glory, He had (as it were) disbanded His legions of Angels, He came on earth without arms, except the arms of truth, meekness, and righteousness, and committed Himself to the world in perfect innocence and sinlessness, and in utter helplessness, as the Lamb of God. In the words of St. Peter, "Who did no sin, neither was guile found in His mouth; who, when He was reviled, reviled not again; when He suffered, He threatened not; but committed Himself to Him that judgeth righteously." [4] Think then, my brethren, of your feelings at cruelty practised upon brute animals, and you will gain one sort of feeling which the history of Christ's Cross and Passion ought to excite within you. And let me add, this is in all cases one good use to which you may turn any accounts you read of wanton and unfeeling acts shown towards the inferior animals; let them remind you, as a picture, of Christ's sufferings. He who is higher than the Angels, deigned to humble Himself even to the state of the brute creation, as the Psalm says, "I am a worm, and no man; a very scorn of men, and the outcast of the people." [5]

2. Take another example, and you will see the same thing

[4] 1 Pet. ii. 22, 23.
[5] Ps. xxii. 6.

still more strikingly. How overpowered should we be, nay
not at the sight only, but at the very hearing of cruelties
shown to a little child, and why so? for the same two reasons,
because it was so innocent, and because it was so unable to
defend itself. I do not like to go into the details of such cruelty,
they would be so heart-rending. What if wicked men took and
crucified a young child? What if they deliberately seized its
poor little frame, and stretched out its arms, nailed them to
a cross bar of wood, drove a stake through its two feet, and
fastened them to a beam, and so left it to die? It is almost too
shocking to say; perhaps, you will actually say it *is* too shocking, and ought not to be said. O, my brethren, you feel the
horror of this, and yet you can bear to read of Christ's sufferings without horror; for what is that little child's agony to His?
and which deserved it more? which is the more innocent?
which the holier? was He not gentler, sweeter, meeker, more
tender, more loving, than any little child? Why are you shocked
at the one, why are you not shocked at the other?

Or take another instance, not so shocking in its circumstances, yet introducing us to another distinction, in which
Christ's passion exceeds that of any innocent sufferers, such as
I have supposed. When Joseph was sent by his father to his
brethren on a message of love, they, when they saw him, said,
"Behold, this dreamer cometh; come now, therefore, and let
us slay him." [6] They did not kill him, however, but they put
him in a pit in spite of the anguish of his soul, and sold him
as a slave to the Ishmaelites, and he was taken down into a
foreign country, where he had no friends. Now this was most
cruel and most cowardly in the sons of Jacob; and what is so
especially shocking in it is, that Joseph was not only innocent
and defenceless, their younger brother whom they ought to
have protected, but besides that, he was so confiding and
loving, that he need not have come to them, that he would not
at all have been in their power, *except* for his desire to do them
service. Now, whom does this history remind us of but of Him

[6] Gen. xxxvii. 19, 20.

concerning whom the Master of the vineyard said, on sending Him to the husbandmen, "They will reverence My Son"? [7] "But when the husbandmen saw the Son, they said among themselves, This is the Heir, come, let us kill Him, and let us seize on His inheritance. And they caught Him, and cast Him out of the vineyard, and slew Him." Here, then, is an additional circumstance of cruelty to affect us in Christ's history, such as is suggested in Joseph's, but which no instance of a brute animal's or of a child's sufferings can have; our Lord was not only guiltless and defenceless, but He had come among His persecutors in love.

3. And now, instead of taking the case of the young, innocent, and confiding, let us take another instance which will present to us our Lord's passion under another aspect. Let us suppose that some aged and venerable person whom we have known as long as we could recollect any thing, and loved and reverenced, suppose such a one, who had often done us kindnesses, who had taught us, who had given us good advice, who had encouraged us, smiled on us, comforted us in trouble, whom we knew to be very good and religious, very holy, full of wisdom, full of heaven, with grey hairs and awful countenance, waiting for Almighty God's summons to leave this world for a better place; suppose, I say, such a one whom we have ourselves known, and whose memory is dear to us, rudely seized by fierce men, stripped naked in public, insulted, driven about here and there, made a laughing-stock, struck, spit on, dressed up in other clothes in ridicule, then severely scourged on the back, then laden with some heavy load till he could carry it no longer, pulled and dragged about, and at last exposed with all his wounds to the gaze of a rude multitude who came and jeered him, what would be our feelings? Let us in our mind think of this person or that, and consider how we should be overwhelmed and pierced through and through by such a hideous occurrence.

But what is all this to the suffering of the holy Jesus, which

[7] Matt. xxi. 37—39.

we bear to read of as a matter of course! Only think of Him, when in His wounded state, and without garment on, He had to creep up the ladder, as He could, which led Him up the cross high enough for His murderers to nail Him to it; and consider *who* it was that was in that misery. Or again, view Him dying, hour after hour bleeding to death; and how? in peace? no; with His arms stretched out, and His face exposed to view, and any one who pleased coming and staring at Him, mocking Him, and watching the gradual ebbing of His strength, and the approach of death. These are some of the appalling details which the Gospels contain, and surely they were not recorded for nothing; but that we might dwell on them.

Do you think that those who saw these things had much heart for eating or drinking or enjoying themselves? On the contrary, we are told that even "the people who came together to that sight, smote their breasts and returned." [8] If these were the feelings of the people, what were St. John's feelings, or St. Mary Magdalene's, or St. Mary's, our Lord's blessed mother? Do we desire to be of this company? do we desire, according to His own promise, to be rather blessed than the womb that bare Him, and the paps that He sucked? do we desire to be as His brother, and sister, and mother? [9] Then, surely, ought we to have some portion of that mother's sorrow! When He was on the cross and she stood by, then, according to Simeon's prophecy, "a sword pierced through her soul." [10] What is the use of our keeping the memory of His cross and passion, unless we lament and are in sorrow with her? I can understand people who do not keep Good Friday at all; they are indeed very ungrateful, but I know what they mean; I understand them. But I do not understand at all, I do not at all see what men mean who *do* profess to keep it, yet do not sorrow, or at least try to sorrow. Such a spirit of grief and lamentation is ex-

[8] Luke xxiii. 48.
[9] Matt. xii. 46, &c.
[10] Luke ii. 35.

pressly mentioned in Scripture as a characteristic of those who turn to Christ. If then *we* do not sorrow, have *we* turned to Him? "I will pour upon the house of David," says the merciful Saviour Himself, before He came on earth, speaking of what was to come, "upon the inhabitants of Jerusalem, the spirit of grace and of supplications; and they shall look upon Me whom they have pierced, and they shall *mourn* for Him, as one mourneth for his only son, and shall be in bitterness for Him, as one that is in bitterness for his first-born." [11]

One thing I will add:—if there be persons here present who are conscious to themselves that they do not feel the grief which this season should cause them, who feel now as they do at other times, let them consider with themselves whether perhaps this defect does not arise from their having neglected to come to church, whether during this season or at other times, as often as they might. Our feelings are not in our own power; God alone can rule our feelings; God alone can make us sorrow, when we would but cannot sorrow; but *will* He, if we have not diligently sought Him according to our opportunities in this house of grace? I speak of those who might come to prayers more frequently, and do not. I know well that many cannot come. I speak of those who can, if they will. Even if they come as often as they are able, I know well they will not be *satisfied* with their own feelings; they will be conscious even then that they ought to grieve more than they do; of course none of us feels the great event of this day as he ought, and therefore we all *ought* to be dissatisfied with ourselves. However, if this is not our own fault, we need not be out of heart, for God will mercifully lead us forward in His own time; but if it arises from our not coming to prayers here as often as we might, then our coldness and deadness *are* our own fault, and I beg you all to consider that that fault is not a slight one. It is said in the Book of Revelation, "Behold He cometh with clouds; and every eye shall see Him, and they also which pierced Him: and all kindreds of the earth shall wail because

[11] Zech. xii. 10.

of Him." [12] We, my brethren, every one of us, shall one day rise from our graves, and see Jesus Christ; we shall see Him who hung on the cross, we shall see His wounds, we shall see the marks in His hands, and in His feet, and in His side. Do we wish to be of those, then, who wail and lament, or of those who rejoice? If we would not lament at the sight of Him then, we must lament at the thought of Him now. Let us prepare to meet our God; let us come into His Presence whenever we can; let us try to fancy as if we saw the Cross and Him upon it; let us draw near to it; let us beg Him to look on us as He did on the penitent thief, and let us say to Him, "Lord remember me when Thou comest into Thy kingdom." [13]

Let this be added to the prayer, my brethren, with which you are about to leave this church. After I have given the blessing, you will say to yourselves a short prayer. Well; fancy you see Jesus Christ on the cross, and say to Him with the penitent thief, "Lord, remember me when Thou comest into Thy kingdom;" that is, "Remember me, Lord, in mercy, remember not my sins, but Thine own cross; remember Thine own sufferings, remember that Thou sufferedst for me, a sinner; remember in the last day that I, during my lifetime, felt Thy sufferings, that I suffered on my cross by Thy side. Remember me then, and make me remember Thee now."

[*March 25, 1842.*]

[12] Rev. i. 7.
[13] Luke xxiii. 42.

VI

THE CHRISTIAN CHURCH AN
IMPERIAL POWER [1]

*"And it shall come to pass in the last days, that the mountain of
the Lord's house shall be established in the top of the mountains,
and shall be exalted above the hills; and all nations shall flow unto
it."*—Isaiah ii. 2.

WHEN CHRIST CAME AND TOOK POSSESSION of His own
House, it could not be but that some great changes
would take place in its economy, and its condition.
And such there were; it was exalted and established above all
earthly power, and became a refuge and home for all nations.
It remained what it had been before, a Church, in its inward
and characteristic structure the same; but it became what it
had never been before, or only in a partial measure in the time
of David and some other princes, and that in type of what was
to come, it became an imperial Church. It was the head of an
empire.

And hence so much stress is laid upon its being a kingdom,
and Christ a King. It was a prophecy even among the heathen
at the time of His coming, that they who were to rule the world
were to issue from Judæa. Much more had Micah, with the
voice of inspiration, said of Bethlehem, "Though thou be little
among the thousands of Judah, yet out of thee shall He come
forth unto Me, that is to be ruler in Israel." [2] And Daniel saw
"one like the Son of man," "brought near before" the Ancient

[1] From *Sermons Bearing on Subjects of the Day*, No. 16. [Ed.]
[2] Micah v. 2.

49

of days, "and there was given Him dominion and glory, and a kingdom, that all people, nations, and languages, should serve Him." [3] And the patriarch Jacob, long before them, had said, "The sceptre shall not depart from Judah, nor a lawgiver from between his feet, until Shiloh come, and unto Him shall the gathering of the people be." [4] Well, then, might His own brethren rejoice and shout for joy, and sing Hosanna, when their King came unto them, "just and having salvation, lowly, and riding upon an ass, and upon a colt the foal of an ass." [5] And for Him, His first and last words were about His kingdom, or empire, as we now speak. For He began His ministry with the words, "Repent, for the kingdom of heaven is at hand." [6] And before He ascended, He committed the work to His disciples, "being seen of them forty days," says St. Luke, "and speaking of the things pertaining to the kingdom of God." [7]

1. When He was ascending, He said, "All power is given unto Me in heaven, and *in earth*." We believe in His power in heaven, but, strange to say, it is usual with us to grudge Him His power upon earth. We believe that He exercises His powerful intercession with the Father in heaven; but we seem to think that the Mediator has no earthly kingdom. As God indeed, of course, we accord Him a rule upon earth; but that rule He had from the time He created land and sea, and all things therein. But on His resurrection as Mediator, a kingdom was given unto Him; do we believe that He has a kingdom? We know what is meant by a kingdom. It means a body politic, bound together by common laws, ruled by one head, holding intercourse part with part, acting together. We know what is meant by the kingdom of Chaldea, or of Persia, or of Rome, which the Prophet Daniel mentions; do we believe that Christ now has a kingdom, as those earthly powers once had?

[3] Dan. vii. 13, 14.
[4] Gen. xlix. 10.
[5] Zech. ix. 9.
[6] Matt. iv. 17.
[7] Acts i. 3.

"Yes;" we reply, "He has a kingdom; it is an invisible kingdom." An *invisible* kingdom on *earth?* what is meant by an invisible kingdom? A kingdom is an organized body: do we mean then a secret society? no; what we really mean by the words is, that He has no earthly kingdom at all. We admit a truth and explain it away. We explain away His words into a mere metaphor, as when we speak of the animal kingdom, or the vegetable kingdom. When we say that Christ has an invisible kingdom, we mean, I suppose, that He has servants on earth, and gives them laws; that He interposes in the world's history, and punishes the guilty; but all this surely He did before He came in the flesh; and all this surely does not come up to the idea, does not answer to the name, of kingdom. It is as unmeaning to speak of an invisible kingdom on earth, as of invisible chariots and horsemen, invisible swords and spears, invisible palaces: to be a kingdom at all it must be visible, if the word has any true meaning.

But it may be said, that Christ Himself, the King, is invisible, and therefore His kingdom may well be invisible also. It is true, He is the *invisible* King of a *visible* kingdom; for it does not at all follow, because a monarch is withdrawn from view, that therefore His kingdom must cease to be a fact in the face of day also. It is seldom that the monarch of any kingdom is seen, and then not by many, except on certain occasions. Kings are within their palaces, yet their power is in the public world. It is seldom they rule by themselves; they rule by instruments. Such is Christ's mode of governing; He is away; He has not resigned His rule; He does not simply abandon it to His servants: but still He rules *through* His appointed servants, and has committed His subjects to *them*. He resembles earthly sovereigns, not only in having a kingdom, but in His mode of governing it.

Now this description of Christ's kingdom is what He gives us of it Himself. "*The kingdom of heaven,*" He says, "is as a man travelling into a far country, who called his own servants, and *delivered unto them his goods.* And unto one he gave five talents, to another two, and to another one." [8] Another parable, spoken in warning, represents the officers of the kingdom under the image of a steward: "Who then is that faithful and wise steward, whom his lord shall make ruler over his household, to give them their portion of meat in due season? ...If that servant say in his heart, My Lord delayeth His coming, and shall begin to beat the men-servants and maidens, and to eat and drink, and to be drunken, the Lord of that servant will come in a day when he looketh not for Him, and at an hour when he is not aware." [9]

2. So much is spoken in general; but next *who* are spoken of as the rulers in the kingdom, Christ's viceroys? the Twelve Apostles, and first of all Peter. To him our Lord addressed these wonderful words: "I say unto thee, That thou art Peter, and upon this rock I will build My Church; and the gates of hell shall not prevail against it. And I will give unto thee the keys of the kingdom of heaven: and whatsoever thou shalt bind on earth shall be bound in heaven; and whatsoever thou shalt loose on earth shall be loosed in heaven." [10] By the "Church" must be meant a community or polity of men, and you see that St. Peter had the keys of this Church or kingdom, or the power of admitting into it, and excluding from it: and besides that, an awful power of binding and loosing, about which it does not fall within our present subject to inquire.

What is here spoken of St. Peter, is elsewhere spoken of the other Apostles. They too are rulers in Christ's kingdom. Christ said to them all, "Whatsoever ye shall bind on earth shall be bound in heaven, and whatsoever ye shall loose on earth shall be loosed in heaven." [11]

And more distinctly on another occasion: "I appoint unto you a kingdom, as My Father hath appointed unto Me, that ye may eat and drink at My table, in My kingdom, and sit on

[8] Matt. xxv. 14, 15.
[9] Luke xii. 42, 45, 46.
[10] Matt. xvi. 18, 19.
[11] Matt. xviii. 18.

thrones, judging the twelve tribes of Israel." [12] It had been prophesied of Christ that He should sit on the throne of David. Accordingly, they too, as His representatives, in His absence, were to sit on twelve thrones.

And their authority was equal to that of Him who appointed them. "He that receiveth you," He saith, "receiveth Me; and he that receiveth Me, receiveth Him that sent Me." [13] And as He had said to the seventy, "He that heareth you, heareth Me; and he that despiseth you, despiseth Me; and he that despiseth Me, despiseth Him that sent Me." [14] Nay, it would seem as if their authority were even greater than that which it pleased our Lord to possess in the days of His flesh; for, whereas He breathed on them and said, "Receive ye the Holy Ghost," He had formerly said, "Whosoever speaketh a word against the Son of man, it shall be forgiven him; but whosoever speaketh against the Holy Ghost, it shall not be forgiven him, neither in this world, neither in the world to come." [15] Thus the Apostles, the ministers of the kingdom, as being the organs of the Spirit, were arrayed in more awful sanctions even than the King Himself during His abode upon earth; and hence St. Paul says, "He that despiseth, despiseth not man, but God; who hath also given unto us His Holy Spirit." [16] And when St. Peter inflicted judgment upon Ananias, he said, "Thou hast not lied unto men, but unto God." [17]

Moreover, this kingdom was to extend all over the earth; "Go ye therefore and teach all nations," [18] or rather, "make disciples of all nations, baptizing them." And, especially, consider the parable of the mustard seed. "The kingdom of heaven," says our Lord, "is like to a grain of mustard seed,

[12] Luke xxii. 29, 30.
[13] Matt. x. 40.
[14] Luke x. 16.
[15] Matt. xii. 32.
[16] 1 Thess. iv. 8.
[17] Acts v. 4.
[18] Matt. xxviii. 19.

which a man took and sowed in his field; which indeed is the least of all seeds; but when it is grown, it is the greatest among herbs, and becometh a tree; so that the birds of the air come and lodge in the branches thereof." Now what is especially remarkable here, is the concluding clause, which seems to refer us, by way of parallel, to the Chaldean power, as described by the Prophet Daniel, of which Nebuchadnezzar was the head. "The tree grew and was strong, and the height thereof reached unto heaven . . . the beasts of the field had shadow under it, and the fowls of the heaven dwelt in the boughs thereof." [19] The parable then of the mustard seed, not only represents the kingdom of Christ as the greatest of kingdoms, but, like Nebuchadnezzar's, as a kingdom under which things external to it find shelter, or as an empire.

And further, let it be observed, that the visible appearance and display of this one kingdom in all lands, seems to have been intended as the means (which no doubt it really was in the event) by which all lands were to be converted. For our Lord prays for His followers, that they may be *one; "that* the world may *believe* that Thou hast sent Me." Again, "that they may be made perfect in one, *that* the world may *know* that Thou hast sent Me, and hast loved them as Thou hast loved Me." [20]

3. Now the only question that can here arise is this: whether this imperial power was vested only in the Twelve Apostles, or in others besides and after them.

I answer, we must conclude that the power was vested in others also, from the size of the empire; for a few persons, though inspired, cannot be supposed to have been equal to the care of all the Churches. As Moses found his charge too great for him, and was permitted to have associates in his office, so doubtless would it be with the Apostles.

But again, it is expressly said, that the Church is to last to the end of time, and the gates of hell are to fail in their warfare

[19] Dan. iv. 11, 12. *Vide* also Ezek. xvii. 23; xxxi. 6.
[20] John xvii. 21, 23.

against it. But the Apostles were soon cut off; therefore the Church's power was vested in others besides the Apostles.

But further, let this be observed, that the promise was neither made nor fulfilled exactly to the Twelve Apostles; one of them fell, and another took his place. Again, St. Paul was "not a whit behind the very chiefest Apostles," yet he was added to their original company. Further, when, after His resurrection, He breathed on the Apostles, and gave them power to remit sins, St. Thomas was not present; was he then without the power which the rest had? Surely not; therefore others had it besides them on whom our Lord personally or primarily bestowed it. It appears from all this, that the Twelve to whom our Lord first spake, were but representatives of the full number of His ministers, not commensurate with them.

This conclusion is strengthened by considering our Lord's language on another occasion, which certainly seems to show that the Apostles were not regarded by Christ in a personal light, but as representatives of others, or rather, I should say, of Himself. He truly is the only One, properly speaking, who sits on the throne of the kingdom; He is the sole Ruler in His empire, though invisible. They are but regents, or viceroys, in His absence; and whatever be their power, it is not their own, it comes from Him; and as it did not begin in them, so with them it did not terminate. They were but the accidental, though specially favoured, organs of His wonder-working operation. The text I allude to is as follows:—"Be not ye called Rabbi, for One is your Master, even Christ, and all ye are brethren. . . . Call no man your father upon the earth; for One is your Father, which is in heaven. Neither be ye called masters; for One is your Master, even Christ." [21] What words can be clearer to show, that no honours which were accorded to the Apostles, were accorded to them for their own sake, or were, strictly speaking, vested in *them?* that they were theirs only as being instruments of Him who, being "immortal, invisible," governs His kingdom in every age in His own

[21] Matt. xxiii. 8–10.

way, the one Master, the one Lord, the one Teacher, the one Priest, alone glorified in all His saints, while they live and when they die? Whatever honours, then, and powers the Apostles possessed, needed not to die with them, for they never had really belonged to them.

It would seem then, that the ecclesiastical power held by the Apostles was intended for others also; but let us suppose the contrary, and see what will follow. This will follow: that we have no warrant in Scripture for any ministry under the Gospel at all; a ministry like the Apostles' being the only ministry for which we have *any* precedent in the New Testament. If we will be scriptural in our view of the Church, we must consider that it is a kingdom, that its officers have great powers and high gifts, that they are charged with the custody of Divine Truth, that they are all united together, and that the nations are subject to them. If we reject this kind of ministry, as inapplicable to the present day, we shall in vain go to Scripture to find another. If we will form to ourselves a ministry and a Church bereft of the august power which I have mentioned, it will be one of our own devising; and let us pretend no more to draw our religion from the Bible. Rather, we are like Jeroboam, who made his own religion. "Jesus I know, and Paul I know," said the evil spirit in the demoniac; "but who are ye?" Men now-a-days consider the Christian minister to be merely one who teaches the unlearned, rouses the sinful, consoles the afflicted, and relieves the poor. Great and Gospel offices these indeed, but who made them the privilege of a particular order of men? Great and Gospel offices, so great, so full of Gospel savour, that they are the prerogatives of all Christians, and may not be confined to a class. If the ministerial office consist in these alone, then all Christians are ministers. Men have a notion, that the mere function of reading prayers in public worship, and preaching sermons, constitutes a minister of Christ: where is this found in Scripture? Let us be honest; we are but deceiving ourselves, if we keep up the name of a Church, and deny its Scripture definition.

4. These then being the characteristics of the Christian Church, as we find them stated in the New Testament, let us next turn to the Prophets of the Old, and observe whether the same are not represented to us even more explicitly in their inspired pages. If even from the texts which have been cited from the Gospels we might infer the imperial nature of Christ's kingdom, much more is this peculiarity of it drawn out in the prophetical writings. By an imperial state, or an empire, is meant a power which has wide extent over the earth, and that beyond its own limits. Thus, the kingdom of which we are subjects is small, consisting of two islands; but the empire vested in that kingdom extends all over the earth, consisting of our colonies, dependencies, fortified places, subject and tributary nations, and such allies as are materially under our influence and authority. It is the peculiarity of an imperial state to bear rule over other states; and it is another peculiarity, not indeed essential, but almost necessary, that it should be always in movement, advancing or retiring, never stationary, aggression being the condition of its existence. Conquest is almost of the essence of an empire, and when it ceases to conquer it ceases to be.

Such is an empire of this world; and it is not difficult to show from Scripture, that such also in its substance is the kingdom of Christ. "In the days of these kings," says Daniel, speaking of the heathen empires, "shall the God of heaven set up a kingdom, which shall never be destroyed; and the kingdom shall not be left to other people, but it shall break in pieces and consume all these kingdoms, and it shall stand for ever." [22] Christ's religion was not a mere creed or philosophy. A creed or a philosophy need not have interfered with kingdoms of this world; but might have existed under the Roman empire or under the Persian. No; Christ's kingdom was a counter kingdom. It occupied ground; it claimed to rule over those whom hitherto this world's governments ruled over without rival; and if this world's governments would not themselves

[22] Dan. ii. 44.

acknowledge and submit to its rule, and rule under and according to its laws, it "broke in pieces" those governments—not by carnal weapons, but by Divine Power—"without hands," to use the Prophet Daniel's language. Or, as another Prophet expresses it, "The nation and kingdom that will not serve thee shall perish; yea, those nations shall be utterly wasted." [23]

The royal Prophet and the other Psalmists give the same account of the promised kingdom, as an enterprising, active, advancing power, or empire, conquering and ruling. "Gird Thee with Thy sword upon Thy thigh, O Thou Most Mighty, according to Thy worship and renown.... Thy arrows are very sharp, and the people shall be subdued unto Thee; even in the midst, among the King's enemies." [24] And while conquest is spoken of, and sharp weapons, in order to conquest, it is also signified that these weapons are of a heavenly nature; "Ride on, because of the word of truth, of meekness, and righteousness." Again, "A sceptre of righteousness is the sceptre of Thy kingdom; Thou hast loved righteousness and hated iniquity." [25] Parallel to this are the passages in the book of Revelation, where our Lord is represented as on a white horse, the emblem of holiness: "I saw, and behold a white horse; and He that sat on him had a bow, and a crown was given unto Him; and He went forth conquering and to conquer." [26] Again: "I saw heaven opened, and behold a white horse; and He that sat upon him was called Faithful and True, and in righteousness He doth judge and make war.... And the armies which were in heaven followed Him upon white horses, clothed in fine linen, white and clean. And out of His mouth goeth a sharp sword, that with it He should smite the nations; and He shall rule them with a rod of iron." [27]

These last words remind us of another celebrated Psalm, in

[23] Isa. lx. 12.
[24] Ps. xlv. 4, 6.
[25] Heb. i. 8, 9.
[26] Rev. vi. 2.
[27] Rev. xix. 11, 14, 15.

which the conflict is described between Christ and the world, and the conquest of Christ predicted. "The kings of the earth stand up, and the rulers take counsel together, against the Lord and against His Anointed. . . . Thou shalt bruise them with a rod of iron, and break them in pieces like a potter's vessel. Be wise now, therefore, O ye kings; be learned, ye that are judges of the earth. Serve the Lord in fear, and rejoice unto Him with reverence." [28] You see that Christ breaks whom He does not bend; and that it is the wisdom of kings of the earth to bow down to Christ.

In another Psalm: "They that dwell in the wilderness shall kneel before Him. His enemies shall lick the dust. . . . All kings shall fall down before Him; all nations shall do Him service. For He shall deliver the poor when he crieth, the needy also, and him that hath no helper." [29] You see that Christ persuades or destroys; and that kings of the earth must fall down before Him, or lick the dust.

Again: "Let the saints be joyful with glory; let them rejoice in their beds. Let the praises of God be in their mouth, and a two-edged sword in their hands; to be avenged of the heathen, and to rebuke the people; to bind their kings in chains, and their nobles with links of iron." [30] Such is the battle of the Saints, such the victory of the Christian army, though their weapons be not carnal.

Once more: "Let God arise, and let His enemies be scattered: let them also that hate Him flee before Him. . . . The chariots of God are twenty thousand, even thousands of Angels; and the Lord is among them, as in the holy place of Sinai. . . . God shall wound the head of His enemies, and the hairy scalp of such a one as goeth on still in his wickedness. The Lord hath said, I will bring My people again, as I did from Basan; Mine own will I bring again, as I did sometime from the deep of the sea. . . . When He hath scattered the people that delight in

[28] Ps. ii. 2, 9–11.
[29] Ps. lxxii. 9, 11, 12.
[30] Ps. cxlix. 5–9.

war, then shall the princes come out of Egypt; the Morian's land shall soon stretch out her hands unto God." [31] You see God promised to fight for His people, and His people were to make progress, and to spread while He fought as of old time.

If we next take up the book of the Prophet Isaiah, we shall find promises made to the kingdom of Christ so many, and so high and awful, that there is neither time nor necessity to quote them at length. Thus in the text: "It shall come to pass in the last days, that the mountain of the Lord's house shall be established in the top of the mountains, and shall be exalted above the hills; and all nations shall flow unto it. . . . And He shall judge among the nations, and shall rebuke many people; and they shall beat their swords into ploughshares, and their spears into pruninghooks. . . . The lofty looks of man shall be humbled, and the haughtiness of men shall be bowed down, and the Lord alone shall be exalted in that day." [32] "In that day there shall be a root of Jesse, which shall stand for an ensign of the people: to it shall the Gentiles seek: and His rest shall be glorious." [33] Again, "The extortioner is at an end, the spoiler ceaseth, the oppressors are consumed out of the land. And in mercy shall the throne be established, and He shall sit upon it in truth, in the tabernacle of David, judging and seeking judgment, and hasting righteousness." [34]

But, you will say, such passages in the Prophet speak rather of the victory of the faith than of the Church; and that the faith might spread, even though there were no Church. Let us, then, consider the following passages in addition, and see whether, taken all together, they admit of being thus explained. "Arise, shine," says the Prophet to the Church, "for thy light is come, and the glory of the Lord is risen upon thee. . . . And the Gentiles shall come to thy light, and kings to the brightness of thy rising. . . . The sons of strangers shall build up thy walls,

---

[31] Ps. lxviii. 1, 17, 21, 22, 30, 31.
[32] Isa. ii. 2, 4, 11.
[33] Isa. xi. 10.
[34] Isa. xvi. 4, 5.

and their kings shall minister unto thee.... The nation and kingdom that will not serve thee shall perish; yea, those nations shall be utterly wasted. . . . The sons also of them that afflicted thee shall come bending unto thee; and all they that despised thee shall bow themselves down at the soles of thy feet." [35] Again, "Behold I will make thee a new sharp threshing instrument, having teeth; thou shalt thresh the mountains, and beat them small, and shalt make the hills as chaff." Again, "Enlarge the place of thy tent, and let them stretch forth the curtains of thine habitations: spare not, lengthen thy cords, and strengthen thy stakes. For thou shalt break forth on the right hand and on the left; and thy seed shall inherit the Gentiles, and make the desolate cities to be inhabited. . . . No weapon that is formed against thee shall prosper; and every tongue that shall rise against thee in judgment thou shalt condemn." [36] Again, "Strangers shall stand and feed your flocks, and the sons of the alien shall be your plowmen and your vine-dressers. But ye shall be named the priests of the Lord, men shall call you the ministers of our God; for ye shall eat the riches of the Gentiles, and in their glory shall ye boast yourselves." And again, "Kings shall be thy nursing fathers, and their queens thy nursing mothers: they shall bow down to thee with their face toward the earth, and lick up the dust of thy feet." [37]

What is wanting in such passages to the picture of a great empire, comprising all that a great empire ordinarily exhibits? Extended dominion, and that not only over its immediate subjects, but over the kings of other kingdoms; aggression and advance; a warfare against enemies; acts of judgment upon the proud; acts of triumph over the defeated; high imperial majesty towards the suppliant; clemency towards the repentant; parental care of the dutiful. Again, these passages imply, in the subjects of the kingdom, a multitude of various conditions and dispositions; some of them loyal, some restrained by fear, some

[35] Isa. lx. 1, 3, 10, 12, 14.
[36] Isa. liv. 2, 3, 17.
[37] Isa. xlix. 23.

by interest, some partly subjected, some indirectly influenced. They involve, in consequence, though they do not mention, a complex organization, and a combination of movements, and a variety and opposition of interests, and other similar results of extended sway. Of course, too, they involve vicissitudes of fortune, and all those other characteristics of the history of a temporal power which ever will attend it, while men are men, whether, as in the case of the Jews, they are under a supernatural Providence or no.

5. After this view of the Gospel Church, as set before us in our Lord's announcements, and in the prophecies which preceded His coming, let us turn, in conclusion, to its history, and see whether they have not been most exactly and marvellously fulfilled.

Even in the Apostles' life-time the Gospel had spread east, west, and south, far and wide, and the Church with it. Multitudes had been converted in all nations, and the Apostles were the acknowledged rulers of those multitudes. So wide and well-connected a polity there was not on the earth, even before their martyrdom, except the Roman Empire itself, which was the seat of it.

And much more have the prophecies been fulfilled in later times. Many persons among us think that the history of the Church has been the fulfilment of those dark and fearful predictions, which speak of the city of confusion, and the man of sin. Now here I put the matter to a simple issue. Here are two sets of prophecies: one about the Gospel Dispensation, in the Prophet Isaiah and his brethren; the other in Daniel, St. Paul, and St. John, about the great enemy of the Gospel. I ask, then, *which* of the two sets of prophecy is the more *literally* fulfilled in the history of the Church? In which have we the less need to betake ourselves to allegories, and explanations, and forced statements? which of the two has the fewer difficulties? Has there not, in fact, been a great corporation, or continuous body politic, all over the world, from the Apostles' days to our own, bearing the name of Church—one, and one only? Has it not spread in spite of all opposition, and maintained itself marvellously against the power of the world? Has it not ever taken the cause of the poor and friendless against the great and proud? Has it not succeeded by the use of weapons, not earthly and carnal, but by righteousness and mercy, as was foretold? Has it not broken in pieces numberless kingdoms and conquerors which opposed it, and risen again, and flourished more than before, after the most hopeless reverses? Has it not ever been at war with the spirit of the world, with pride, and luxury, and cruelty, and tyranny, and profaneness? Let us, then, glorify our Lord and Saviour for what He has said, what He has done. Surely we may use, and with fuller reason, if it be possible, the words of Solomon, "Blessed be the Lord, that hath given rest unto His people Israel, according to all that He promised; *there hath not failed one word* of all His good promise, which He promised by the hand of Moses His servant. The Lord our God be with us, as He was with our fathers: let Him not leave us, nor forsake us: that He may incline our hearts unto Him, to walk in all His ways, and to keep His commandments, and His statutes, and His judgments which He commanded our fathers; . . . that He maintain the cause of His servant and the cause of His people Israel, at all times, as the matter shall require; that all the people of the earth may know that the Lord is God, and that there is none else." [38]

[*November 27, 1842.*]

[38] 1 Kings viii. 56–60.

VII

THE THEORY OF DEVELOPMENTS IN RELIGIOUS DOCTRINE [1]

"But Mary kept all these things, and pondered them in her heart."
—Luke ii. 19.

LITTLE IS TOLD US IN SCRIPTURE concerning the Blessed Virgin, but there is one grace of which the Evangelists make her the pattern, in a few simple sentences,—of Faith. Zacharias questioned the Angel's message, but "Mary said, Behold the handmaid of the Lord; be it unto me according to thy word." Accordingly Elisabeth, speaking with an apparent allusion to the contrast thus exhibited between her own highly-favoured husband, righteous Zacharias, and the still more highly-favoured Mary, said, on receiving her salutation, "Blessed art thou among women, and blessed is the fruit of thy womb; Blessed is she that believed, for there shall be a performance of those things which were told her from the Lord."

2. But Mary's faith did not end in a mere acquiescence in Divine providences and revelations: as the text informs us, she "pondered" them. When the shepherds came, and told of the vision of Angels which they had seen at the time of the Nativity, and how one of them announced that the Infant in her arms was "the Saviour, which is Christ the Lord," while others did but wonder, "Mary kept all these things, and pondered them in her heart." Again, when her Son and Saviour had come to the age of twelve years, and had left her for awhile

[1] Preached on the Feast of the Purification. From *Oxford University Sermons,* No. 15. [Ed.]

for His Father's service, and had been found, to her surprise, in the Temple, amid the doctors, both hearing them and asking them questions, and had, on her addressing Him, vouchsafed to justify His conduct, we are told, "His mother kept all these sayings in her heart." And accordingly, at the marriage-feast in Cana, her faith anticipated His first miracle, and she said to the servants, "Whatsoever He saith unto you, do it."

3. Thus St. Mary is our pattern of Faith, both in the reception and in the study of Divine Truth. She does not think it enough to accept, she dwells upon it; not enough to possess, she uses it; not enough to assent, she developes it; not enough to submit the Reason, she reasons upon it; not indeed reasoning first, and believing afterwards, with Zacharias, yet first believing without reasoning, next from love and reverence, reasoning after believing. And thus she symbolizes to us, not only the faith of the unlearned, but of the doctors of the Church also, who have to investigate, and weigh, and define, as well as to profess the Gospel; to draw the line between truth and heresy; to anticipate or remedy the various aberrations of wrong reason; to combat pride and recklessness with their own arms; and thus to triumph over the sophist and the innovator.

4. If, then, on a Day dedicated to such high contemplations as the Feast which we are now celebrating, it is allowable to occupy the thoughts with a subject not of a devotional or practical nature, it will be some relief of the omission to select one in which St. Mary at least will be our example,—the use of Reason in investigating the doctrines of Faith; a subject, indeed, far fitter for a volume than for the most extended notice which can here be given to it; but one which cannot be passed over altogether in silence, in any attempt at determining the relation of Faith to Reason.

5. The overthrow of the wisdom of the world was one of the earliest, as well as the noblest of the triumphs of the Church; after the pattern of her Divine Master, who took His place among the doctors before He preached His new Kingdom, or opposed Himself to the world's power. St. Paul, the

learned Pharisee, was the first fruits of that gifted company, in whom the pride of science is seen prostrated before the foolishness of preaching. From his day to this the Cross has enlisted under its banner all those great endowments of mind, which in former times had been expended on vanities, or dissipated in doubt and speculation. Nor was it long before the schools of heathenism took the alarm, and manifested an unavailing jealousy of the new doctrine, which was robbing them of their most hopeful disciples. They had hitherto taken for granted that the natural home of the Intellect was the Garden or the Porch; and it reversed their very first principles to be called on to confess, what yet they could not deny, that a Superstition, as they considered it, was attracting to itself all the energy, the keenness, the originality, and the eloquence of the age. But these aggressions upon heathenism were only the beginning of the Church's conquests; in the course of time the whole mind of the world, as I may say, was absorbed into the philosophy of the Cross, as the element in which it lived, and the form upon which it was moulded. And how many centuries did this endure, and what vast ruins still remain of its dominion! In the capitals of Christendom the high cathedral and the perpetual choir still witness to the victory of Faith over the world's power. To see its triumph over the world's wisdom, we must enter those solemn cemeteries in which are stored the relics and the monuments of ancient Faith—our libraries. Look along their shelves, and every name you read there is, in one sense or other, a trophy set up in record of the victories of Faith. How many long lives, what high aims, what single-minded devotion, what intense contemplation, what fervent prayer, what deep erudition, what untiring diligence, what toilsome conflicts has it taken to establish its supremacy! This has been the object which has given meaning to the life of Saints, and which is the subject-matter of their history. For this they have given up the comforts of earth and the charities of home, and surrendered themselves to an austere rule, nay, even to confessorship and persecution, if so be they could

make some small offering, or do some casual service, or provide some additional safeguard towards the great work which
was in progress. This has been the origin of controversies, long
and various, yes, and the occasion of much infirmity, the test
of much hidden perverseness, and the subject of much bitterness and tumult. The world has been moved in consequence
of it, populations excited, leagues and alliances formed, kingdoms lost and won: and even zeal, when excessive, evinced
a sense of its preciousness; nay, even rebellions in some sort
did homage to it, as insurgents imply the actual sovereignty of
the power which they are assailing. Meanwhile the work went
on, and at length a large fabric of divinity was reared, irregu-
lar in its structure, and diverse in its style, as beseemed the
slow growth of centuries; nay, anomalous in its details, from
the peculiarities of individuals, or the interference of strangers,
but still, on the whole, the development of an idea, like itself,
and unlike any thing else, its most widely-separated parts having relations with each other, and betokening a common
origin.

6. Let us quit this survey of the general system, and descend
to the history of the formation of any Catholic dogma. What
a remarkable sight it is, as almost all unprejudiced persons will
admit, to trace the course of the controversy, from its first dis-
orders to its exact and determinate issue. Full of deep interest,
to see how the great idea takes hold of a thousand minds by
its living force, and will not be ruled or stinted, but is "like
a burning fire," as the Prophet speaks, "shut up" within them,
till they are "weary of forbearing, and cannot stay," and grows
in them, and at length is born through them, perhaps in a
long course of years, and even successive generations; so that
the doctrine may rather be said to use the minds of Christians,
than to be used by them. Wonderful it is to see with what
effort, hesitation, suspense, interruption,—with how many
swayings to the right and to the left—with how many reverses,
yet with what certainty of advance, with what precision in its
march, and with what ultimate completeness, it has been

evolved; till the whole truth "self-balanced on its centre hung," part answering to part, one, absolute, integral, indissoluble, while the world lasts! Wonderful, to see how heresy has but thrown that idea into fresh forms, and drawn out from it farther developments, with an exuberance which exceeded all questioning, and a harmony which baffled all criticism, like Him, its Divine Author, who, when put on trial by the Evil One, was but fortified by the assault, and is ever justified in His sayings, and overcomes when He is judged.

7. And this world of thought is the expansion of a few words, uttered, as if casually, by the fishermen of Galilee. Here is another topic which belongs more especially to that part of the subject to which I propose to confine myself. Reason has not only submitted, it has ministered to Faith; it has illustrated its documents; it has raised illiterate peasants into philosophers and divines; it has elicited a meaning from their words which their immediate hearers little suspected. Stranger surely is it that St. John should be a theologian, than that St. Peter should be a prince. This is a phenomenon proper to the Gospel, and a note of divinity. Its half sentences, its overflowings of language, admit of development; [2] they have a life in them which shows itself in progress; a truth, which has the token of consistency; a reality, which is fruitful in resources; a depth, which extends into mystery: for they are representations of what is actual, and has a definite location and necessary bearings and a meaning in the great system of things, and a harmony in what it is, and a compatibility in what it involves. What form of Paganism can furnish a parallel? What philosopher has left his words to posterity as a talent which could be put to usury, as a mine which could be wrought? Here, too, is the badge of heresy; its dogmas are unfruitful; it has no theology; so far forth as it is heresy, it has none. Deduct its remnant of Catholic theology, and what remains? Polemics, explanations, protests. It turns to Biblical Criticism, or to the Evidences of Religion, for want of a province. Its *formulæ*

[2] *Vide* Butler's *Analogy*, part ii. ch. iii.

end in themselves, without development, because they are words; they are barren, because they are dead. If they had life, they would increase and multiply; or, if they do live and bear fruit, it is but as "sin, when it is finished, bringeth forth death." It developes into dissolution; but it creates nothing, it tends to no system, its resultant dogma is but the denial of all dogmas, any theology, under the Gospel. No wonder it denies what it cannot attain.

8. Heresy denies to the Church what is wanting in itself. Here, then, we are brought to the subject to which I wish to give attention. It need not surely formally be proved that this disparagement of doctrinal statements, and in particular of those relating to the Holy Trinity and Incarnation, is especially prevalent in our times. There is a suspicion widely abroad,— felt, too, perhaps, by many who are unwilling to confess it,— that the development of ideas and formation of dogmas is a mere abuse of Reason, which, when it attempted such sacred subjects, went beyond its powers, and could do nothing more than multiply words without meaning, and deductions which come to nothing. The conclusion follows, that such an attempt does but lead to mischievous controversy, from that discordance of doctrinal opinions, which is its immediate consequence; that there is, in truth, no necessary or proper connexion between inward religious belief and scientific expositions; and that charity, as well as good sense, is best consulted by reducing creeds to the number of private opinions, which, if individuals will hold for themselves, at least they have no right to impose upon others.

9. It is my purpose, then, in what follows, to investigate the connexion between Faith and Dogmatic Confession, as far as relates to the sacred doctrines which were just now mentioned, and to show the office of the Reason in reference to it; and, in doing so, I shall make as little allusion as may be to erroneous views on the subject, which have been mentioned only for the sake of perspicuity; following rather the course which the discussion may take, and pursuing those issues on

which it naturally opens. Nor am I here in any way concerned with the question, who is the legitimate framer and judge of these dogmatic inferences under the Gospel, or if there be any. Whether the Church is infallible, or the individual, or the first ages, or none of these, is not the point here, but the theory of developments itself.

10. Theological dogmas are propositions expressive of the judgments which the mind forms, or the impressions which it receives, of Revealed Truth. Revelation sets before it certain supernatural facts and actions, beings and principles; these make a certain impression or image upon it; and this impression spontaneously, or even necessarily, becomes the subject of reflection on the part of the mind itself, which proceeds to investigate it, and to draw it forth in successive and distinct sentences. Thus the Catholic doctrine of Original Sin, or of Sin after Baptism, or of the Eucharist, or of Justification, is but the expression of the inward belief of Catholics on these several points, formed upon an analysis of that belief.[3] Such, too, are the high doctrines with which I am especially concerned.

11. Now, here I observe, first of all, that, naturally as the inward idea of divine truth, such as has been described, passes into explicit form by the activity of our reflective powers, still such an actual delineation is not essential to its genuineness and perfection. A peasant may have such a true impression, yet be unable to give any intelligible account of it, as will easily be understood. But what is remarkable at first sight is this, that there is good reason for saying that the impression made upon the mind need not even be recognized by the parties possessing it. It is no proof that persons are not possessed, because they are not conscious, of an idea. Nothing is of more

[3] The controversy between the English Church and the Church of Rome lies, it is presumed, *in the matter of fact,* whether such and such developments are true, (e. g. Purgatory a true development of the doctrine of sin after baptism,) not in the *principle* of development itself.

frequent occurrence, whether in things sensible or intellectual, than the existence of such unperceived impressions. What do we mean when we say, that certain persons do not know themselves, but that they are ruled by views, feelings, prejudices, objects which they do not recognize? How common is it to be exhilarated or depressed, we do not recollect why, though we are aware that something has been told us, or has happened, good or bad, which accounts for our feeling, could we recall it! What is memory itself, but a vast magazine of such dormant, but present and excitable ideas? Or consider, when persons would trace the history of their own opinions in past years, how baffled they are in the attempt to fix the date of this or that conviction, their system of thought having been all the while in continual, gradual, tranquil expansion; so that it were as easy to follow the growth of the fruit of the earth, "first the blade, then the ear, after that the full corn in the ear," as to chronicle changes, which involved no abrupt revolution, or reaction, or fickleness of mind, but have been the birth of an idea, the development, in explicit form, of what was already latent within it. Or, again, critical disquisitions are often written about the idea which this or that poet might have in his mind in certain of his compositions and characters; and we call such analysis the philosophy of poetry, not implying thereby of necessity that the author wrote upon a theory in his actual delineation, or knew what he was doing; but that, in matter of fact, he was possessed, ruled, guided by an unconscious idea. Moreover, it is a question whether that strange and painful feeling of unreality, which religious men experience from time to time, when nothing seems true, or good, or right, or profitable, when Faith seems a name, and duty a mockery, and all endeavours to do right, absurd and hopeless, and all things forlorn and dreary, as if religion were wiped out from the world, may not be the direct effect of the temporary obscuration of some master vision, which unconsciously supplies the mind with spiritual life and peace.

12. Or, to take another class of instances which are to the

point so far as this, that at least they are real impressions, even though they be not influential. How common is what is called vacant vision, when objects meet the eye, without any effort of the judgment to measure or locate them; and that absence of mind, which recollects minutes afterwards the occurrence of some sound, the striking of the hour, or the question of a companion, which passed unheeded at the time it took place! How, again, happens it in dreams, that we suddenly pass from one state of feeling, or one assemblage of circumstances to another, without any surprise at the incongruity, except that, while we are impressed first in this way, then in that, we take no active cognizance of the impression? And this, perhaps, is the life of inferior animals, a sort of continuous dream, impressions without reflections; such, too, seems to be the first life of infants; nay, in heaven itself, such may be the high existence of some exalted orders of blessed spirits, as the Seraphim, who are said to be, not Knowledge, but all Love.

13. Now, it is important to insist on this circumstance, because it suggests the reality and permanence of inward knowledge, as distinct from explicit confession. The absence, or partial absence, or incompleteness of dogmatic statements is no proof of the absence of impressions or implicit judgments, in the mind of the Church. Even centuries might pass without the formal expression of a truth, which had been all along the secret life of millions of faithful souls. Thus, not till the thirteenth century was there any direct and distinct avowal, on the part of the Church, of the numerical Unity of the Divine Nature, which the language of some of the principal Greek fathers, *primâ facie,* though not really, denies. Again, the doctrine of the Double Procession was no Catholic dogma in the first ages, though it was more or less clearly stated by individual Fathers; yet, if it is now to be received, as surely it must be, as part of the Creed, it was really held every where from the beginning, and therefore, in a measure, held as a mere religious impression, and perhaps an unconscious one.

14. But, further, if the ideas may be latent in the Christian mind, by which it is animated and formed, it is less wonderful that they should be difficult to elicit and define; and of this difficulty we have abundant proof in the history whether of the Church, or of individuals. Surely it is not at all wonderful, that, when individuals attempt to analyze their own belief, they should find the task arduous in the extreme, if not altogether beyond them; or, again, a work of many years; or, again, that they should shrink from the true developments, if offered to them, as foreign to their thoughts. This may be illustrated in a variety of ways.

15. It will often happen, perhaps from the nature of things, that it is impossible to master and express an idea in a short space of time. As to individuals, sometimes they find they cannot do so at all; at length, perhaps, they recognize, in some writer they meet with, the very account of their own thoughts, which they desiderate; and then they say, that "here is what they have felt all along, and wanted to say, but could not," or "what they have ever maintained, only better expressed." Again, how many men are burdened with an idea, which haunts them through a great part of their lives, and of which only at length, with much trouble, do they dispossess themselves? I suppose most of us have felt at times the irritation, and that for a long period, of thoughts and views which we felt, and felt to be true, only dimly showing themselves, or flitting before us; which at length we understood must not be forced, but must have their way, and would, if it were so ordered, come to light in their own time. The life of some men, and those not the least eminent among divines and philosophers, has centred in the development of one idea; nay, perhaps has been too short for the process. Again, how frequently it happens, that, on first hearing a doctrine propounded, a man hesitates, first acknowledges, then disowns it; then says that he has always held it, but finds fault with the mode in which it is presented to him, accusing it of paradox or over-refinement; that is, he cannot at the moment analyze his own opinions,

and does not know whether he holds the doctrine or not, from the difficulty of mastering his thoughts.

16. Another characteristic, as I have said, of dogmatic statements, is the difficulty of recognizing them, even when attained, as the true representation of our meaning. This happens for many reasons; sometimes, from the faint hold we have of the impression itself, whether its nature be good or bad, so that we shrink from principles in substance, which we acknowledge in influence. Many a man, for instance, is acting on utilitarian principles, who is shocked at them in set treatises, and disowns them. Again, in sacred subjects, the very circumstance that a dogma professes to be a direct contemplation, and, if so be, a definition of what is infinite and eternal, is painful to serious minds. Moreover, from the hypothesis, it is the representation of an idea in a medium not native to it, not as originally conceived, but, as it were, in projection; no wonder, then, that, though there be an intimate correspondence, part by part, between the impression and the dogma, yet there should be an harshness in the outline of the latter; as, for instance, a want of harmonious proportion; and yet this is unavoidable, from the infirmities of our intellectual powers.

17. Again, another similar peculiarity in developments in general, is the great remoteness of the separate results of a common idea, or rather at first sight the absence of any connexion. Thus it often happens that party spirit is imputed to persons, merely because they agree with one another in certain points of opinion and conduct, which are thought too minute, distant, and various, in the large field of religious doctrine and discipline, to proceed from any but an external influence and a positive rule; whereas an insight into the wonderfully expansive power and penetrating virtue of theological or philosophical ideas would have shown, that what is apparently arbitrary in rival or in kindred schools of thought, is after all rigidly determined by the original hypothesis. The remark has been made, for instance, that rarely have persons

maintained the sleep of the soul before the Resurrection, without falling into more grievous errors; again, those who deny the Lutheran doctrine of Justification, commonly have tendencies towards a ceremonial religion; again, it is a serious fact that Protestantism has at various times unexpectedly developed into an allowance or vindication of polygamy; and heretics in general, however opposed in tenets, are found to have an inexplicable sympathy for each other, and never wake up from their ordinary torpor, but to exchange courtesies and meditate coalitions. One other remark is in point here, and relates to the length to which statements run, though, before we attempted them, we fancied our idea could be expressed in one or two sentences. Explanations grow under our hands, in spite of our effort at compression. Such, too, is the contrast between conversation and epistolary correspondence. We speak our meaning with little trouble; our voice, manner, and half words completing it for us; but in writing, when details must be drawn out, and misapprehensions anticipated, we seem never to be rid of the responsibility of our task. This being the case, it is surprising that the Creeds are so short, not surprising that they need a comment.

18. The difficulty, then, and hazard of developing doctrines implicitly received, must be fully allowed; and this is often made a ground for inferring that they have no proper developments at all; that there is no natural connexion between certain dogmas and certain impressions; and that theological science is a matter of time, and place, and accident, though inward belief is ever and every where one and the same. But surely the instinct of every Christian revolts from such a position; for the very first impulse of his faith is to try to express itself about the "great sight" which is vouchsafed to it; and this seems to argue that a science there is, whether the mind is equal to its discovery or no. And, indeed, what science is open to every chance inquirer? which is not recondite in its principles? which requires not special gifts of mind for its just formation? All subject-matters admit of true theories and

false, and the false are no prejudice to the true. Why should this class of ideas be different from all other? Principles of philosophy, physics, ethics, politics, taste, admit both of implicit reception and explicit statement; why should not the ideas, which are the secret life of the Christian, be recognized also as fixed and definite in themselves, and as capable of scientific analysis? Why should not there be that real connexion between science and its subject-matter in religion, which exists in other departments of thought? No one would deny that the philosophy of Zeno or Pythagoras was the exponent of a certain mode of viewing things; or would affirm that Platonist and Epicurean acted on one and the same idea of nature, life, and duty, and meant the same thing, though they verbally differed, merely because a Plato or an Epicurus was needed to detect the abstruse elements of thought, out of which each philosophy was eventually constructed. A man surely may be a Peripatetic or an Academic in his feelings, views, aims, and acts, who never heard the names. Granting, then, extreme cases, when individuals who would analyze their views of religion are thrown entirely upon their own reason, and find that reason unequal to the task, this will be no argument against a general, natural, and ordinary correspondence between the dogma and the inward idea. Surely, if Almighty God is ever one and the same, and is revealed to us as one and the same, the true inward impression of Him, made on the recipient of the revelation, must be one and the same; and, since human nature proceeds upon fixed laws, the statement of that impression must be one and the same, so that we may as well say that there are two Gods as two Creeds. And considering the strong feelings and energetic acts and severe sufferings which age after age have been involved in the maintenance of the Catholic dogmas, it is surely a very shallow philosophy to account such maintenance a mere contest about words, and a very abject philosophy to attribute it to mere party spirit, or to personal rivalry, or to ambition, or to covetousness.

19. Reasonable, however, as is this view of doctrinal developments in general, it cannot be denied that those which relate to the Objects of Faith, of which I am particularly speaking, have a character of their own, and must be considered separately. Let us, then, consider how the case stands, as regards the sacred doctrines of the Trinity and the Incarnation.

20. The Apostle said to the Athenians, "Whom ye ignorantly worship, Him declare I unto you;" and the mind which is habituated to the thought of God, of Christ, of the Holy Spirit, naturally turns, as I have said, with a devout curiosity to the contemplation of the Object of its adoration, and begins to form statements concerning Him before it knows whither, or how far, it will be carried. One proposition necessarily leads to another, and a second to a third; then some limitation is required; and the combination of these opposites occasions some fresh evolutions from the original idea, which indeed can never be said to be entirely exhausted. This process is its development, and results in a series, or rather body of dogmatic statements, till what was at first an impression on the Imagination has become a system or creed in the Reason.

21. Now such impressions are obviously individual and complete above other theological ideas, *because* they are the impressions of Objects. Ideas and their developments are commonly not identical, the development being but the carrying out of the idea into its consequences. Thus the doctrine of Penance may be called a development of the doctrine of Baptism, yet still is a distinct doctrine; whereas the developments in the doctrines of the Holy Trinity and the Incarnation are mere portions of the original impression, and modes of representing it. As God is one, so the impression which He gives us of Himself is one; it is not a thing of parts; it is not a system; nor is it any thing imperfect, and needing a counterpart. It is the vision of an object. When we pray, we pray, not to an assemblage of notions, or to a creed, but to One Individual Being; and when we speak of Him we speak of a Person, not of a Law or a Manifestation. This being the case,

all our attempts to delineate our impression of Him go to bring out one idea, not two or three or four; not a philosophy, but an individual idea in its separate aspects.

22. This may be fitly compared to the impressions made on us through the senses. Material objects are whole, and individual; and the impressions which they make on the mind, by means of the senses, are of a corresponding nature, complex and manifold in their relations and bearings, but considered in themselves integral and one. And in like manner the ideas which we are granted of Divine Objects under the Gospel, from the nature of the case and because they are ideas, answer to the Originals so far as this, that they are whole, indivisible, substantial, and may be called real, as being images of what is real. Objects which are conveyed to us through the senses, stand out in our minds, as I may say, with dimensions and aspects and influences various, and all of these consistent with one another, and many of them beyond our memory or even knowledge, while we contemplate the objects themselves; thus forcing on us a persuasion of their reality from the spontaneous congruity and coincidence of these accompaniments, as if they could not be creations of our minds, but were the images of external and independent beings. This of course will take place in the case of the sacred ideas which are the objects of our faith. Religious men, according to their measure, have an idea or vision of the Blessed Trinity in Unity, of the Son Incarnate and of His Presence, not as a number of qualities, attributes, and actions, not as the subject of a number of propositions, but as one, and individual, and independent of words, as an impression conveyed through the senses.

23. Particular propositions, then, which are used to express portions of the great idea vouchsafed to us, can never really be confused with the idea itself, which all such propositions taken together can but reach, and cannot exceed. As definitions are not intended to go beyond their subject, but to be adequate to it, so the dogmatic statements of the Divine Na-

ture used in our confessions, however multiplied, cannot say more than is implied in the original idea, considered in its completeness, without the risk of heresy. Creeds and dogmas live in the one idea which they are designed to express, and which alone is substantive; and are necessary only because the human mind cannot reflect upon it, except piecemeal, cannot use it in its oneness and entireness, nor without resolving it into a series of aspects and relations. And in matter of fact these expressions are never equivalent to it; we are able, indeed, to define the creations of our own minds, for they are what we make them and nothing else; but it were as easy to create what is real as to define it; and thus the Catholic dogmas are, after all, but symbols of a Divine fact, which, far from being compassed by those very propositions, would not be exhausted, nor fathomed, by a thousand.

24. Now of such sacred ideas and their attendant expressions, I observe:—

(1) First, that an impression of this intimate kind seems to be what Scripture means by "knowledge." "This is life eternal," says our Saviour, "that they might know Thee the only True God, and Jesus Christ whom Thou hast sent." In like manner St. Paul speaks of willingly losing all things, "for the excellency of the knowledge of Christ Jesus;" and St. Peter of "the knowledge of Him who hath called us to glory and virtue." [4] Knowledge is the possession of those living ideas of sacred things, from which alone change of heart or conduct can proceed. This awful vision is what Scripture seems to designate by the phrases "Christ in us," "Christ dwelling in us by faith," "Christ formed in us," and "Christ manifesting Himself unto us." And though it is faint and doubtful in some minds, and distinct in others, as some remote object in the twilight or in the day, this arises from the circumstances of the particular mind, and does not interfere with the perfection of the gift itself.

25. (2) This leads me next, however, to observe, that these

[4] John xvii. 3. Phil. iii. 8. 2 Pet. i. 3.

religious impressions differ from those of material objects, in the mode in which they are made. The senses are direct, immediate, and ordinary informants, and act spontaneously without any will or effort on our part; but no such faculties have been given us, as far as we know, for realizing the Objects of Faith. It is true that inspiration may be a gift of this kind to those who have been favoured with it; nor would it be safe to deny to the illuminating grace of Baptism a power, at least of putting the mind into a capacity for receiving impressions; but the former of these is not ordinary, and both are supernatural. The secondary and intelligible means by which we receive the impression of Divine Verities, are, for instance, the habitual and devout perusal of Scripture, which gradually acts upon the mind; again, the gradual influence of intercourse with those who are in themselves in possession of the sacred ideas; again, the study of Dogmatic Theology, which is our present subject; again, a continual round of devotion; or again, sometimes, in minds both fitly disposed and apprehensive, the almost instantaneous operation of a keen faith. This obvious distinction follows between sensible and religious ideas, that we put the latter into language in order to fix, teach, and transmit them, but not the former. No one defines a material object by way of conveying to us what we know so much better by the senses, but we form creeds as a chief mode of perpetuating the impression.

26. (3) Further, I observe, that though the Christian mind reasons out a series of dogmatic statements, one from another, this it has ever done, and always must do, not from those statements taken in themselves, as logical propositions, but as being itself enlightened and (as if) inhabited by that sacred impression which is prior to them, which acts as a regulating principle, ever present, upon the reasoning, and without which no one has any warrant to reason at all. Such sentences as "the Word was God," or "the Only-begotten Son who is in the bosom of the Father," or "the Word was made flesh," or "the Holy Ghost which proceedeth from the Father," are not a mere

letter which we may handle by the rules of art at our own will, but august tokens of most simple, ineffable, adorable facts, embraced, enshrined according to its measure in the believing mind. For though the development of an idea is a deduction of proposition from proposition, these propositions are ever formed in and round the idea itself (so to speak), and are in fact one and all only aspects of it. Moreover, this will account both for the mode of arguing from particular texts or single words of Scripture, practised by the early Fathers, and for their fearless decision in practising it; for the great Object of Faith on which they lived both enabled them to appropriate to itself particular passages of Scripture, and became to them a safeguard against heretical deductions from them. Also, it will account for the charge of weak reasoning, commonly brought against those Fathers; for never do we seem so illogical to others as when we are arguing under the continual influence of impressions to which they are insensible.

27. (4) Again, it must of course be remembered, as I have just implied, (though as being an historical matter it hardly concerns us here), that Revelation itself has provided in Scripture the main outlines and also large details of the dogmatic system. Inspiration has superseded the exercise of human Reason in great measure, and left it but the comparatively easy task of finishing the sacred work. The question, indeed, at first sight occurs, why such inspired statements are not enough without further developments; but in truth, when Reason has once been put on the investigation, it cannot stop till it has finished it; one dogma creates another, by the same right by which it was itself created; the Scripture statements are sanctions as well as informants in the inquiry; they begin and they do not exhaust.

28. (5) Scripture, I say, begins a series of developments which it does not finish; that is to say, in other words, it is a mistake to look for every separate proposition of the Catholic doctrine in Scripture. This is plain from what has gone before. For instance, the Athanasian Creed professes to lay down the

right faith, which we must hold on its most sacred subjects, in order to be saved. This must mean that there is one view concerning the Holy Trinity, or concerning the Incarnation, which is true, and distinct from all others; one definite, consistent, entire view, which cannot be mistaken, not contained in any certain number of propositions, but held as a view by the believing mind, and not held, but denied by Arians, Sabellians, Tritheists, Nestorians, Monophysites, Socinians, and other heretics. That idea is not enlarged, if propositions are added, nor impaired if they are withdrawn: if they are added, this is with a view of conveying that one integral view, not of amplifying it. That view does not depend on such propositions: it does not consist in them; they are but specimens and indications of it. And they may be multiplied without limit. They are necessary, but not needful to it, being but portions or aspects of that previous impression which has at length come under the cognizance of Reason and the terminology of science. The question, then, is not whether this or that proposition of the Catholic doctrine is *in terminis* in Scripture, unless we would be slaves to the letter, but whether that one view of the Mystery, of which all such are the exponents, be not there; a view which would be some other view, and not itself, if any one of such propositions, if any one of a number of similar propositions, were not true. Those propositions imply each other, as being parts of one whole; so that to deny one is to deny all, and to invalidate one is to deface and destroy the view itself. One thing alone has to be impressed on us by Scripture, the Catholic idea, and in it they all are included. To object, then, to the number of propositions, upon which an anathema is placed, is altogether to mistake their use; for their multiplication is not intended to enforce many things, but to express one,—to form within us that one impression concerning Almighty God, as the ruling principle of our minds, and that, whether we can fully recognize our own possession of it or no. And surely it is no paradox to say that such ruling ideas may exert a most powerful influence, at least in their various aspects, on our moral character, and on the whole man: as no one would deny in the case of belief or disbelief of a Supreme Being.

29. (6) And here we see the ordinary mistake of doctrinal innovators, viz. to go away with this or that proposition of the Creed, instead of embracing that one idea which all of them together are meant to convey; it being almost a definition of heresy, that it fastens on some one statement as if the whole truth, to the denial of all others, and as the basis of a new faith; erring rather in what it rejects, than in what it maintains: though, in truth, if the mind deliberately rejects any portion of the doctrine, this is a proof that it does not really hold even that very statement for the sake of which it rejects the others. Realizing is the very life of true developments; it is peculiar to the Church, and the justification of her definitions.

30. Enough has now been said on the distinction, yet connexion, between the implicit knowledge and the explicit confession of the Divine Objects of Faith, as they are revealed to us under the Gospel. An objection, however, remains, which cannot be satisfactorily treated in a few words. And what is worse than prolixity, the discussion may bear with it some appearance of unnecessary or even wanton refinement; unless, indeed, it is thrown into the form of controversy, a worse evil. Let it suffice to say, that my wish is, not to discover difficulties in any subject, but to solve them.

31. It may be asked, then, whether the mistake of words and names for things is not incurred by orthodox as well as heretics, in dogmatizing at all about the "secret things which belong unto the Lord our God," inasmuch as the idea of a supernatural object must itself be supernatural, and since no such ideas are claimed by ordinary Christians, no knowledge of Divine Verities is possible to them. How should any thing of this world convey ideas which are beyond and above this world? How can teaching and intercourse, how can human

words, how can earthly images, convey to the mind an idea of the Invisible? They cannot rise above themselves. They can suggest no idea but what is resolvable into ideas natural and earthly. The words "Person," "Substance," "Consubstantial," "Generation," "Procession," "Incarnation," "Taking of the manhood into God," and the like, have either a very abject and human meaning, or none at all. In other words, there is no such inward view of these doctrines, distinct from the dogmatic language used to express them, as was just now supposed. The metaphors by which they are signified are not mere symbols of ideas which exist independently of them, but their meaning is coincident and identical with the ideas. When, indeed, we have knowledge of a thing from other sources, then the metaphors we may apply to it are but accidental appendages to that knowledge; whereas our ideas of Divine things are just co-extensive with the figures by which we express them, neither more nor less, and without them are not; and when we draw inferences from those figures, we are not illustrating one existing idea, but drawing mere logical inferences. We speak, indeed, of material objects freely, because our senses reveal them to us apart from our words; but as to these ideas about heavenly things, we learn them from words, yet (it seems) we are to say what we, without words, conceive of them, as if words could convey what they do not contain. It follows that our anathemas, our controversies, our struggles, our sufferings, are merely about the poor ideas conveyed to us in certain figures of speech.

32. Some obvious remarks suggest themselves in answer to this representation. First, it is difficult to determine what divine grace may not do for us, if not in immediately implanting new ideas, yet in refining and elevating those which we gain through natural informants. If, as we all acknowledge, grace renews our moral feelings, yet through outward means, if it opens upon us new ideas about virtue and goodness and heroism and heavenly peace, it does not appear why, in a certain sense, it may not impart ideas concerning the nature

of God. Again, the various terms and figures which are used in the doctrine of the Holy Trinity or of the Incarnation, surely may by their combination create ideas which will be altogether new, though they are still of an earthly character. And further, when it is said that such figures convey no knowledge of the Divine Nature itself, beyond those figures, whatever they are, it should be considered whether our senses can be proved to suggest any real idea of matter. All that we know, strictly speaking, is the existence of the impressions our senses make on us; and yet we scruple not to speak as if they conveyed to us the knowledge of material substances. Let, then, the Catholic dogmas, as such, be freely admitted to convey no true idea of Almighty God, but only an earthly one, gained from earthly figures, provided it be allowed, on the other hand, that the senses do not convey to us any true idea of matter, but only an idea commensurate with sensible impressions.

33. Nor is there any reason why this should not be fully granted. Still there may be a certain correspondence between the idea, though earthly, and its heavenly archetype, such, that that idea belongs to the archetype, in a sense in which no other earthly idea belongs to it, as being the nearest approach to it which our present state allows. Indeed Scripture itself intimates the earthly nature of our present ideas of Sacred Objects, when it speaks of our now "seeing in a glass *darkly, ἐν αἰνίγματι,* but then face to face;" and it has ever been the doctrine of divines that the Beatific Vision, or true sight of Almighty God, is reserved for the world to come. Meanwhile we are allowed such an approximation to the truth as earthly images and figures may supply to us.

34. It must not be supposed that this is the only case in which we are obliged to receive information needful to us, through the medium of our existing ideas, and consequently with but a vague apprehension of its subject-matter. Children, who are made our pattern in Scripture, are taught, by an accommodation, on the part of their teachers, to their imma-

ture faculties and their scanty vocabulary. To answer their
questions in the language which we should use towards grown
men, would be simply to mislead them, if they could construe
it at all. We must dispense and "divide" the word of truth,
if we would not have it changed, as far as they are concerned,
into a word of falsehood; for what is short of truth in the
letter may be to them the most perfect truth, that is, the nearest approach to truth, compatible with their condition.[5] The
case is the same as regards those who have any natural defect
or deprivation which cuts them off from the circle of ideas
common to mankind in general. To speak to a blind man of
light and colours, in terms proper to those phenomena, would
be to mock him; we must use other media of information
accommodated to his circumstances, according to the well-
known instance in which his own account of scarlet was to
liken it to the sound of a trumpet. And so again, as regards
savages, or the ignorant, or weak, or narrow-minded, our representations and arguments must take a certain form, if they
are to gain admission into their minds at all, and to reach
them. Again, what impediments do the diversities of language
place in the way of communicating ideas! Language is a sort
of analysis of thought; and, since ideas are infinite, and infinitely combined, and infinitely modified, whereas language is
a method definite and limited, and confined to an arbitrary se-
lection of a certain number of these innumerable materials,
it were idle to expect that the courses of thought marked out
in one language should, except in their great outlines and main
centres, correspond to those of another. Multitudes of ideas
expressed in the one do not even enter into the other, and can
only be conveyed by some economy or accommodation, by
circumlocutions, phrases, limiting words, figures, or some bold
and happy expedient. And sometimes, from the continual de-

---

[5] Hence it is not more than an hyperbole to say that, in certain cases,
a lie is the nearest approach to the truth. [*Vide Hist. of Arians,* Chap. I,
iii, 4 &c. Edit. 3.] We are told that "God is not the son of man, that He
should repent;" yet "it repented the Lord that He had made man."

mand, foreign words become naturalized. Again, the difficulty is extreme, as all persons know, of leading certain individuals (to use a familiar phrase) to understand one another; their habits of thought turning apparently on points of mutual repulsion. Now this is always in a measure traceable to moral diversities between the parties; still, in many cases, it arises mainly from difference in the principle on which they have divided and subdivided that world of ideas, which comes before them both. They seem ever to be dodging each other, and need a common measure or economy to mediate between them.

35. Fables, again, are economies or accommodations, being truths and principles cast into that form in which they will be most vividly recognized; as in the well-known instance attributed to Menenius Agrippa. Again, mythical representations, at least in their better form, may be considered facts or narratives, untrue, but like the truth, intended to bring out the action of some principle, point of character, and the like. For instance, the tradition that St. Ignatius was the child whom our Lord took in His arms, may be unfounded; but it realizes to us his special relation to Christ and His Apostles, with a keenness peculiar to itself. The same remark may be made upon certain narratives of martyrdoms, or of the details of such narratives, or of certain alleged miracles, or heroic acts, or speeches, all which are the spontaneous produce of religious feeling under imperfect knowledge. If the alleged facts did not occur, they ought to have occurred (if I may so speak); they are such as might have occurred, and would have occurred, under circumstances; and they belong to the parties to whom they are attributed, potentially, if not actually; or the like of them did occur; or occurred to others similarly circumstanced, though not to those very persons. Many a theory or view of things, on which an institution is founded, or a party held together, is of the same kind. Many an argument, used by zealous and earnest men, has this economical character, being not the very ground on which they act, (for

they continue in the same course, though it be refuted,) yet, in a certain sense, a representation of it, a proximate description of their feelings in the shape of argument, on which they can rest, to which they can recur when perplexed, and appeal when questioned. Now, in this reference to accommodation or economy in human affairs, I do not meddle with the question of casuistry, viz. which of such artifices, as they may be called, are innocent, or where the line is to be drawn. That some are immoral, common sense tells us; but it is enough for my purpose, if some are necessary, as the same common sense will allow; and then the very necessity of the use will account for the abuse and perversion.

36. Even between man and man, then, constituted, as men are, alike, various distinct instruments, keys, or *calculi* of thought obtain, on which their ideas and arguments shape themselves respectively, and which we must use, if we would reach them. The cogitative method, as it may be called, of one man is notoriously very different from that of another; of the lawyer from that of the soldier, of the rich from that of the poor. The territory of thought is portioned out in a hundred different ways. Abstractions, generalizations, definitions, propositions, all are framed on distinct standards; and if this is found in matters of this world between man and man, surely much more must it exist between the ideas of men, and the thoughts, ways, and works of God.

37. One of the obvious instances of this contrariety is seen in the classifications we make of the subjects of the animal or vegetable kingdoms. Here a very intelligible order has been observed by the Creator Himself; still one of which we have not, after all, the key. We are obliged to frame one of our own; and when we apply it, we find that it will not exactly answer the Divine idea of arrangement, as it discovers itself to us; there being phenomena which we cannot locate, or which, upon our system of division, are anomalies in the general harmony of the Creation.

38. Mathematical science will afford us a more extended illustration of this distinction between supernatural and eternal laws, and our attempts to represent them, that is, our economies. Various methods or *calculi* have been adopted to embody those immutable principles and dispositions of which the science treats, which are really independent of any, yet cannot be contemplated or pursued without one or other of them. The first of these instruments of investigation employs the medium of extension; the second, that of number; the third, that of motion; the fourth proceeds on a more subtle hypothesis, that of increase. These methods are very distinct from each other, at least the geometrical and the differential; yet they are, one and all, analyses, more or less perfect, of those same necessary truths, for which we have not a name, of which we have no idea, except in the terms of such economical representations. They are all developments of one and the same range of ideas; they are all instruments of discovery as to those ideas. They stand for real things, and we can reason with them, though they be but symbols, as if they were the things themselves, for which they stand. Yet none of them carries out the lines of truth to their limits; first, one stops in the analysis, then another; like some calculating tables which answer for a thousand times, and miss in the thousand and first. While they answer, we can use them just as if they were the realities which they represent, and without thinking of those realities; but at length our instrument of discovery issues in some great impossibility or contradiction, or what we call in religion, a mystery. It has run its length; and by its failure shows that all along it has been but an expedient for practical purposes, not a true analysis or adequate image of those recondite laws which are investigated by means of it. It has never fathomed their depth, because it now fails to measure their course. At the same time, no one, because it cannot do every thing, would refuse to use it within the range in which it will act; no one would say that it was a system of empty

symbols, though it be but a shadow of the unseen. Though we use it with caution, still we use it, as being the nearest approximation to the truth which our condition admits.

39. Let us take another instance, of an outward and earthly form, or economy, under which great wonders unknown seem to be typified; I mean musical sounds, as they are exhibited most perfectly in instrumental harmony. There are seven notes in the scale; make them fourteen; yet what a slender outfit for so vast an enterprise! What science brings so much out of so little? Out of what poor elements does some great master in it create his new world! Shall we say that all this exuberant inventiveness is a mere ingenuity or trick of art, like some game or fashion of the day, without reality, without meaning? We may do so; and then, perhaps, we shall also account the science of theology to be a matter of words; yet, as there is a divinity in the theology of the Church, which those who feel cannot communicate, so is there also in the wonderful creation of sublimity and beauty of which I am speaking. To many men the very names which the science employs are utterly incomprehensible. To speak of an idea or a subject seems to be fanciful or trifling, to speak of the views which it opens upon us to be childish extravagance; yet is it possible that that inexhaustible evolution and disposition of notes, so rich yet so simple, so intricate yet so regulated, so various yet so majestic, should be a mere sound, which is gone and perishes? Can it be that those mysterious stirrings of heart, and keen emotions, and strange yearnings after we know not what, and awful impressions from we know not whence, should be wrought in us by what is unsubstantial, and comes and goes, and begins and ends in itself? It is not so; it cannot be. No; they have escaped from some higher sphere; they are the outpourings of eternal harmony in the medium of created sound; they are echoes from our Home; they are the voice of Angels, or the Magnificat of Saints, or the living laws of Divine Governance, or the Divine Attributes; something are they besides themselves, which we cannot compass, which we

cannot utter,—though mortal man, and he perhaps not otherwise distinguished above his fellows, has the gift of eliciting them.

40. So much on the subject of musical sound; but what if the whole series of impressions, made on us through the senses, be, as I have already hinted, but a Divine economy suited to our need, and the token of realities distinct from themselves, and such as might be revealed to us, nay, more perfectly, by other senses, different from our existing ones as they from each other? What if the properties of matter, as we conceive of them, are merely relative to us, so that facts and events, which seem impossible when predicated concerning it in terms of those impressions, are impossible only in those terms, not in themselves,—impossible only because of the imperfection of the idea, which, in consequence of those impressions, we have conceived of material substances? If so, it would follow that the laws of physics, as we consider them, are themselves but generalizations of economical exhibitions, inferences from figure and shadow, and not more real than the phenomena from which they are drawn. Scripture, for instance, says that the sun moves and the earth is stationary; and science, that the earth moves, and the sun is comparatively at rest. How can we determine which of these opposite statements is the very truth, till we know what motion is? If our idea of motion be but an accidental result of our present senses, neither proposition is true, and both are true; neither true philosophically, both true for certain practical purposes in the system in which they are respectively found; and physical science will have no better meaning when it says that the earth moves, than plane astronomy when it says that the earth is still.

41. And should any one fear lest thoughts such as these should tend to a dreary and hopeless scepticism, let him take into account the Being and Providence of God, the Merciful and True; and he will at once be relieved of his anxiety. All is dreary till we believe, what our hearts tell us, that we are

subjects of His Governance; nothing is dreary, all inspires hope and trust, directly we understand that we are under His hand, and that whatever comes to us is from Him, as a method of discipline and guidance. What is it to us whether the knowledge He gives us be greater or less, if it be He who gives it? What is it to us whether it be exact or vague, if He bids us trust it? What have we to care whether we are or are not given to divide substance from shadow, if He is training us heavenwards by means of either? Why should we vex ourselves to find whether our deductions are philosophical or no, provided they are religious? If our senses supply the media by which we are put on trial, by which we are all brought together, and hold intercourse with each other, and are disciplined and are taught, and enabled to benefit others, it is enough. We have an instinct within us, impelling us, we have external necessity forcing us, to trust our senses, and we may leave the question of their substantial truth for another world, "till the day break, and the shadows flee away." [6] And what is true of reliance on our senses, is true of all the information which it has pleased God to vouchsafe to us, whether in nature or in grace.

42. Instances, then, such as these, will be found both to sober and to encourage us in our theological studies,—to impress us with a profound sense of our ignorance of Divine Verities, when we know most; yet to hinder us from relinquishing their contemplation, though we know so little. On the one hand, it would appear that even the most subtle questions of the schools may have a real meaning, as the most intricate

[6 The senses convey to the mind "substantial truth," in so far as they bring home to us that certain things are, and *in confuso* what they are. But has a man born blind, by means of hearing, smelling, taste, and touch, such an idea of physical nature, as may be called *substantially* true, or, on the contrary, an idea which at best is but the *shadow* of the truth? for, in whichever respect, whether as in substance or by a shadow, the blind man knows the objects of sight, in the same are those things, in "which eye has not seen, nor ear heard," apprehended by us now, "in a glass darkly," *per speculum, in ænigmate.*]

formulæ in analytics; and since we cannot tell how far our instrument of thought reaches in the process of investigation, and
at what point it fails us, no questions may safely be despised.
"Whether God was any where before creation?" "whether
He knows all creatures in Himself?" "whether the blessed
see all things possible and future in Him?" "whether relation
is the form of the Divine Persons?" "in what sense the Holy
Spirit is Divine Love?" these, and a multitude of others, far
more minute and remote, are all sacred from their subject.

43. On the other hand, it must be recollected that not
even the Catholic reasonings and conclusions, as contained
in Confessions, and most thoroughly received by us, are
worthy of the Divine Verities which they represent, but are
the truth only in as full a measure as our minds can admit it;
the truth as far as they go, and under the conditions of thought
which human feebleness imposes. It is true that God is without beginning, if eternity may worthily be considered to imply
succession; in every place, if He who is a Spirit can have relations with space. It is right to speak of His Being and Attributes, if He be not rather super-essential: it is true to say that
He is wise or powerful, if we may consider Him as other than
the most simple Unity. He is truly Three, if He is truly One;
He is truly One, if the idea of Him falls under earthly number.
He has a triple Personality, in the sense in which the Infinite
can be understood to have Personality at all. If we know any
thing of Him,—if we may speak of Him in any way,—if we
may emerge from Atheism or Pantheism into religious faith,
—if we would have any saving hope, any life of truth and holiness within us,—this only do we know, with this only confession, we must begin and end our worship—that the Father
is the One God, the Son the One God, and the Holy Ghost
the One God; and that the Father is not the Son, the Son not
the Holy Ghost, and the Holy Ghost not the Father.

44. The fault, then, which we must guard against in receiving such Divine intimations, is the ambition of being wiser
than what is written; of employing the Reason, not in carrying

out what is told us, but in impugning it; not in support, but in prejudice of Faith. Brilliant as are such exhibitions of its powers, they bear no fruit. Reason can but ascertain the profound difficulties of our condition, it cannot remove them; it has no work, it makes no beginning, it does but continually fall back, till it is content to be a little child, and to follow where Faith guides it.

45. What remains, then, but to make our prayer to the Gracious and Merciful God, the Father of Lights, that in all our exercises of Reason, His gift, we may thus use it,—as He would have us, in the obedience of Faith, with a view to His glory, with an aim at His Truth, in dutiful submission to His will, for the comfort of His elect, for the edification of Holy Jerusalem, His Church, and in recollection of His own solemn warning, "Every idle word that men shall speak, they shall give account thereof in the day of judgment; for by thy words thou shalt be justified, and by thy words thou shalt be condemned."

[*February 2, 1843.*]

VIII

THE APOSTOLICAL CHRISTIAN [1]

"Know ye not, that they which run in a race run all, but one receiveth the prize? so run, that ye may obtain."—1 Corinthians ix. 24.

THERE WAS ONE who came running to Christ, and kneeled to Him, yet he did not obtain; for that haste of his and hurry was no type of the inward earnestness with which the true soul goes sedately forward unto salvation. He was one of the many who, in some sort, run the race, yet do not receive the prize, because they run in self-will, or lightness of mind. "If a man strive for masteries, yet is he not crowned, except he strive lawfully." "I have not sent" them, says the Lord by His Prophet, "yet they ran." [2] Many there are, who are not open sinners, who do not deny Christ, who honour Him with their lips—nay, in some sort with their lives—who, like the young man, are religious in a certain sense, and yet obtain not the crown. For they are not of those who, with the blessed Apostle who speaks in the text, observe the rules of the contest. They have no claim upon the prize, because they run on their own ground, or at their own time; or, in other respects, after their own pleasure. They make a religion for themselves, and they have a private idea what a Christian ought to be; and they never get beyond, even if they attain, the regulation of their lives and conduct upon this self-devised standard of truth. They can never be said to have "finished their course," for, in truth, they have never entered on it. Or they begin it, and turn

---

[1] From *Sermons Bearing on Subjects of the Day*, No. 19. [Ed.]
[2] 2 Tim. ii. 5. Jer. xxiii. 21.

aside in some other direction, mistaking the path. "Ye did run well," says St. Paul to the Galatians; "who did hinder you that ye should not obey the truth?" [3]

Let us then, with this thought before us, leave for a while our own private judgment of what is pleasing to God and not pleasing, and turn to consider the picture which Scripture gives us of the true Christian life, and then attempt to measure our own life by it. He alone who gives us eternal happiness, has the power of determining the conditions for attaining it. Let us not take it for granted that we shall know them by our own common sense. Let us betake ourselves to Scripture to learn them.

Now it is very certain, that the New Testament abounds in notices, suggestions, and descriptions of the temper and mode of living of the disciples of Christ; that is, as they were characterized at the time when it was written. The idea of a Christian, as set forth in Scripture, is something very definite. We may conceive we have some general notion from Scripture what a Jew was, but we know much more what a Christian was. As a Jew had a very peculiar character, as an Englishman has a character all his own, so the Christian, as described in the inspired writings, is like himself, and unlike any one else. He is not like Pharisee, not like Sadducee, not like Herodian, not like Greek, not like Roman, not like Samaritan; but he is like a follower of Christ, and none but him. Now, whether Christians at this day need be like what Christians were in the primitive times, is a further question. I want, in the first place, to consider *what* the primitive Christians were like, as represented in Scripture. As an historical question, as a matter of fact, thus only I would consider the subject; afterwards will be time enough for us to apply it to our own case, and to settle how far it is necessary for men of this day to conform their lives to the pattern given them once for all by inspiration.

Now so far is certain, that this one peculiar Christian char-

[3] Gal. v. 7.

acter and life, and none but it, is attributed in Scripture to our Lord, to St. John Baptist, to the Apostles, and to Christians generally. Very different is our Lord from St. John Baptist; very different St. John from the Apostles; very different the Apostles from private Christians. John came in the garb of an ascetic, dressed in a garment of camel's hair, and eating locusts and wild honey. Our Lord came eating and drinking; He lived in the world as St. John in the desert. The Apostles were the teachers of grace, as St. John of repentance; and Christians in general were hearers, not preachers; numbers of them besides were women, and thereby still more unlike Christ and St. John and the Apostles: and yet on the whole one only character distinguishes all of them in Scripture; Christ Himself, and the Baptist, and St. Peter, and St. John, and St. Paul, and the Christian multitude, men and women. And now to draw out what that character is; though, in doing so, I shall say nothing, my brethren, but what you know well already, and shall be doing little more than quoting texts of Scripture. And yet you have heard these texts so often, that perhaps they fall dead upon your ear, and they leave you as they found you, impressing no definite image of their meaning upon your minds.

1. Now the first great and obvious characteristic of a Bible Christian, if I may use that much abused term, is to be without worldly ties or objects, to be living in this world, but not for this world. St. Paul says, "our conversation is in heaven," [4] or in other words, heaven is our city. We know what it is to be a citizen of this world; it is to have interests, rights, privileges, duties, connexions, in some particular town or state; to depend upon it, and to be bound to defend it; to be part of it. Now all this the Christian is in respect to heaven. Heaven is his city, earth is not. Or, at least, so it was as regards the Christians of Scripture. "Here," as the same Apostle says in another place, "we have no continuing city, but we seek one

[4] Phil. iii. 20.

to come." [5] And therefore he adds to the former of these texts, "from whence also we look for the Saviour, the Lord Jesus Christ." This is the very definition of a Christian,—one who looks for Christ; not who looks for gain, or distinction, or power, or pleasure, or comfort, but who looks "for the Saviour, the Lord Jesus Christ." This, according to Scripture, is the essential mark, this is the foundation of a Christian, from which every thing else follows; whether he is rich or poor, high or low, is a further matter, which may be considered apart; but he surely is a primitive Christian, and he only, who has no aim of this world, who has no wish to be other in this world than he is; whose thoughts and aims have relation to the unseen, the future world; who has lost his taste for this world, sweet and bitter being the same to him; who fulfils the same Apostle's exhortation in another Epistle, "Set your affection on things above, not on things on the earth, for ye are dead, and your life is hid with Christ in God. When Christ, who is our life, shall appear, then shall ye also appear with Him in glory." [6]

Hence it follows, that watching is a special mark of the Scripture Christian, as our Lord so emphatically sets before us: "Watch therefore, for ye know not what hour your Lord doth come. . . . Be ye also ready, for in such an hour as ye think not the Son of man cometh." [7] "At midnight there was a cry made, Behold, the bridegroom cometh, go ye out to meet Him. . . . Watch therefore, for ye know neither the day nor the hour wherein the Son of man cometh." [8] "Watch ye therefore, for ye know not when the Master of the house cometh, at even, or at midnight, or at the cockcrowing, or in the morning; lest coming suddenly he find you sleeping; and what I say unto you, I say unto all, Watch."[9] And St. Peter, who once suffered

[5] Heb. xiii. 14.
[6] Col. iii. 2–4.
[7] Matt. xxiv. 42, 44.
[8] Matt. xxv. 6, 13.
[9] Mark xiii. 35–37.

for lack of watching, repeats the lesson: "The end of all things is at hand: be ye therefore sober, and watch unto prayer."[10]

And accordingly, prayer, as St. Peter enjoins in the last text, is another characteristic of Christians as described in Scripture. They knew not what hour their Lord would come, and therefore they watched and prayed in every hour, lest they should enter into temptation. "They were continually in the temple praising and blessing God." [11] "These all continued with one accord in prayer and supplication with the women." [12] "They, continuing daily with one accord in the temple, and breaking bread from house to house, did eat their meat with gladness and singleness of heart." [13] "They were all with one accord in one place," [14] at "the third hour of the day." Again, "Peter and John went up together into the temple at the hour of prayer, being the ninth hour." [15] "Cornelius, . . . a devout man, . . . which gave much alms to the people, and prayed to God alway," saw "in a vision evidently about the ninth hour of the day an angel of God;" [16] and he says himself, "I was fasting until this hour, and at the ninth hour I prayed in my house." "Peter went up upon the house-top to pray about the sixth hour." "At midnight Paul and Silas prayed, and sang praises unto God." [17] "And they all brought us on our way, with wives and children, till we were out of the city; and we kneeled down on the shore, and prayed." [18] This habit of prayer then, recurrent prayer, morning, noon, and night, is one discriminating point in Scripture Christianity, as arising from the text with which I began, "our conversation is in heaven."

[10] 1 Pet. iv. 7.
[11] Luke xxiv. 53.
[12] Acts i. 14.
[13] Acts ii. 46.
[14] Acts ii. 1.
[15] Acts iii. 1.
[16] Acts x. 1–3.
[17] Acts xvi. 25.
[18] Acts xxi. 5.

In a word, there was no barrier, no cloud, no earthly object, interposed between the soul of the primitive Christian and its Saviour and Redeemer. Christ was in his heart, and therefore all that came from his heart, his thoughts, words, and actions, savoured of Christ. The Lord was his light, and therefore he shone with the illumination. For, "The light of the body is the eye: if therefore thine eye be single, thy whole body shall be full of light. But if thine eye be evil, thy whole body shall be full of darkness." [19] And, "Out of the abundance of the heart the mouth speaketh. A good man out of the good treasure of the heart bringeth forth good things: and an evil man out of the evil treasure, bringeth forth evil things." [20] Or, as Christ says elsewhere, "Cleanse first that which is within the cup and platter, that the outside of them may be clean also." [21] Observe this well, my brethren; religion, you see, begins with the heart, but it does not end with the heart. It begins with the conversion of the heart from earth to heaven, the stripping off and casting away all worldly aims; but it does not end there; it did not end there in the Christians whom Scripture describes, whom our Lord's precepts formed: it drew up all the faculties of the soul, all the members of the body, to Him who was in their heart. Let us then now go on to see in what that inward Christianity issued; what Christians then, in that early time, looked like outwardly, who were citizens of heaven within.

2. Christians, then, were a simple, innocent, grave, humble, patient, meek, and loving body, without earthly advantages or worldly influence, as every page of the New Testament shows us. A description of them is given in the beginning of the Acts: "The multitude of them that believed were of one heart and of one soul; neither said any of them that ought of the things which he possessed was his own, but they had all

[19] Matt. vi. 22, 23.
[20] Matt. xii. 34, 35.
[21] Matt. xxiii. 26.

things common. . . . Neither was there any among them that lacked: for as many as were possessors of lands or houses sold them, and brought the prices of the things that were sold, and laid them down at the Apostles' feet: and distribution was made unto every man according as he had need." [22]

Such, of course, was the natural consequence of a deep conviction of the nothingness of this world, and the all-importance of the other. Those who understood that they were "fellow-citizens with the saints, and of the household of God," could not but show it in their actions. In circumstances like theirs they would have been using idle words, had they said that their conversation was in heaven, yet had gone on eating, and drinking, and conversing like children of men. But here our Lord's words may well take the place of ours. Consider, then, how solemnly He had warned them.

"As the days of Noe were, so shall also the coming of the Son of man be. For as in the days that were before the flood, they were eating and drinking, marrying and giving in marriage, until the day that Noe entered into the ark, and knew not until the flood came, and took them all away; so shall also the coming of the Son of man be." [23] "They did eat, they drank, they married wives, they were given in marriage, until the day that Noe entered into the ark, and the flood came, and destroyed them all. Likewise also as it was in the days of Lot; they did eat, they drank, they bought, they sold, they planted, they builded; but the same day that Lot went out of Sodom, it rained fire and brimstone from heaven, and destroyed them all." [24] Again, "They all with one consent began to make excuse. The first said unto him, I have bought a piece of ground, and I must needs go and see it: I pray thee have me excused. And another said, I have bought five yoke of oxen, and I go to prove them: I pray thee have me excused. And

[22] Acts iv. 32–35.
[23] Matt. xxiv. 37–39.
[24] Luke xvii. 27–29.

another said, I have married a wife, and therefore I cannot come." [25] Again, "There was a certain rich man, which was clothed in purple and fine linen, and fared sumptuously every day." [26] Again, "Take heed and beware of covetousness. . . . The ground of a certain rich man brought forth plenti-fully; . . . and he said . . . I will say to my soul, Soul, thou hast much goods laid up for many years; take thine ease, eat, drink, and be merry. But God said unto him, Thou fool, this night thy soul shall be required of thee." Again, "Sell that ye have, and give alms: provide yourselves bags which wax not old, a treasure in the heavens that faileth not, where no thief ap-proacheth, neither moth corrupteth; for where your treasure is, there will your heart be also. Let your loins be girded about, and your lights burning." [27] Again, "How hardly shall they that have riches enter into the kingdom of God!" [28] Again, "Take no thought, saying, What shall we eat? or, What shall we drink? or, Wherewithal shall we be clothed?" [29] And hence St. Paul, after the pattern of his Lord and Saviour, is careful to remind us that "the time is short;" [30]—we are labour-ers in the eleventh hour of the day. "The time is short; it re-maineth that both they that have wives be as though they had none; and they that weep, as though they wept not; and they that rejoice, as though they rejoiced not; and they that buy, as though they possessed not; and they that use this world, as not abusing it, for the fashion of this world passeth away." And again, "No man that warreth entangleth himself with the affairs of this life; that he may please him who hath chosen him to be a soldier." [31]

This separation from the world which marked the Christian character as drawn by Christ and His Apostles, is displayed

[25] Luke xiv. 18–20.
[26] Luke xvi. 19.
[27] Luke xii. 15–20, 33–35.
[28] Mark x. 23.
[29] Matt. vi. 31.
[30] 1 Cor. vii. 29.
[31] 2 Tim. ii. 4.

in a variety of details scattered up and down the sacred
volume. "Love not the world, neither the things that are in
the world," [32] says St. John. "Be not conformed to this world,
but be ye transformed by the renewing of your mind," [33] says
St. Paul. Again, of himself, "By the Cross of Christ . . . the
world is crucified unto me, and I unto the world." [34] The
first Christians were separated from their earthly kindred
and friends. "Henceforth," says he, "know we no man after
the flesh; yea, though we have known Christ after the flesh,
yet now henceforth know we Him no more. Therefore, if any
man be in Christ, he is a new creature: old things are passed
away, behold all things are become new." [35] Or, in our Lord's
words, "He that loveth father or mother more than Me, is
not worthy of Me; and he that loveth son or daughter more
than Me, is not worthy of Me." [36] They parted with property:
"Every one that hath forsaken houses, . . . or lands, for My
Name's sake, shall receive an hundredfold, and shall inherit
everlasting life." [37] They put off from them things personal:
"Provide neither gold, nor silver, nor brass, in your purses,
nor scrip for your journey, neither two coats, neither shoes,
nor yet staves: for the workman is worthy of his meat." [38]
They sacrificed to Christ their dearest wishes and objects,
things nearer and closer to them than the very garments they
had on them: "If thy hand or thy foot offend thee," says our
Lord, in figurative language, "cut them off, and cast them
from thee; it is better for thee to enter into life halt or maimed,
rather than having two hands or two feet to be cast into
everlasting fire. And if thine eye offend thee, pluck it out, and
cast it from thee: it is better for thee to enter into life with
one eye, rather than having two eyes to be cast into hell

[32] 1 John ii. 15.
[33] Rom. xii. 2.
[34] Gal. vi. 14.
[35] 2 Cor. v. 16, 17.
[36] Matt. x. 37.
[37] Matt. xix. 29.
[38] Matt. x. 9, 10.

fire." [39] They forfeited the common sympathy of humanity, and were cruelly used, or rather, hunted down, as some separate race of beings less than man: "Ye shall be hated of all men for My Name's sake. . . . The disciple is not above his Master, nor the servant above his Lord. . . . If they have called the Master of the house Beelzebub, how much more shall they call them of his household!" [40]

This, to speak briefly on a great subject, is the picture of a Christian as drawn in the New Testament. Christians are those who profess to have the love of the truth in their hearts; and when Christ asks them whether they so love Him as to be able to drink of His cup, and partake of His Baptism, they answer, "We are able," and their profession issues in a wonderful fulfilment. They love God and they give up the world.

3. And here we are brought to a third and last characteristic of the Christianity of the New Testament, which necessarily follows from the other two. If the first disciples so unreservedly gave up the world, and if, secondly, they were so strictly and promptly taken at their word, what do you think would follow, if they were true men and not hypocrites? this —they would rejoice to be so taken. This, then, is the third chief grace of primitive Christianity—joy in all its forms; not only a pure heart, not only a clean hand, but, thirdly, a cheerful countenance. I say joy in all its forms, for in true joyfulness many graces are included; joyful people are loving; joyful people are forgiving; joyful people are munificent. Joy, if it be Christian joy, the refined joy of the mortified and persecuted, makes men peaceful, serene, thankful, gentle, affectionate, sweet-tempered, pleasant, hopeful; it is graceful, tender, touching, winning. All this were the Christians of the New Testament, for they had obtained what they desired. They had desired to sacrifice the kingdom of the world and all its pomps for the love of Christ, whom they had seen, whom they loved, in whom they believed, in whom they delighted; and

[39] Matt. xviii. 8, 9.
[40] Matt. x. 22, 24, 25.

when their wish was granted, they could but "rejoice in that day, and leap for joy, for, behold, their reward was great in heaven": [41] blessed were they, thrice blessed, because they in their lifetime had evil things,[42] and their consolation was to come hereafter.

Such, I say, was the joy of the first disciples of Christ, to whom it was granted to suffer shame and to undergo toil for His Name's sake; and such holy, gentle graces were the fruit of this joy, as every part of the Gospels and Epistles shows us. "We glory in tribulations," says St. Paul, "knowing that tribulation worketh patience, and patience experience, and experience hope, and hope maketh not ashamed, because the love of God is shed abroad in our hearts by the Holy Ghost which is given unto us." [43] Again, "Even unto this present hour we both hunger and thirst, and are naked, and are buffeted, and have no certain dwelling-place, and labour working with our own hands: being reviled, we bless; being persecuted, we suffer it; being defamed, we intreat; we are made as the filth of the earth, and are the off-scouring of all things unto this day." [44] How is the very same character set before us in the Beatitudes, so holy, so tender, so serene, so amiable! "Blessed are the poor in spirit, for theirs is the kingdom of heaven; blessed are they that mourn, for they shall be comforted; blessed are the meek, they which do hunger and thirst after righteousness, the merciful, the pure in heart, the peace-makers, they which are persecuted for righteousness' sake." [45] And again, "Let your communication be yea, yea, nay, nay; for whatsoever is more than these cometh of evil." [46] "I say unto you, That ye resist not evil; but whosoever shall smite thee on thy right cheek, turn to him the other also:" "love

[41] Luke vi. 23.
[42] Luke xvi. 25.
[43] Rom. v. 3—5.
[44] 1 Cor. iv. 11—13.
[45] Matt. v. 3—10.
[46] Matt. v. 37.

your enemies, bless them that curse you, do good to them that hate you, and pray for them which despitefully use you and persecute you; that ye may be the children of your Father which is in heaven." Again, "Judge not, that ye be not judged; . . . and why beholdest thou the mote that is in thy brother's eye, but considerest not the beam that is in thine own eye?" [47] And again, "In your patience possess ye your souls." [48] Again, "If I then, your Lord and Master, have washed your feet, ye also ought to wash one another's feet." [49] Again, "By this shall all men know that ye are My disciples, if ye have love one to another." And again, "Peace I leave with you, My peace I give unto you, not as the world giveth, give I unto you. Let not your heart be troubled, neither let it be afraid." [50] Or again, consider the special prayer which the Lord Himself taught us, as a pattern of all prayer, and see how it corresponds to that one idea of a Christian which I have been drawing out. It consists of seven petitions; three have reference to Almighty God, four to the petitioners; and could any form of words be put together which so well could be called the Prayer of the Pilgrim? We often hear it said, that the true way of serving God is to serve man, as if religion consisted merely in acting well our part in life, not in direct faith, obedience, and worship: how different is the spirit of this prayer! Evil round about him, enemies and persecutors in his path, temptation in prospect, help for the day, sin to be expiated, God's will in his heart, God's Name on his lips, God's kingdom in his hopes: this is the view it gives us of a Christian. What simplicity! what grandeur! and what definiteness! how one and the same, how consistent with all that we read of him elsewhere in Scripture!

Alas! my brethren, so it is, when you have subjects like this dwelt upon, too many of you are impatient of them, and

[47] Matt. vii. 1. 3.
[48] Luke xxi. 19.
[49] John xiii. 14.
[50] John xiv. 27.

wish to hurry past them, and are eager to be reminded by the preacher in the same breath with his presenting them—nay, you remind yourselves—that you of this day can have no immediate interest in them,—that times are changed. Times *are* changed, I grant; but without going on to the question of the obligation now of such a profession of the Gospel as I have been describing, do persuade yourselves, I entreat you, to contemplate the picture. Do not shut your eyes, do not revolt from it, do not fret under it, but look at it. Bear to look at the Christianity of the Bible; bear to contemplate the idea of a Christian, traced by inspiration, without gloss, or comment, or tradition of man. Bear to hear read to you a number of texts; texts which might be multiplied sevenfold; texts which can be confronted by no others; which are no partial selections, but a specimen of the whole of the New Testament. Before you go forward to the question, "How do they affect us, must we obey them, or why need we not?" prevail on yourselves to realize the idea of a Scriptural Christian, and the fact that the first Christians really answered to it. Granting you have to apply and modify the pattern given you, before you can use it yourselves, which I am not denying, yet after all, your pattern it is; you have no other pattern of a Christian any where. No other view of Christianity is given you in Scripture. If Scripture is used, you must begin with accepting that pattern; how can you apply what you will not study? Study what a Bible Christian is; be silent over it; pray for grace to comprehend it, to accept it.

And next ask yourselves this question, and be honest in your answer. This model of a Christian, though not commanding your literal imitation, still is it not the very model which has been fulfilled in others in every age since the New Testament was written? You will ask me in whom? I am loth to say; I have reason to ask you to be honest and candid; for so it is, as if from consciousness of the fact, and dislike to have it urged upon us, we and our forefathers have been accustomed to scorn and ridicule these faithful, obedient persons, and, in our Saviour's very words, to "cast out their *name* as evil, for the Son of man's sake." But, if the truth must be spoken, what are the humble monk, and the holy nun, and other regulars, as they are called, but Christians after the very pattern given us in Scripture? What have they done but this—perpetuate in the world the Christianity of the Bible? Did our Saviour come on earth suddenly, as He will one day visit it, in whom would He see the features of the Christians whom He and His Apostles left behind them, but in them? Who but these give up home and friends, wealth and ease, good name and liberty of will, for the kingdom of heaven? Where shall we find the image of St. Paul, or St. Peter, or St. John, or of Mary the mother of Mark, or of Philip's daughters, but in those who, whether they remain in seclusion, or are sent over the earth, have calm faces, and sweet plaintive voices, and spare frames, and gentle manners, and hearts weaned from the world, and wills subdued; and for their meekness meet with insult, and for their purity with slander, and for their gravity with suspicion, and for their courage with cruelty; yet meet with Christ every where—Christ, their all-sufficient, everlasting portion, to make up to them, both here and hereafter, all they suffer, all they dare, for His Name's sake?

And, lastly, apply this pattern to yourselves; for there only will you have power to apply it rightly. You know very well, most of us know it too well, that such precepts and examples do not directly apply to every one of us. We are not severally bound to give up the world by so literal a surrender. The case of Ananias and Sapphira is enough to show us this. Their sin lay in professing to do what they need not have done; in making pretence of a voluntary renunciation which they did not execute. They kept back part of the price of the land which they made a show of giving up: and St. Peter urged it against them. "Whiles it remained, was it not thine own? and after it was sold, was it not in thine own power?" A most awful warning to every one, not to affect greater sanctity or self-denial than he attempts; but a proof withal, that those great surrenders which Scripture speaks of, are not incumbent on all Christians. They could not be voluntary if they were duties; they could not be meritorious if they were not voluntary. But though they are not duties to all, they may be duties to you; and though they are voluntary, you may have a call to them. It may be your duty to follow after merit. And whether it is you cannot learn, till first you have fairly surrendered your mind to the contemplation of that Christianity which Scripture delineates. After all, it may prove to be your duty to remain as others, and you may serve Him best and most acceptably in a secular life. But you cannot tell till you inquire; enough do we hear of private judgment in matters of doctrine; alas! that we will not exercise it where it is to a certain extent allowable and religious; in points, not public and ecclesiastical and eternal and independent of ourselves, but personal,—in the choice of life, in matters of duty!

[*February 5 (or 12?), 1843.*]

WISDOM AND INNOCENCE [1]

"Behold, I send you forth as sheep in the midst of wolves; be ye therefore wise as serpents, and harmless as doves."—Matthew x. 16.

SHEEP ARE DEFENCELESS, wolves are strong and fierce. How prompt, how frightful, how resistless, how decisive, would be the attack of a troop of wolves on a few straggling sheep which fell in with them! and how lively, then, is the image which our Lord uses to express the treatment which His followers were to receive from the world! He himself was the great Exemplar of all such sufferings. When He was in the hands of His enemies, surrounded by a mad multitude, gazed on by relentless enemies, jeered at, struck, hurried along, tormented by rude soldiers, and at length nailed to the cross, what was He emphatically but a sheep among wolves? "He is brought as a lamb to the slaughter, and as a sheep before her shearers is dumb, so He openeth not His mouth." And what He foretold of His followers, that the Psalmist had declared of them at an earlier time, and His Apostle applies it to them on its fulfilment. "As it is written," says St. Paul, "For Thy sake we are killed all the day long; we are accounted as sheep for the slaughter." [2] Such was the Church of Christ in its beginnings, and such has it been in every age in proportion to its purity. The purer it has been, the more defenceless; whenever it has been pure, it has, in one way or another, been defenceless. The less worldly it has been, and the more it has cultivated its proper gifts, and the less it has relied upon

[1] From *Sermons Bearing on Subjects of the Day*, No. 20. [Ed.]
[2] Rom. viii. 36.

sword and bow, chariots and horses, and arm of man, the more it has been exposed to ill-usage; the more it has invited oppression, the more it has irritated the proud and powerful. This, I say, is exemplified in every age. Seasons of peace, indeed, have been vouchsafed to it from the first, and in the most fearful times; but not an age of peace. A reign of temporal peace it can hardly enjoy, except under the reign of corruption, and in an age of faithlessness. Peace and rest are future.

Now, then, what is it natural to suppose will be the conduct of those who are helpless and persecuted, as the Holy Spouse of Christ? Pain and hardship and disrepute are pleasant to no man; and though they are to be gloried in when they are undergone, yet they will rather, if possible, be shunned or averted. Such avoidance is sanctioned, nay, commanded, by our Lord. When trials are inevitable, we must cheerfully bear them; but when they can be avoided without sin, we ought to prevent them. But how were Christians to prevent them when they might not fight? I answer, they were allowed the arms, that is, the arts, of the defenceless. Even the inferior animals will teach us how wonderfully the Creator has compensated to the weak their want of strength, by giving them other qualities which may avail in their struggle with the strong. They have the gift of fleetness; or they have a certain make and colour; or certain habits of living; or some natural cunning, which enables them either to elude or even to destroy their enemies. Brute force is countervailed by flight, brute passion by prudence and artifice. Instances of a similar kind occur in our own race. Those nations which are destitute of material force, have recourse to the arts of the unwarlike; they are fraudulent and crafty; they dissemble, negotiate, procrastinate, evading what they cannot resist, and wearing out what they cannot crush. Thus is it with a captive, effeminate race, under the rule of the strong and haughty. So is it with slaves; so is it with ill-used and oppressed children; who learn to be cowardly and deceitful towards their tyrants. So is it with the subjects of a despot, who encounter his axe or bowstring with the secret influence of intrigue and conspiracy, the dagger and the poisoned cup. They exercise the unalienable right of self-defence by such methods as they best may; only, since human nature is unscrupulous, guilt or innocence is all the same to them, if it works their purpose.

Now, our Lord and Saviour did not forbid us the exercise of that instinct of self-defence which is born with us. He did not forbid us to defend ourselves, but He forbad certain *modes* of defence. All sinful means, of course, He forbad, as is plain without mentioning. But, besides these, He forbad us what is not sinful, but allowable by nature, though not in that more excellent and perfect way which He taught—He forbad us to defend ourselves by force, to return blow for blow. "Ye have heard," He says, "that it hath been said, An eye for an eye, and a tooth for a tooth; but I say unto you, That ye resist not evil: but whosoever shall smite thee on thy right cheek, turn to him the other also. And if any man will sue thee at the law, and take away thy coat, let him have thy cloke also. And whosoever shall compel thee to go a mile, go with him twain." Thus the servants of Christ are forbidden to defend themselves by violence; but they are not forbidden other means; direct means are not allowed them, but others are even commanded. For instance, *foresight;* "beware of men:" [3] *avoidance,* "when they persecute you in this city, flee ye into another:" *prudence and skill,* as in the text, "be ye wise as serpents."

Here we are reminded of the awful history with which the sacred volume opens. In the beginning, "the serpent was more subtle than any beast of the field which the Lord God had made." First, observe then, our Lord in the text sanctions that very reference which I have been making to the instincts and powers of the inferior animals, and puts them forth as our example. As we are to learn industry from the ant, and reliance on Him from the ravens, so the dove is our pattern of innocence, and the serpent our pattern of wisdom. But, more-

[3] Matt. x. 17.

over, considering that the serpent was chosen by the Enemy of mankind, as the instrument of his temptations in Paradise, it is very remarkable that Christ should choose it as the pattern of wisdom for His followers. It is as if He appealed to the whole world of sin, and to the bad arts by which the feeble gain advantages here over the strong. It is as if He set before us the craft, the treachery, the perfidy of the captive and the slave, and bade us extract a lesson even from so great an evil. It is as if the more we are forbidden violence, the more we are exhorted to prudence; as if it were our bounden duty to rival the wicked in endowments of mind, and to excel them in their exercise. And He makes a reference of this very kind in one of His parables, where "the lord commended the unjust steward, because he had done wisely; for the children of this world are in their generation wiser than the children of light." "Be ye wise as serpents," He said; then, knowing how dangerous such wisdom is, especially in times of temptation, if a severe conscientiousness is not awake, He added, "and harmless as doves." "Behold, I send you forth as sheep in the midst of wolves; be ye therefore wise as serpents, and harmless as doves."

It needs very little knowledge of the history of the Church, to understand how remarkably this exhortation to wisdom has been fulfilled in it. If there be one reproach more than another which has been cast upon it, it is that of fraud and cunning—cast upon it, even from St. Paul's day, whose word was accused of being "yea and nay;" [4] and himself of "walking in craftiness, and handling the word of God deceitfully:" [5] of being a "deceiver," though he was "true;" [6] of "terrifying by letters;" [7] and of "being crafty," and "catching" his converts "with guile." [8] Nay, cast upon it in the person of our Lord, who was

[4] 2 Cor. i. 17.
[5] 2 Cor. iv. 2.
[6] 2 Cor. vi. 8.
[7] 2 Cor. x. 9.
[8] 2 Cor. xii. 16.

called "a deceiver," and said to "deceive the people." Priest-craft has ever been considered the badge, and its imputation is a kind of note of the Church; and in part, indeed, truly, because the presence of powerful enemies, and the sense of their own weakness, has sometimes tempted Christians to the abuse, instead of the use of Christian wisdom, to be wise without being harmless; but partly—nay, for the most part—not truly, but slanderously, and merely because the world called their wisdom craft, when it was found to be a match for its own numbers and power. Christians were called crafty, because "they were, in fact, so strong, though professing to be weak." And next, in mere consistency, they were called hypocritical, because "they were, forsooth, so crafty, professing to be innocent." And thus whereas they have ever, in accordance with our Lord's words, been wise and harmless, they have ever been called instead crafty and hypocritical. The words "craft" and "hypocrisy" are but the version of "wisdom" and "harmlessness," in the language of the world.

It is remarkable, however, that not only is harmlessness the corrective of wisdom, securing it against the corruption of craft and deceit, as stated in the text; but innocence, simplicity, implicit obedience to God, tranquillity of mind, contentment, these and the like virtues are themselves a sort of wisdom;—I mean, they produce the same results as wisdom, because God works for those who do not work for themselves; and thus Christians especially incur the charge of craft at the hands of the world, because they pretend to so little, yet effect so much. This circumstance admits dwelling on.

By innocence, or harmlessness, is meant simplicity in act, purity in motive, honesty in aim; acting conscientiously and religiously, according to the matter in hand, without caring for consequences or appearances; doing what appears one's duty, and being obedient for obedience' sake, and leaving the event to God. This is to be innocent as the dove; yet this conduct is the truest wisdom; and this conduct accordingly has pre-eminently the appearance of craft.

It appears to be craft, and is wisdom, in many ways.

1. First: sobriety, self-restraint, control of word and feeling, which religious men exercise, have about them an appearance of being artificial, because they are not natural; and of being artful, because artificial. I do not deny there is something very engaging in a frank and unpremeditating manner; some persons have it more than others; in some persons it is a great grace. But it must be recollected that I am speaking of times of persecution and oppression to Christians, such as the text foretells; and then surely frankness will become nothing else than indignation at the oppressor, and vehemence of speech, if it is permitted. Accordingly, as persons have deep feelings, so they will find the necessity of self-control, lest they should say what they ought not. All this stands to reason, without enlarging upon it. And to this must be added, that those who would be holy and blameless, the sons of God, find so much in the world to unsettle and defile them, that they are necessarily forced upon a strict self-restraint, lest they should receive injury from such intercourse with it as is unavoidable; and this self-restraint is the first thing which makes holy persons seem wanting in openness and manliness.

2. Next let it be considered that the world, the gross, carnal, unbelieving world, is blind to the peculiar feelings, objects, hopes, fears, affections of religious people. It cannot understand them. Religious men are a mystery to it; and, being a mystery, they will be called by the world, in mere self-defence, mysterious, dark, subtle, designing; and that the more, because, as living to God, they are at no pains to justify themselves to the world, or to open their hearts, or account to it for their conduct. The world will impute motives, either because it cannot find any, or because it simply will not believe those motives to be the real ones which are such, and are avowed as such. It cannot believe that men will deliberately sacrifice this life to the next; and when they profess to do so, it thinks that of necessity there must be something behind which they do not divulge. And, again, all the reasons which

religious men allege, seem to the world unreal, and all the feelings fantastical and strained; and this strengthens it in its idea that it has not fathomed them, and that there is some secret to be found out. And indeed it has not fathomed them, and there is a secret; but it is the power of Divine grace, their state of heart, which is the secret; not their motives or their ends, which the world is told to the full. Here is a second reason why the dove seems but a serpent. Christians give up worldly advantages; they sacrifice rank or wealth; they prefer obscurity to station; they do penance rather than live delicately; and the world says, "Here are effects without causes sufficient for them; here is craft."

3. Further, let this be considered. The precept given us is, that "we resist not evil;" that we yield to worldly authority, and "give place unto wrath." This the early Christians did in an especial way. But it is very difficult to make the world understand the difference between an outward obedience, and an interior assent. When the Christians obeyed the heathen magistrate in all things not sinful, it was not that they thought the heathen right; they knew them to be idolaters. There are a multitude of cases, and very various, where it is our duty to obey those who nevertheless have no power over our belief or conviction. When, however, religious men outwardly conform, on the score of duty, to "the powers that be," the world is easily led into the mistake that they have renounced their opinions as well as submitted their actions; and it feels or affects surprise, to learn that their opinions remain; and this it considers or calls an inconsistency, or a duplicity. It argues that they are breaking promise, cherishing what they disown, or resuming what they professed to abandon. And thus the very fact that they are so harmless, so inoffensive, that they do so much in the way of compliance, becomes a ground of complaint against them, that they do not do more—that they do not do more than they have a right to do. They yield outwardly; to assent inwardly would be to betray the faith; yet

they are called deceitful and double-dealing, because they do as much as they can, and not more than they may.

4. Again: the cheerfulness, contentment, and readiness with which religious men resign their cause into God's hands, and are well-pleased that the world should seem to triumph over them, have still further an appearance of craft and deceit. For why should they be so satisfied to give up their wishes, unless they knew something which others did not know, or were really gaining while they seemed to lose? Other men make a great clamour and lamentation over their idols; there is no mistaking that they have lost them, and that they have no hope. But Christians resign themselves. They are silent; silence itself is suspicious—even silence is mystery. Why do they not speak out? why do they not show a natural, an honest indignation? The submitting to calumny is a proof that it is too true. They would set themselves right, if they could. Still more strange and suspicious is the confidence which religious men show, in spite of apparent weakness, that their cause will triumph. The boldness, decisiveness, calmness of speech, which are necessarily the result of Christian faith and hope, lead the world to the surmise of some hidden reliance, some secret support, to account for them; as if God's word, when received and dwelt on, were not a greater encouragement to the lonely combatant than any word of man, however powerful, or any conspiracy, however far-spreading.

5. And still stronger is this delusion on the part of the world, when the event justifies the confidence of religious men. The truest wisdom is to stand still and trust in God, and to the world it is also the strongest evidence of craft. God fights for those who do not fight for themselves; such is the great truth, such is the gracious rule, which is declared and exemplified in the Gospel: "Dearly beloved, avenge not yourselves," says St. Paul, "but rather give place unto wrath, for it is written, Vengeance is Mine, I will repay, saith the Lord." [9] Do

[9] Rom. xii. 19.

nothing, and you have done every thing. The less you do, the more God will do for you. The more you submit to the violence of the world, the more powerfully will He rise against the world, who is irresistible. The less you ward off the world's blows from you, the more heavy will be His blows upon the world, if not in your cause, at least in His own. When, then, the world at length becomes sensible that it is faring ill, and receiving more harm than it inflicts, yet is unwilling to humble itself under the mighty hand of God, what is left but to attribute its failure to the power of those who seem to be weak? that is, to their craft, who pretend to be weak when really they are strong.

6. To this must be added, that the truth has in itself the gift of spreading, without instruments; it makes its way in the world, under God's blessing, by its own persuasiveness and excellence; "So is the kingdom of God," says our Lord, "as if a man should cast seed into the ground, and should sleep, and rise night and day, and the seed should spring and grow up, he *knoweth not* how." [10] The Word, when once uttered, runs its course. He who speaks it has done his work in uttering it, and cannot recall it if he would. It runs its course; it prospers in the thing whereunto God sends it. It seizes many souls at once, and subdues them to the obedience of faith. Now when bystanders see these effects and see no cause, for they will not believe that the Word itself is the cause, which is to them a dead-letter—when it sees many minds moved in one way in many places, it imputes to secret management that uniformity which is nothing but the echo of the One Living and True Word.

7. And of course all this happens to the surprise of Christians as well as of the world; they can but marvel and praise God, but cannot account for it more than the world. "When the Lord turned again the captivity of Sion," says the Psalmist, "then were we like unto them that dream." [11] Or as the

[10] Mark iv. 26, 27.
[11] Ps. cxxvi. 1.

Prophet says of the Church, "Thine heart shall fear and be enlarged; because the abundance of the sea shall be converted unto thee, the forces of the Gentiles shall come unto thee," [12] and here again the Christian's true wisdom looks like craft. It is true wisdom to leave the event to God; but when they are prospered, it looks like deceit to show surprise, and to disclaim the work themselves. Moreover, meekness, gentleness, patience, and love, have in themselves a strong power to melt the heart of those who witness them. Cheerful suffering, too, leads spectators to sympathy, till, perhaps, a reaction takes place in the minds of men, and they are converted by the sight, and glorify their Father which is in heaven. But it is easy to insinuate, when men are malevolent, that those who triumph through meekness have affected the meekness to secure the triumph.

8. Here a very large subject opens upon us, to which I shall but allude. Those who surrender themselves to Christ in implicit faith are graciously taken into His service; and, "as men under authority," they do great things without knowing it, by the Wisdom of their Divine Master. They act on conscience, perhaps in despondency, and without foresight; but what is obedience in them, has a purpose with God, and they are successful, when they do but mean to be dutiful. But what duplicity does the world think it, to speak of conscience, or honour, or propriety, or delicacy, or to give other tokens of personal motives, when the event seems to show that a calculation of results has been the actuating principle at bottom! It is God who designs, but His servants seem designing; and that the more, should it so happen that they really do themselves catch glimpses of their own position in His providential course. For then what they do from the heart, approves itself to their reason, and they are able to recognize the expedience of obedience.

How frequently is this remark in point in the history—nay, in the very constitution of the Church! Jacob, for instance,

[12] Isa. lx. 5.

is thought worldly-wise in his dealings with Laban, whereas he was a "plain man," simply obedient to the Angel who "spake unto him in a dream," who took care of his worldly interests for him, and protected him against his avaricious kinsman. Moses, again, is sometimes called sagacious and shrewd in his measures or his laws, as if wise acts might not come from the Source of wisdom, and provisions were proved to be human, when they could be shown to be advisable. And so, again, in the Christian Church, bishops have been called hypocritical in submitting and yet opposing themselves to the civil power, in a matter of plain duty, if a popular movement was the consequence; and then hypocritical again, if they did their best to repress it. And in like manner, theological doctrines or ecclesiastical usages are styled politic if they are but salutary; as if the Lord of the Church, who has willed her sovereignty, might not effect it by secondary causes. What, for instance, though we grant that sacramental confession and the celibacy of the clergy do tend to consolidate the body politic in the relation of rulers and subjects, or, in other words, to aggrandize the priesthood? for how can the Church be one body without such relation, and why should not He, who has decreed that there should be unity, take measures to secure it? Marks of design are not elsewhere assumed as disproofs of His interference. Why should not the Creator, who has given us the feeling of hunger that we may eat and not die, and sentiments of compassion and benevolence for the welfare of our brethren, when He would form a more integral power than mankind had yet seen, adopt adequate means, and use His old world to create a new one? and why must His human instruments set out with a purpose, because they accomplish one? Nothing is safe in Revelation on such an interpretation. As the expedience of its provisions is made an objection to their honesty, so the beauty of its facts becomes an argument against their truth. The narratives in the Gospels have lately been viewed as mythical representations from their very perfection; as if a

Divine work could not be most beautiful on the one hand and most expedient on the other.

The reason is this: men do not like to hear of the interposition of Providence in the affairs of the world; and they invidiously ascribe ability and skill to His agents, to escape the thought of an Infinite Wisdom and an Almighty Power. They will be unjust to their brethren, that they may not be just to Him; they will be wanton in their imputations, rather than humble themselves to a confession.

But for us, let us glory in what they disown; let us beg of our Divine Lord to take to Him His great power, and manifest Himself more and more, and reign both in our hearts and in the world. Let us beg of Him to stand by us in trouble, and guide us on our dangerous way. May He, as of old, choose "the foolish things of the world to confound the wise, and the weak things of the world to confound the things which are mighty"! May He support us all the day long, till the shades lengthen, and the evening comes, and the busy world is hushed, and the fever of life is over, and our work is done! Then in His mercy may He give us a safe lodging, and a holy rest, and peace at the last!

[*February 19, 1843.*]

X

THE PARTING OF FRIENDS [1]

"Man goeth forth to his work and to his labour until the evening."
—Psalm civ. 23.

WHEN THE SON OF MAN, the First-born of the creation
of God, came to the evening of His mortal life, He
parted with His disciples at a feast. He had borne
"the burden and heat of the day;" yet, when "wearied with
His journey," He had but stopped at the well's side, and
asked a draught of water for His thirst; for He had "meat to
eat which" others "knew not of." His meat was "to do the will
of Him that sent Him, and to finish His work;" "I must work
the works of Him that sent Me," said He, "while it is day; the
night cometh, when no man can work." [2] Thus passed the
season of His ministry; and if at any time He feasted with
Pharisee or publican, it was in order that He might do the
work of God more strenuously. But "when the even was come
He sat down with the Twelve." "And He said unto them,
With desire have I desired to eat this Passover with you, before
I suffer." [3] He was about to suffer more than man had ever
suffered or shall suffer. But there is nothing gloomy, churlish,
violent, or selfish in His grief; it is tender, affectionate, social.
He calls His friends around Him, though He was as Job
among the ashes; He bids them stay by Him, and see Him suffer; He desires their sympathy; He takes refuge in their love.

---

[1] Preached on the anniversary of the consecration of a chapel. From
Sermons Bearing on Subjects of the Day, No. 26. [Ed.]

[2] John iv. 6, 34; ix. 4.

[3] Matt. xxvi. 20.   Luke xxii. 15.

He first feasted them, and sung a hymn with them, and washed their feet; and when His long trial began, He beheld them and kept them in His presence, till they in terror shrank from it. Yet, on St. Mary and St. John, His Virgin Mother and His Virgin Disciple, who remained, His eyes still rested; and in St. Peter, who was denying Him in the distance, His sudden glance wrought a deep repentance. O wonderful pattern, the type of all trial and of all duty under it, while the Church endures.

We indeed to-day have no need of so high a lesson and so august a comfort. We have no pain, no grief which calls for it; yet, considering it has been brought before us in this morning's service,[4] we are naturally drawn to think of it, though it be infinitely above us, under certain circumstances of this season and the present time. For now are the shades of evening falling upon the earth, and the year's labour is coming to its end. In Septuagesima the labourers were sent into the vineyard; in Sexagesima the sower went forth to sow;—that time is over; "the harvest is passed, the summer is ended,"[5] the vintage is gathered. We have kept the Ember-days for the fruits of the earth, in self-abasement, as being unworthy even of the least of God's mercies; and now we are offering up of its corn and wine as a propitiation, and are eating and drinking of them with thanksgiving.

"All things come of Thee, and of Thine own have we given Thee."[6] If we have had the rain in its season, and the sun shining in its strength, and the fertile ground, it is of Thee. We give back to Thee what came from Thee. "When Thou givest it them, they gather it, and when Thou openest Thy hand, they are filled with good. When Thou hidest Thy face, they are troubled; when Thou takest away their breath, they die, and are turned again to their dust. When Thou lettest Thy breath go forth, they shall be made, and Thou shalt renew

4 Sept. 25, 1843.
5 Jer. viii. 20.
6 1 Chron. xxix. 14.

the face of the earth." [7] He gives, He takes away. "Shall we receive good at the hand of God, and shall we not receive evil?" [8] May He not "do what He will with His own?" [9] May not His sun set as it has risen? and must it not set, if it is to rise again? and must not darkness come first, if there is ever to be morning? and must not the sky be blacker, before it can be brighter? And cannot He, who can do all things, cause a light to arise even in the darkness? "I have thought upon Thy Name, O Lord, in the night season, and have kept Thy Law;" "Thou also shalt light my candle, the Lord my God shall make my darkness to be light;" or as the Prophet speaks, "At the evening time it shall be light." [10]

"All things come of Thee," says holy David, "for we are strangers before Thee and sojourners, as were all our fathers; our days on the earth are as a shadow, and there is none abiding." [11] All is vanity, vanity of vanities, and vexation of spirit. "What profit hath a man of all his labour which he taketh under the sun? One generation passeth away, and another generation cometh; but the earth abideth for ever; the sun also ariseth, and the sun goeth down; . . . all things are full of labour, man cannot utter it; . . . that which is crooked cannot be made straight, and that which is wanting cannot be numbered." [12] "To every thing there is a season, and a time to every purpose under heaven; a time to be born and a time to die; a time to plant and a time to pluck up that which is planted; a time to kill and a time to heal; a time to break down and a time to build up; . . . a time to get and a time to lose; a time to keep and a time to cast away." [13] And time, and matter, and motion, and force, and the will of man, how vain are they all, except as instruments of the grace of God, bless-

[7] Ps. civ. 28–30.
[8] Job ii. 10.
[9] Matt. xx. 15.
[10] Zech. xiv. 7.
[11] 1 Chron. xxix. 15.
[12] Eccles. i. 3–15.
[13] Eccles. iii. 1–6.

ing them and working with them! How vain are all our pains, our thought, our care, unless God uses them, unless God has inspired them! how worse than fruitless are they, unless directed to His glory, and given back to the Giver!

"Of Thine own have we given Thee," says the royal Psalmist, after he had collected materials for the Temple. Because "the work was great," and "the palace, not for man, but for the Lord God," therefore he "prepared with all his might for the house of his God," gold, and silver, and brass, and iron, and wood, "onyx stones, and stones to be set, glistering stones, and of divers colours, and all manner of precious stones, and marble stones in abundance." [14] And "the people rejoiced, for that they offered willingly; ... and David the king also rejoiced with great joy." We too, at this season, year by year, have been allowed in our measure, according to our work and our faith, to rejoice in God's Presence, for this sacred building which He has given us to worship Him in. It was a glad time when we first met here,—many of us now present recollect it; nor did our rejoicing cease, but was renewed every autumn, as the day came round. It has been "a day of gladness and feasting, and a good day, and of sending portions one to another." [15] We have kept the feast heretofore with merry hearts; we have kept it seven full years unto "a perfect end;" now let us keep it, even though in haste, and with bitter herbs, and with loins girded, and with a staff in our hand, as they who have "no continuing city, but seek one to come." [16]

So was it with Jacob, when with his staff he passed over that Jordan. He too kept feast before he set out upon his dreary way. He received a father's blessing, and then was sent afar; he left his mother, never to see her face or hear her voice again. He parted with all that his heart loved, and turned his face towards a strange land. He went with the doubt, whether he should have bread to eat, or raiment to put on. He came to "the

[14] 1 Chron. xxix. 1, 2, 9.
[15] Esther ix. 19.
[16] Heb. xiii. 14.

people of the East," and served a hard master twenty years.
"In the day the drought consumed him, and the frost by night;
and his sleep departed from his eyes." [17] O little did he think,
when father and mother had forsaken him, and at Bethel he
lay down to sleep on the desolate ground, because the sun was
set and even had come, that there was the house of God and
the gate of heaven, that the Lord was in that place, and would
thence go forward with him whithersoever he went, till He
brought him back to that river in "two bands," who was then
crossing it forlorn and solitary!

So had it been with Ishmael; though the feast was not to him
a blessing, yet he feasted in his father's tent, and then was sent
away. That tender father, who, when a son was promised him
of Sarah, cried out to his Almighty Protector, "O that Ishmael
might live before Thee!" [18]—he it was, who, under a divine direction, the day after the feast, "rose up early in the morning,
and took bread, and a bottle of water, and gave it unto Hagar,
putting it on her shoulder, and the child, and sent her away.
And she departed, and wandered in the wilderness of Beer-
sheba." [19] And little thought that fierce child, when for feasting
came thirst and weariness and wandering in the desert, that
this was not the end of Ishmael, but the beginning. And little
did Hagar read his coming fortunes, when "the water was
spent in the bottle, and she cast the child under one of the
shrubs, and she went and sat her down over against him a good
way off; . . . for she said, Let me not see the death of the child.
And she sat over against him, and lift up her voice, and wept."

So had it been with Naomi, though she was not quitting,
but returning to her home, and going, not to a land of famine,
but of plenty. In a time of distress, she had left her country,
and found friends and made relatives among the enemies of
her people. And when her husband and her children died,
Moabitish women, who had once been the stumbling-block of

[17] Gen. xxxi. 40.
[18] Gen. xvii. 18.
[19] Gen. xxi. 14.

Israel, became the support and comfort of her widowhood. Time had been when, at the call of the daughters of Moab, the chosen people had partaken their sacrifices, and "bowed down to their gods. And Israel joined himself unto Baal-peor, and the anger of the Lord was kindled against Israel." Centuries had since passed away, and now of Moabites was Naomi mother; and to their land had she given her heart, when the call of duty summoned her back to Bethlehem. "She had heard in the country of Moab, how that the Lord had visited His people in giving them bread. Wherefore she went forth out of the place where she was, and her two daughters-in-law with her, and they went on the way to return unto the land of Judah." [20]

Forlorn widow, great was the struggle in her bosom, whether shall she do?—leave behind her the two heathen women, in widowhood and weakness like herself, her sole stay, the shadows of departed blessings? or shall she selfishly take them as fellow-sufferers, who could not be protectors? Shall she seek sympathy where she cannot gain help? shall she deprive them of a home, when she has none to supply? So she said, "Go, return each to her mother's house: the Lord deal kindly with you, as ye have dealt with the dead and with me!" Perplexed Naomi, torn with contrary feelings; which tried her the more, —Orpah who left her, or Ruth who remained? Orpah who was a pain, or Ruth who was a charge? "They lifted up their voice and wept again; and Orpah kissed her mother-in-law, but Ruth clave unto her. And she said, Behold, thy sister-in-law is gone back unto her people and unto her gods; return thou after thy sister-in-law. And Ruth said, Entreat me not to leave thee, or to return from following after thee: for whither thou goest, I will go; and where thou lodgest, I will lodge: thy people shall be my people, and thy God my God. Where thou diest, will I die, and there will I be buried; the Lord do so to me, and more also, if aught but death part thee and me." [21]

Orpah kissed Naomi, and went back to the world. There was

[20] Ruth i. 6–8, 14, 15.
[21] Ruth i. 14–17.

sorrow in the parting, but Naomi's sorrow was more for Orpah's
sake than for her own. Pain there would be, but it was the pain
of a wound, not the yearning regret of love. It was the pain we
feel when friends disappoint us, and fall in our esteem. That
kiss of Orpah was no loving token; it was but the hollow profession of those who use smooth words, that they may part company with us with least trouble and discomfort to themselves.
Orpah's tears were but the dregs of affection; she clasped her
mother-in-law once for all, that she might not cleave to her.
Far different were the tears, far different the embrace, which
passed between those two religious friends recorded in the
book which follows, who loved each other with a true love
unfeigned, but whose lives ran in different courses. If Naomi's
grief was great when Orpah kissed her, what was David's
when he saw the last of him, whose "soul had from the first
been knit with his soul," so that "he loved him as his own
soul"? [22] "I am distressed for thee, my brother Jonathan," he
says; "very pleasant hast thou been unto me; thy love to me
was wonderful, passing the love of women." [23] What woe was
upon that "young man," "of a beautiful countenance and goodly
to look to," and "cunning in playing, and a mighty valiant man,
and a man of war, and prudent in matters;" [24] when his devoted affectionate loyal friend, whom these good gifts have
gained, looked upon him for the last time! O hard destiny,
except that the All-merciful so willed it, that such companions
might not walk in the house of God as friends! David must
flee to the wilderness, Jonathan must pine in his father's hall;
Jonathan must share that stern father's death in battle, and
David must ascend the vacant throne. Yet they made a
covenant on parting: "Thou shalt not only," said Jonathan,
"while yet I live, show me the kindness of the Lord, that I die
not; but also thou shalt not cut off thy kindness from my house
for ever; no, not when the Lord hath cut off the enemies of

[22] 1 Sam. xviii. 1–3.
[23] 2 Sam. i. 26.
[24] 1 Sam. xvi. 12, 18.

David, every one from the face of the earth.... And Jonathan caused David to swear again, because he loved him, for he loved him as he loved his own soul." And then, while David hid himself, Jonathan made trial of Saul, how he felt disposed to David; and when he found that "it was determined of his father to slay David," he "arose from the table in fierce anger, and did eat no meat the second day of the month; for he was grieved for David, because his father had done him shame." Then in the morning he went out into the field, where David lay, and the last meeting took place between the two. "David arose out of a place toward the south, and fell on his face to the ground, and bowed himself three times; and they kissed one another, and wept one with another, till David exceeded. And Jonathan said to David, Go in peace, forasmuch as we have sworn both of us in the Name of the Lord, saying, The Lord be between me and thee, and between my seed and thy seed for ever. And he arose and departed; and Jonathan went into the city." [25]

David's affection was given to a single heart; but there is another spoken of in Scripture, who had a thousand friends and loved each as his own soul, and seemed to live a thousand lives in them, and died a thousand deaths when he must quit them: that great Apostle, whose very heart was broken when his brethren wept; who "lived if they stood fast in the Lord;" who "was glad when he was weak and they were strong;" and who was "willing to have imparted unto them his own soul, because they were dear unto him." [26] Yet we read of his bidding farewell to whole Churches, never to see them again. At one time, to the little ones of the flock: "When we had accomplished those days," says the Evangelist, "we departed, and went our way,... with wives and children, till we were out of the city; and we kneeled down on the shore and prayed. And when we had taken our leave one of another, we took ship, and they returned home again." At another time, to the

[25] 1 Sam. xx. 14–42.
[26] Acts xxi. 21, 22. 1 Thess. ii. 8; iii. 8. 2 Cor. xiii. 9.

rulers of the Church: "And now behold," he says to them, "I know that ye all, among whom I have gone preaching the kingdom of God, shall see my face no more. Wherefore, I take you to record this day, that I am pure from the blood of all men, for I have not shunned to declare unto you all the counsel of God. . . . I have coveted no man's silver, or gold, or apparel; . . . I have showed you all things, how that so labouring he ought to support the weak; and to remember the words of the Lord Jesus, how he said, It is more blessed to give than to receive." And then, when he had finished, "he kneeled down, and prayed with them all. And they all wept sore, and fell on Paul's neck, and kissed him; sorrowing most of all for the words which he spake, that they should see his face no more. And they accompanied him unto the ship." [27]

There was another time, when he took leave of his "own son in the faith," Timothy, in words more calm, and still more impressive, when his end was nigh: "I am now ready to be offered," he says, "and the time of my departure is at hand. I have fought a good fight, I have finished my course, I have kept the faith. Henceforth there is laid up for me a crown of righteousness, which the Lord, the Righteous Judge, shall give me at that day." [28]

And what are all these instances but memorials and tokens of the Son of Man, when His work and His labour were coming to an end? Like Jacob, like Ishmael, like Elisha, like the Evangelist whose day is just passed, He kept feast before His departure; and, like David, He was persecuted by the rulers in Israel; and, like Naomi, He was deserted by His friends; and, like Ishmael, He cried out, "I thirst" in a barren and dry land; and at length, like Jacob, He went to sleep with a stone for His pillow, in the evening. And, like St. Paul, He had "finished the work which God gave Him to do," and had "witnessed a good confession;" and, beyond St. Paul, "the

[27] Acts xxi. 5, 6; xx. 25–27, 33, 35, 36–38.
[28] 2 Tim. iv. 6–8.

Prince of this world had come, and had nothing in Him." [29]
"He was in the world, and the world was made by Him, and
the world knew Him not. He came unto His own, and His own
received Him not." [30] Heavily did He leave, tenderly did He
mourn over the country and city which rejected Him. "When
He was come near, He beheld the city, and wept over it,
saying, If thou hadst known, even thou, at least in this thy day,
the things which belong unto thy peace! but now they are hid
from thine eyes." And again: "O Jerusalem, Jerusalem, which
killest the prophets, and stonest them that are sent unto thee,
how often would I have gathered thy children together, as a
hen doth gather her brood under her wings, and ye would not!
Behold, your house is left unto you desolate." [31]

A lesson surely, and a warning to us all, in every place
where He puts His Name, to the end of time; lest we be cold
towards His gifts, or unbelieving towards His word, or jealous
of His workings, or heartless towards His mercies. . . . O mother
of saints! O school of the wise! O nurse of the heroic! of whom
went forth, in whom have dwelt, memorable names of old,
to spread the truth abroad, or to cherish and illustrate it at
home! O thou, from whom surrounding nations lit their lamps!
O virgin of Israel! wherefore dost thou now sit on the ground
and keep silence, like one of the foolish women who were
without oil in the coming of the Bridegroom? Where is now
the ruler in Sion, and the doctor in the Temple, and the ascetic
on Carmel, and the herald in the wilderness, and the preacher
in the market-place? where are thy "effectual fervent prayers,"
offered in secret, and thy alms and good works coming up as
a memorial before God? How is it, O once holy place, that
"the land mourneth, for the corn is wasted, the new wine is
dried up, the oil languisheth, . . . because joy is withered away
from the sons of men?" "Alas for the day! . . . how do the

---

[29] 1 Tim. vi. 13. John xiv. 30.
[30] John i. 10, 11.
[31] Luke xix. 41, 42; xiii. 34, 35.

beasts groan! the herds of cattle are perplexed, because they have no pasture, yea, the flocks of sheep are made desolate." "Lebanon is ashamed and hewn down; Sharon is like a wilderness, and Bashan and Carmel shake off their fruits." [32] O my mother, whence is this unto thee, that thou hast good things poured upon thee and canst not keep them, and bearest children, yet darest not own them? why hast thou not the skill to use their services, nor the heart to rejoice in their love? how is it that whatever is generous in purpose, and tender or deep in devotion, thy flower and thy promise, falls from thy bosom and finds no home within thine arms? Who hath put this note upon thee, to have "a miscarrying womb, and dry breasts," to be strange to thine own flesh, and thine eye cruel towards thy little ones? Thine own offspring, the fruit of thy womb, who love thee and would toil for thee, thou dost gaze upon with fear, as though a portent, or thou dost loathe as an offence;—at best thou dost but endure, as if they had no claim but on thy patience, self-possession, and vigilance, to be rid of them as easily as thou mayest. Thou makest them "stand all the day idle," as the very condition of thy bearing with them; or thou biddest them be gone, where they will be more welcome; or thou sellest them for nought to the stranger that passes by. And what wilt thou do in the end thereof? . . .

Scripture is a refuge in any trouble; only let us be on our guard against seeming to use it further than is fitting, or doing more than sheltering ourselves under its shadow. Let us use it according to our measure. It is far higher and wider than our need; and its language veils our feelings while it gives expression to them. It is sacred and heavenly; and it restrains and purifies, while it sanctions them.

And now, my brethren, "bless God, praise Him and magnify Him, and praise Him for the things which He hath done unto you in the sight of all that live. It is good to praise God, and exalt His Name, and honourably to show forth the works of

[32] Joel i. 10–18. Isa. xxxiii. 9.

God; therefore be not slack to praise Him." "All the works of the Lord are good; and He will give every needful thing in due season; so that a man cannot say, This is worse than that; for in time they shall all be well approved. And therefore praise ye the Lord with the whole heart and mouth, and bless the Name of the Lord." [33]

"Leave off from wrath, and let go displeasure; flee from evil, and do the thing that is good." "Do that which is good, and no evil shall touch you." "Go your way; eat your bread with joy, and drink your wine with a merry heart, for God now accepteth your works; let your garments be always white, and let your head lack no ointment." [34]

And, O my brethren, O kind and affectionate hearts, O loving friends, should you know any one whose lot it has been, by writing or by word of mouth, in some degree to help you thus to act; if he has ever told you what you knew about yourselves, or what you did not know; has read to you your wants or feelings, and comforted you by the very reading; has made you feel that there was a higher life than this daily one, and a brighter world than that you see; or encouraged you, or sobered you, or opened a way to the inquiring, or soothed the perplexed; if what he has said or done has ever made you take interest in him, and feel well inclined towards him; remember such a one in time to come, though you hear him not, and pray for him, that in all things he may know God's will, and at all times he may be ready to fulfil it.

[*September 25, 1843.*]

[33] Tob. xii. 6.   Ecclus. xxxix. 33–35.
[34] Ps. xxxvii. 8. 27.   Tob. xii. 7.   Eccles. ix. 7, 8.

XI

PURITY AND LOVE[1]

WE FIND TWO ESPECIAL MANIFESTATIONS of divine grace in the human heart, whether we turn to Scripture for instances of it, or to the history of the Church; whether we trace it in the case of Saints, or in persons of holy and religious life: and the two are even found among our Lord's Apostles, being represented by the two foremost of that favoured company, St. Peter and St. John. St. John is the Saint of purity, and St. Peter is the Saint of love. Not that love and purity can ever be separated; not as if a Saint had not all virtues in him at once; not as if St. Peter were not pure as well as loving, and St. John loving, for all he was so pure. The graces of the Spirit cannot be separated from each other; one implies the rest; what is love but a delight in God, a devotion to Him, a surrender of the whole self to Him? what is impurity, on the other hand, but the turning to something of this world, something sinful, as the object of our affections instead of God? What is it but a deliberate abandonment of the Creator for the creature, and seeking pleasure in the shadow of death, not in the all-blissful Presence of light and holiness? The impure then cannot love God; and those who are without love of God cannot really be pure. Purity prepares the soul for love, and love confirms the soul in purity. The flame of love will not be bright unless the substance which feeds it be pure and unadulterate; and the most dazzling purity is but as iciness and desolation unless it draws its life from fervent love.

[1] From *Discourses to Mixed Congregations* (1849), No. 4. [Ed.]

134

Yet, certain as this is, it is certain also that the spiritual works of God show differently from each other to our eyes, and that they display, in their character and their history, some of them this virtue more than other virtues, and some that. In other words, it pleases the Giver of grace to endue His Saints specially with certain gifts, for His glory, which light up and beautify one particular portion or department of their souls, so as to cast their other excellences into the shade. And then this special gift of grace becomes their characteristic, and we put it first in our thoughts of them, and consider what they have besides, as included in it, or dependent upon it, and speak of them as if they had not the rest, though we know they really have them; and we give them some title or description taken from that particular grace which is so emphatically theirs. And in this way we may speak, as I intend to do in what I am going to say, of two chief classes of Saints, whose emblems are the lily and the rose, who are bright with angelic purity or who burn with divine love.

The two St. Johns are the great instances of the Angelic life. Whom, my brethren, can we conceive to have such majestic and severe sanctity as the Holy Baptist? He had a privilege which reached near upon the prerogative of the Most Blessed Mother of God; for, if she was conceived without sin, at least without sin he was born. She was all-pure, all-holy, and sin had no part in her: but St. John was in the beginning of his existence a partaker of Adam's curse: he lay under God's wrath, deprived of that grace which Adam had received, and which is the life and strength of human nature. Yet as soon as Christ, his Lord and Saviour, came to him, and Mary saluted his own mother, Elizabeth, forthwith the grace of God was given to him, and the original guilt was wiped away from his soul. And therefore it is that we celebrate the nativity of St. John; nothing unholy does the Church celebrate; not St. Peter's nor St. Paul's, nor St. Augustine's, nor St. Gregory's, nor St. Bernard's, nor St. Aloysius's, nor the nativity of any other Saint, however glorious, because they were all born in sin. She celebrates their conversions, their prerogatives, their martyrdoms, their deaths, their translations, but not their birth, because in no case was it holy. Three nativities alone does she commemorate, our Lord's, His Mother's, and lastly, St. John's. What a special gift was this, my brethren, separating the Baptist off, and distinguishing him from all prophets and preachers, who ever lived, however holy, except perhaps the prophet Jeremias! And such as was his commencement, was the course of his life. He was carried away by the Spirit into the desert, and there he lived on the simplest fare, in the rudest clothing, in the caves of wild beasts, apart from men, for thirty years, leading a life of mortification and of meditation, till he was called to preach penance, to proclaim the Christ, and to baptize Him; and then having done his work, and having left no act of sin on record, he was laid aside as an instrument which had lost its use, and languished in prison, till he was suddenly cut off by the sword of the executioner. Sanctity is the one idea of him impressed upon us from first to last; a most marvellous Saint, a hermit from his childhood, then a preacher to a fallen people, and then a Martyr. Surely such a life fulfils the expectation, which the salutation of Mary raised concerning him before his birth.

Yet still more beautiful, and almost as majestic, is the image of his namesake, that great Apostle, Evangelist, and Prophet of the Church, who came so early into our Lord's chosen company, and lived so long after all his fellows. We can contemplate him in his youth and in his venerable age; and on his whole life, from first to last, as his special gift, is marked purity. He is the virgin Apostle, who on that account was so dear to his Lord, "the disciple whom Jesus loved," who lay on His Bosom, who received His Mother from Him when upon the Cross, who had the vision of all the wonders which were to come to pass in the world to the end of time. "Greatly to be honoured," says the Church, "is blessed John, who on the Lord's Breast lay at supper, to whom, a virgin, did Christ

on the Cross commit his Virgin Mother. He was chosen a
virgin by the Lord, and was more beloved than the rest. The
special prerogative of chastity had made him meet for his
Lord's larger love, because, being chosen by Him a virgin, a
virgin he remained unto the end." He it was who in his youth
professed his readiness to drink Christ's chalice with Him;
who wore away a long life as a desolate stranger in a foreign
land; who was at length carried to Rome and plunged into
the hot oil, and then was banished to a far island, till his days
drew near their close.

O how impossible it is worthily to conceive of the sanctity
of these two great servants of God, so different is their whole
history, in their lives and in their deaths, yet agreeing together
in their seclusion from the world, in their tranquillity, and in
their all but sinlessness! Mortal sin had never touched them,
and we may well believe that even from deliberate venial
sin they were ever exempt; nay, that at particular seasons or
on certain occasions they did not sin at all. The rebellion of
the reason, the waywardness of the feelings, the disorder of the
thoughts, the fever of passion, the treachery of the senses, these
evils did the all-powerful grace of God subdue in them. They
lived in a world of their own, uniform, serene, abiding; in
visions of peace, in communion with heaven, in anticipation of
glory; and, if they spoke to the world without, as preachers
or as confessors, they spoke as from some sacred shrine, not
mixing with men while they addressed them, as "a voice crying
in the wilderness" or "in the Spirit on the Lord's Day." And
therefore it is we speak of them rather as patterns of sanctity
than of love, because love regards an external object, runs
towards it and labours for it, whereas such Saints came so
close to the Object of their love, they were granted so to
receive Him into their breasts, and so to make themselves
one with Him, that their hearts did not so much love heaven
as were themselves a heaven, did not so much see light as
were light; and they lived among men as those Angels in the
old time, who came to the patriarchs and spake as though

they were God, for God was in them, and spake by them. Thus these two were almost absorbed in the Godhead, living an angelical life, as far as man could lead one, so calm, so still, so raised above sorrow and fear, disappointment and regret, desire and aversion, as to be the most perfect images that earth has seen of the peace and immutability of God. Such too are the many virgin Saints whom history records for our veneration, St. Joseph, the great St. Antony, St. Cecilia who was waited on by Angels, St. Nicholas of Bari, St. Peter Celestine, St. Rose of Viterbo, St. Catherine of Sienna, and a host of others, and above all, the Virgin of Virgins, and Queen of Virgins, the Blessed Mary, who, though replete and overflowing with the grace of love, yet for the very reason that she was the "seat of wisdom," and the very "ark of the covenant," is more commonly represented under the emblem of the lily than of the rose.

But now, my brethren, let us turn to the other class of Saints. I have been speaking of those who in a wonderful, sometimes in a miraculous way, have been defended from sin, and conducted from strength to strength, from youth till death; but now suppose it has been the will of God to shed the light and power of His Spirit upon those who have misused the talents, and quenched the grace already given them, and who therefore have a host of evils within them of which they are to be dispossessed, who are under the dominion of obstinate habits, indulged passions, false opinions; who have served Satan, not as infants before their baptism, but with their will, with their reason, with their faculties responsible, and their hearts alive and conscious. Is He to draw these elect souls to Him without themselves, or by means of themselves? Is He to change them at His word, as He created them, as He will make them die, as He will raise them from the grave, or is He to enter into their souls, to address Himself to them, to persuade them, and so to win them? Doubtless He might have been urgent with them, and masterful; He might by a blessed violence have come upon them, and

so turned them into Saints; He might have superseded any
process of conversion, and out of the very stones have raised
up children to Abraham. But He has willed otherwise; else,
why did He manifest Himself on earth? Why did He surround Himself on His coming with so much that was touching and attractive and subduing? Why did He bid His angels
proclaim that He was to be seen as a little infant, in a manger
and in a Virgin's bosom, at Bethlehem? Why did He go
about doing good? Why did He die in public, before the
world, with His mother and His beloved disciple by Him?
Why does He now tell us how He is exalted in Heaven with
a host of glorified Saints, who are our intercessors, about His
throne? Why does He give us His own Mother Mary for our
mother, the most perfect image after Himself of what is
beautiful and tender, and gentle and soothing, in human nature? Why does He manifest Himself by an ineffable condescension on our Altars, still humbling Himself, though He
reigns on high? What does all this show, but that, when souls
wander away from Him, He reclaims them by means of themselves, "by cords of Adam," or of human nature, as the
prophet speaks,—conquering us indeed at His will, saving us
in spite of ourselves,—and yet by ourselves, so that the very
reason and affections of the old Adam, which have been made
"the instruments of iniquity unto sin," should, under the power
of His grace, become "the instruments of justice unto God"?

Yes, doubtless He draws us "by cords of Adam," and what
are those cords, but, as the prophet speaks in the same verse,
"the cords," or "the twine of love"? It is the manifestation
of the glory of God in the Face of Jesus Christ; it is that
view of the attributes and perfections of Almighty God; it is
the beauty of His sanctity, the sweetness of His mercy, the
brightness of His heaven, the majesty of His law, the harmony
of His providences, the thrilling music of His voice, which is
the antagonist of the flesh, and the soul's champion against
the world and the devil. "Thou hast seduced me, O Lord,"
says the prophet, "and I was seduced; Thou art stronger than

I, and hast prevailed;" Thou hast thrown Thy net skilfully, and its subtle threads are entwined round each affection of my heart, and its meshes have been a power of God, "bringing into captivity the whole intellect to the service of Christ." If the world has its fascinations, so surely has the Altar of the living God; if its pomps and vanities dazzle, so much more should the vision of Angels ascending and descending on the heavenly ladder; if sights of earth intoxicate, and its music is a spell upon the soul, behold Mary pleads with us, over against them, with her chaste eyes, and offers the Eternal Child for our caress, while sounds of cherubim are heard all round singing from out the fulness of the Divine Glory. Has divine hope no emotion? Has divine charity no transport? "How dear are Thy tabernacles, O Lord of hosts!" says the prophet; "my soul doth lust, and doth faint for the courts of the Lord; my heart and my flesh have rejoiced in the living God. Better is one day in Thy courts above a thousand: I have chosen to be an abject in the house of my God, rather than to dwell in the tabernacles of sinners."

So is it, as a great Doctor and penitent has said, St. Augustine; "It is not enough to be drawn by the will; thou art also drawn by the sense of pleasure. What is it to be drawn by pleasure? 'Delight thou in the Lord, and He will give thee the petitions of thy heart.' There is a certain pleasure of heart, when that heavenly Bread is sweet to a man. Moreover, if the poet saith, 'Every one is drawn by his own pleasure,' not by necessity, but by pleasure; not by obligation, but by delight; how much more boldly ought we to say, that man is drawn to Christ, when he is delighted with truth, delighted with bliss, delighted with justice, delighted with eternal life, all which is Christ? Have the bodily senses their pleasures, and is the mind without its own? If so, whence is it said, 'The sons of men shall hope under the covering of Thy wings; they shall be intoxicate with the richness of Thy house, and with the torrent of Thy pleasure shalt thou give them to drink: for with Thee is the well of life, and in Thy light we shall see light'? 'He, whom the

Father draweth, cometh to Me' "? he continues; "Whom hath the Father drawn? him who said, 'Thou art Christ, the Son of the living God.' You present a green branch to the sheep, and you draw it forward; fruits are offered to the child, and he is drawn; in that he runs, he is drawn, he is drawn by loving, drawn without bodily hurt, drawn by the bond of the heart. If then it be true that the sight of earthly delight draws on the lover, doth not Christ too draw us when revealed by the Father? For what doth the soul desire more strongly than truth?"

Such are the means which God has provided for the creation of the Saint out of the sinner; He takes him as he is, and uses him against himself: He turns his affections into another channel, and extinguishes a carnal love by infusing a heavenly charity. Not as if He used him as a mere irrational creature, who is impelled by instincts and governed by external incitements without any will of his own, and to whom one pleasure is the same as another, the same in kind, though different in degree. I have already said, it is the very triumph of His grace, that He enters into the heart of man, and persuades it, and prevails with it, while He changes it. He violates in nothing that original constitution of mind which He gave to man: He treats him as man; He leaves him the liberty of acting this way or that; He appeals to all his powers and faculties, to his reason, to his prudence, to his moral sense, to his conscience: He rouses his fears as well as his love; He instructs him in the depravity of sin, as well as in the mercy of God; but still, on the whole, the animating principle of the new life, by which it is both kindled and sustained, is the flame of charity. This only is strong enough to destroy the old Adam, to dissolve the tyranny of habit, to quench the fires of concupiscence, and to burn up the strongholds of pride.

And hence it is that love is presented to us as the distinguishing grace of those who were sinners before they were Saints; not that love is not the life of all Saints, of those who have never needed a conversion, of the Most Blessed Virgin, of the

two St. Johns, and of those others, many in number, who are
"first-fruits unto God and the Lamb;" but that, while in those
who have never sinned gravely love is so contemplative as
almost to resolve itself into the sanctity of God Himself; in
those, on the contrary, in whom it dwells as a principle of re-
covery, it is so full of devotion, of zeal, of activity, and good
works, that it gives a visible character to their history, and is
ever associating itself with our thoughts of them.

Such was the great Apostle, on whom the Church is built,
and whom I contrasted, when I began, with his fellow-Apostle
St. John: whether we contemplate him after his first calling,
or on his repentance, he who denied his Lord, out of all the
Apostles, is the most conspicuous for his love of Him. It was
for this love of Christ, flowing on, as it did, from its impetuosity and exuberance, into love of the brethren, that he was
chosen to be the chief Pastor of the fold. "Simon, son of John,
lovest thou Me more than these?" was the trial put on him by
his Lord; and the reward was, "Feed My lambs, feed My
sheep." Wonderful to say, the Apostle whom Jesus loved, was
yet surpassed in love for Jesus by a brother Apostle, not virginal as he; for it is not John of whom our Lord asked this
question, and who was rewarded with this commission, but
Peter.

Look back at an earlier passage of the same narrative; there,
too, the two Apostles are similarly contrasted in their respective characters; for when they were in the boat, and their
Lord spoke to them from the shore, and "they knew not that
it was Jesus," first "that disciple, whom Jesus loved, said to
Peter, It is the Lord," for "the clean of heart shall see God;"
and then at once "Simon Peter," in the impetuosity of his love,
"girt his tunic about him, and cast himself into the sea," to
reach Him the quicker. St. John beholds and St. Peter acts.

Thus the very presence of Jesus kindled Peter's heart, and
at once drew him unto Him; also at a former time, when he
saw his Lord walking on the sea, his very first impulse was,
as in the passage to which I have been referring, to leave the

vessel and hasten to His side: "Lord, if it be Thou, bid me come to Thee upon the waters." And when he had been betrayed into his great sin, the very Eye of Jesus brought him to himself: "And the Lord turned and looked upon Peter; and Peter remembered the word of the Lord, and he went out and wept bitterly." Hence, on another occasion, when many of the disciples fell away, and "Jesus said to the twelve, Do ye too wish to go away?" St. Peter answered, "Lord, to whom shall we go? Thou hast the words of eternal life; and we have believed and have known that Thou art Christ, the Son of God."

Such, too, was that other great Apostle, who, in so many ways, is associated with St. Peter—the Doctor of the Gentiles. He indeed was converted miraculously, by our Lord's appearing to him, when he was on his way to carry death to the Christians of Damascus: but how does he speak? "Whether we are beside ourselves," he says, "it is to God; or whether we be sober, it is for you: for the charity of Christ constraineth us. If, therefore, any be a new creature in Christ, old things have passed away, behold, all things are made new." And so again: "With Christ am I nailed to the cross; but I live, yet no longer I, but Christ liveth in me; and the life I now live in the flesh, I live by the faith of the Son of God, who loved me, and gave Himself for me." And again: "I am the least of the Apostles, who am not worthy to be called an Apostle, because I persecuted the Church of God. But by the grace of God I am what I am; and His grace in me hath not been void, but I laboured more abundantly than they all, yet not I, but the grace of God with me." And once more: "Whether we live, unto the Lord we live; whether we die, unto the Lord we die; whether we live or whether we die, we are the Lord's." You see, my brethren, the character of St. Paul's love; it was a love fervent, eager, energetic, active, full of great works, "strong as death," as the Wise Man says, a flame which "many waters could not quench, nor the streams drown," which lasted to the end, when he could say, "I have fought the good fight, I have finished the course, I have kept the faith; henceforth is laid up for me the crown of justice, which the Lord will render to me at that day, the just Judge."

And there is a third, my brethren, there is an illustrious third in Scripture, whom we must associate with these two great Apostles, when we speak of the saints of penance and love. Who is it but the loving Magdalen? Who is it so fully instances what I am showing, as "the woman who was a sinner," who watered the Lord's feet with her tears, and dried them with her hair, and anointed them with precious ointment? What a time for such an act! She, who had come into the room as if for a festive purpose, to go about an act of penance! It was a formal banquet, given by a rich Pharisee, to honour, yet to try, our Lord. Magdalen came, young and beautiful, and "rejoicing in her youth," "walking in the ways of her heart and the gaze of her eyes:" she came as if to honour that feast, as women were wont to honour such festive doings, with her sweet odours and cool unguents for the forehead and hair of the guests. And he, the proud Pharisee, suffered her to come, so that she touched not him; let her come, as we might suffer inferior animals to enter our apartments, without caring for them; suffered her as a necessary embellishment of the entertainment, yet as having no soul, or as destined to perdition, but anyhow as nothing to him. He, proud being, and his brethren like him, might "compass sea and land to make one proselyte;" but, as to looking into that proselyte's heart, pitying its sin, and trying to heal it, this did not enter into the circuit of his thoughts. No, he thought only of the necessities of his banquet, and he let her come to do her part, such as it was, careless what her life was, so that she did that part well, and confined herself to it. But, lo, a wondrous sight! was it a sudden inspiration, or a mature resolve? was it an act of the moment, or the result of a long conflict?—but behold, that poor, many-coloured child of guilt approaches to crown with her sweet ointment the head of Him to whom the feast was given; and see, she has stayed her hand. She has looked, and she discerns the Immaculate, the Virgin's Son, "the brightness of the Eternal Light, and the spotless mirror of God's majesty." She looks, and she recognizes the Ancient of Days, the Lord of life and death, her Judge; and again she looks, and she sees in His face and in His mien a beauty, and a sweetness, awful, serene, majestic, more than that of the sons of men, which paled all the splendour of that festive room. Again she looks, timidly yet eagerly, and she discerns in His eye, and in His smile, the loving-kindness, the tenderness, the compassion, the mercy of the Saviour of man. She looks at herself, and oh! how vile, how hideous is she, who but now was so vain of her attractions!—how withered is that comeliness, of which the praises ran through the mouths of her admirers!—how loathsome has become the breath, which hitherto she thought so fragrant, savouring only of those seven bad spirits which dwell within her! And there she would have stayed, there she would have sunk on the earth, wrapped in her confusion and in her despair, had she not cast one glance again on that all-loving, all-forgiving Countenance. He is looking at her: it is the Shepherd looking at the lost sheep, and the lost sheep surrenders herself to Him. He speaks not, but He eyes her; and she draws nearer to Him. Rejoice, ye Angels, she draws near, seeing nothing but Him, and caring neither for the scorn of the proud, nor the jests of the profligate. She draws near, not knowing whether she shall be saved or not, not knowing whether she shall be received, or what will become of her; this only knowing that He is the Fount of holiness and truth, as of mercy, and to whom should she go, but to Him who hath the words of eternal life? "Destruction is thine own, O Israel; in Me only is thy help. Return unto Me, and I will not turn away My face from thee: for I am holy, and will not be angry for ever." "Behold we come unto Thee; for Thou art the Lord our God. Truly the hills are false, and the multitude of the mountains: Truly the Lord our God is the salvation of Israel." Wonderful meeting between what was most base and what is most pure! Those wanton hands, those polluted lips, have touched, have kissed the feet of the Eternal, and He shrank not from the homage. And as she hung over them, and as she moistened them from her full eyes, how did her love for One so great, yet so gentle, wax vehement within her, lighting up a flame which never was to die from that moment even for ever! and what excess did it reach, when He recorded before all men her forgiveness, and the cause of it! "Many sins are forgiven her, for she loved much; but to whom less is forgiven, the same loveth less. And He said unto her, Thy sins are forgiven thee; thy faith hath made thee safe, go in peace."

Henceforth, my brethren, love was to her, as to St. Augustine and to St. Ignatius Loyola afterwards, (great penitents in their own time), as a wound in the soul, so full of desire as to become anguish. She could not live out of the presence of Him in whom her joy lay: her spirit languished after Him, when she saw Him not; and waited on Him silently, reverently, wistfully, when she was in His blissful Presence. We read of her, on one occasion, sitting at His feet, and listening to His words; and He testified to her that she had chosen that best part which should not be taken away from her. And, after His resurrection, she, by her perseverance, merited to see Him even before the Apostles. She would not leave the sepulchre, when Peter and John retired, but stood without, weeping; and when the Lord appeared to her, and held her eyes that she should not know Him, she said piteously to the supposed keeper of the garden, "Tell me where thou hast laid Him, and I will take Him away." And when at length He made Himself known to her, she turned herself, and rushed impetuously to embrace His feet, as at the beginning, but He, as if to prove the dutifulness of her love, forbade her: "Touch Me not," He said, "for I have not yet ascended to My Father; but go to My brethren, and say to them, I ascend to My Father and your Father, to My God and your God." And so she was left to long for the time when she should see Him, and hear His voice, and enjoy His smile, and be allowed to minister to Him, for ever in heaven.

Such then is the second great class of Saints, as viewed in contrast with the first. Love is the life of both: but while the love of the innocent is calm and serene, the love of the penitent is ardent and impetuous, commonly engaged in contest with the world, and active in good works. And this is the love which you, my brethren, must have in your measure, if you would have a good hope of salvation. For you were once sinners; either by open and avowed contempt of religion, or by secret transgression, or by carelessness and coldness, or by some indulged bad habit, or by setting your heart on some object of this world, and doing your own will instead of God's, I think I may say you have needed, or now need, a reconciliation to Him. You have needed, or you need, to be brought near to Him, and to have your sins washed away in His blood, and your pardon recorded in Heaven. And what will do this for you, but contrition? and what is contrition without love? I do not say that you must have the love which Saints have, in order to your forgiveness, the love of St. Peter or of St. Mary Magdalen; but still without your portion of that same heavenly grace, how can you be forgiven at all? If you would do works meet for penance, they must proceed from a living flame of charity. If you would secure perseverance to the end, you must gain it by continual loving prayer to the Author and Finisher of faith and obedience. If you would have a good prospect of His acceptance of you in your last moments, still it is love alone which secures His love, and blots out sin. My brethren, at that awful hour you may be unable to obtain the last Sacraments; death may come on you suddenly, or you may be at a distance from a Priest. You may be thrown on yourselves, simply on your own compunction of heart, your own repentance, your own resolutions of amendment. You may have been weeks and weeks at a distance from spiritual aid; you may have to meet your God without the safeguard, the compensation, the mediation of any holy rite; and oh! what will save you in such disadvantage, but the exercise of divine love "poured over your hearts by the Holy Ghost who is given to you"? At that hour nothing but a firm habit of charity, which has kept you from mortal sins, or a powerful act of charity which blots them out, will be of any avail to you. Nothing but charity can enable you to live well or to die well. How can you bear to lie down at night, how can you bear to go a journey, how can you bear the presence of pestilence, or the attack of ever so slight an indisposition, if you are ill provided in yourselves with divine love against that change, which will come on you some day, yet when and how you know not? Alas! how will you present yourselves before the judgment-seat of Christ, with the imperfect mixed feelings which now satisfy you, with a certain amount of faith, and trust, and fear of God's judgments, but with nothing of that real delight in Him, in His attributes, in His will, in His commandments, in His service, which Saints possess in such fulness, and which alone can give the soul a comfortable title to the merits of His death and passion?

How different is the feeling with which the loving soul, on its separation from the body, approaches the judgment-seat of its Redeemer! It knows how great a debt of punishment remains upon it, though it has for many years been reconciled to Him; it knows that purgatory lies before it, and that the best it can reasonably hope for is to be sent there. But to see His face, though for a moment! to hear His voice, to hear Him speak, though it be to punish! O Saviour of men, it says, I come to Thee, though it be in order to be at once remanded from Thee; I come to Thee who art my Life and my All; I come to Thee on the thought of whom I have lived all my life long. To Thee I gave myself when first I had to take a part in the world; I sought Thee for my chief good early, for early didst Thou teach me, that good elsewhere there was none. Whom have I in heaven but Thee? whom have I desired on earth, whom have I had on earth, but Thee? whom shall I have amid the sharp flame but Thee? Yea, though I be now descending thither, into "a land desert, pathless and without water," I will fear no ill, for Thou art with me. I have

seen Thee this day face to face, and it sufficeth; I have seen
Thee, and that glance of Thine is sufficient for a century of
sorrow, in the nether prison. I will live on that look of Thine,
though I see Thee not, till I see Thee again, never to part
from Thee. That eye of Thine shall be sunshine and comfort
to my weary, longing soul; that voice of Thine shall be everlasting music in my ears. Nothing can harm me, nothing shall
discompose me: I will bear the appointed years, till my end
come, bravely and sweetly. I will raise my voice, and chant
a perpetual *Confiteor* to Thee and to Thy Saints in that dreary
valley;—"to God Omnipotent, and to the Blessed Mary Ever-
Virgin," (Thy Mother and mine, immaculate in her conception), "and to blessed Michael Archangel," (created in his
purity by the very hand of God), and "to Blessed John Baptist," (sanctified even in his mother's womb); and after these
three, "to the Holy Apostles Peter and Paul," (penitents, who
compassionate the sinner from their experience of sin); "to
all Saints," (whether they have lived in contemplation or in
toil, during the days of their pilgrimage), will I address my
supplication, begging them to "remember me, since it is well
with them, and to do mercy by me, and to make mention of
me unto the King that He bring me out of that prison." And
then at length "God shall wipe away every tear from my eyes,
and death shall be no longer, nor mourning, nor crying, nor
pain any more, for the former things are passed away."

XII

GOD'S WILL THE END OF LIFE [1]

I AM GOING TO ASK YOU A QUESTION, my dear brethren, so trite, and therefore so uninteresting at first sight, that you may wonder why I put it, and may anticipate that nothing profitable can be made of it. It is this:—"Why were you sent into the world?" Yet, after all, it is perhaps a thought more obvious than it is common, more easy than it is familiar; I mean it ought to come into your minds, but it does not, and you never had more than a distant acquaintance with it, though that sort of acquaintance with it you have had for many years. Nay, once or twice, perhaps you have been thrown across the thought somewhat intimately, for a short season, but this was an accident which did not last. There are those who recollect the first time, as it would seem, when it came home to them. They were but little children, and they were by themselves, and they spontaneously asked themselves, or rather God spake in them, "Why am I here? how came I here? who brought me here? What am I to do here?" Perhaps it was the first act of reason, the beginning of their real responsibility, the commencement of their trial; perhaps from that day they may date their capacity, their awful power, of choosing between good and evil, and of committing mortal sin. And so, as life goes on, the thought comes vividly, from time to time, for a short season across their conscience; whether in illness, or in some anxiety, or at some season of

[1] From *Discourses to Mixed Congregations* (1849), No. 6. [Ed.]

solitude, or on hearing some preacher, or reading some religious work. A vivid feeling comes over them of the vanity
and unprofitableness of the world, and then the question re-
curs, "Why then am I sent into it?"

And a great contrast indeed does this vain, unprofitable,
yet overbearing world, present with such a question as that.
It seems out of place to ask such a question in so magnificent,
so imposing a presence, as that of the great Babylon. The
world professes to supply all that we need, as if we were sent
into it for the sake of being sent here, and for nothing beyond
the sending. It is a great favour to have an introduction to
this august world. This is to be our exposition, forsooth, of
the mystery of life. Every man is doing his own will here,
seeking his own pleasure, pursuing his own ends, and that
is why he was brought into existence. Go abroad into the
streets of the populous city, contemplate the continuous out-
pouring there of human energy, and the countless varieties of
human character, and be satisfied! The ways are thronged,
carriage-way and pavement; multitudes are hurrying to and
fro, each on his own errand, or are loitering about from list-
lessness, or from want of work, or have come forth into the
public concourse, to see and to be seen, for amusement or for
display, or on the excuse of business. The carriages of the
wealthy mingle with the slow wains laden with provisions or
merchandise, the productions of art or the demands of luxury.
The streets are lined with shops, open and gay, inviting
customers, and widen now and then into some spacious square
or place, with lofty masses of brick-work or of stone, gleaming
in the fitful sunbeam, and surrounded or fronted with what
simulates a garden's foliage. Follow them in another direction,
and you find the whole groundstead covered with large build-
ings, planted thickly up and down, the homes of the mechanical arts. The air is filled, below, with a ceaseless, importunate,
monotonous din, which penetrates even to your most inner-
most chamber, and rings in your ears even when you are not

conscious of it; and overhead, with a canopy of smoke, shrouding God's day from the realms of obstinate sullen toil. This is the end of man!

Or stay at home, and take up one of those daily prints, which are so true a picture of the world; look down the columns of advertisements, and you will see the catalogue of pursuits, projects, aims, anxieties, amusements, indulgences which occupy the mind of man. He plays many parts: here he has goods to sell, there he wants employment; there again he seeks to borrow money, here he offers you houses, great seats or small tenements; he has food for the million, and luxuries for the wealthy, and sovereign medicines for the credulous, and books, new and cheap, for the inquisitive. Pass on to the news of the day, and you will learn what great men are doing at home and abroad: you will read of wars and rumours of wars; of debates in the Legislature; of rising men, and old statesmen going off the scene; of political contests in this city or that county; of the collision of rival interests. You will read of the money market, and the provision market, and the market for metals; of the state of trade, the call for manufactures, news of ships arrived in port, of accidents at sea, of exports and imports, of gains and losses, of frauds and their detection. Go forward, and you arrive at discoveries in art and science, discoveries (so called) in religion, the court and royalty, the entertainments of the great, places of amusement, strange trials, offences, accidents, escapes, exploits, experiments, contests, ventures. Oh this curious, restless, clamorous, panting being, which we call life!—and is there to be no end to all this? Is there no object in it? It never has an end, it is forsooth its own object!

And now, once more, my brethren, put aside what you see and what you read of the world, and try to penetrate into the hearts, and to reach the ideas and the feelings of those who constitute it; look into them as closely as you can; enter into their houses and private rooms; strike at random through the streets and lanes: take as they come, palace and hovel, office or factory, and what will you find? Listen to their words, witness, alas! their works; you will find in the main the same lawless thoughts, the same unrestrained desires, the same un-governed passions, the same earthly opinions, the same wilful deeds, in high and low, learned and unlearned; you will find them all to be living for the sake of living; they one and all seem to tell you, "We are our own centre, our own end." Why are they toiling? why are they scheming? for what are they living? "We live to please ourselves; life is worthless except we have our own way; we are not *sent* here at all, but we find ourselves here, and we are but slaves unless we can think what we will, believe what we will, love what we will, hate what we will, do what we will. We detest interference on the part of God or man. We do not bargain to be rich or to be great; but we do bargain, whether rich or poor, high or low, to live for ourselves, to live for the lust of the moment, or, according to the doctrine of the hour, thinking of the future and the unseen just as much or as little as we please."

Oh, my brethren, is it not a shocking thought, but who can deny its truth? The multitude of men are living without any aim beyond this visible scene; they may from time to time use religious words, or they may profess a communion or a worship, as a matter of course, or of expedience, or of duty, but, if there was any sincerity in such profession, the course of the world could not run as it does. What a contrast is all this to the end of life, as it is set before us in our most holy Faith! If there was one among the sons of men, who might allowably have taken His pleasure, and have done His own will here below, surely it was He who came down on earth from the bosom of the Father, and who was so pure and spotless in that human nature which He put on Him, that He could have no human purpose or aim inconsistent with the will of His Father. Yet He, the Son of God, the Eternal Word, came, not to do His own will, but His who sent Him, as you know very well is told us again and again in Scripture. Thus the Prophet in the Psalter, speaking in His person, says, "Lo,

I come to do Thy will, O God." And He says in the Prophet Isaias, "the Lord God hath opened Mine ear, and I do not resist; I have not gone back." And in the Gospel, when He had come on earth, "My food is to do the will of Him that sent Me, and to finish His work." Hence, too, in His agony He cried out, "Not My will, but Thine, be done;" and St. Paul, in like manner, says, that "Christ pleased not Himself;" and elsewhere, that, "though He was God's Son, yet learned He obedience by the things which He suffered." Surely so it was; as being indeed the Eternal Co-equal Son, His will was one and the same with the Father's will, and He had no submission of will to make; but He chose to take on Him man's nature, and the will of that nature; He chose to take on Him affections, feelings, and inclinations proper to man, a will innocent indeed and good, but still a man's will, distinct from God's will; a will, which, had it acted simply according to what was pleasing to its nature, would, when pain and toil were to be endured, have held back from an active co-operation with the will of God. But, though He took on Himself the nature of man, He took not on Him that selfishness, with which fallen man wraps himself round, but in all things He devoted Himself as a ready sacrifice to His Father. He came on earth, not to take His pleasure, not to follow His taste, not for the mere exercise of human affection, but simply to glorify His Father and to do His will. He came charged with a mission, deputed for a work; He looked not to the right nor to the left, He thought not of Himself, He offered Himself up to God.

Hence it is that He was carried in the womb of a poor woman, who, before His birth, had two journeys to make, of love and of obedience, to the mountains and to Bethlehem. He was born in a stable, and laid in a manger. He was hurried off to Egypt to sojourn there; then He lived till He was thirty years of age in a poor way, by a rough trade, in a small house, in a despised town. Then, when He went out to preach, He had not where to lay His head; He wandered up and down the country, as a stranger upon earth. He was driven out into the wilderness, and dwelt among the wild beasts. He endured heat and cold, hunger and weariness, reproach and calumny. His food was coarse bread, and fish from the lake, or depended on the hospitality of strangers. And as He had already left His Father's greatness on high, and had chosen an earthly home; so again, at that Father's bidding, He gave up the sole solace given Him in this world, and denied Himself His Mother's presence. He parted with her who bore Him; He endured to be strange to her; He endured to call her coldly "woman," who was His own undefiled one, all beautiful, all gracious, the best creature of His hands, and the sweet nurse of His infancy. He put her aside, as Levi, His type, merited the sacred ministry, by saying to His parents and kinsmen, "I know you not." He exemplified in His own person the severe maxim, which He gave to His disciples, "He that loveth mother more than Me is not worthy of Me." In all these many ways He sacrificed every wish of His own; that we might understand, that, if He, the Creator, came into His own world, not for His own pleasure, but to do His Father's will, we too have most surely some work to do, and have seriously to bethink ourselves what that work is.

Yes, so it is; realize it, my brethren;—every one who breathes, high and low, educated and ignorant, young and old, man and woman, has a mission, has a work. We are not sent into this world for nothing; we are not born at random; we are not here, that we may go to bed at night, and get up in the morning, toil for our bread, eat and drink, laugh and joke, sin when we have a mind, and reform when we are tired of sinning, rear a family and die. God sees every one of us; He creates every soul, He lodges it in the body, one by one, for a purpose. He needs, He deigns to need, every one of us. He has an end for each of us; we are all equal in His sight, and we are placed in our different ranks and stations, not to get what we can out of them for ourselves, but to labour in them for Him. As Christ has His work, we too have ours; as He rejoiced to do His work, we must rejoice in ours also.

St. Paul on one occasion speaks of the world as a scene in a theatre. Consider what is meant by this. You know, actors on a stage are on an equality with each other really, but for the occasion they assume a difference of character; some are high, some are low, some are merry, and some sad. Well, would it not be a simple absurdity in any actor to pride himself on his mock diadem, or his edgeless sword, instead of attending to his part? what, if he did but gaze at himself and his dress? what, if he secreted, or turned to his own use, what was valuable in it? Is it not his business, and nothing else, to act his part well? common sense tells us so. Now we are all but actors in this world; we are one and all equal, we shall be judged as equals as soon as life is over; yet, equal and similar in ourselves, each has his special part at present, each has his work, each has his mission,—not to indulge his passions, not to make money, not to get a name in the world, not to save himself trouble, not to follow his bent, not to be selfish and self-willed, but to do what God puts on him to do.

Look at that poor profligate in the Gospel, look at Dives; do you think he understood that his wealth was to be spent, not on himself, but for the glory of God?—yet for forgetting this, he was lost for ever and ever. I will tell you what he thought, and how he viewed things:—he was a young man, and had succeeded to a good estate, and he determined to enjoy himself. It did not strike him that his wealth had any other use than that of enabling him to take his pleasure. Lazarus lay at his gate; he might have relieved Lazarus; *that* was God's will; but he managed to put conscience aside, and he persuaded himself he should be a fool, if he did not make the most of this world, while he had the means. So he resolved to have his fill of pleasure; and feasting was to his mind a principal part of it. "He fared sumptuously every day;" everything belonging to him was in the best style, as men speak; his house, his furniture, his plate of silver and gold, his attendants, his establishments. Everything was for enjoyment, and for show too; to attract the eyes of the world, and to gain the applause and admiration of his equals, who were the companions of his sins. These companions were doubtless such as became a person of such pretensions; they were fashionable men; a collection of refined, high-bred, haughty men, eating, not gluttonously, but what was rare and costly; delicate, exact, fastidious in their taste, from their very habits of indulgence; not eating for the mere sake of eating, or drinking for the mere sake of drinking, but making a sort of science of their sensuality; sensual, carnal, as flesh and blood can be, with eyes, ears, tongue, steeped in impurity, every thought, look, and sense, witnessing or ministering to the evil one who ruled them; yet, with exquisite correctness of idea and judgment, laying down rules for sinning;—heartless and selfish, high, punctilious, and disdainful in their outward deportment, and shrinking from Lazarus, who lay at the gate, as an eyesore, who ought for the sake of decency to be put out of the way. Dives was one of such, and so he lived his short span, thinking of nothing, loving nothing, but himself, till one day he got into a fatal quarrel with one of his godless associates, or he caught some bad illness; and then he lay helpless on his bed of pain, cursing fortune and his physician, that he was no better, and impatient that he was thus kept from enjoying his youth, trying to fancy himself mending when he was getting worse, and disgusted at those who would not throw him some word of comfort in his suspense, and turning more resolutely from his Creator in proportion to his suffering;—and then at last his day came, and he died, and (O miserable!) "was buried in hell." And so ended he and his mission.

This was the fate of your pattern and idol, oh ye, if any of you be present, young men, who, though not possessed of wealth and rank, yet affect the fashions of those who have them. You, my brethren, have not been born splendidly or nobly; you have not been brought up in the seats of liberal education; you have no high connexions; you have not learned the manners nor caught the tone of good society; you have no share of the largeness of mind, the candour, the romantic sense of honour, the correctness of taste, the consideration for others, and the gentleness which the world puts forth as its highest type of excellence; you have not come near the courts or the mansions of the great; yet you ape the sin of Dives, while you are strangers to his refinement. You think it the sign of a gentleman to set yourselves above religion, to criticize the religious and professors of religion, to look at Catholic and Methodist with impartial contempt, to gain a smattering of knowledge on a number of subjects, to dip into a number of frivolous publications, if they are popular, to have read the latest novel, to have heard the singer and seen the actor of the day, to be well up with the news, to know the names, and, if so be, the persons of public men, to be able to bow to them, to walk up and down the street with your heads on high, and to stare at whatever meets you;—and to say and do worse things, of which these outward extravagances are but the symbol. And this is what you conceive you have come upon earth for! The Creator made you, it seems, O my children, for this work and office, to be a bad imitation of polished ungodliness, to be a piece of tawdry and faded finery, or a scent which has lost its freshness, and does but offend the sense! Oh, that you could see how absurd and base are such pretences in the eyes of any but yourselves! No calling of life but is honourable; no one is ridiculous who acts suitably to his calling and estate; no one, who has good sense and humility, but may, in any station of life, be truly well-bred and refined; but ostentation, affectation, and ambitious efforts are, in every station of life, high or low, nothing but vulgarities. Put them aside, despise them yourselves, O my very dear sons whom I love, and whom I would fain serve;—oh, that you could feel that you have souls! oh, that you would have mercy on your souls! oh, that, before it is too late, you would betake yourselves to Him who is the Source of all that is truly high and magnificent and beautiful, all that is bright and pleasant, and secure what you ignorantly seek, in Him whom you so wilfully, so awfully despise!

He alone, the Son of God, "the brightness of the Eternal Light, and the spotless mirror of His Majesty," is the source of all good and all happiness to rich and poor, high and low. If you were ever so high, you would need Him; if you were ever so low, you could offend Him. The poor can offend Him; the poor man can neglect his divinely appointed mission as well as the rich. Do not suppose, my brethren, that what I have said against the upper or the middle class, will not, if you happen to be poor, also lie against you. Though a man were as poor as Lazarus, he could be as guilty as Dives. If you are resolved to degrade yourselves to the brutes of the field, who have no reason and no conscience, you need not wealth or rank to enable you to do so. Brutes have no wealth; they have no pride of life; they have no purple and fine linen, no splendid table, no retinue of servants, and yet they are brutes. They are brutes by the law of their nature: they are the poorest among the poor; there is not a vagrant and outcast who is so poor as they; they differ from him, not in their possessions, but in their want of a soul, in that he has a mission and they have not, he can sin and they can not. O my brethren, it stands to reason, a man may intoxicate himself with a cheap draught, as well as with a costly one; he may steal another's money for his appetites, if he does not waste his own upon them; he may break through the natural and social laws which encircle him, and profane the sanctity of family duties, though he be, not a child of nobles, but a peasant or artisan,—nay, and perhaps he does so more frequently than they. This is not the poor's blessedness, that he has less temptations to self-indulgence, for he has as many, but that from his circumstances he receives the penances and corrections of self-indulgence. Poverty is the mother of many pains and sorrows in their season, and these are God's messengers to lead the soul to repentance; but, alas! if the poor man indulges his passions, thinks little of religion, puts off repentance, refuses to make an effort, and dies without conversion, it matters nothing that he was poor in this world, it matters nothing that he was less daring than the rich, it matters not that he promised himself God's favour, that he sent for the Priest when death came, and received the last Sacraments; Lazarus too, in that case, shall be buried with Dives in hell, and shall have had his consolation neither in this world nor in the world to come.

My brethren, the simple question is, whatever a man's rank in life may be, does he in that rank perform the work which God has given him to do? Now then, let me turn to others, of a very different description, and let me hear what they will say, when the question is asked them;—why, they will parry it thus:—"You give us no alternative," they will say to me, "except that of being sinners and Saints. You put before us our Lord's pattern, and you spread before us the guilt and the ruin of the deliberate transgressor; whereas we have no intention of going so far one way or the other; we do not aim at being Saints, but we have no desire at all to be sinners. We neither intend to disobey God's will, nor to give up our own. Surely there is a middle way, and a safe one, in which God's will and our will may both be satisfied. We mean to enjoy both this world and the next. We will guard against mortal sin; we are not obliged to guard against venial; indeed it would be endless to attempt it. None but Saints do so; it is the work of a life; we need have nothing else to do. We are not monks, we are in the world, we are in business, we are parents, we have families; we must live for the day. It is a consolation to keep from mortal sin; that we do, and it is enough for salvation. It is a great thing to keep in God's favour; what indeed can we desire more? We come at due time to the Sacraments; this is our comfort and our stay; did we die, we should die in grace, and escape the doom of the wicked. But if we once attempted to go further, where should we stop? how will you draw the line for us; the line between mortal and venial sin is very distinct; we understand that; but do you not see that, if we

attended to our venial sins, there would be just as much reason
to attend to one as to another? If we began to repress our
anger, why not also repress vainglory? why not also guard
against niggardness? why not also keep from falsehoods? from
gossiping, from idling, from excess in eating? And, after all,
without venial sin we never can be, unless indeed we have
the prerogative of the Mother of God, which it would be almost heresy to ascribe to any one but her. You are not asking
us to be converted; that we understand; we *are* converted, we
were converted a long time ago. You bid us aim at an indefi-
nite vague something, which is less than perfection, yet more
than obedience, and which, without resulting in any tangible
advantage, debars us from the pleasures and embarrasses us
in the duties of this world."

This is what you will say; but your premises, my brethren,
are better than your reasoning, and your conclusions will not
stand. You have a right view why God has sent you into the
world, viz., in order that you may get to heaven; it is quite
true also that you would fare' well indeed if you found yourselves there, you could desire nothing better; nor, it is true,
can you live any time without venial sin. It is true also that you
are not obliged to aim at being Saints; it is no sin not to aim at
perfection. So much is true and to the purpose; but it does not
follow from it that you, with such views and feelings as you
have expressed, are using sufficient exertions even for attaining to purgatory. Has your religion any difficulty in it, or is it
in all respects easy to you? Are you simply taking your own
pleasure in your mode of living, or do you find your pleasure
in submitting yourself to God's pleasure? In a word, is your
religion a work? for if it be not, it is not religion at all. Here
at once, before going into your argument, is a proof that it
is an unsound one, because it brings you to the conclusion
that, whereas Christ came to do a work, and all Saints, nay,
nay, and sinners do a work too, you, on the contrary, have no
work to do, because, forsooth, you are neither sinners nor
Saints; or, if you once had a work, at least you have despatched

it already, and you have nothing upon your hands. You have attained your salvation, it seems, before your time, and have nothing to occupy you, and are detained on earth too long. The work-days are over, and your perpetual holiday is begun. Did then God send you, above all other men, into the world to be idle in spiritual matters? Is it your mission only to find pleasure in this world, in which you are but as pilgrims and sojourners? Are you more than sons of Adam, who, by the sweat of their brow, are to eat bread till they return to the earth out of which they are taken? Unless you have some work in hand, unless you are struggling, unless you are fighting with yourselves, you are no followers of those who "through many tribulations entered into the kingdom of God." A fight is the very token of a Christian. He is a soldier of Christ; high or low, he is this and nothing else. If you have triumphed over all mortal sin, as you seem to think, then you must attack your venial sins; there is no help for it; there is nothing else to do, if you would be soldiers of Jesus Christ. But, O simple souls! to think you have gained any triumph at all! No: you cannot safely be at peace with any, even the least malignant, of the foes of God; if you are at peace with venial sins, be certain that in their company and under their shadow mortal sins are lurking. Mortal sins are the children of venial, which, though they be not deadly themselves, yet are prolific of death. You may think that you have killed the giants who had possession of your hearts, and that you have nothing to fear, but may sit at rest under your vine and under your fig-tree; but the giants will live again, they will rise from the dust, and, before you know where you are, you will be taken captive and slaughtered by the fierce, powerful, and eternal enemies of God.

The end of a thing is the test. It was our Lord's rejoicing in His last solemn hour, that He had done the work for which He was sent. "I have glorified Thee on earth," He says in His prayer, "I have finished the work which Thou gavest Me to do; I have manifested Thy name to the men whom Thou hast given Me out of the world." It was St. Paul's consolation also; "I have fought the good fight, I have finished the course, I have kept the faith; henceforth there is laid up for me a crown of justice, which the Lord shall render to me in that day, the just Judge." Alas! alas! how different will be our view of things when we come to die, or when we have passed into eternity, from the dreams and pretences with which we beguile ourselves now! What will Babel do for us then? Will it rescue our souls from the purgatory or the hell to which it sends them? If we were created, it was that we might serve God; if we have His gifts, it is that we may glorify Him; if we have a conscience, it is that we may obey it; if we have the prospect of heaven, it is that we may keep it before us; if we have light, that we may follow it; if we have grace, that we may save ourselves by means of it. Alas! alas! for those who die without fulfilling their mission! who were called to be holy, and lived in sin; who were called to worship Christ, and who plunged into this giddy and unbelieving world; who were called to fight, and who remained idle; who were called to be Catholics, and who did but remain in the religion of their birth! Alas for those who have had gifts and talents, and have not used, or have misused, or abused them; who have had wealth, and have spent it on themselves; who have had abilities, and have advocated what was sinful, or ridiculed what was true, or scattered doubts against what was sacred; who have had leisure, and have wasted it on wicked companions, or evil books, or foolish amusements! Alas! for those, of whom the best that can be said is, that they are harmless and naturally blameless, while they never have attempted to cleanse their hearts or to live in God's sight!

The world goes on from age to age, but the holy Angels and blessed Saints are always crying alas! alas! and woe! woe! over the loss of vocations, and the disappointment of hopes, and the scorn of God's love, and the ruin of souls. One generation succeeds another, and whenever they look down upon earth from their golden thrones, they see scarcely anything but a multitude of guardian spirits, downcast and sad, each following his own charge, in anxiety, or in terror, or in despair, vainly endeavouring to shield him from the enemy, and failing because he will not be shielded. Times come and go, and man will not believe, that that is to be which is not yet, or that what now is only continues for a season, and is not eternity. The end is the trial; the world passes; it is but a pageant and a scene; the lofty palace crumbles, the busy city is mute, the ships of Tarshish have sped away. On heart and flesh death is coming; the veil is breaking. Departing soul, how hast thou used thy talents, thy opportunities, the light poured around thee, the warnings given thee, the grace inspired into thee? O my Lord and Saviour, support me in that hour in the strong arms of Thy Sacraments, and by the fresh fragrance of Thy consolations. Let the absolving words be said over me, and the holy oil sign and seal me, and Thy own Body be my food, and Thy Blood my sprinkling; and let my sweet Mother Mary breathe on me, and my Angel whisper peace to me, and my glorious Saints, and my own dear Father, Philip, smile on me; that in them all, and through them all, I may receive the gift of perseverance, and die, as I desire to live, in Thy faith, in Thy Church, in Thy service, and in Thy love.

XIII

NATURE AND GRACE [1]

I N THE PARABLE OF THE GOOD SHEPHERD our Lord sets before us a dispensation or state of things, which is very strange in the eyes of the world. He speaks of mankind as consisting of two bodies, distinct from each other, divided by as real a line of demarcation as the fence which encloses the sheepfold. "I am the Door," He says, "by Me if any man shall have entered in, he shall be saved: and he shall go in and go out, and shall find pastures. My sheep hear My voice, and I know them, and they follow Me, and I give them life everlasting; and they shall not perish for ever, and no man shall snatch them out of My Hand." And in His last prayer for His disciples to His Eternal Father, He says, "I have manifested Thy Name to the men whom Thou hast given Me out of the world. Thine they were, and Thou hast given them to Me, and they have kept Thy word. I pray for them, I pray not for the world, but for those whom Thou hast given Me, for they are Thine. Holy Father, keep them in Thy Name whom Thou hast given Me, that they may be one, as We also." Nor are these passages solitary or singular; "Fear not, little flock," He says by another Evangelist, "for it hath pleased your Father to give you the kingdom." And again, "I thank Thee, Father, Lord of heaven and earth, that Thou hast hid these things from the wise and prudent, and hast revealed them unto little ones;" and again, "How narrow is the gate, and strait the way which leadeth to life, and few there are who find it!" St. Paul repeats

[1] From *Discourses to Mixed Congregations* (1849), No. 8. [Ed.]

165

and insists on this doctrine of his Lord, "Ye were once darkness, but now are light in the Lord;" "He hath delivered us
from the power of darkness, and hath translated us into the
kingdom of the Son of His love." And St. John, "Greater is He
that is in you than he that is in the world. They are of the
world, we are of God." Thus there are two parties on this
earth, and two only, if we view men in their religious aspect;
those, the few, who hear Christ's words and follow Him, who
are in the light, and walk in the narrow way, and have the
promise of heaven; and those, on the other hand, who are the
many, for whom Christ prays not, though He has died for
them, who are wise and prudent in their own eyes, who are
possessed by the Evil One, and are subject to his rule.

And such is the view taken of mankind, as by their Maker
and Redeemer, so also by the small company in whom He
lives and is glorified; but far differently does the larger body,
the world itself, look upon mankind at large, upon its own vast
multitudes, and upon those whom God has taken out of it for
His own special inheritance. It considers that all men are pretty
much on a level, or that, differ though they may, they differ by
such fine shades from each other, that it is impossible, because
it would be untrue and unjust, to divide them into two bodies,
or to divide them at all. Each man is like himself and no one
else; each man has his own opinions, his own rule of faith and
conduct, his own worship; if a number join together in a religious form, this is an accident, for the sake of convenience;
for each is complete in himself; religion is simply a personal
concern; there is no such thing really as a common or joint
religion, that is, one in which a number of men, strictly speaking, partake; it is all matter of private judgment. Hence, as
men sometimes proceed even to avow, there is no such thing
as a true religion or a false; that is true to each, which each
sincerely believes to be true; and what is true to one, is not
true to his neighbour. There are no special doctrines, necessary to be believed in order to salvation; it is not very difficult to be saved; and most men may take it for granted that

they shall be saved. All men are in God's favour, except so far as, and while, they commit acts of sin; but when the sin is over, they get back into His favour again, naturally and as a thing of course, no one knows how, owing to God's infinite indulgence, unless indeed they persevere and die in a course of sin, and perhaps even then. There is no such place as hell, or at least punishment is not eternal. Predestination, election, grace, perseverance, faith, sanctity, unbelief, and reprobation are strange ideas, and, as they think, very false ones. This is the cast of opinion of men in general, in proportion as they exercise their minds on the subject of religion, and think for themselves; and if in any respect they depart from the easy, cheerful, and tranquil temper of mind which it expresses, it is when they are led to think of those who presume to take the contrary view, that is, who take the view set forth by Christ and His Apostles. On these they are commonly severe, that is, on the very persons whom God acknowledges as His, and is training heavenward,—on Catholics, who are the witnesses and preachers of those awful doctrines of grace, which condemn the world and which the world cannot endure.

In truth the world does not know of the existence of grace; nor is it wonderful, for it is ever contented with itself, and has never turned to account the supernatural aids bestowed upon it. Its highest idea of man lies in the order of nature; its pattern man is the natural man; it thinks it wrong to be anything else than a natural man. It sees that nature has a number of tendencies, inclinations, and passions; and because these are natural, it thinks that each of them may be indulged for its own sake, so far as it does no harm to others, or to a person's bodily, mental, and temporal well-being. It considers that want of moderation, or excess, is the very definition of sin, if it goes so far as to recognize that word. It thinks that he is the perfect man who eats, and drinks, and sleeps, and walks, and diverts himself, and studies, and writes, and attends to religion, in moderation. The devotional feeling and the intellect, and the flesh, have each its claim upon us, and each must have play, if the Creator is to be duly honoured. It does not understand, it will not admit, that impulses and propensities, which are found in our nature, as God created it, may nevertheless, if indulged, become sins, on the ground that He has subjected them to higher principles, whether these principles be in our nature, or be superadded to our nature. Hence it is very slow to believe that evil thoughts are really displeasing to God, and incur punishment. Works, indeed, tangible actions, which are seen and which have influence, it will allow to be wrong; but it will not believe even that deeds are sinful, or that they are more than reprehensible, if they are private or personal; and it is blind utterly to the malice of thoughts, of imaginations, of wishes, and of words. Because the wild emotions of anger, desire, greediness, craft, cruelty, are no sin in the brute creation, which has neither the means nor the command to repress them, therefore they are no sins in a being who has a diviner sense and a controlling power. Concupiscence may be indulged, because it is in its first elements natural.

Behold here the true origin and fountain-head of the warfare between the Church and the world; here they join issue, and diverge from each other. The Church is built upon the doctrine that impurity is hateful to God, and that concupiscence is its root; with the Prince of the Apostles, her visible Head, she denounces "the corruption of concupiscence which is in the world," or, that corruption in the world which comes of concupiscence; whereas the corrupt world defends, nay, I may even say, sanctifies that very concupiscence which is the world's corruption. Its bolder and more consistent teachers, as you know, my brethren, make the laws of this physical creation so supreme, as to disbelieve the existence of miracles, as being an unseemly violation of them; well, and in like manner, it deifies and worships human nature and its impulses, and denies the power and the grant of grace. This is the source of the hatred which the world bears to the Church; it finds a whole catalogue of sins brought into light and denounced, which it would fain believe to be no sins at all; it finds itself, to its indignation and impatience, surrounded with sin, morning, noon, and night; it finds that a stern law lies against it, where it believed that it was its own master and need not think of God; it finds guilt accumulating upon it hourly, which nothing can prevent, nothing remove, but a higher power, the grace of God. It finds itself in danger of being humbled to the earth as a rebel, instead of being allowed to indulge its self-dependence and self-complacency. Hence it takes its stand on nature, and denies or rejects divine grace. Like the proud spirit in the beginning, it wishes to find its supreme good in its own self, and nothing above it; it undertakes to be sufficient for its own happiness; it has no desire for the supernatural, and therefore does not believe in it. And because nature cannot rise above nature, it will not believe that the narrow way is possible; it hates those who enter upon it as if pretenders and hypocrites, or laughs at their aspirations as romance and fanaticism;—lest it should have to believe in the existence of grace.

Now you may think, my brethren, from the way in which I have been contrasting nature and grace, that they cannot possibly be mistaken for each other; but I wish to show you, in the next place, how grace may be mistaken for nature, and nature mistaken for grace. They may easily be mistaken for each other, because, as it is plain from what I have said, the difference is in a great measure an inward, and therefore a secret one. Grace is lodged in the heart; it purifies the thoughts and motives, it raises the soul to God, it sanctifies the body, it corrects and exalts human nature in regard to those sins of which men are ashamed, and do not make a public display. Accordingly, in outward show, in single actions, in word, in profession, in teaching, in the social and political virtues, in striking and heroical exploits, on the public transitory scene of things, nature may counterfeit grace, nay even to the deception of the man himself in whom the counterfeit occurs. Recollect that it is by nature, not by grace, that man has the gifts of reason and conscience; and mere reason and con-science will lead him to discover, and in a measure pursue, objects which are, properly speaking, supernatural and divine. The natural reason is able, from the things which are seen, from the voice of tradition, from the existence of the soul, and from the necessity of the case, to infer the existence of God. The natural heart can burst forth by fits and starts into emo-tions of love towards Him; the natural imagination can depict the beauty and glory of His attributes; the natural conscience may ascertain and put in order the truths of the great moral law, nay even to the condemnation of that concupiscence, which it is too weak to subdue, and is therefore persuaded to tolerate. The natural will can do many things really good and praiseworthy; nay, in particular cases, or at particular seasons, when temptation is away, it may seem to have a strength which it has not, and to be imitating the austerity and purity of a Saint. One man has no temptation to hoard; another has no temptation to gluttony and drunkenness; another has no temptation to ill-humour; another has no temptation to be ambitious and overbearing. Hence human nature may often show to great advantage; it may be meek, amiable, kind, benevolent, generous, honest, upright, and tem-perate; and, as seen in its happier specimens, it may become quite a trial to faith, seeing that in its best estate it has really no relationship to the family of Christ, and no claim whatever to a heavenly reward,—though it can talk of Christ and heaven too, read Scripture, and "do many things willingly" in consequence of reading it, and can exercise a certain sort of belief, however different from that faith which is imparted to us by grace.

Certainly, it is a most mournful, often quite a piercing thought, to contemplate the conduct and the character of those who have never received the elementary grace of God in the Sacrament of Baptism. They are sometimes so benevolent, so active and untiring in their benevolence; they may be so wise and so considerate; they may have so much in them to engage the affections of those who see them! Well, let us leave them to God; His grace is over all the earth; if that grace comes to good effect and bears fruit in the hearts of the unbaptized, He will reward it; but, where grace is not, there doubtless what looks so fair has its reward in this world, for such good as is in it, but has no better claim on a heavenly reward than skill in any art or science, than eloquence or wit. And moreover, it often happens, that, where there is much that is specious and amiable, there is also much that is sinful, and frightfully so. Men show their best face in the world; but for the greater part of their time, the many hours of the day and the night, they are shut up in their own thoughts. They are their own witnesses, none see them besides, save God and His Angels; therefore in such cases we can only judge of what we actually see, and can only admire what is in itself good, without having any means of determining the real moral condition of those who display it. Just as children are caught by the mere good-nature and familiarity with which they are treated by some grown man, and have no means or thought of forming a judgment about him in other respects, and may be surprised, when they grow up, to find how unworthy he is of their respect or affection; as the uneducated, who have seen very little of the world, have no faculties for distinguishing between one rank of men and another, and consider all persons on a level who are respectably dressed, whatever be their accent, their carriage, or their countenance; so all of us, not children only or the uncultivated, are but novices, or less than novices, in the business of deciding what is the real state in God's sight of this or that man, who is external to the Church, yet in character or conduct resembles her true sons. Not entering then upon this point, which is beyond us, so much we even can see and are sure of, that human nature is, in a degree beyond all words, inconsistent, and that we must not take for granted that it can do anything at all more than it actually does, or that those, in whom it shows most plausibly, are a whit better than they look. We see the best, and (as far as moral excellence goes) the whole of them. We cannot argue from what we see in favour of what we do not see; we cannot take what we see as a specimen of what they really are. Sad, then, as the spectacle of such a man is to a Catholic, he is no difficulty to him. He may be benevolent, and kind-hearted, and generous, upright and honourable, candid, dispassionate, and forbearing, yet he may have nothing of a special Christian cast about him, meekness, purity, or devotion. He may like his own way intensely, have a great opinion of his own powers, scoff at faith and religious fear, and seldom or never have said a prayer in his life. Nay, even outward gravity of deportment is no warrant that there is not within an habitual indulgence of evil thoughts, and secret offences odious to Almighty God. We admire then whatever is excellent in the ancient heathen (as in moderns, who are often in their condition); we acknowledge without jealousy whatever they have done virtuous and praiseworthy, but we understand as little of the character or destiny of the being in whom that goodness is found, as we understand the nature of the material substances which present themselves to us under the outward garb of shape and color. They are to us as unknown causes which have influenced or disturbed the world, and which manifest themselves in certain great effects, political, social, or ethical; they are to us as pictures, which appeal to the eye, but not to the touch. We do not know that they would prove to be more real than a painting, if we could touch them. Thus much we know, that, if they have attained to heaven, it has been by the grace of God and their co-operation with it; if they have lived and died without that grace, they will never see life; and, if they have lived and died in mortal sin, they are in the state of bad Catholics, and will for ever see death.

Yet, taking the mere outward appearance of things, and the more felicitous, though partial and occasional, efforts of human nature, how great it is, how amiable, how brilliant,—that is, if we may pretend to the power of viewing it distinct from

the supernatural influences which have ever haunted it! How
great are the old Greek lawgivers and statesmen, whose histories and works are known to some of us, and whose names
to many more! How great are those stern Roman heroes, who
conquered the world, and prepared the way for Christ! How
wise, how profound, are those ancient teachers and sages!
what power of imagination, what a semblance of prophecy,
is manifest in their poets! The present world is in many respects not so great as in that old time, but even now there
is enough in it to show both the strength of human nature
in this respect, and its weakness. Consider the solidity of our
own political fabric at home, and the expansion of our empire abroad, and you will have matter enough spread out before you to occupy many a long day in admiration of the
genius, the virtues, and the resources of human nature. Take
a second meditation upon it; alas! you will find nothing of
faith there, but only expedience as the measure of right and
wrong, and only temporal well-being as the end of action.
Again, many are the tales and poems written now-a-days,
expressing high and beautiful sentiments; I dare say some of
you, my brethren, have fallen in with them, and perhaps you
have thought to yourselves, that he must be a man of deep
religious feeling and high religious profession who could
write so well. Is it so in fact, my brethren? it is not so; why?
because after all it is *but* poetry, not religion; it is human
nature exerting the powers of imagination and reason, which
it has, till it seems also to have powers which it has not. There
are, you know, in the animal world various creatures, which
are able to imitate the voice of man; nature in like manner is
often a mockery of grace. The truth is, the natural man sees
this or that principle to be good or true from the light of
conscience; and then, since he has the power of reasoning, he
knows that, if this be true, many other things are true likewise; and then, having the power of imagination, he pictures
to himself those other things as true, though he does not really
understand them. And then he brings to his aid what he has

read and gained from others who *have* had grace, and thus he completes his sketch; and then he throws his feelings and his heart into it, meditates on it, and kindles in himself a sort of enthusiasm, and thus he is able to write beautifully and touchingly about what to others indeed may be a reality, but to him is nothing more than a fiction. Thus some can write about the early Martyrs, and others describe some great Saint of the Middle Ages, not exactly as a Catholic, but as if they had a piety and a seriousness to which really they are strangers. So, too, actors on a stage can excite themselves till they think they are the persons they represent; and, as you know, prejudiced persons, who wish to quarrel with another, impute something to him, which at first they scarcely believe themselves; but they wish to believe it and act as if it were true, and raise and cherish anger at the thought of it, till at last they come simply to believe it. So it is, I say, in the case of many an author in verse and prose; readers are deceived by his fine writing; they not only praise this or that sentiment, or argument, or description, in what they read, which happens to be true, but they put faith in the writer himself; and they believe sentiments or statements which are false on the credit of the true. Thus it is that people are led away into false religions and false philosophies; a preacher or speaker, who is in a state of nature, or has fallen from grace, is able to say many things to touch the heart of a sinner or to strike his conscience, whether from his natural powers, or from what he has read in books; and the latter forthwith takes him for his prophet and guide, on the warrant of these accidental truths which it required no supernatural gifts to discover and enforce.

Scripture provides us an instance of such a prophet, (nay, of one far more favoured and honoured than any false teacher is now,) who nevertheless was the enemy of God; I mean the prophet Balaam. He went forth to curse the chosen people in spite of an express prohibition from heaven, and that for money; and at length he died fighting against them in battle.

Such was he in his life and in his death; such were his deeds; but what were his words? most religious, most conscientious, most instructive. "If Balac," he says, "shall give me his house full of silver and gold, I cannot alter the word of the Lord my God." Again, "Let my soul die the death of the just, and let my end be like to theirs!" And again, "I will show thee, O man, what is good, and what the Lord requireth of thee; to do judgment and to love mercy, and to walk heedfully with thy God." Here is a man, who is not in a state of grace, speaking so religiously, that at first sight you might have thought he was to be followed in whatever he said, and that your soul would have been safe with his.

And thus it often happens, that those who seem so amiable and good, and so trustworthy, when we only know them from their writings, disappoint us so painfully, if at length we come to have a personal acquaintance with them. We do not recognize in the living being the eloquence or the wisdom which so much enchanted us. He is rude, perhaps, and unfeeling; he is selfish, he is dictatorial, he is sensual, he is empty-minded and frivolous; while we in our simplicity had antecedently thought him the very embodiment of purity and tenderness, or an oracle of heavenly truth.

Now, my dear brethren, I have been engaged in bringing before you what human nature can do, and what it can appear, without being reconciled to God, without any hope of heaven, without any security against sin, without any pardon of the original curse, nay, in the midst of mortal sin; but it is a state which has never existed in fact, without great modifications. No one has ever been deprived of the assistance of grace, both for illumination and conversion; even the heathen world as a whole had to a certain extent its darkness relieved by these fitful and recurrent gleams of light; but I have thought it useful to get you to contemplate what human nature is, viewed in itself, for various reasons. It explains how it is that men look so like each other as they do,—grace being imitated, and, as it were, rivalled by nature, both in society at large, and in the hearts of particular persons. Hence the world will not believe the separation really existing between it and the Church, and the smallness of the flock of Christ. And hence too it is, that numbers who have heard the Name of Christ, and profess to believe in the Gospel, will not be persuaded as regards themselves that they are exterior to the Church, and do not enjoy her privileges; merely because they do their duty in some general way, or because they are conscious to themselves of being benevolent or upright. And this is a point which concerns Catholics too, as I now proceed to show you.

Make yourselves quite sure then, my brethren, of the matter of fact, before you go away with the belief, that you are not confusing, in your own case, nature and grace, and taking credit to yourselves for supernatural works, which merit heaven, when you are but doing the works of a heathen, are unforgiven, and lie under an eternal sentence. Oh, it is a dreadful thought, that a man may deceive himself with the notion that he is secure, merely because he is a Catholic, and because he has some kind of love and fear of God, whereas he may be no better than many a Protestant round about him, who either never was baptized, or threw himself once for all out of grace on coming to years of understanding. This idea is entirely conceivable; it is well if it be not true in matter of fact. You know, it is one opinion entertained among divines and holy men, that the number of Catholics that are to be saved will on the whole be small. Multitudes of those who never knew the Gospel will rise up in the judgment against the children of the Church, and will be shown to have done more with scantier opportunities. Our Lord speaks of His people as a small flock, as I cited His words when I began: He says "Many are called, few are chosen." St. Paul, speaking, in the first instance, of the Jews, says that but "a remnant is saved according to the election of grace." He speaks even of the possibility of his own reprobation. What a thought in an Apostle! yet it is one with which Saints are familiar; they fear both for themselves and for others. It is related in the history of my own dear Patron, St. Philip Neri, that some time after his death he appeared to a holy religious, and bade him take a message of consolation to his children, the Fathers of the Oratory. The consolation was this, that, by the grace of God, up to that day not one of the Congregation had been lost. "None of them lost!" a man may cry out; "well, had his consolation for his children been, that they were all in paradise, having escaped the dark lake of purgatory, that would have been something worth telling; but all he had to say was, that none of them were in hell! Strange if they were! Here was a succession of men, who had given up the world for a religious life, who had given up self for God and their neighbour, who had passed their days in prayer and good works, who had died happily with the last Sacraments, and it is revealed about them, as a great consolation, that none of them were lost!" Still such after all is our holy Father's consolation; and, that it should be such, only proves that salvation is not so easy a matter, or so cheap a possession, as we are apt to suppose. It is not obtained by the mere wishing. And, if it was a thing so to be coveted by men, who had made sacrifices for Christ, and were living in sanctity, how much more rare and arduous of attainment is it in those who have confessedly loved the world more than God, and have never dreamed of doing any duty to which the Church did not oblige them!

Tell me, what is the state of your souls and the rule of your lives? You come to Confession, once a year, four times a year, at the Indulgences; you communicate as often; you do not miss Mass on days of obligation; you are not conscious of any great sin.—There you come to an end; you have nothing more to say. What? do you not take God's name in vain? only when you are angry;—that is, I suppose, you are subject to fits of violent passion, in which you use every shocking word which the devil puts into your mouth, and abuse and curse, and perhaps strike the objects of your anger?—Only now and then, you say, when you are in liquor. Then it seems you are given to intoxication?—you answer, you never drink so much as not to know what you are doing. Well, have you improved in these respects in the course of several years past? You cannot say you have, but such sins are not mortal at the most. Then, I suppose, you have not lately fallen into mortal sin at all? You pause, and then you are obliged to confess that you have, and that once and again; and the more I question you, perhaps the longer becomes the catalogue of offences which have separated you from God. But this is not all; your sole idea of sin is, the sinning in act and in deed; sins of habit, which cling so close to you that they are difficult to detect, and manifest themselves in slight but continual influences on your thoughts, words, and works, do not engage your attention at all. You are selfish, and obstinate, and worldly, and self-indulgent; you neglect your children; you are fond of idle amusements; you scarcely ever think of God from day to day, for I cannot call your hurried prayers morning and night any thinking of Him at all. You are friends with the world, and live a good deal among those who have no sense of religion.

Now what have you to tell me which will set against this? what good have you done? in what is your hope of heaven? whence do you gain it? You perhaps answer me, that the Sacrament of Penance reconciles you from time to time to God; that you live in the world; that you are not called to the religious state; that it is true you love the world more than God, but that you love God sufficiently for salvation, and that you rely in the hour of death upon the powerful intercession of the Blessed Mother of God. Then besides, you have a number of good points, which you go through, and which are to you signs that you *are* in the grace of God; you conceive that your state at worst is one of tepidity. Tepidity! I tell you, you have no marks of tepidity; do you wish to know what a tepid person is? one who has begun to lead almost the life of a Saint, and has fallen from his fervour; one who retains his good practices, but does them without devotion; one who does so much, that we only blame him for not doing more.

No, you need not confess tepidity, my brethren;—do you wish to have the judgment which I am led to form about you? it is, that probably you are not in the grace of God at all. The probability is, that for a long while past you have gone to Confession without the proper dispositions, without real grief, and without sincere purpose of amendment for your sins. You are probably such, that were you to die this night, you would be lost for ever. What do you do more than nature does? You do certain good things; "what reward have ye? do not even the publicans so? what do ye more than others? do not even the heathen so?" You have the ordinary virtues of human nature, or some of them; you are what nature made you, and care not to be better. You may be naturally kind-hearted, and then you do charitable actions to others; you have a natural strength of character,—if so, you are able to bring your passions under the power of reason; you have a natural energy, and you labour for your family; you are naturally mild, and so you do not quarrel; you have a dislike of intemperance, and therefore you are sober. You have the virtues of your Protestant neighbours, and their faults too; what are you better than they?

Here is another grave matter against you, that you are so well with the Protestants about you; I do not mean to say that you are not bound to cultivate peace with all men, and to do them all the offices of charity in your power. Of course you are, and if they respect, esteem, and love you, it redounds to your praise and will gain you a reward; but I mean more than this; they do *not* respect you, but they like you, because they think of you as of themselves, they see no difference between themselves and you. This is the very reason why they so often take your part, and assert or defend your political rights. Here again, there is a sense of course in which our civil rights may be advocated by Protestants without any reflection on us, and with honour to them. We are like others in this, that we are men; that we are members of the same state with them, subjects, contented subjects, of the same Sovereign, that we have a dependence on them, and have them dependent on us; that, like them, we feel pain when ill-used, and are grateful when well-treated. We need not be ashamed of a fellowship like this, and those who recognize it in us are generous in doing so. But we have much cause to be ashamed, and much cause to be anxious what God thinks of us, if we gain their support by giving them a false impression in our persons of what the Catholic Church is, and what Catholics are bound to be, what bound to believe, and to do; and is not this the case often, my brethren, that the world takes up your interest, because you share its sins?

Nature is one with nature, grace with grace; the world then witnesses against you by being good friends with you; you could not have got on with the world so well, without surrendering something which was precious and sacred. The world likes you, all but your professed creed; distinguishes you from your creed in its judgment of you, and would fain separate you from it in fact. Men say, "These persons are better than their Church; we have not a word to say for their Church; but Catholics are not what they were, they are very much like other men now. Their Creed certainly is bigoted and cruel, but what would you have of them? You cannot expect them to confess this; let them change quietly, no one changes in public, be satisfied that they are changed. They are as fond of the world as we are; they take up political objects as warmly; they like their own way just as well; they do not like strictness a whit better; they hate spiritual thraldom, and they are half ashamed of the Pope and his Councils. They hardly believe any miracles now, and are annoyed when their own brethren officiously proclaim them; they never speak of purgatory; they are sore about images; they avoid the subject of Indulgences; and they will not commit themselves to the doctrine of exclusive salvation. The Catholic doctrines are now mere badges of party. Catholics think for themselves and judge for themselves, just as we do; they are kept in their

Church by a point of honour, and a reluctance at seeming to abandon a fallen cause."

Such is the judgment of the world, and you, my brethren, are shocked to hear it;—but may it not be, that the world knows more about you than you know about yourselves? "If ye had been of the world," says Christ, "the world would love its own; but because ye are not of the world, but I have chosen you out of the world, therefore the world hateth you." So speaks Christ of His Apostles. How run His words when applied to you? "If ye be of the world, the world will love its own; therefore ye *are* of the world, and I have *not* chosen you out of the world, because the world loveth you." Do not complain of the world's imputing to you more than is true; those who live as the world give colour to those who think them of the world, and seem to form but one party with them. In proportion as you put off the yoke of Christ, so does the world by a sort of instinct recognize you, and think well of you accordingly. Its highest compliment is to tell you that you disbelieve. Oh, my brethren, there is an eternal enmity between the world and the Church. The Church declares by the mouth of an Apostle, "Whoso will be a friend of the world, becomes an enemy of God;" and the world retorts, and calls the Church apostate, sorceress, Beelzebub, and Antichrist. She is the image and the mother of the predestinate, and, if you would be found among her children when you die, you must have part in her reproach while you live. Does not the world scoff at all that is glorious, all that is majestic, in our holy religion? Does it not speak against the special creations of God's grace? Does it not disbelieve the possibility of purity and chastity? Does it not slander the profession of celibacy? Does it not deny the virginity of Mary? Does it not cast out her very name as evil? Does it not scorn her as a dead woman, whom you know to be the Mother of all living, and the great Intercessor of the faithful? Does it not ridicule the Saints? Does it not make light of their relics? Does it not despise the

Sacraments? Does it not blaspheme the awful Presence which dwells upon our altars, and mock bitterly and fiercely at our believing that what it calls bread and wine is that very same Body and Blood of the Lamb, which lay in Mary's womb and hung on the Cross? What are we, that we should be better treated than our Lord, and His Mother, and His servants, and His works? Nay, what are we, if we *be* better treated, but the friends of those who treat us well, and who ill-treat Him?

Oh, my dear brethren, be children of grace, not of nature; be not seduced by this world's sophistries and assumptions; it pretends to be the work of God, but in reality it comes of Satan. "I know My sheep," says our Lord, "and Mine know Me, and they follow Me." "Show me, O Thou whom my soul loveth," says the Bride in the Canticle, "where Thou feedest, where Thou restest at noon;" and He answers her, "Go forth, and follow after the steps of the flocks, and feed thy kids beside the shepherds' tents." Let us follow the Saints, as they follow Christ; so that, when He comes in judgment, and the wretched world sinks to perdition, "on us sinners, His servants, hoping in the multitude of His mercies, He may vouchsafe to bestow some portion and fellowship with his Holy Apostles and Martyrs, with John, Stephen, Matthias, Barnabas, Ignatius, Alexander, Marcelline, Peter, Felicity, Perpetua, Agatha, Lucy, Agnes, Cicely, Anastasia, and all His Saints, not for the value of our merit, but according to the bounty of His pardon, through the same Christ our Lord."

XIV

FAITH AND PRIVATE JUDGMENT [1]

WHEN WE CONSIDER THE BEAUTY, the majesty, the completeness, the resources, the consolations, of the Catholic Religion, it may strike us with wonder, my brethren, that it does not convert the multitude of those who come in its way. Perhaps you have felt this surprise yourselves; especially those of you who have been recently converted, and can compare it, from experience, with those religions which the millions of this country choose instead of it. You know, from experience, how barren, unmeaning, and baseless those religions are; what poor attractions they have, and how little they have to say for themselves. Multitudes, indeed, are of no religion at all; and you may not be surprised that those who cannot even bear the thought of God, should not feel drawn to His Church; numbers, too, hear very little about Catholicism, or a great deal of abuse and calumny against it, and you may not be surprised that they do not all at once become Catholics; but what may fairly surprise those who enjoy the fulness of Catholic blessings is, that those who see the Church ever so distantly, who see even gleams or the faint lustre of her majesty, nevertheless should not be so far attracted by what they see as to seek to see more,—should not at least put themselves in the way to be led on to the Truth, which of course is not ordinarily recognized in its divine authority except by degrees. Moses, when he saw the burning bush, turned aside to see "that great sight;" Nathanael, though

[1] From *Discourses to Mixed Congregations* (1849), No. 10. [Ed.]

he thought no good could come out of Nazareth, at least
followed Philip to Christ, when Philip said to him, "Come and
see;" but the multitudes about us see and hear, in some
measure, surely,—many in ample measure,—and yet are not
persuaded thereby to see and hear more, are not moved to
act upon their knowledge. Seeing they see not, and hearing
they hear not; they are contented to remain as they are: they
are not drawn to inquire, or at least not drawn on to embrace.

Many explanations may be given of this difficulty; I will
proceed to suggest to you one, which will sound like a truism,
but yet has a meaning in it. Men do not become Catholics,
because they have not faith. Now you may ask me, how this
is saying more than that men do not believe the Catholic
Church *because* they do not believe it; which is saying nothing
at all. Our Lord, for instance, says, "He who cometh to Me
shall not hunger, and he who believeth in Me shall never
thirst;"—to believe then and to come are the same thing. If
they had faith, of course, they would join the Church, for the
very meaning, the very exercise of faith, is joining the Church.
But I mean something more than this: faith is a state of mind,
it is a particular mode of thinking and acting, which is exercised, always indeed towards God, but in very various ways.
Now I mean to say, that the multitude of men in this country
have not this habit or character of mind. We could conceive,
for instance, their believing in their own religions, even if
they did not believe in the Church; this would be faith,
though a faith improperly directed; but they do not believe
even their own religions; they do not believe in anything at
all. It is a definite defect in their minds: as we might say that
a person had not the virtue of meekness, or of liberality, or
of prudence, quite independently of this or that exercise of
the virtue, so there is such a virtue as faith, and there is such
a defect as the absence of it. Now I mean to say that the great
mass of men in this country have not this particular virtue
called faith, have not this virtue at all. As a man might be
without eyes or without hands, so they are without faith; it is

a distinct want or fault in their soul; and what I say is, that
since they have not this faculty of believing, no wonder they
do not embrace that, which cannot really be embraced without it. They do not believe any teaching at all in any true
sense; and therefore they do not believe the Church in particular.

Now, in the first place, what is faith? it is assenting to a
doctrine as true, which we do not see, which we cannot prove,
because God says it is true, who cannot lie. And further than
this, since God says it is true, not with his His own voice, but
by the voice of His messengers, it is assenting to what man
says, not simply viewed as a man, but to what he is commis-
sioned to declare, as a messenger, prophet, or ambassador
from God. In the ordinary course of this world we account
things true either because we see them, or because that we
can perceive that they follow and are deducible from what we
do see; that is, we gain truth by sight or by reason, not by
faith. You will say indeed, that we accept a number of things
which we cannot prove or see, on the word of others; certainly; but then we accept what they say only as the word of
man; and we have not commonly that absolute and unreserved
confidence in them, which nothing can shake. We know that
man is open to mistake, and we are always glad to find some
confirmation of what he says, from other quarters, in any
important matter; or we receive his information with negli-
gence and unconcern, as something of little consequence, as
a matter of opinion; or, if we act upon it, it is as a matter of
prudence, thinking it best and safest to do so. We take his
word for what it is worth, and we use it either according to
our necessity, or its probability. We keep the decision in our
own hands, and reserve to ourselves the right of re-opening
the question whenever we please. This is very different from
divine faith; he who believes that God is true, and that this is
His word, which He has committed to man, has no doubt at
all. He is as certain that the doctrine taught is true, as that
God is true; and he is certain, *because* God is true, *because*

God has spoken, not because he sees its truth or can prove its truth. That is, faith has two peculiarities;—it is most certain, decided, positive, immoveable in its assent, and it gives this assent not because it sees with eye, or sees with the reason, but because it receives the tidings from one who comes from God.

This is what faith was in the time of the Apostles, as no one can deny; and what it was then, it must be now, else it ceases to be the same thing. I say, it certainly was this in the Apostles' time, for you know they preached to the world that Christ was the Son of God, that He was born of a Virgin, that He had ascended on high, that He would come again to judge all, the living and the dead. Could the world see all this? could it prove it? how then were men to receive it? why did so many embrace it? on the word of the Apostles, who were, as their powers showed, messengers from God. Men were told to submit their reason to a living authority. Moreover, whatever an Apostle said, his converts were bound to believe; when they entered the Church, they entered it in order to learn. The Church was their teacher; they did not come to argue, to examine, to pick and choose, but to accept whatever was put before them. No one doubts, no one can doubt this, of those primitive times. A Christian was bound to take without doubting all that the Apostles declared to be revealed; if the Apostles spoke, he had to yield an internal assent of his mind; it would not be enough to keep silence, it would not be enough not to oppose; it was not allowable to credit in a measure; it was not allowable to doubt. No; if a convert had his own private thoughts of what was said, and only kept them to himself, if he made some secret opposition to the teaching, if he waited for farther proof before he believed it, this would be a proof that he did not think the Apostles were sent from God to reveal His will; it would be a proof that he did not in any true sense believe at all. Immediate, implicit submission of the mind was, in the lifetime of the Apostles, the only, the necessary token of faith; then there was no room whatever for what is now called private judgment. No one could say,

"I will choose my religion for myself, I will believe this, I will not believe that; I will pledge myself to nothing; I will believe just as long as I please and no longer; what I believe to-day I will reject to-morrow, if I choose. I will believe what the Apostles have as yet said, but I will not believe what they shall say in time to come." No; either the Apostles were from God, or they were not; if they were, everything that they preached was to be believed by their hearers; if they were not, there was nothing for their hearers to believe. To believe a little, to believe more or less, was impossible; it contradicted the very notion of believing: if one part was to be believed, every part was to be believed; it was an absurdity to believe one thing and not another; for the word of the Apostles, which made the one true, made the other true too; they were nothing in themselves, they were all things, they were an infallible authority, as coming from God. The world had either to become Christian, or to let it alone; there was no room for private tastes and fancies, no room for private judgment.

Now surely this is quite clear from the nature of the case; but it is also clear from the words of Scripture. "We give thanks to God," says St. Paul, "without ceasing, because when ye had received from us the word of hearing, which is of God, ye received it, not as the word of men, but (as it is indeed) the word of God." Here you see St. Paul expresses what I have said above; that the word comes from God, that it is spoken by men, that it must be received, not as man's word, but as God's word. So in another place he says, "He who despiseth these things, despiseth not man, but God, who hath also given in us His Holy Spirit." Our Saviour had made a like declaration already, "He that heareth you, heareth Me; and he that despiseth you, despiseth Me; and he that despiseth Me, despiseth Him that sent Me." Accordingly St. Peter on the day of Pentecost said, "Men of Israel, *hear* these words, God hath raised up this Jesus, whereof *we* are *witnesses*. Let all the house of Israel *know most certainly* that God hath made this Jesus, whom we have crucified, both Lord and

Christ." At another time he said, "We ought to obey God, rather than man; we are *witnesses* of these things, and so *is the Holy Ghost,* whom God hath given to all who obey Him." And again, "He commanded us to preach to the people, and to testify that it is He (Jesus) who hath been appointed by God to be the Judge of the living and of the dead." And you know that the continual declaration of the first preachers was, "Believe, and thou shalt be saved:" they do not say, "prove our doctrine by your own reason," nor "wait till you see before you believe;" but, "believe without seeing and without proving, because our word is not our own, but God's word." Men might indeed use their reason in inquiring into the pretensions of the Apostles; they might inquire whether or not they did miracles; they might inquire whether they were predicted in the Old Testament as coming from God; but when they had ascertained this fairly in whatever way, they were to take all the Apostles said for granted without proof; they were to exercise their faith, they were to be saved by hearing. Hence, as you perhaps observed, St. Paul significantly calls the revealed doctrine "the word of hearing," in the passage I quoted; men came to hear, to accept, to obey, not to criticize what was said; and in accordance with this he asks elsewhere, "How shall they believe Him, whom they have not heard? and how shall they hear without a preacher? Faith cometh by hearing, and hearing by the word of Christ."

Now, my dear brethren, consider, are not these two states or acts of mind quite distinct from each other;—to believe simply what a living authority tells you; and to take a book, such as Scripture, and to use it as you please, to master it, that is, to make yourself the master of it, to interpret it for yourself, and to admit just what you choose to see in it, and nothing more? Are not these two procedures distinct in this, that in the former you submit, in the latter you judge? At this moment I am not asking you which is the better, I am not asking whether this or that is practicable now, but are they not two ways of taking up a doctrine, and not one? is not submission quite contrary to judging? Now, is it not certain that faith in the time of the Apostles consisted in submitting? and is it not certain that it did not consist in judging for one's self? It is in vain to say that the man who judges from the Apostles' writings, does submit to those writings in the first instance, and therefore has faith in them; else why should he refer to them at all? There is, I repeat, an essential difference between the act of submitting to a living oracle, and to his book; in the former case there is no appeal from the speaker, in the latter the final decision remains with the reader. Consider how different is the confidence with which you report another's words in his presence and in his absence. If he be absent, you boldly say that he holds so and so, or said so and so; but let him come into the room in the midst of the conversation, and your tone is immediately changed. It is then, "I *think* I have heard you say something *like* this, or what I *took* to be this;" or you modify considerably the statement or the fact to which you originally pledged him, dropping one-half of it for safety-sake, or retrenching the most startling portions of it; and then after all you wait with some anxiety to see whether he will accept any portion of it at all. The same sort of process takes place in the case of the written document of a person now dead. I can fancy a man magisterially expounding St. Paul's Epistle to the Galatians or to the Ephesians, who would be better content with the writer's absence than his sudden re-appearance among us, lest the Apostle should take his own meaning out of his commentator's hands and explain it for himself. In a word, though he says he has faith in St. Paul's writings, he confessedly has no faith in St. Paul; and though he may speak much about truth as found in Scripture, he has no wish at all to have been one of the Christians who are found there.

I think I may assume that this virtue, which was exercised by the first Christians, is not known at all among Protestants now; or at least if there are instances of it, it is exercised towards those, I mean their teachers and divines, who expressly disclaim that they are fit objects of it, and who exhort their people to judge for themselves. Protestants, generally speaking, have not faith, in the primitive meaning of that word; this is clear from what I have been saying, and here is a confirmation of it. If men believed now, as they did in the times of the Apostles, they could not doubt nor change. No one can doubt whether a word spoken by God is to be believed; of course it is; whereas any one, who is modest and humble, may easily be brought to doubt of his own inferences and deductions. Since men now-a-days deduce from Scripture, instead of believing a teacher, you may expect to see them waver about; they will feel the force of their own deductions more strongly at one time than at another, they will change their minds about them, or perhaps deny them altogether; whereas this cannot be, while a man has faith, that is, belief, that what a preacher says to him comes from God. This is what St. Paul especially insists on, telling us that Apostles, prophets, evangelists, pastors, and teachers, are given us that, "we may all attain to unity of faith," and, on the contrary, in order "that we be *not* as children tossed to and fro, and carried about by every gale of doctrine." Now, in matter of fact, do not men in this day change about in their religious opinions without any limit? Is not this, then, a proof that they have not that faith which the Apostles demanded of their converts? If they had faith, they would not change. Once believe that God has spoken, and you are sure He cannot unsay what He has already said; He cannot deceive; He cannot change; you have received it once for all; you will believe it ever.

Such is the only rational, consistent account of faith; but so far are Protestants from professing it, that they laugh at the very notion of it. They laugh at the notion itself of men pinning their faith (as they express themselves) upon Pope or Council; they think it simply superstitious and narrow-minded, to profess to believe just what the Church believes, and to assent to whatever she shall say in time to come on matters of doctrine. That is, they laugh at the bare notion of doing what Christians undeniably did in the time of the Apostles. Observe, they do not merely ask whether the Catholic Church has a claim to teach, has authority, has the gifts;—this is a reasonable question;—no, they think that the very state of mind, which such a claim involves in those who admit it, namely, the disposition to accept without reserve or question, that this is slavish. They call it priestcraft to insist on this surrender of the reason, and superstition to make it. That is, they quarrel with the very state of mind which all Christians had in the age of the Apostles; nor is there any doubt, (who will deny it?) that those who thus boast of not being led blindfold, of judging for themselves, of believing just as much and just as little as they please, of hating dictation, and so forth, would have found it an extreme difficulty to hang on the lips of the Apostles, had they lived at their date, or rather would have simply resisted the sacrifice of their own liberty of thought, would have thought life eternal too dearly purchased at such a price, and would have died in their unbelief. And they would have defended themselves on the plea that it was absurd and childish to ask them to believe without proof, to bid them give up their education, and their intelligence, and their science, and, in spite of all those difficulties which reason and sense find in the Christian doctrine, in spite of its mysteriousness, its obscurity, its strangeness, its unacceptableness, its severity, to require them to surrender themselves to the teaching of a few unlettered Galilæans, or a learned indeed but fanatical Pharisee. This is what they would have said then; and if so, is it wonderful they do not become Catholics now? The simple account of their remaining as they are, is, that they lack one thing,—they have not faith; it is a state of mind, it is a virtue, which they do not recognize to be praiseworthy, which they do not aim at possessing.

What they feel now, my brethren, is just what both Jew and Greek felt before them in the time of the Apostles, and what the natural man has felt ever since. The great and wise men of the day looked down upon faith, then as now, as if it were unworthy the dignity of human nature, "See your vocation, brethren, that there are not," among you "many wise according to the flesh, not many mighty, not many noble; but the foolish things of the world hath God chosen to confound the strong, and the mean things of the world, and the things that are contemptible, hath God chosen, and things that are not, that He might destroy the things that are, that no flesh might glory in His sight." Hence the same Apostle speaks of "the foolishness of preaching." Similar to this is what our Lord had said in His prayer to the Father; "I thank Thee, Father, Lord of heaven and earth, because Thou hast hid these things from the wise and prudent, and hast revealed them unto little ones." Now is it not plain that men of this day have just inherited the feelings and traditions of these falsely wise and fatally prudent persons in our Lord's day? They have the same obstruction in their hearts to entering the Catholic Church, which Pharisees and Sophists had before them; it goes against them to believe her doctrine, not so much for want of evidence that she is from God, as because, if so, they shall have to submit their minds to living men, who have not their own cultivation or depth of intellect, and because they must receive a number of doctrines, whether they will or no, which are strange to their imagination and difficult to their reason. The very characteristic of the Catholic teaching and of the Catholic teacher is to them a preliminary objection to their becoming Catholics, so great, as to throw into the shade any argument however strong, which is producible in behalf of the mission of those teachers and the origin of that teaching. In short, they have not faith.

They have not in them the principle of faith; and I repeat, it is nothing to the purpose to urge that at least they firmly believe Scripture to be the word of God. In truth, it is much to be feared that their acceptance of Scripture itself is nothing better than a prejudice or inveterate feeling impressed on them when they were children. A proof of it is this; that, while they profess to be so shocked at Catholic miracles, and

are not slow to call them "lying wonders," they have no difficulty at all about Scripture narratives, which are quite as
difficult to the reason as any miracles recorded in the history
of the Saints. I have heard on the contrary of Catholics who
have been startled at first reading in Scripture the narrative
of the ark in the deluge, of the tower of Babel, of Balaam and
Balac, of the Israelites' flight from Egypt and entrance into
the promised land, and of Esau's and Saul's rejection; which
the bulk of Protestants receive without any effort of mind.
How, then, do these Catholics accept them? by faith. They
say, "God is true, and every man a liar." How come Protestants
so easily to receive them? by faith? Nay, I conceive that in
most cases there is no submission of the reason at all; simply
they are so familiar with the passages in question, that the
narrative presents no difficulties to their imagination; they have
nothing to overcome. If, however, they *are* led to contemplate
these passages in themselves, and to try them in the balance
of probability, and to begin to question about them, as will
happen when their intellect is cultivated, then there is nothing
to bring them back to their former habitual or mechanical
belief; they know nothing of submitting to authority, that is,
they know nothing of faith; for they have no authority to
submit to. They either remain in a state of doubt without any
great trouble of mind, or they go on to ripen into utter disbelief on the subjects in question, though they may say nothing
about it. Neither before they doubt, nor when they doubt,
is there any token of the presence in them of a power sub-
jecting reason to the word of God. No; what looks like faith,
is a mere hereditary persuasion, not a personal principle: it
is a habit which they have learned in the nursery, which has
never changed into anything higher, and which is scattered
and disappears, like a mist, before the light, such as it is, of
reason. If, however, there are Protestants, who are not in one
or other of these two states, either of credulity or of doubt,
but who firmly believe in spite of all difficulties, they certainly
have some claim to be considered under the influence of faith;

but there is nothing to show that such persons, where they are found, are not in the way to become Catholics, and perhaps they are already called so by their friends, showing in their own examples the logical, indisputable connexion which exists between possessing faith and joining the Church.

If, then, faith be now the same faculty of mind, the same sort of habit or act, which it was in the days of the Apostles, I have made good what I set about showing. But it must be the same; it cannot mean two things; the word cannot have changed its meaning. Either say that faith is not necessary now at all, or take it to be what the Apostles meant by it, but do not say that you have it, and then show me something quite different, which you have put in the place of it. In the Apostles' days the peculiarity of faith was submission to a living authority; this is what made it so distinctive; this is what made it an act of submission at all; this is what destroyed private judgment in matters of religion. If you will not look out for a living authority, and will bargain for private judgment, then say at once that you have not Apostolic faith. And in fact you have it not; the bulk of this nation has it not; confess you have it not; and then confess that this is the reason why you are not Catholics. You are not Catholics because you have not faith. Why do not blind men see the sun? because they have no eyes; in like manner it is vain to discourse upon the beauty, the sanctity, the sublimity of the Catholic doctrine and worship, where men have no faith to accept them as divine. They may confess their beauty, sublimity, and sanctity, without believing them; they may acknowledge that the Catholic religion is noble and majestic; they may be struck with its wisdom, they may admire its adaptation to human nature, they may be penetrated by its tender and winning bearing, they may be awed by its consistency. But to commit themselves to it, that is another matter; to choose it for their portion, to say with the favoured Moabitess, "Whithersoever thou shalt go, I will go; and where thou shalt dwell, I will dwell; thy people shall be my people, and thy

God my God," this is the language of faith. A man may revere, a man may extol, who has no tendency whatever to obey, no notion whatever of professing. And this often happens in fact: men are respectful to the Catholic religion; they acknowledge its services to mankind, they encourage it and its professors; they like to know them, they are interested in hearing of their movements, but they are not, and never will be Catholics. They will die, as they have lived, out of the Church, because they have not possessed themselves of that faculty by which the Church is to be approached. Catholics who have not studied them or human nature, will wonder they remain where they are; nay, they themselves, alas for them! will sometimes lament they cannot become Catholics. They will feel so intimately the blessedness of being a Catholic, that they will cry out, "Oh, what would I give to be a Catholic! oh, that I could believe what I admire! but I do not, and I can no more believe merely because I wish to do so, than I can leap over a mountain. I should be much happier were I a Catholic; but I am not; it is no use deceiving myself; I am what I am; I revere, I cannot accept."

Oh, deplorable state! deplorable because it is utterly and absolutely their own fault, and because such great stress is laid in Scripture, as they know, on the necessity of faith for salvation. Faith is there made the foundation and commencement of all acceptable obedience. It is described as the "argument" or "proof of things not seen;" by faith men have understood that God is, that He made the world, that He is a rewarder of those who seek Him, that the flood was coming, that their Saviour was to be born. "Without faith it is impossible to please God;" "by faith we stand;" "by faith we walk;" "by faith we overcome the world." When our Lord gave to the Apostles their commission to preach all over the world, He continued, "He that believeth and is baptized, shall be saved; but he that believeth not, shall be condemned." And He declared to Nicodemus, "He that believeth in the Son, is not judged; but he that doth not believe is already judged, because he believeth not in the Name of the Only-begotten Son of God." He said to the Pharisees, "If you believe not that I am He, ye shall die in your sins." To the Jews, "Ye believe not, because ye are not of My sheep." And you may recollect that before His miracles, He commonly demands faith of the supplicant; "All things are possible," He says, "to him that believeth;" and we find in one place "He could not do any miracle," on account of the unbelief of the inhabitants.

Has faith changed its meaning, or is it less necessary now? Is it not still what it was in the Apostles' day, the very characteristic of Christianity, the special instrument of renovation, the first disposition for justification, one out of the three theological virtues? God might have renewed us by other means, by sight, by reason, by love, but He has chosen to "purify our hearts by faith;" it has been His will to select an instrument which the world despises, but which is of immense power. He preferred it, in His infinite wisdom, to every other; and if men have it not, they have not the very element and rudiment, out of which are formed, on which are built, the Saints and Servants of God. And they have it not, they are living, they are dying, without the hopes, without the aids of the Gospel, because, in spite of so much that is good in them, in spite of their sense of duty, their tenderness of conscience on many points, their benevolence, their uprightness, their generosity, they are under the dominion (I must say it) of a proud fiend; they have this stout spirit within them, they will be their own masters in matters of thought, about which they know so little; they consider their own reason better than any one's else; they will not admit that any one comes from God who contradicts their own view of truth. What! is none their equal in wisdom anywhere? is there none other whose word is to be taken on religion? is there none to wrest from them their ultimate appeal to themselves? Have they in no possible way the occasion or opportunity of faith? Is it a virtue, which in consequence of their transcendent sagacity, their prerogative of omniscience, they must despair of exercising?

If the pretensions of the Catholic Church do not satisfy them, let them go somewhere else, if they can. If they are so fastidious that they cannot trust her as the oracle of God, let them find another more certainly from Him than the House of His own institution, which has ever been called by His Name, has ever maintained the same claims, has ever taught one substance of doctrine, and has triumphed over those who preached any other. Since Apostolic faith was reliance on man's word as being God's word, since what faith was in the beginning such it is now, since faith is necessary for salvation, let them attempt to exercise it towards another, if they will not accept the Bride of the Lamb. Let them, if they can, put faith in some of those religions which have lasted a whole two or three centuries in a corner of the earth. Let them stake their eternal prospects on kings and nobles and parliaments and soldiery, let them take some mere fiction of the law, or abortion of the schools, or idol of a populace, or upstart of a crisis, or oracle of lecture-rooms, as the prophet of God. Alas! they are hardly bestead if they must possess a virtue, which they have no means of exercising,—if they must make an act of faith, they know not on whom, and know not why!

What thanks ought we to render to Almighty God, my dear brethren, that He has made us what we are! It is a matter of grace. There are, to be sure, many cogent arguments to lead one to join the Catholic Church, but they do not force the will. We may know them, and not be moved to act upon them. We may be convinced without being persuaded. The two things are quite distinct from each other, seeing you ought to believe, and believing; reason, if left to itself, will bring you to the conclusion that you have sufficient grounds for believing, but belief is the gift of grace. You are then what you are, not from any excellence or merit of your own, but by the grace of God who has chosen you to believe. You might have been as the barbarian of Africa, or the freethinker of Europe, with grace sufficient to condemn you, because it had not furthered your salvation. You might have had strong inspirations of grace and have resisted them, and then additional grace might not have been given to overcome your resistance. God gives not the same measure of grace to all. Has He not visited you with over abundant grace? and was it not necessary for your hard hearts to receive more than other people? Praise and bless Him continually for the benefit; do not forget, as time goes on, that it is of grace; do not pride yourselves upon it; pray ever not to lose it; and do your best to make others partakers of it.

And you, my brethren, also, if such be present, who are not as yet Catholics, but who by your coming hither seem to show your interest in our teaching, and your wish to know more about it, you too remember, that though you may not yet have faith in the Church, still God has brought you into the way of obtaining it. You are under the influence of His grace; He has brought you a step on your journey; He wishes to bring you farther, He wishes to bestow on you the fulness of His blessings, and to make you Catholics. You are still in your sins; probably you are laden with the guilt of many years, the accumulated guilt of many a deep mortal offence, which no contrition has washed away, and to which no Sacrament has been applied. You at present are troubled with an uneasy conscience, a dissatisfied reason, an unclean heart, and a divided will; you need to be converted. Yet now the first suggestions of grace are working in your souls, and are to issue in pardon for the past and sanctity for the future. God is moving you to acts of faith, hope, love, hatred of sin, repentance; do not disappoint Him, do not thwart Him, concur with Him, obey Him. You look up, and you see, as it were, a great mountain to be scaled; you say, "How can I possibly find a path over these giant obstacles, which I find in the way of my becoming Catholic? I do not comprehend this doctrine, and I am pained at that; a third seems impossible; I never can be familiar with one practice, I am afraid of another; it is one maze and discomfort to me, and I am led to sink down in despair." Say not so, my dear brethren, look up in hope, trust in Him who calls you forward. "Who art thou, O great mountain, before Zorobabel? but a plain." He will lead you forward step by step, as He has led forward many a one before you. He will make the crooked straight and the rough plain. He will turn the streams, and dry up the rivers, which lie in your path. "He shall strengthen your feet like harts' feet, and set you up on high places. He shall widen your steps under you, and your tread shall not be weakened." "There is no God like the God of the righteous; He that mounts the heaven is thy Helper; by His mighty working the clouds disperse. His dwelling is above, and underneath are the everlasting arms; He shall cast out the enemy from before thee, and shall say, Be brought to nought." "The young shall faint, and youths shall fall; but they that hope in the Lord shall be new-fledged in strength, they shall take feathers like eagles, they shall run and not labour, they shall walk and not faint."

FAITH AND DOUBT[1]

THOSE WHO ARE DRAWN BY CURIOSITY or a better motive to inquire into the Catholic Religion, sometimes put to us a strange question,—whether, if they took up the profession of it, they would be at liberty, when they felt inclined, to reconsider the question of its divine authority; meaning, by "reconsideration" an inquiry springing from doubt of it, and possibly ending in a denial. The same question, in the form of an objection, is often asked by those who have no thoughts at all of becoming Catholics, and who enlarge upon it, as something terrible, that whoever once enters the pale of the Church, on him the door of egress is shut for ever; that, once a Catholic, he never, never can doubt again; that, whatever his misgivings may be, he must stifle them, nay must start from them as the suggestions of the evil spirit; in short, that he must give up altogether the search after truth, and do a violence to his mind, which is nothing short of immoral. This is what is said, my brethren, by certain objectors, and their own view is, or ought to be, if they are consistent, this,—that it is a fault ever to make up our mind once for all on any religious subject whatever; and that, however sacred a doctrine may be, and however evident to us,—let us say, for instance, the divinity of our Lord, or the existence of God,— we ought always to reserve to ourselves the liberty of doubting about it. I cannot help thinking that so extravagant a position, as this is, confutes itself; however, I will consider the

[1] From *Discourses to Mixed Congregations* (1849), No. 11. [Ed.]

contrary (that is, the Catholic) view of the subject, on its own merits, though without admitting the language in which it was just now stated by its opponents.

It is, then, perfectly true, that the Church does not allow her children to entertain any doubt of her teaching; and that, first of all, simply for this reason, because they are Catholics only while they have faith, and faith is incompatible with doubt. No one can be a Catholic without a simple faith, that what the Church declares in God's name, is God's word, and therefore true. A man must simply believe that the Church is the oracle of God; he must be as certain of her mission, as he is of the mission of the Apostles. Now, would any one ever call him certain that the Apostles came from God, if, after professing his certainty, he added, that, for what he knew, he might doubt one day about their mission? Such an anticipation would be a real, though latent, doubt, betraying that he was not certain of it at present. A person who says, "I believe just at this moment, but perhaps I am excited without knowing it, and I cannot answer for myself, that I shall believe to-morrow," does not believe. A man who says, "Perhaps I am in a kind of delusion, which will one day pass away from me, and leave me as I was before;" or, "I believe as far as I can tell, but there may be arguments in the background which will change my view," such a man has not faith at all. When, then, Protestants quarrel with us for saying that those who join us must give up all ideas of ever doubting the Church in time to come, they do nothing else but quarrel with us for insisting on the necessity of faith in her. Let them speak plainly; our offence is that of demanding faith in the Holy Catholic Church; it is this, and nothing else. I must insist upon this: faith implies a confidence in a man's mind, that the thing believed is really true; but, if it is once true, it never can be false. If it is true that God became man, what is the meaning of my anticipating a time when perhaps I shall not believe that God became man? this is nothing short of anticipating a time when I shall disbelieve a truth. And if I bargain to be allowed in time to come not to believe, or to doubt, that God became man, I am but asking to be allowed to doubt or to disbelieve what is an eternal truth. I do not see the privilege of such a permission at all, or the meaning of wishing to secure it:—if at present I have no doubt whatever about it, then I am but asking leave to fall into error; if at present I have doubts about it, then I do not believe it at present, that is, I have not faith. But I cannot both really believe it now, and yet look forward to a time when perhaps I shall not believe it; to make provision for future doubt, is to doubt at present. It proves I am not in a fit state to become a Catholic now. I may love by halves, I may obey by halves; I cannot believe by halves: either I have faith, or I have it not.

And so again, when a man has become a Catholic, were he to set about following out a doubt which has occurred to him, he has already disbelieved. *I* have not to warn him against losing his faith, he is not merely in danger of losing it, he has lost it; from the nature of the case he has already lost it; he fell from grace at the moment when he deliberately entertained and pursued his doubt. No one can determine to doubt what he is sure of; but if he is not sure that the Church is from God, he does not believe it. It is not I who forbid him to doubt; he has taken the matter into his own hands when he determined on asking for leave; he has begun, not ended, in unbelief; his very wish, his purpose, is his sin. I do not make it so, it is such from the very state of the case. You sometimes hear, for example, of Catholics falling away, who will tell you it arose from reading the Scriptures, which opened their eyes to the "unscripturalness," so they speak, of the Church of the Living God. No; Scripture did not make them disbelieve (impossible!); they disbelieved *when* they opened the Bible; they opened it in an unbelieving spirit, and for an unbelieving purpose; they would not have opened it, had they not anticipated—I might say, hoped—that they should find things there inconsistent with Catholic teaching. They begin in self·will and disobedience, and they end in apostasy. This, then, is

the direct and obvious reason why the Church cannot allow
her children the liberty of doubting the truth of her word.
He who really believes in it now, cannot imagine the future
discovery of reasons to shake his faith; if he imagines it, he
has not faith; and that so many Protestants think it a sort of
tyranny in the Church to forbid any children of hers to doubt
about her teaching, only shows they do not know what faith
is—which is the case; it is a strange idea to them. Let a man
cease to inquire, or cease to call himself her child.

This is my first remark, and now I go on to a second. You
may easily conceive, my brethren, that they who are entering
the Church, or at least those who have entered it, have more
than faith; that they have some portion of divine love also.
They have heard in the Church of the charity of Him who
died for them, and who has given them His Sacraments as
the means of conveying the merits of His death to their souls,
and they have felt more or less in those poor souls of theirs
the beginnings of a responsive charity drawing them to Him.
Now, does it stand with a loving trust, better than with faith,
for a man to anticipate the possibility of doubting or denying
the great mercies in which he is rejoicing? Take an instance;
what would you think of a friend whom you loved, who could
bargain that, in spite of his present trust in you, he might be
allowed some day to doubt you? who, when a thought came
into his mind, that you were playing a game with him, or
that you were a knave, or a profligate, did not drive it from
him with indignation, or laugh it away for its absurdity, but
considered that he had an evident right to indulge it, nay,
should be wanting in duty to himself, unless he did? Would
you think that your friend trifled with truth, that he was unjust to his reason, that he was wanting in manliness, that he
was hurting his mind, if he shrank from it? or would you not
call him cruel and miserable if he did not? For me, my
brethren, if he took the latter course, may I never be intimate
with so unpleasant a person; suspicious, jealous minds, minds
that keep at a distance from me, that insist on their rights,

fall back on their own centre, are ever fancying offences, and are cold, censorious, wayward, and uncertain, these are often to be borne as a cross; but give me for my friend one who will unite heart and hand with me, who will throw himself into my cause and interest, who will take my part when I am attacked, who will be sure beforehand that I am in the right, and, if he is critical, as he may have cause to be towards a being of sin and imperfection, will be so from very love and loyalty, from anxiety that I should always show to advantage, and a wish that others should love me as heartily as he does. I should not say a friend trusted me, who listened to every idle story against me; and I should like his absence better than his company, if he gravely told me that it was a duty he owed to himself to encourage his misgivings of my honour.

Well, pass on to a higher subject;—could a man be said to trust in God, and to love God, who was familiar with doubts whether there was a God at all, or who bargained that, just as often as he pleased, he might be at liberty to doubt whether God was good, or just or almighty; and who maintained that, unless he did this, he was but a poor slave, that his mind was in bondage, and could render no free acceptable service to his Maker;—that the very worship which God approved was one attended with a *caveat*, on the worshipper's part, that he did not promise to render it to-morrow, that he would not answer for himself that some argument might not come to light, which he had never heard before, which would make it a grave moral duty in him to suspend his judgment and his devotion? Why, I should say, my brethren, that that man was worshipping his own mind, his own dear self, and not God; that his idea of God was a mere accidental form which his thoughts took at this time or that, for a long period or a short one, as the case might be, not an image of the great Eternal Object, but a passing sentiment or imagination which meant nothing at all. I should say, and most men would agree with me, did they choose to give attention to the matter, that the person in question was a very self-conceited, self-wise man, and had neither love, nor faith, nor fear, nor anything supernatural about him; that his pride must be broken, and his heart new-made, before he was capable of any religious act at all. The argument is the same, in its degree, when applied to the Church; she comes to us as a messenger from God,—how can a man who feels this, who comes to her, who falls at her feet as such, make a reserve, that he may be allowed to doubt her at some future day? Let the world cry out, if it will, that his reason is in fetters; let it pronounce that he is a bigot, unless he reserves his right of doubting; but he knows full well himself that he would be an ingrate and a fool, if he did. Fetters, indeed! yes, "the cords of Adam," the fetters of love, these are what bind him to the Holy Church; he is, with the Apostle, the slave of Christ, the Church's Lord; united, (never to part, as he trusts, while life lasts,) to her Sacraments, to her Sacrifices, to her Saints, to the Blessed Mary her advocate, to Jesus, to God.

The truth is, that the world, knowing nothing of the blessings of the Catholic faith, and prophesying nothing but ill concerning it, fancies that a convert, after the first fervour is over, feels nothing but disappointment, weariness, and offence in his new religion, and is secretly desirous of retracing his steps. This is at the root of the alarm and irritation which it manifests at hearing that doubts are incompatible with a Catholic's profession, because it is sure that doubts will come upon him, and then how pitiable will be his state! That there can be peace, and joy, and knowledge, and freedom, and spiritual strength in the Church, is a thought far beyond its imagination; for it regards her simply as a frightful conspiracy against the happiness of man, seducing her victims by specious professions, and, when they are once hers, caring nothing for the misery which breaks upon them, so that by any means she may detain them in bondage. Accordingly, it conceives we are in perpetual warfare with our own reason, fierce objections ever rising within us, and we forcibly repressing them. It believes that, after the likeness of a vessel which has met with some accident at sea, we are ever baling out the water which rushes in upon us, and have hard work to keep afloat; we just manage to linger on, either by an unnatural strain on our minds, or by turning them away from the subject of religion. The world disbelieves our doctrines itself, and cannot understand our own believing them. It considers them so strange, that it is quite sure, though we will not confess it, that we are haunted day and night with doubts, and tormented with the apprehension of yielding to them. I really do think it is the world's judgment, that one principal part of a confessor's work is the putting down such misgivings in his penitents. It fancies that the reason is ever rebelling, like the flesh; that doubt, like concupiscence, is elicited by every sight and sound, and that temptation insinuates itself in every page of letter-press, and through the very voice of a Protestant polemic. When it sees a Catholic Priest, it looks hard at him, to make out how much there is of folly in his composition, and how much of hypocrisy. But, my dear brethren, if these are your thoughts, you are simply in error. Trust me, rather than the world, when I tell you, that it is no difficult thing for a Catholic to believe; and that unless he grievously mismanages himself, the difficult thing is for him to doubt. He has received a gift which makes faith easy; it is not without an effort, a miserable effort, that any one who has received that gift, unlearns to believe. He does violence to his mind, not in exercising, but in withholding his faith. When objections occur to him, which they may easily do if he lives in the world, they are as odious and unwelcome to him as impure thoughts are to the virtuous. He does certainly shrink from them, he flings them away from him, but why? not in the first instance, because they are dangerous, but because they are cruel and base. His loving Lord has done everything for him, and has He deserved such a return? *Popule meus, quid feci tibi?* "O My people, what have I done to thee, or in what have I molested thee? answer thou Me. I brought thee out of the land of Egypt, and delivered thee out of the house of slaves; and I sent before thy face Moses, and Aaron, and Mary; I fenced thee in, and planted thee with the choicest vines; and what is there that I ought to do more to My vineyard that I have not done to it?" He has poured on us His grace, He has been with us in our perplexities, He has led us on from one truth to another, He has forgiven us our sins, He has satisfied our reason, He has made faith easy, He has given us His Saints, He shows before us day by day His own Passion; why should I leave Him? What has He ever done to me but good? Why must I re-examine what I have examined once for all? Why must I listen to every idle word which flits past me against Him, on pain of being called a bigot and a slave, when, if I did, I should be behaving to the Most High, as you yourselves, who so call me, would not behave towards a human friend or benefactor? If I am convinced in my reason, and persuaded in my heart, why may I not be allowed to remain unmolested in my worship?

I have said enough on the subject; still there is a third point of view in which it may be useful to consider it. Personal prudence is not the first or second ground for refusing to hear objections to the Church, but a motive it is, and that from the peculiar nature of divine faith, which cannot be treated as an ordinary conviction or belief. Faith is the gift of God, and not a mere act of our own, which we are free to exert when we will. It is quite distinct from an exercise of reason, though it follows upon it. I may feel the force of the argument for the divine origin of the Church; I may see that I ought to believe; and yet I may be unable to believe. This is no imaginary case; there is many a man who has ground enough to believe, who wishes to believe, but who cannot believe. It is always indeed his own fault, for God gives grace to all who ask for it, and use it, but still such is the fact, that conviction is not faith. Take the parallel case of obedience; many a man knows he ought to obey God, and does not and cannot,—through his own fault indeed, but still he cannot; for through grace alone can he obey. Now, faith is

not a mere conviction in reason, it is a firm assent, it is a clear
certainty greater than any other certainty; and this is wrought
in the mind by the grace of God, and by it alone. As then
men may be convinced, and not act according to their conviction, so may they be convinced, and not believe according
to their conviction. They may confess that the argument is
against them, that they have nothing to say for themselves,
and that to believe is to be happy; and yet, after all, they
avow they cannot believe, they do not know why, but they
cannot; they acquiesce in unbelief, and they turn away from
God and His Church. Their reason is convinced, and their
doubts are moral ones, arising in their root from a fault of
the will. In a word, the arguments for religion do not compel
any one to believe, just as arguments for good conduct do not
compel any one to obey. Obedience is the consequence of
willing to obey, and faith is the consequence of willing to
believe; we may see what is right, whether in matters of faith
or obedience, of ourselves, but we cannot will what is right
without the grace of God. Here is the difference between other
exercises of reason, and arguments for the truth of religion.
It requires no act of faith to assent to the truth that two
and two make four; we cannot help assenting to it; and hence
there is no merit in assenting to it; but there is merit in believing that the Church is from God; for though there are
abundant reasons to prove it to us, yet we can, without an
absurdity, quarrel with the conclusion; we may complain that
it is not clearer, we may suspend our assent, we may doubt
about it, if we will, and grace alone can turn a bad will into
a good one.

And now you see why a Catholic dare not in prudence attend to such objections as are brought against his faith; he has
no fear of their proving that the Church does not come from
God, but he is afraid, if he listened to them without reason,
lest God should punish him by the loss of his supernatural
faith. This is one cause of that miserable state of mind, to
which I have already alluded, in which men would fain be

Catholics, and are not. They have trifled with conviction, they have listened to arguments against what they knew to be true, and a deadness of mind has fallen on them; faith has failed them, and, as time goes on, they betray in their words and their actions, the Divine judgment, with which they are visited. They become careless and unconcerned, or restless and unhappy, or impatient of contradiction; ever asking advice and quarrelling with it when given; not attempting to answer the arguments urged against them, but simply not believing. This is the whole of their case, they do not believe. And then it is quite an accident what becomes of them; perhaps they continue on in this perplexed and comfortless state, lingering about the Church, yet not of her; not knowing what they believe and what they do not, like blind men, or men deranged, who are deprived of the eye, whether of body or mind, and cannot guide themselves in consequence; ever exciting hopes of a return, and ever disappointing them;—or, if they are men of more vigorous minds, they launch forward in a course of infidelity, not really believing less, as they proceed, for from the first they believed nothing, but taking up, as time goes on, more and more consistent forms of error, till sometimes, if a free field is given them, they even develope into atheism. Such is the end of those who, under the pretence of inquiring after truth, trifle with conviction.

Here then are some of the reasons why the Catholic Church cannot consistently allow her children to doubt the divinity and the truth of her words. Mere investigation indeed into the grounds of our faith is not to doubt; nor is it doubting to consider the arguments urged against it, when there is good reason for doing so; but I am speaking of a real doubt, or a wanton entertainment of objections. Such a procedure the Church denounces, and not only for the reasons which I have assigned, but because it would be a plain abandonment of her office and character to act otherwise. How can she, who has the prerogative of infallibility, allow her children to doubt of her gift? It would be a simple inconsistency in her, who is the sure oracle of truth and messenger of heaven, to look with indifference on rebels to her authority. She simply does what the Apostles did before her, whom she has succeeded. "He that despiseth," says St. Paul, "despiseth not man, but God, who hath also given in us His Holy Spirit." And St. John, "We are of God; he that knoweth God, heareth us; he that is not of God, heareth us not; by this we know the spirit of truth and the spirit of error." Take, again, an instance from the Old Testament:—When Elias was taken up into heaven, Eliseus was the only witness of the miracle; on his coming back then to the sons of the Prophet, they doubted what had become of his master, and wished to search for him; and, though they acknowledged Eliseus as his successor, they in this instance refused to take his word on the subject. Eliseus had struck the waters of Jordan, they had divided, and he had passed over; here, surely, was ground enough for faith, and accordingly "the sons of the Prophets at Jericho, who were over against him, seeing it, said, The spirit of Elias hath rested upon Eliseus; and they came to meet him, and worshipped him, falling to the ground." What could they require more? they confessed that Eliseus had the spirit of his great master, and, in confessing it, they implied that that master was taken away; yet, they proceed, from infirmity of mind, to make a request indicative of doubt; "Behold, there are with thy servants fifty strong men, that can go and search for thy master, lest perhaps the Spirit of the Lord hath taken him up, and cast him upon some mountain or into some valley." Now here was a request to follow up a doubt into an inquiry; did Eliseus allow it? he knew perfectly well that the inquiry would but end, as it really did end, in confirmation of the truth, but it was indulging a wrong spirit to engage in it, and he would not allow it. These religious men were, as he would feel, strangely inconsistent: they were doubting his word whom they had just now worshipped as a Prophet, and, not only so, but they were doubting his supreme authority, for they implied that Elias was still among them. Accordingly he forbade their request; "He said, Send not." This is what the world would call stifling an inquiry; it was, forsooth, tyrannical and oppressive to oblige them to take on his word what they might ascertain for themselves; yet he could not do otherwise without being unfaithful to his divine mission, and sanctioning them in a fault. It is true when "they pressed him, he consented, and said, Send;" but we must not suppose this to be more than a condescension to their weakness, or a concession in displeasure, like that which Almighty God gave to Balaam, who pressed his request in a similar way. When Balaam asked to go with the ancients of Moab, God said, "Thou shalt not go with them;" when Balaam asked Him "once more," "God said to him, Arise and go with them;" then it is added, "Balaam went with them, and God was angry." Here in like manner, the prophet said, Send; "and they sent fifty men, and they sought three days, but found him not;" yet though the inquiry did but prove that Elias was removed, Eliseus showed no satisfaction at it, even when it had confirmed his authority: but "he said to them, Said I not to you, Send not?" It is thus that the Church ever forbids inquiry in those who already acknowledge her authority; but if they will inquire, she cannot hinder it; but they are not justified in doing so.

And now I think you see, my brethren, why inquiry precedes faith, and does not follow it. You inquired before you joined the Church; you were satisfied, and God rewarded you with the grace of faith; were you now determined to inquire further, you would lead us to think you had lost it again, for inquiry and faith are in their very nature incompatible. I will add, what is very evident, that no other religious body has a right to demand such an exercise of faith in them, and a right to forbid you further inquiry, but the Catholic Church; and for this simple reason, that no other body even claims to be infallible, let alone the proof of such a claim. Here is the defect at first starting, which disqualifies them, one and all, from ever competing with the Church of God. The sects about us, so far from demanding your faith, actually call on you to inquire and to doubt freely about their own merits; they protest that they are but voluntary associations, and would be sorry to be taken for anything else; they beg and pray you not to mistake their preachers for anything more than mere sinful men, and they invite you to take the Bible with you to their sermons, and to judge for yourselves whether their doctrine is in accordance with it. Then, as to the Established Religion, grant that there are those in it who forbid inquiry into its claims; yet still, dare they maintain that it is infallible? If they do not, (and no one does,) how can they forbid inquiry about it, or claim for it the absolute faith of any of its members? Faith under these circumstances is not really faith, but obstinacy. Nor do they commonly venture to demand it; they will say, negatively, "Do not inquire;" but they cannot say positively, "Have faith;" for in whom are their members to have faith? of whom can they say, whether individual or collection of men, "He or they are gifted with infallibility, and cannot mislead us"? Therefore, when pressed to explain themselves, they ground their duty of continuance in their communion, not on faith in it, but on attachment to it, which is a very different thing; utterly different, for there are very many reasons why they should feel a very great liking for the religion in which they have been brought up. Its portions of Catholic teaching, its "decency and order," the pure and beautiful English of its prayers, its literature, the piety found among its members, the influence of superiors and friends, its historical associations, its domestic character, the charm of a country life, the remembrance of past years,—there is all this and much more to attach the mind to the national worship. But attachment is not trust, nor is to obey the same as to look up to, and to rely upon; nor do I think that any thoughtful or educated man can simply believe or confide in the *word* of the Established Church. I never met any such person who did, or said he did, and I do not think that such a person is possible. Its defenders would believe if they could; but their highest confidence is qualified by a misgiving. They obey, they are silent before the voice of their superiors, but they do not profess to believe. Nothing is clearer than this, that if faith in God's word is required of us for salvation, the Catholic Church is the only medium by which we can exercise it.

And now, my brethren, who are not Catholics, perhaps you will tell me, that, if all inquiry is to cease when you become Catholics, you ought to be very sure that the Church is from God before you join it. You speak truly; no one should enter the Church without a firm purpose of taking her word in all matters of doctrine and morals, and that, on the ground of her coming directly from the God of Truth. You must look the matter in the face, and count the cost. If you do not come in this spirit, you may as well not come at all; high and low, learned and ignorant, must come to learn. If you are right as far as this, you cannot go very wrong; you have the foundation; but, if you come in any other temper, you had better wait till you have got rid of it. You must come, I say, to the Church to learn; you must come, not to bring your own notions to her, but with the intention of ever being a learner; you must come with the intention of taking her for your portion and of never leaving her. Do not come as an experiment; do not come as you would take sittings in a chapel, or tickets for a lecture-room; come to her as to your home, to the school of your souls, to the Mother of Saints, and to the vestibule of heaven. On the other hand do not distress yourselves with thoughts whether, when you have joined her, your faith will last; this is a suggestion of your enemy to hold you back. He who has begun a good work in you, will perfect it; He who has chosen you, will be faithful to you; put your cause into His hand, wait upon Him, and you will surely persevere. What good work will you ever begin, if you bargain first to see the end of it? If you wish to do all at once, you will do nothing; he has done half the work, who has begun it well; you will not gain your Lord's praise at the final reckoning by hiding His talent. No; when He brings you from error to truth, He will have done the more difficult work (if aught is difficult to Him), and surely He will preserve you from returning from truth to error. Take the experience of those who have gone before you in the same course; they had many fears that their faith would fail them, before taking the great step, but those fears vanished on their taking it; they had fears, before the grace of faith, lest, after receiving it, they should lose it again, but no fears (except on the ground of their general frailness) after it was actually given.

Be convinced in your reason that the Catholic Church is a teacher sent to you from God, and it is enough. I do not wish you to join her, till you are. If you are half convinced, pray for a full conviction, and wait till you have it. It is better indeed to come quickly, but better slowly than carelessly; and sometimes, as the proverb goes, the more haste, the worse speed. Only make yourselves sure that the delay is not from any fault of yours, which you can remedy. God deals with us very differently; conviction comes slowly to some men, quickly to others; in some it is the result of much thought and many reasonings, in others of a sudden illumination. One man is convinced at once, as in the instance described by St. Paul: "If all prophesy," he says, speaking of exposition of doctrine, "and there come in one that believeth not, or one unlearned, he is convinced of all, he is judged of all. The secrets of his heart are made manifest; and so, falling down on his face, he will worship God, and say that God is among you of a truth." The case is the same now; some men are converted merely by entering a Catholic Church; others are converted by reading one book; others by one doctrine. They feel the weight of their sins, and they see that that religion must come from God which alone has the means of forgiving them. Or they are touched and overcome by the evident sanctity, beauty, and (as I may say) fragrance of the Catholic Religion. Or they long for a guide amid the strife of tongues; and the very doctrine of the Church about faith, which is so hard to many, is conviction to them. Others, again, hear many objections to the Church, and follow out the whole subject far and wide;

conviction can scarcely come to them except as at the end of a long inquiry. As in a court of justice, one man's innocence may be proved at once, another's is the result of a careful investigation; one has nothing in his conduct or character to explain, another has many presumptions against him at first sight; so Holy Church presents herself very differently to different minds who are contemplating her from without. God deals with them differently; but, if they are faithful to their light, at last, in their own time, though it may be a different time to each, He brings them to that one and the same state of mind, very definite and not to be mistaken, which we call *conviction*. They will have no doubt, whatever difficulties may still attach to the subject, that the Church is from God; they may not be able to answer this objection or that, but they will be certain in spite of it.

This is a point which should ever be kept in view: conviction is a state of mind, and it is something beyond and distinct from the mere arguments of which it is the result; it does not vary with their strength or their number. Arguments lead to a conclusion, and when the arguments are stronger, the conclusion is clearer; but conviction may be felt as strongly in consequence of a clear conclusion, as of one which is clearer. A man may be so sure upon six reasons, that he does not need a seventh, nor would feel surer if he had it. And so as regards the Catholic Church: men are convinced in very various ways,—what convinces one, does not convince another; but this is an accident; the time comes anyhow, sooner or later, when a man ought to be convinced, and is convinced, and then he is bound not to wait for any more arguments, though more arguments be producible. He will find himself in a condition when he may even refuse to hear more arguments in behalf of the Church; he does not wish to read or think more on the subject, his mind is quite made up. In such a case it is his duty to join the Church at once; he must not delay; let him be cautious in counsel, but prompt in execution. This it is that makes Catholics so anxious about him: it is not that they wish him to be precipitate; but knowing the temptations which the evil one ever throws in our way, they are lovingly anxious for his soul, lest he has come to the point of conviction, and is passing it, and is losing his chance of conversion. If so, it may never return; God has not chosen every one to salvation: it is a rare gift to be a Catholic; it may be offered to us once in our lives and never again; and, if we have not seized on the "accepted time," nor known "in our day the things which are for our peace," oh, the misery for us! What shall we be able to say when death comes, and we are not converted, and it is directly and immediately our own doing that we are not?

"Wisdom preacheth abroad, she uttereth her voice in the streets: How long, ye little ones, love ye childishness, and fools covet what is hurtful to them, and the unwise hate knowledge? Turn ye at My reproof; behold, I will bring forth to you My Spirit, and I will show My words unto you. Because I have called, and ye refused, I stretched out My hand, and there was none who regarded, and ye despised all My counsel and neglected My chidings; I also will laugh in your destruction, and will mock when that shall come to you which you feared; when a sudden storm shall rush on you, and destruction shall thicken as a tempest, when tribulation and straitness shall come upon you. Then shall they call on Me, and I will not hear; they shall rise betimes, but they shall not find Me; for that they hated discipline, and took not on them the fear of the Lord, nor acquiesced in My counsel, but made light of My reproof, therefore shall they eat the fruit of their own way, and be filled with their own devices."

Oh, the misery for us, as many of us as shall be in that number! Oh, the awful thought for all eternity! Oh, the remorseful sting, "I was called, I might have answered, and I did not!" And oh, the blessedness, if we can look back on the time of trial, when friends implored and enemies scoffed, and say,—The misery for me, which would have been, had I not followed on, had I hung back, when Christ called! Oh, the utter confusion of mind, the wreck of faith and opinion, the blackness and void, the dreary scepticism, the hopelessness, which would have been my lot, the pledge of the outer darkness to come, had I been afraid to follow Him! I have lost friends, I have lost the world, but I have gained Him, who gives in Himself houses and brethren and sisters and mothers and children and lands a hundred-fold; I have lost the perishable, and gained the Infinite; I have lost time, and I have gained eternity; "O Lord, my God, I am Thy servant, and the son of Thine handmaid; Thou hast broken my bonds. I will sacrifice to Thee the sacrifice of praise, and I will call on the Name of the Lord."

XVI

THE INFINITUDE OF THE DIVINE
ATTRIBUTES [1]

WE ALL KNOW WELL, and firmly hold, that our Lord Jesus Christ, the Son of God, died on the Cross in satisfaction for our sins. This truth is the great foundation of all our hopes, and the object of our most earnest faith and most loving worship. And yet, however well we know it, it is a subject which admits of drawing out, and insisting on in detail, in a way which most persons will feel profitable to themselves. I shall now attempt to do this in some measure, and to follow the reflections to which it leads; though at this season [2] many words would be out of place.

Christ died for our sins, for the sins of the whole world; but He need not have died, for the Almighty God might have saved us all, might have saved the whole world, without His dying. He might have pardoned and brought to heaven every individual child of Adam without the incarnation and death of His Son. He might have saved us without any ransom and without any delay. He might have abolished original sin, and restored Adam at once. His word had been enough; with Him to say is to do. "All things art possible to Thee," was the very reason our Lord gave in His agony for asking that the chalice might pass from Him. As in the beginning He said, "Let light be made, and it was made;" so might He have spoken again,

---

[1] From *Discourses to Mixed Congregations* (1849), No. 15. [Ed.]
[2] Passion-tide.

and sin would have vanished from the soul, and guilt with
it. Or He might have employed a mediator less powerful than
His own Son; He might have accepted the imperfect satisfaction of some mere man. He wants not for resources; but He
willed otherwise. He who ever does the best, saw in His infinite wisdom that it was expedient and fitting to take a ransom. As He has not hindered the reprobate from resisting His
grace and rejecting redemption, so He has not pardoned any
who are to enter His eternal kingdom without a true and sufficient satisfaction for their sin. Both in the one case and the
other, He has done, not what was possible merely, but what
was best. And this is why the coming of the Word was necessary; for if a true satisfaction was to be made, then nothing
could accomplish this short of the incarnation of the All-holy.

You see, then, my brethren, how voluntary was the mission
and death of our Lord; if an instance can be imagined of
voluntary suffering, it is this. He came to die when He need
not have died; He died to satisfy for what might have been
pardoned without satisfaction; He paid a price which need
not have been asked, nay, which needed to be accepted [3]
when paid. It may be said with truth, that, rigorously speaking, one being can never, by his own suffering, simply dis-
charge the debt of another's sin.[4] Accordingly, He died, not

[3] Dicendum videtur satisfactionem Christi, licet fuerit rigorosa quoad
æqualitatem et condignitatem pretii soluti, non tamen fuisse rigorosam
quoad modum solutionis, sed indiguisse aliquâ *gratiâ liberâ* Dei. . . . Si
aliquis ita peccavit, ut justè puniatur exilio unius mensis, et velit redimere
pecuniâ illud exilium, offeratque summam æquivalentem, immo exceden-
tem, non dubium quin satisfiat rigori justitiæ vindicativæ, si attendas ad
mensuram pœnæ; non tamen satisfit, si attendas ad modum; si enim judex
gratiosè non admittat illam compensationem, *jus habet* ex rigore justitiæ
punitivæ ad exigendum exilium, quantumvis alia æqualis et longè major
pœna offeratur.—*De Lug. Incarn.* iii. 10.

[4] Qui redemit captivum solvendo pretium, solvit quantum domino
debetur ex justitiâ, solum enim debetur illi pretium ex contractu et con-
ventione inter ipsum et redemptorem. . . . Nullum est justitiæ debitum
cui non satisfiat per solutionem illius pretii. At vero pro *injuriâ* non solum

in order to exert a peremptory claim on the divine justice, if I may so speak,—as if He were bargaining in the market-place, or pursuing a plea in a court of law;—but in a more loving, generous, munificent way, did He shed that blood, which was worth ten thousand lives of men, worth more than the blood of all the sons of Adam poured out together, in accordance with His Father's will, who, for wise reasons unrevealed, exacted it as the condition of their pardon.

Nor was this all;—one drop of His blood had been sufficient to satisfy for our sins; He might have offered His circumcision as an atonement, and it would have been sufficient; one moment of His agony of blood had been sufficient, one stroke of the scourge might have wrought a sufficient satisfaction. But neither circumcision, agony, nor scourging was our redemption, because He did not offer them as such. The price He paid was nothing short of the whole treasure of His blood, poured forth to the last drop from His veins and sacred heart. He shed His whole life for us; He left Himself empty of His all. He left His throne on high; He gave up His home on earth; He parted with His Mother, He gave His strength and His toil, He gave His body and soul, He offered up His passion, His crucifixion, and His death, that man should not be bought for nothing. This is what the Apostle intimates in saying that we are "bought with a *great* price"; and the Prophet, while he declares that "with the Lord there is mercy, and with Him a *copious*" or "plenteous redemption."

This is what I wished to draw out distinctly, my brethren, for your devout meditation. We might have been pardoned without the humiliation of the Eternal Word; again, we might have been redeemed by one single drop of His blood; but still on earth He came, and a death He died, a death of inconceivable suffering; and all this He did as a free offering to

---

debetur ex justitiâ satisfactio utcunque, sed *exhibenda ab ipso offensore* ... sicut nec qui abstulit librum, satisfacit adæquatè reddendo pretium æquivalens.—*Ibid.* iv. 2.

His Father, not as forcing His acceptance of it. From beginning to the end it was in the highest sense a voluntary work; and this is what is so overpowering to the mind in the thought of it. It is as if He delighted in having to suffer; as if He wished to show all creatures, what would otherwise have seemed impossible, that the Creator could practise, in the midst of His heavenly blessedness, the virtues of a creature, self-abasement and humility. It is, as if He wished, all-glorious as He was from all eternity, as a sort of addition (if we may so speak) to His perfections, to submit to a creature's condition in its most afflictive form. It is, if we may use human language, a prodigality of charity, or that heroic love of toil and hardship, which is poorly shadowed out in the romantic defenders of the innocent or the oppressed, whom we read of in history or in fable, who have gone about the earth, nobly exposing themselves to peril for any who asked their aid.

Or rather, and that is what I wish to insist upon, it suggests to us, as by a specimen, the infinitude of God. We all confess that He is infinite; He has an infinite number of perfections, and He is infinite in each of them. This we shall confess at once; but, we ask, what is infinity? what is meant by saying He is infinite? We seem to wish to be told, as if we had nothing given us to throw light on the question. Why, my brethren, we have much given us; the outward exhibition of infinitude is mystery; and the mysteries of nature and of grace are nothing else than the mode in which His infinitude encounters us and is brought home to our minds. Men confess that He is infinite, yet they start and object, as soon as His infinitude comes in contact with their imagination and acts upon their reason. They cannot bear the fulness, the superabundance, the inexhaustible flowing forth, and "vehement rushing," [5] and encompassing flood of the divine attributes. They restrain and limit them to their own comprehension, they measure them by their own standard, they fashion them by

[5] Tanquam advenientis spiritûs vehementis.

their own model; and when they discern aught of the unfathomable depth, the immensity, of any single excellence or
perfection of the Divine Nature, His love, or His justice, or
His power, they are at once offended, and turn away, and refuse to believe.

Now, this instance of our Lord's humiliation is a case in
point. What would be profusion and extravagance in man, is
but suitable or necessary, if I may say so, in Him whose resources are illimitable. We read in history accounts of oriental
munificence, which sound like fiction, and which would gain,
not applause but contempt in Europe, where wealth is not
concentrated, as in the east, upon a few out of a whole people.
"Royal munificence" has become a proverb, from the idea that
a king's treasures are such, as to make the giving of large
presents and bounties, not allowable only, but appropriate
in him. He, then, who is infinite, may be only doing what is
best, and holiest, and wisest, in doing what to man seems infinitely to exceed the necessity; for He cannot exceed His own
powers or resources. Man has limited means and definite
duties; it would be waste in him to lavish a thousand pieces
of gold on one poor man, when with the same he might have
done substantial good to many; but God is as rich, as profound and vast, as infinite, after He has done a work of infinite
bounty, as before He set about it. "Knowest thou not," He
says, "or hast thou not heard? the Everlasting God, the Lord,
who has created the ends of the earth, shall not faint, nor
weary; nor is there searching of His wisdom." He cannot do a
small work; He cannot act by halves; He ever does whole
works, great works. Had Christ been incarnate for one single
soul, who ought to have been surprised? who ought not to
have praised and blessed Him for telling us in one instance,
and by a specimen, what that love and bounty are, which fill
the heavens? and in like manner, when in fact He has taken
flesh for those, who might have been saved without it, though
more suitably to His glorious majesty with it, and moreover
has shed His whole blood in satisfaction, when a drop might

have sufficed, shall we think such teaching strange and hard to receive, and not rather consider it consistent, and merely consistent, with that great truth, which we all start with admitting, that He is infinite? Surely it would be most irrational in us, to admit His infinitude in the general, and to reject the examples of it in particular; to maintain that He is mystery, yet to deny that His acts can be mysterious.

We must not, then, bring in our economical theories, borrowed from the schools of the day, when we would reason about the Eternal God. The world is ever doing so, when it speaks of religion. It will not allow the miracles of the Saints, because it pretends that those wrought by the Apostles were sufficient for the purpose which miracles had, or ought forsooth to have, in view. I wonder how the world comes to admit that such multitudes of human beings are born and die in infancy; or that a profusion of seeds is cast over the face of the earth, some of which fall by the way-side, some on the rock, some among thorns, and only a remnant on the good ground. How wasteful was that sower! so thinks the world, but an Apostle cries out, "Oh, the depth of the riches of the wisdom and of the knowledge of God! how incomprehensible are His judgments, and how unsearchable His ways!"

The world judges of God's condescension as it judges of His bounty. We know from Scripture that "the teaching of the Cross" was in the beginning "foolishness" to it; grave thinking men scoffed at it as impossible, that God, who is so high, should humble Himself so low, and that One who died a malefactor's death should be worshipped on the very instrument of His punishment. Voluntary humiliation they did not understand then, nor do they now. They do not indeed express their repugnance to the doctrine so openly now, because what is called public opinion does not allow them; but you see what they really think of Christ, by the tone which they adopt towards those who in their measure follow Him. Those who are partakers of His fulness, are called on, according as the gift is given them, whether by His ordinary suggestions or by particular inspiration, to imitate His pattern; they are carried on to the sacrifice of self, and thus they come into collision with the maxims of the world. A voluntary or gratuitous mortification in one shape or another, voluntary chastity, voluntary poverty, voluntary obedience, vows of perfection, all this is the very point of contest between the world and the Church, the world hating it, and the Church counselling it. "Why cannot they stop with me?" says the world; "why will they give up their station or position, when it is certain they might be saved where they are? Here is a lady of birth; she might be useful at home, she might marry well, she might be an ornament to society, she might give her countenance to religious objects, and she has perversely left us all; she has cut off her hair, and put on a coarse garment, and is washing the feet of the poor. There is a man of name and ability, who has thrown himself out of his sphere of influence, and he lives in a small room, in a place where no one knows who he is; and he is teaching little children their catechism." The world is touched with pity, and shame, and indignation at the sight, and moralizes over persons who act so unworthily of their birth or education, and are so cruel towards themselves. And worse still, "here is a Saint, and what must he do but practise eccentricities?"—as they really would be in others, though in him they are but the necessary antagonists to the temptations which otherwise would come on him from "the greatness of the revelations," or are but tokens of the love with which he embraces the feet of his Redeemer. And "here again is another, and she submits her flesh to penances shocking to think of, and wearies herself out in the search after misery, and all from some notion that she is assimilating her condition to the voluntary self-abasement of the Word." Alas, for the world! which is simply forgetful that God is great in all He does, great in His sufferings, and that He makes Saints and holy men in their degree partakers of that greatness.

Here, too, is another instance in point. If there is one divine attribute rather than another, which forces itself upon the mind from the contemplation of the material world, it is the glory, harmony, and beauty of its Creator. This lies on the surface of the creation, like light on a countenance, and addresses itself to all. To few men indeed is it given to penetrate into the world's system and order so deeply, as to perceive, in addition, the wonderful skill and goodness of the Divine Artificer; but the grace and loveliness which beam from the very face of the visible creation are cognizable by all, rich and poor, learned and ignorant. It is indeed so beautiful, that those same philosophers, who devote themselves to its investigation, come to love it idolatrously, and to think it too perfect for them to allow of its infringement or alteration, or to tolerate even that idea. Not looking up to the Infinite Creator, who could make a thousand fairer worlds, and who has made the fairest portion of this the most perishable,—blooming, as it does, to-day, and to-morrow burning in the oven,—loving, I say, the creature more than the Creator, they have taken on them in all ages to disbelieve the possibility of interruptions of physical order, and have denied the miracles of Revelation. They have denied the miracles of Apostles and Prophets, on the ground of their marring and spoiling what is so perfect and harmonious, as if the visible world were some work of human art, too exquisite to be wantonly dashed on the ground. But He, my brethren, the Eternal Maker of time and space, of matter and sense, as if to pour contempt upon the forward and minute speculations of His ignorant creatures about His works and His will, in order to a fuller and richer harmony, and a higher and nobler order, confuses the laws of this physical universe and untunes the music of the spheres. Nay, He has done more, He has gone farther still; out of the infinitude of His greatness, He has defaced His own glory, and wounded and deformed His own beauty,—not indeed as it is in itself, for He is ever the same, transcendently perfect and unchangeable, but in the contemplation of His creatures,—by the unutterable condescension of His incarnation.

Semetipsum exinanivit, "He made Himself void or empty,"

as the earth had been "void and empty" at the beginning; He seemed to be unbinding and letting loose the assemblage of attributes which made Him God, and to be destroying the idea which He Himself had implanted in our minds. The God of miracles did the most awful of signs and wonders, by revoking and contradicting, as it were, all His perfections, though He remained the while one and the same. Omnipotence became an abject; the Life became a leper; the first and only Fair came down to us with an "inglorious visage," and an "unsightly form," bleeding and (I may say) ghastly, lifted up in nakedness and stretched out in dislocation before the eyes of sinners. Not content with this, He perpetuates the history of His humiliation; men of this world, when they fall into trouble, and then recover themselves, hide the memorials of it. They conceal their misfortunes in prospect, as long as they can; bear them perforce, when they fall into them; and, when they have overcome them, affect to make light of them. Kings of the earth, when they have rid themselves of their temporary conquerors, and are reinstated on their thrones, put all things back into their former state, and remove from their palaces, council-rooms, and cities, whether statue or picture or inscription or edict, all which bears witness to the suspension of their power. Soldiers indeed boast of their scars, but it is because their foes were well-matched with them, and their conflicts were necessary, and the marks of what they have suffered is a proof of what they have done; but He, who *oblatus est, quia voluit*, who "was offered, for He willed it," who exposed Himself to the powers of evil, yet could have saved us without that exposure, who was neither weak in that He was overcome, nor strong in that He overcame, proclaims to the whole world what He has gone through, without the tyrant's shame, without the soldier's pride;—He (wonderful it is) has raised up on high, He has planted over the earth, the memorial, that that Evil One whom He cast out of heaven in the beginning, has in the hour of darkness inflicted agony upon Him. For in truth, by consequence of the infinitude of

His glory, He is more beautiful in His weakness than in His strength; His wounds shine like stars of light; His very Cross becomes an object of worship; the instruments of His passion, the nails and the thorny crown, are replete with miraculous power. And so He bids the commemoration of His Bloody Sacrifice to be made day by day all over the earth, and He Himself is there in Person to quicken and sanctify it; He rears His bitter but saving Cross in every Church and over every Altar; He shows Himself torn and bleeding upon the wood at the corners of each street and in every village market-place; He makes it the symbol of His religion; He seals our foreheads, our lips, and our breast with this triumphant sign; with it He begins and ends our days, and with it He consigns us to the tomb. And when He comes again, that Sign of the Son of Man will be seen in heaven; and when He takes His seat in judgment, the same glorious marks will be seen by all the world in His hands, Feet, and Side, which were dug into them at the season of His degradation. Thus "hath King Solomon made Himself a litter of the wood of Libanus. The pillars thereof He made of silver, the seat of gold, the going up of purple; the midst He covered with charity for the daughters of Jerusalem. Go forth, ye daughters of Sion; and see King Solomon in the diadem, wherewith His mother crowned Him in the day of His espousals, and in the day of His heart's joy."

I must not conclude this train of thought, without alluding to a sterner subject, on which it seems to throw some light. There is a class of doctrines which to the natural man are an especial offense and difficulty; I mean those connected with the divine judgments. Why has the Almighty assigned an endless punishment to the impenitent sinner? Why is it that vengeance has its hold on him when he passes out of this life, and there is no remedy? Why, again, is it that even the beloved children of God, that holy souls who leave this life in His grace and in His favour, are not at once admitted to His face; but, if there be an outstanding debt against them, first enter purgatory and exhaust it? Men of the world shrink from a doctrine like this as impossible, and religious men answer that it is a mystery; and a mystery it is,—that is, it is but another of those instances which Nature and Revelation bring before us of the Divine Infinitude; it is but one of the many overpowering manifestations of the Almighty, when He acts, which remind us, which are intended to remind us, that He is infinite, and above and beyond human measure and understanding,—which lead us to bow the head and adore Him, as Moses did, when He passed by, and with him awfully to proclaim His Name, as "the Lord God, who hath dominion, keeping mercy for thousands, and returning the iniquity of the fathers upon the children and children's children to the third and fourth generation."

Thus the attributes of God, though intelligible to us on their surface,—for from our own sense of mercy and holiness and patience and consistency, we have general notions of the All-merciful and All-holy and All-patient, and of all that is proper to His Essence,—yet, for the very reason that they are infinite, transcend our comprehension, when they are dwelt upon, when they are followed out, and can only be received by faith. They are dimly shadowed out, in this very respect, by the great agents which He has created in the material world. What is so ordinary and familiar to us as the elements, what so simple and level to us, as their presence and operation? yet how their character changes, and how they overmaster us, and triumph over us, when they come upon us in their fulness! The invisible air, how gentle is it, and intimately ours! we breathe it momentarily, nor could we live without it; it fans our cheek, and flows around us, and we move through it without effort, while it obediently recedes at every step we take, and obsequiously pursues us as we go forward. Yet let it come in its power, and that same silent fluid, which was just now the servant of our necessity or caprice, takes us up on its wing with the invisible power of an Angel, and carries us forth into the regions of space, and flings us down headlong upon the earth. Or go to the spring, and draw thence at your pleasure, for your cup or your pitcher, in supply of your wants; you have a ready servant, a domestic ever at hand, in large quantity or in small, to satisfy your thirst, or to purify you from the dust and mire of the world. But go from home, reach the coast: and you will see that same humble element transformed before your eyes. You were equal to it in its condescension, but who shall gaze without astonishment at its vast expanse in the bosom of the ocean? who shall hear without awe the dashing of its mighty billows along the beach? who shall without terror feel it heaving under him, and swelling and mounting up, and yawning wide, till he, its very sport and mockery, is thrown to and fro, hither and thither, at the mere mercy of a power which was just now his companion and almost his slave? Or, again, approach the flame: it warms you, and it enlightens you; yet approach not too near, presume not, or it will change its nature. That very element which is so beautiful to look at, so brilliant in its light, so graceful in its figure, so soft and lambent in its motion, will be found in its essence to be of a keen resistless kind; it tortures, it consumes, it reduces to ashes that, of which it was just before the illumination and the life. So is it with the attributes of God; our knowledge of them serves us for our daily welfare; they give us light and warmth and food and guidance and succour; but go forth with Moses upon the mount and let the Lord pass by, or with Elias stand in the desert amid the wind, the earthquake, and the fire, and all is mystery and darkness; all is but a whirling of the reason, and a dazzling of the imagination, and an overwhelming of the feelings, reminding us that we are but mortal men and He is God, and that the outlines which Nature draws for us are not His perfect image, nor to be pronounced inconsistent with those further lights and depths with which it is invested by Revelation.

Say not, my brethren, that these thoughts are too austere for this season, when we contemplate the self-sacrificing, self-consuming charity wherewith God our Saviour has visited us. It is for that very reason that I dwell on them; the higher He is, and the more mysterious, so much the more glorious and the more subduing is the history of His humiliation. I own it, my brethren, I love to dwell on Him as the Only-begotten Word; nor is it any forgetfulness of His sacred humanity to contemplate His Eternal Person. It is the very idea, that He is God, which gives a meaning to His sufferings; what is to me a man, and nothing more, in agony, or scourged, or crucified? There are many holy martyrs, and their torments were terrible. But here I see One dropping blood, gashed by the thong, and stretched upon the Cross, and He is God. It is no tale of human woe which I am reading here; it is the record of the passion of the great Creator. The Word and Wisdom of the Father, who dwelt in His bosom in bliss ineffable from all eternity, whose very smile has shed radiance and grace over the whole creation, whose traces I see in the starry heavens and on the green earth, this glorious living God, it is He who looks at me so piteously, so tenderly from the Cross. He seems to say,—I cannot move, though I am omnipotent, for sin has bound Me here. I had had it in mind to come on earth among innocent creatures, more fair and lovely than them all, with a face more radiant than the Seraphim, and a form as royal as that of Archangels, to be their equal yet their God, to fill them with My grace, to receive their worship, to enjoy their company, and to prepare them for the heaven to which I destined them; but, before I carried My purpose into effect, they sinned, and lost their inheritance, and so I come indeed, but come, not in that brightness in which I went forth to create the morning stars and to fill the sons of God with melody, but in deformity and in shame, in sighs and tears, with blood upon My cheek, and with My limbs laid bare and rent. Gaze on Me, O My Children, if you will, for I am helpless; gaze on your Maker, whether in contempt, or in faith and love. Here I wait, upon the Cross, the appointed time, the time of grace and mercy; here I wait till the end of the world, silent and motionless, for the conversion of the sinful and the consolation of the just; here I remain in weakness and shame, though

I am so great in heaven, till the end, patiently expecting My full catalogue of souls, who, when time is at length over, shall be the reward of My passion and the triumph of My grace to all eternity.

XVII

MENTAL SUFFERINGS OF OUR LORD IN HIS PASSION [1]

EVERY PASSAGE IN THE HISTORY of our Lord and Saviour is of unfathomable depth, and affords inexhaustible matter of contemplation. All that concerns Him is infinite, and what we first discern is but the surface of that which begins and ends in eternity. It would be presumptuous for any one short of Saints and Doctors to attempt to comment on His words and deeds, except in the way of meditation; but meditation and mental prayer are so much a duty in all who wish to cherish true faith and love towards Him, that it may be allowed us, my brethren, under the guidance of holy men who have gone before us, to dwell and enlarge upon what otherwise would more fitly be adored than scrutinized. And certain times of the year, this especially,[2] call upon us to consider, as closely and minutely as we can, even the more sacred portions of the Gospel history. I would rather be thought feeble or officious in my treatment of them, than wanting to the season; and so I now proceed, because the religious usage of the Church requires it, and though any individual preacher may well shrink from it, to direct your thoughts to a subject, especially suitable now, and about which many of us perhaps think very little, the sufferings which our Lord endured in His innocent and sinless soul.

You know, my brethren, that our Lord and Saviour, though

---

[1] From *Discourses to Mixed Congregations* (1849), No. 16. [Ed.]
[2] Passion-tide.

He was God, was also perfect man; and hence He had not only a body, but a soul likewise, such as ours, though pure from all stain of evil. He did not take a body without a soul, God forbid! for that would not have been to become man. How would He have sanctified our nature if He had taken a nature which was not ours? Man without a soul is on a level with the beasts of the field; but our Lord came to save a race capable of praising and obeying Him, possessed of immortality, yet dispossessed of that hope of an immortality of bliss. Man was created in the image of God, and that image is in his soul; when then his Maker, by an unspeakable condescension, came in his nature, He took on Himself a soul in order to take on Him a body; He took on Him a soul as the means of His union with a body; He took on Him in the first place the soul, then the body of man, both at once, but in this order, the soul and the body; He Himself created the soul which He took on Himself, while He took His body from the flesh of the Blessed Virgin, His Mother. Thus He became perfect man with body and soul; and, as He took on Him a body of flesh and nerves, which admitted of wounds and death, and was capable of suffering, so did He take a soul too, which was susceptible of that suffering, and moreover was susceptible of the pain and sorrow which are proper to a human soul; and, as His atoning passion was undergone in the body, so it was undergone in the soul also.

As the solemn days proceed, we shall be especially called on, my brethren, to consider His sufferings in the body, His seizure, His forced journeyings to and fro, His blows and wounds, His scourging, the crown of thorns, the nails, the Cross. They are all summed up in the Crucifix itself, as it meets our eyes; they are represented all at once on His sacred flesh, as it hangs up before us,—and meditation is made easy by the spectacle. It is otherwise with the sufferings of His soul, they cannot be painted for us, nor can they even be duly investigated: they are beyond both sense and thought; and yet they anticipated His bodily sufferings. The agony, a pain of the soul, not of the body, was the first act of His tremendous sacrifice; "My soul is sorrowful even unto death," He said; nay; if He suffered in the body, it really was in the soul, for the body did but convey the infliction on to that, which was the true recipient and seat of the anguish.

This it is very much to the purpose to insist upon; I say, it was not the body that suffered, but the soul in the body; it was the soul and not the body which was the seat of the suffering of the Eternal Word. Consider, then, there is no real pain, though there may be apparent suffering, when there is no kind of inward sensibility or spirit to be the seat of it. A tree, for instance, has life, organs, growth, and decay; it may be wounded and injured; it droops, and is killed; but it does not suffer, because it has no mind or sensible principle within it. But wherever this gift of an immaterial principle is found, there pain is possible, and greater pain according to the quality of the gift. Had we no spirit of any kind, we should feel as little as a tree feels; had we no soul, we should not feel pain more acutely than a brute feels it; but, being men, we feel pain in a way in which none but those who have souls can feel it.

Living beings, I say, feel more or less according to the spirit which is in them; brutes feel far less than man, because they cannot think of what they feel; they have no advertence or direct consciousness of their sufferings. This it is that makes pain so trying, viz., that we cannot help thinking of it, while we suffer it. It is before us, it possesses the mind, it keeps our thoughts fixed upon it. Whatever draws the mind off the thought of it lessens it; hence friends try to amuse us when we are in pain, for amusement is a diversion. If the pain is slight, they sometimes succeed with us; and then we are, so to say, without pain, even while we suffer. And hence it continually happens that in violent exercise or labour, men meet with blows or cuts, so considerable and so durable in their effect, as to bear witness to the sufferings which must have attended their infliction, of which nevertheless they recollect nothing. And in quarrels and in battles wounds are received which, from the excitement of the moment, are brought home to the consciousness of the combatant, not by the pain at the time of receiving them, but by the loss of blood that follows.

I will show you presently, my brethren, how I mean to apply what I have said to the consideration of our Lord's sufferings; first I will make another remark. Consider, then, that hardly any one stroke of pain is intolerable; it is intolerable when it continues. You cry out perhaps that you cannot bear more; patients feel as if they could stop the surgeon's hand, simply because he continues to pain them. Their feeling is that they have borne *as much* as they can bear; as if the continuance and not the intenseness was what made it too much for them. What does this mean, but that the memory of the foregoing moments of pain acts upon and (as it were) edges the pain that succeeds? If the third or fourth or twentieth moment of pain could be taken by itself, if the succession of the moments that preceded it could be forgotten, it would be no more than the first moment, as bearable as the first; but what makes it unbearable is, that it *is* the twentieth; that the first, the second, the third, on to the nineteenth moment of pain, are all concentrated in the twentieth; so that every additional moment of pain has all the weight, the ever-increasing weight, of all that has preceded it. Hence, I repeat, it is that brute animals would seem to feel so little pain, because, that is, they have not the power of reflection or of consciousness. They do not know they exist; they do not contemplate themselves; they do not look backwards or forwards; every moment as it succeeds, is their all; they wander over the face of the earth, and see this thing and that, and feel pleasure and pain, but still they take everything as it comes, and then let it go again, as men do in dreams. They have memory, but not the memory of an intellectual being; they put together nothing, they make nothing properly one and individual to themselves out of the particular sensations which they receive; nothing is to them a reality or has a substance beyond those sensations; they are but sensible of a number of successive impressions. And hence, as their other feelings, so their feeling of pain is but faint and dull, in spite of their outward manifestations of it. It is the intellectual comprehension of pain, as a whole diffused through successive moments, which gives it its special power and keenness, and it is the soul only, which a brute has not, which is capable of that comprehension.

Now apply this to the sufferings of our Lord;—do you recollect their offering Him wine mingled with myrrh, when He was on the point of being crucified? He would not drink of it; why? because such a portion would have stupefied His mind, and He was bent on bearing the pain in all its bitterness. You see from this, my brethren, the character of His sufferings; He would have fain escaped them, had that been His Father's will; "If it be possible," He said, "let this chalice pass from Me;" but since it was not possible, He says calmly and decidedly to the Apostle, who would have rescued Him from suffering, "The chalice which my Father hath given Me, shall I not drink it?" If He was to suffer, He gave Himself to suffering; He did not come to suffer as little as He could; He did not turn away His face from the suffering; He confronted it, or, as I may say, He breasted it, that every particular portion of it might make its due impression on Him. And as men are superior to brute animals, and are affected by pain more than they, by reason of the mind within them, which gives a substance to pain, such as it cannot have in the instance of brutes; so, in like manner our Lord felt pain of the body, with an advertence and a consciousness, and therefore with a keenness and intensity, and with a unity of perception, which none of us can possibly fathom or compass, because His soul was so absolutely in His own power, so simply free from the influence of distractions, so fully directed *upon* the pain, so utterly surrendered, so simply subjected to the suffering. And thus He may truly be said to have suffered the whole of His passion in every moment of it.

Recollect that our Blessed Lord was in this respect different

from us, that, though He was perfect man, yet there was a
power in Him greater than His soul, which ruled His soul,
for He was God. The soul of other men is subjected to its
own wishes, feelings, impulses, passions, perturbations; His
soul was subjected simply to His Eternal and Divine Person.
Nothing happened to His soul, by chance, or on a sudden;
He never was taken by surprise; nothing affected Him without His willing beforehand that it should affect Him. Never
did He sorrow, or fear, or desire, or rejoice in spirit, but He
first willed to be sorrowful, or afraid, or desirous, or joyful.
When we suffer, it is because outward agents and the uncontrollable emotions of our minds bring suffering upon us. We
are brought under the discipline of pain involuntarily, we
suffer from it more or less acutely according to accidental
circumstances, we find our patience more or less tried by it
according to our state of mind, and we do our best to provide
alleviations or remedies of it. We cannot anticipate beforehand how much of it will come upon us, or how far we shall be
able to sustain it; nor can we say afterwards why we have
felt just what we have felt, or why we did not bear the suffering better. It was otherwise with our Lord. His Divine
Person was not subject, could not be exposed, to the influence
of His own human affections and feelings, except so far as He
chose. I repeat, when He chose to fear, He feared; when He
chose to be angry, He was angry; when He chose to grieve,
He was grieved. He was not open to emotion, but He opened
upon Himself voluntarily the influence by which He was
moved. Consequently, when He determined to suffer the pain
of His vicarious passion, whatever He did, He did, as the Wise
Man says, *instanter,* "earnestly," with His might; He did not
do it by halves; He did not turn away His mind from the suffering, as we do;—(how should He, who came to suffer, who
could not have suffered but of His own act?) no, He did not
say and unsay, do and undo; He said and He did; He said,
"Lo, I come to do Thy will, O God; sacrifice and offering
Thou wouldest not, but a body hast Thou fitted to Me." He

took a body in order that He might suffer; He became man, that He might suffer as man; and when His hour was come, that hour of Satan and of darkness, the hour when sin was to pour its full malignity upon Him, it followed that He offered Himself wholly, a holocaust, a whole burnt-offering;—as the whole of His body, stretched out upon the Cross, so the whole of His soul, His whole advertence, His whole consciousness, a mind awake, a sense acute, a living co-operation, a present, absolute intention, not a virtual permission, not a heartless submission, this did He present to His tormentors. His passion was an action; He lived most energetically, while He lay languishing, fainting, and dying. Nor did He die, except by an act of the will; for He bowed His head, in command as well as in resignation, and said, "Father, into Thy hands I commend My Spirit;" He gave the word, He surrendered His soul, He did not lose it.

Thus you see, my brethren, had our Lord only suffered in the body, and in it not so much as other men, still as regards the pain, He would have really suffered indefinitely more, because pain is to be measured by the power of realizing it. God was the sufferer; God suffered in His human nature; the sufferings belonged to God, and were drunk up, were drained out to the bottom of the chalice, because God drank them; not tasted or sipped, not flavoured, disguised by human medicaments, as man disposes of the cup of anguish. And what I have now said will further serve to answer an objection, which I shall proceed to notice, and which perhaps exists latently in the minds of many, and leads them to overlook the part which our Lord's soul had in His gracious satisfaction for sin.

Our Lord said, when His agony was commencing, "My soul is sorrowful unto death;" now you may ask, my brethren, whether He had not certain consolations, peculiar to Himself, impossible in any other, which diminished or impeded the distress of His soul, and caused Him to feel, not more, but less than an ordinary man. For instance, He had a sense of innocence which no other sufferer could have: even His persecutors, even the false apostle who betrayed Him, the judge who sentenced Him, and the soldiers who conducted the execution, testified His innocence. "I have condemned the innocent blood," said Judas; "I am clear from the blood of this just Person," said Pilate; "Truly this was a just Man," cried the centurion. And if even they, sinners, bore witness to His sinlessness, how much more did His own soul! and we know well that even in our own case, sinners as we are, on the consciousness of innocence or of guilt mainly turns our power of enduring opposition and calumny; how much more, you will say, in the case of our Lord, did the sense of inward sanctity compensate for the suffering and annihilate the shame! Again, you may say, that He knew that His sufferings would be short, and that their issue would be joyful, whereas uncertainty of the future is the keenest element of human distress; but He could not have anxiety, for He was not in suspense, nor despondency or despair, for He never was deserted. And in confirmation you may refer to St. Paul who expressly tells us, that "for the joy set before Him," our Lord "despised the shame." And certainly there is a marvellous calm and self-possession in all He does: consider His warning to the Apostles, "Watch and pray, lest ye enter into tempation; the spirit indeed is willing, but the flesh is weak;" or His words to Judas, "Friend, wherefore art thou come?" and "Judas, betrayest thou the Son of Man with a kiss?" or to Peter, "All that take the sword, shall perish with the sword;" or to the man who struck Him, "If I have spoken evil, bear witness of the evil; but if well, why smitest thou Me?" or to His Mother, "Woman, behold thy Son."

All this is true and much to be insisted on; but it quite agrees with, or rather illustrates, what I have been saying. My brethren, you have only said (to use a human phrase) that He was always Himself. His mind was its own centre, and was never in the slightest degree thrown off its heavenly and most perfect balance. What He suffered, He suffered because He put Himself under suffering, and that deliberately and calmly. As He said to the leper, "I will, be thou clean;" and to the paralytic, "Thy sins be forgiven thee;" and to the centurion, "I will come and heal him;" and of Lazarus, "I go to wake him out of sleep;" so He said, "Now I will begin to suffer," and He did begin. His composure is but the proof how entirely He governed His own mind. He drew back, at the proper moment, the bolts and fastenings, and opened the gates, and the floods fell right upon His soul in all their fulness. This is what St. Mark tells us of Him; and he is said to have written it from the very mouth of St. Peter, who was one of three witnesses present at the time. "They came," he says, "to the place which is called Gethsemani; and He saith to His disciples, Sit you here while I pray. And He taketh with Him Peter and James and John, and He *began to be* frightened and to be very heavy." You see how deliberately He acts; He comes to a certain spot; and then, giving the word of command, and withdrawing the support of the God-head from His soul, distress, terror, and dejection at once rush in upon it. Thus He walks forth into a mental agony with as definite an action as if it were some bodily torture, the fire or the wheel.

This being the case, you will see at once, my brethren, that it is nothing to the purpose to say that He would be supported under His trial by the consciousness of innocence and the anticipation of triumph; for His trial consisted in the withdrawal, as of other causes of consolation, so of that very consciousness and anticipation. The same act of the will which admitted the influence upon His soul of any distress at all, admitted all distresses at once. It was not the contest between antagonist impulses and views, coming from without, but the operation of an inward resolution. As men of self-command can turn from one thought to another at their will, so, much more, did He deliberately deny Himself the comfort, and satiate Himself with the woe. In that moment His soul thought not of the future, He thought only of the present burden which was upon Him, and which He had come upon earth to sustain.

And now, my brethren, what was it He had to bear, when He thus opened upon His soul the torrent of this predestinated pain? Alas! He had to bear what is well known to us, what is familiar to us, but what to Him was woe unutterable. He had to bear, that which is so easy a thing to us, so natural, so welcome, that we cannot conceive of it as of a great endurance, but which to Him had the scent and the poison of death; —He had, my dear brethren, to bear the weight of sin; He had to bear your sins; He had to bear the sins of the whole world. Sin is an easy thing to us; we think little of it; we do not understand how the Creator can think much of it; we cannot bring our imagination to believe that it deserves retribution, and, when even in this world punishments follow upon it, we explain them away or turn our minds from them. But consider what sin is in itself; it is rebellion against God; it is a traitor's act who aims at the overthrow and death of His sovereign; it is that, if I may use a strong expression, which, could the Divine Governor of the world cease to be, would be sufficient to bring it about. Sin is the mortal enemy of the All-holy, so that He and it cannot be together; and as the All-holy drives it from His presence into the outer darkness, so, if God could be less than God, it is sin that would have power to make Him so. And here observe, my brethren, that when once Almighty Love, by taking flesh, entered this created system, and submitted Himself to its laws, then forthwith this antagonist of good and truth, taking advantage of the opportunity, flew at that flesh, which He had taken, and fixed on it, and was its death. The envy of the Pharisees, the treachery of Judas, and the madness of the people, were but the instrument or the expression of the enmity which sin felt towards Eternal Purity, as soon as, in infinite mercy towards men, He put Himself within its reach. Sin could not touch His Divine Majesty; but it could assail Him in that way in which He allowed Himself to be assailed, that is, through the medium of His humanity. And in the issue, in the death of God incarnate, you are but taught, my brethren, what sin is in itself, and what it was which then was falling, in its hour and in its strength, upon His human nature, when He allowed that nature to be so filled with horror and dismay at the very anticipation.

There, then, in that most awful hour, knelt the Saviour of the world, putting off the defences of His divinity, dismissing His reluctant Angels, who in myriads were ready at His call, and opening His arms, baring His breast, sinless as He was, to the assault of His foe,—of a foe whose breath was a pestilence, and whose embrace was an agony. There He knelt, motionless and still, while the vile and horrible fiend clad His spirit in a robe steeped in all that is hateful and heinous in human crime, which clung close round His heart, and filled His conscience, and found its way into every sense and pore of His mind, and spread over Him a moral leprosy, till He almost felt Himself to be that which he never could be, and which His foe would fain have made Him. Oh, the horror, when He looked, and did not know Himself, and felt as a foul and loathsome sinner, from His vivid perception of that mass of corruption which poured over His head and ran down even to the skirts of His garments! Oh, the distraction, when He found His eyes, and hands, and feet, and lips, and heart, as if the members of the Evil One, and not of God! Are these the hands of the immaculate Lamb of God, once innocent, but now red with ten thousand barbarous deeds of blood? are these His lips, not uttering prayer, and praise, and holy blessings, but as if defiled with oaths, and blasphemies, and doctrines of devils? or His eyes, profaned as they are by all the evil visions and idolatrous fascinations for which men have abandoned their Adorable Creator? And His ears, they ring with sounds of revelry and of strife; and His heart is frozen with avarice, and cruelty, and unbelief; and His very memory is laden with every sin which has been committed since the fall, in all regions of the earth, with the pride of the old giants, and the lusts of the five cities, and the obduracy of Egypt, and the ambition of Babel, and the unthankfulness and scorn of Israel. Oh, who does not know the misery of a haunting thought which comes again and again, in spite of rejection, to annoy, if it cannot seduce? or of some odious and sickening imagination, in no sense one's own, but forced upon the mind from without? or of evil knowledge, gained with or without a man's fault, but which he would give a great price to be rid of at once and for ever? And adversaries such as these gather around Thee, Blessed Lord, in millions now; they come in troops more numerous than the locust or the palmer-worm, or the plagues of hail, and flies, and frogs, which were sent against Pharaoh. Of the living and of the dead and of the as yet unborn, of the lost and of the saved, of Thy people and of strangers, of sinners and of Saints, all sins are there. Thy dearest are there, Thy Saints and Thy chosen are upon Thee; Thy three Apostles, Peter, James, and John, but not as comforters, but as accusers, like the friends of Job, "sprinkling dust towards heaven," and heaping curses on Thy head. All are there but one; one only is not there, one only; for she, who had no part in sin, she only could console Thee, and therefore she is not nigh. She will be near Thee on the Cross, she is separated from Thee in the garden. She has been Thy companion and Thy confidant through Thy life, she interchanged with Thee the pure thoughts and holy meditations of thirty years; but her virgin ear may not take in, nor may her immaculate heart conceive, what now is in vision before Thee. None was equal to the weight but God; sometimes before Thy Saints Thou hast brought the image of a single sin, as it appears in the light of Thy countenance, a venial sin, perhaps, not a mortal one; and they have told us that the sight did all but kill them, nay, would have killed them, had it not been instantly withdrawn. The Mother of God, for all her

sanctity, nay, by reason of it, could not have borne even one
brood of that innumerable progeny of Satan which compasses
Thee about. It is the long history of a world, and God alone
can bear the load of it. Hopes blighted, vows broken, lights
quenched, warnings scorned, opportunities lost; the innocent
betrayed, the young hardened, the penitent relapsing, the just
overcome, the aged failing; the sophistry of misbelief, the wilfulness of passion, the obduracy of pride, the tyranny of
habit, the canker of remorse, the wasting fever of care, the
anguish of shame, the pining of disappointment, the sickness
of despair; such cruel, such pitiable spectacles, such heart-
rending, revolting, detestable, maddening scenes; nay, the hag-
gard faces, the convulsed lips, the flushed cheek, the dark
brow of the willing victims of rebellion, they are all before
Him now; they are upon Him and in Him. They are with Him
instead of that ineffable peace which has inhabited His soul
since the moment of His conception. They are upon Him,
they are all but His own; He cries to His Father as if He were
the criminal, not the victim; His agony takes the form of guilt
and compunction. He is doing penance, He is making confession, He is exercising contrition with a reality and a virtue
infinitely greater than that of all Saints and penitents together; for He is the One Victim for us all, the sole Satisfaction, the real Penitent, all but the real sinner.

He rises languidly from the earth, and turns around to meet
the traitor and his band, now quickly nearing the deep shade.
He turns, and lo! there is blood upon His garment and in His
footprints. Whence come these first-fruits of the passion of
the Lamb? no soldier's scourge has touched His shoulders,
nor the hangman's nails His hands and feet. My brethren,
He has bled before His time; He has shed blood; yes, and it
is His agonizing soul which has broken up His framework of
flesh and poured it forth. His passion has begun from within.
That tormented Heart, the seat of tenderness and love, began
at length to labour and to beat with vehemence beyond its
nature; "the foundations of the great deep were broken up;"

the red streams rushed forth so copious and fierce as to overflow the veins, and bursting through the pores, they stood in a thick dew over His whole skin; then forming into drops, they rolled down full and heavy, and drenched the ground.

"My soul is sorrowful even unto death," He said. It has been said of that dreadful pestilence which now is upon us, that it begins with death; by which is meant that it has no stages or crisis, that hope is over when it comes, and that what looks like its course is but the death agony and the process of dissolution, and thus our Atoning Sacrifice, in a much higher sense, began with this passion of woe, and only did not die, because at His Omnipotent will His Heart did not break, nor Soul separate from Body, till He had suffered on the Cross.

No; He has not yet exhausted that full chalice, from which at first His natural infirmity shrank. The seizure, and the arraignment, and the buffeting, and the prison, and the trial, and the mocking, and the passing to and fro, and the scourging, and the crown of thorns, and the slow march to Calvary, and the crucifixion, these are all to come. A night and a day, hour after hour, is slowly to run out before the end comes, and the Satisfaction is completed.

And then, when the appointed moment arrived, and He gave the word, as His passion had begun with His soul, with the soul did it end. He did not die of bodily exhaustion, or of bodily pain; His tormented Heart broke, and He commended His Spirit to the Father.

"O Heart of Jesus, all Love, I offer Thee these humble prayers for myself, and for all those who unite themselves with me in spirit to adore Thee. O holiest Heart of Jesus most lovely, I intend to renew and to offer to Thee these acts of adoration and these prayers, for myself a wretched sinner, and for all those who are associated with me in Thy adoration, through all moments while I breathe, even to the end of my life. I recommend to Thee, O my Jesu, Holy Church, Thy dear spouse, and our true Mother, all just souls and all poor sinners, the afflicted, the dying, and all mankind. Let not Thy Blood be shed for them in vain. Finally, deign to apply it in relief of the souls in Purgatory, those in particular, who have practised in the course of their life this holy devotion of adoring Thee."

XVIII

THE GLORIES OF MARY FOR THE
SAKE OF HER SON [1]

WE KNOW, MY BRETHREN, that in the natural world
nothing is superfluous, nothing incomplete, nothing
independent; but part answers to part, and all details combine to form one mighty whole. Order and harmony
are among the first perfections which we discern in this visible
creation; and the more we examine into it, the more widely
and minutely they are found to belong to it. "All things are
double," says the Wise Man, "one against another; and He
hath made nothing defective." It is the very character and
definition of "the heavens and the earth," as contrasted with
the void or chaos which preceded them, that everything is now
subjected to fixed laws; and every motion, and influence, and
effect can be accounted for, and, were our knowledge sufficient, could be anticipated. Moreover, it is plain, on the
other hand, that it is only in proportion to our observation and
our research that this truth becomes apparent; for though a
number of things even at first sight are seen to proceed according to an established and beautiful order, yet in other
instances the law to which they are conformed is with difficulty discovered; and the words "chance," and "hazard," and
"fortune," have come into use as expressions of our ignorance.
Accordingly, you may fancy rash and irreligious minds who
are engaged day after day in the business of the world, suddenly looking out into the heavens or upon the earth, and

[1] From *Discourses to Mixed Congregations* (1849), No. 17. [Ed.]

criticizing the great Architect, arguing that there are creatures in existence which are rude or defective in their constitution, and asking questions which would but evidence their want of scientific education.

The case is the same as regards the supernatural world. The great truths of Revelation are all connected together and form a whole. Every one can see this in a measure even at a glance, but to understand the full consistency and harmony of Catholic teaching requires study and meditation. Hence, as philosophers of this world bury themselves in museums and laboratories, descend into mines, or wander among woods or on the sea-shore, so the inquirer into heavenly truths dwells in the cell and the oratory, pouring forth his heart in prayer, collecting his thoughts in meditation, dwelling on the idea of Jesus, or of Mary, or of grace, or of eternity, and pondering the words of holy men who have gone before him, till before his mental sight arises the hidden wisdom of the perfect, "which God predestined before the world unto our glory," and which He "reveals unto them by His Spirit." And, as ignorant men may dispute the beauty and perfection of the visible creation, so men, who for six days in the week are absorbed in worldly toil, who live for wealth, or name, or self-indulgence, or profane knowledge, and do but give their leisure moments to the thought of religion, never raising their souls to God, never asking for His enlightening grace, never chastening their hearts and bodies, never steadily contemplating the objects of faith, but judging hastily and peremptorily according to their private views or the humour of the hour; such men, I say, in like manner, may easily, or will for certain, be surprised and shocked at portions of revealed truth, as if strange, or harsh, or extreme, or inconsistent, and will in whole or in part reject it.

I am going to apply this remark to the subject of the prerogatives with which the Church invests the Blessed Mother of God. They are startling and difficult to those whose imagination is not accustomed to them, and whose reason has not reflected on them; but the more carefully and religiously they are dwelt on, the more, I am sure, will they be found essential to the Catholic faith, and integral to the worship of Christ. This simply is the point which I shall insist on,—disputable indeed by aliens from the Church, but most clear to her children,—that the glories of Mary are for the sake of Jesus; and that we praise and bless her as the first of creatures, that we may duly confess Him as our sole Creator.

When the Eternal Word decreed to come on earth, He did not purpose, He did not work, by halves; but He came to be a man like any of us, to take a human soul and body, and to make them His own. He did not come in a mere apparent or accidental form, as Angels appear to men; nor did He merely overshadow an existing man, as He overshadows His Saints, and call him by the name of God; but He "was made flesh." He attached to Himself a manhood, and became as really and truly man as He was God, so that henceforth He was both God and man, or, in other words, He was One Person in two natures, divine and human. This is a mystery so marvellous, so difficult, that faith alone firmly receives it; the natural man may receive it for a while, may think he receives it, but never really receives it; begins, as soon as he has professed it, secretly to rebel against it, evades it, or revolts from it. This he has done from the first; even in the lifetime of the beloved disciple men arose, who said that our Lord had no body at all, or a body framed in the heavens, or that He did not suffer, but another suffered in His stead, or that He was but for a time with the human form which was born and which suffered, coming on it at its baptism, and leaving it before its crucifixion, or that He was a mere man. That "in the beginning was the Word, and the Word was with God, and the Word was God, and the word was made flesh and dwelt among us," was too hard a thing for the unregenerate reason.

The case is the same at this day; mere Protestants have seldom any real perception of the doctrine of God and man in one Person. They speak in a dreamy, shadowy way of Christ's divinity; but, when their meaning is sifted, you will find them very slow to commit themselves to any statement sufficient to express the Catholic dogma. They will tell you at once, that the subject is not to be inquired into, for that it is impossible to inquire into it at all, without being technical and subtle. Then when they comment on the Gospels, they will speak of Christ, not simply and consistently as God, but as a being made up of God and man, partly one and partly the other, or between both, or as a man inhabited by a special divine presence. Sometimes they even go on to deny that He was in heaven the Son of God, saying that He became the Son, when he was conceived of the Holy Ghost; and they are shocked, and think it a mark both of reverence and good sense to be shocked, when they hear the Man spoken of simply and plainly as God. They cannot bear to have it said, except as a figure or mode of speaking, that God had a human body, or that God suffered; they think that the "Atonement," and "Sanctification through the Spirit," as they speak, is the sum and substance of the Gospel, and they are shy of any dogmatic expression which goes beyond them. Such, I believe, is the ordinary character of the Protestant notions among us on the divinity of Christ, whether among members of the Anglican communion, or dissenters from it, excepting a small remnant of them.

Now, if you would witness against these unchristian opinions, if you would bring out distinctly and beyond mistake and evasion, the simple idea of the Catholic Church that God is man, could you do it better than by laying down in St. John's words that "God *became* man"? and again could you express this more emphatically and unequivocally than by declaring that He was *born* a man, or that He had a *Mother?* The world allows that God *is* man; the admission costs it little, for God is everywhere, and (as it may say) is everything; but it shrinks from confessing that God is the Son of Mary. It shrinks, for it is at once confronted with a severe fact, which violates and shatters its own unbelieving view of things; the revealed doctrine forthwith takes its true shape, and receives an historical reality; and the Almighty is introduced into His own world at a certain time and in a definite way. Dreams are broken and shadows depart; the divine truth is no longer a poetical expression, or a devotional exaggeration, or a mystical economy, or a mythical representation. "Sacrifice and offering," the shadows of the Law, "Thou wouldest not, but a body hast Thou fitted to Me. That which was from the beginning, which we have heard, which we have seen with our eyes, which we have diligently looked upon, and our hands have handled," "That which we have seen and have heard, declare we unto you;"—such is the record of the Apostle, in opposition to those "spirits" which denied that "Jesus Christ had appeared in the flesh," and which "dissolved" Him by denying either His human nature or His divine. And the confession that Mary is *Deipara*, or the Mother of God, is that safeguard wherewith we seal up and secure the doctrine of the Apostle from all evasion, and that test whereby we detect all the pretences of those bad spirits of "Antichrist which have gone out into the world." It declares that He is God; it implies that He is man; it suggests to us that He is God still, though He has become man, and that He is true man though He is God. By witnessing to the *process* of the union, it secures the reality of the two *subjects* of the union, of the divinity and of the manhood. If Mary is the Mother of God, Christ is understood to be Emmanuel, God with us. And hence it was, that, when time went on, and the bad spirits and false prophets grew stronger and bolder and found a way into the Catholic body itself, then the Church, guided by God, could find no more effectual and sure way of expelling them, than that of using this word *Deipara* against them; and, on the other hand, when they came up again from the realms of darkness, and plotted the utter overthrow of Christian faith in the sixteenth century, then they could find no more certain expedient for their hateful purpose, than that of reviling and blaspheming the prerogatives of Mary, for they knew full sure that, if they could once get the world to dishonour the Mother, the dishonour of the Son would follow close. The Church and Satan agreed together in this, that Son and Mother went together; and the experience of three centuries has confirmed their testimony; for Catholics who have honoured the Mother, still worship the Son, while Protestants, who now have ceased to confess the Son, began then by scoffing at the Mother.

You see then, my brethren, in this particular, the harmonious consistency of the revealed system, and the bearing of one doctrine upon another; Mary is exalted for the sake of Jesus. It was fitting that she, as being a creature, though the first of creatures, should have an office of ministration. She, as others, came into the world to do a work, she had a mission to fulfil; her grace and her glory are not for her own sake, but for her Maker's; and to her is committed the custody of the Incarnation; this is her appointed office,—"A Virgin shall conceive, and bear a Son, and they shall call His Name Emmanuel." As she was once on earth, and was personally the guardian of her Divine Child, as she carried Him in her womb, folded Him in her embrace, and suckled Him at her breast, so now, and to the latest hour of the Church, do her glories and the devotion paid her proclaim and define the right faith concerning Him as God and man. Every Church which is dedicated to her, every altar which is raised under her invocation, every image which represents her, every Litany in her praise, every Hail Mary for her continual memory, does but remind us that there was One who, though He was all-blessed from all eternity, yet for the sake of sinners, "did not shrink from the Virgin's womb." Thus she is the *Turris Davidica,* as the Church calls her, "the Tower of David;" the high and strong defence of the King of the true Israel; and hence the Church also addresses her in the Antiphon, as having "destroyed all heresies in the whole world alone."

And here, my brethren, a fresh thought opens upon us, which is naturally implied in what has been said. If the *Deipara* is to witness of Emmanuel, she must be necessarily more than the *Deipara*. For consider; a defence must be strong in order to be a defence; a tower must be, like that Tower of David, "built with bulwarks;" "a thousand bucklers hang upon it, all the armour of valiant men." It would not have sufficed, in order to bring out and impress on us the idea that God is man, had His Mother been an ordinary person. A mother without a home in the Church, without dignity, without gifts, would have been, as far as the defence of the Incarnation goes, no mother at all. She would not have remained in the memory, or the imagination of men. If she is to witness and remind the world that God became man, she must be on a high and eminent station for the purpose. She must be made to fill the mind, in order to suggest the lesson. When she once attracts our attention, then and not till then, she begins to preach Jesus. "Why should she have such prerogatives," we ask, "unless He be God? and what must He be by nature, when she is so high by grace?" This is why she has other prerogatives besides, namely, the gifts of personal purity and intercessory power, distinct from her maternity; she is personally endowed that she may perform her office well; she is exalted in herself that she may minister to Christ.

For this reason, she has been made more glorious in her person than in her office; her purity is a higher gift than her relationship to God. This is what is implied in Christ's answer to the woman in the crowd, who cried out, when He was preaching, "Blessed is the womb that bare Thee, and the breasts which Thou hast sucked." He replied by pointing out to His disciples a higher blessedness; "Yea, rather blessed," He said, "are they who hear the word of God and keep it." You know, my brethren, that Protestants take these words in disparagement of our Lady's greatness, but they really tell the other way. For consider them; He lays down a principle, that it is more blessed to keep His commandments than to be His Mother; but who even of Protestants will say that she did *not* keep His commandments? She kept them surely, and our Lord does but say that such obedience was in a higher line of privilege than her being His Mother; she was more blessed in her detachment from creatures, in her devotion to God, in her virginal purity, in her fulness of grace, than in her maternity. This is the constant teaching of the Holy Fathers: "More blessed was Mary," says St. Augustine, "in receiving Christ's faith, than in conceiving Christ's flesh;" and St. Chrysostom declares, that she would not have been blessed, though she had borne Him in the body, had she not heard the word of God and kept it. This of course is an impossible case; for she was made holy, that she might be made His Mother, and the two blessednesses cannot be divided. She who was chosen to supply flesh and blood to the Eternal Word, was first filled with grace in soul and body; still, she had a double blessedness, of office and of qualification for it, and the latter was the greater. And it is on this account that the Angel calls her blessed; *"Full of grace,"* he says, "Blessed among women;" and St. Elizabeth also, when she cries out, "Blessed thou that has *believed.*" Nay, she herself bears like testimony, when the Angel announced to her the high favour which was coming on her. Though all Jewish women in each successive age had been hoping to be Mother of the Christ, so that marriage was honourable among them, celibacy a reproach, she alone had put aside the desire and the thought of so great a dignity. She alone, who was to bear the Christ, all but refused to bear Him; He stooped to her, she turned from Him; and why? because she had been inspired, the first of womankind, to dedicate her virginity to God, and she did not welcome a privilege which seemed to involve a forfeiture of her vow. How shall this be, she asked, seeing I am separate from man? Nor, till the Angel told her that the conception would be miraculous and from the Holy Ghost, did she put aside her "trouble" of mind, recognize him securely as God's messenger, and bow her head in awe and thankfulness to God's condescension.

Mary then is a specimen, and more than a specimen, in the

purity of her soul and body, of what man was before his fall, and what he would have been, had he risen to his full perfection. It had been hard, it had been a victory for the Evil One, had the whole race passed away, nor any one instance in it occurred to show what the Creator had intended it to be in its original state. Adam, you know, was created in the image and after the likeness of God; his frail and imperfect nature, stamped with a divine seal, was supported and exalted by an indwelling of divine grace. Impetuous passion did not exist in him, except as a latent element and a possible evil; ignorance was dissipated by the clear light of the Spirit; and reason, sovereign over every motion of his soul, was simply subjected to the will of God. Nay, even his body was preserved from every wayward appetite and affection, and was promised immortality instead of dissolution. Thus he was in a supernatural state; and, had he not sinned, year after year would he have advanced in merit and grace, and in God's favour, till he passed from paradise to heaven. But he fell; and his descendants were born in his likeness; and the world grew worse instead of better, and judgment after judgment cut off generations of sinners in vain, and improvement was hopeless, "because man was flesh," and, "the thoughts of his heart were bent upon evil at all times." However, a remedy had been determined in heaven; a Redeemer was at hand; God was about to do a great work, and he purposed to do it suitably; "where sin abounded, grace was to abound more." Kings of the earth, when they have sons born to them, forthwith scatter some large bounty, or raise some high memorial; they honour the day, or the place, or the heralds of the auspicious event, with some corresponding mark of favour; nor did the coming of Emmanuel innovate on the world's established custom. It was a season of grace and prodigy, and these were to be exhibited in a special manner in the person of His Mother. The course of ages was to be reversed; the tradition of evil was to be broken; a gate of light was to be opened amid the darkness, for the coming of the Just;—a

Virgin conceived and bore Him. It was fitting, for His honour and glory, that she, who was the instrument of His bodily presence, should first be a miracle of His grace; it was fitting that she should triumph, where Eve had failed, and should "bruise the serpent's head" by the spotlessness of her sanctity. In some respects, indeed, the course was not reversed; Mary came into a fallen world, and resigned herself to its laws; she, as also the Son she bore, was exposed to pain of soul and body, she was subjected to death; but she was not put under the power of sin. As grace was infused into Adam from the first moment of his creation, so that he never had experience of his natural poverty, till sin reduced him to it; so was grace given from the first in still ampler measure to Mary, and she never incurred, in fact, Adam's deprivation. She began where others end, whether in knowledge or in love. She was from the first clothed in sanctity, sealed for perseverance, luminous and glorious in God's sight, and incessantly employed in meritorious acts, which continued till her last breath. Hers was emphatically "the path of the just, which, as the shining light goeth forward and increaseth even to the perfect day;" and sinlessness in thought, word, and deed, in small things as well as great, in venial matters as well as grievous, is surely but the natural and obvious sequel of such a beginning. If Adam might have kept himself from sin in his first state, much more shall we expect immaculate perfection in Mary.

Such is her prerogative of sinless perfection, and it is, as her maternity, for the sake of Emmanuel; hence she answered the Angel's salutation *Gratia plena,* with the humble acknowledgment, *Ecce ancilla Domini,* "Behold the handmaid of the Lord." And like to this is her third prerogative, which follows both from her maternity and from her purity, and which I will mention as completing the enumeration of her glories. I mean her intercessory power. For, if "God heareth not sinners, but if a man be a worshipper of Him, and do His will, him He heareth;" if "the continual prayer of a just man availeth much;"

if faithful Abraham was required to pray for Abimelech, "for he was a prophet;" if patient Job was to "pray for his friends," for he had "spoken right things before God;" if meek Moses, by lifting up his hands, turned the battle in favour of Israel against Amalec; why should we wonder at hearing that Mary, the only spotless child of Adam's seed, has a transcendent influence with the God of grace? And if the Gentiles at Jerusalem sought Philip, because he was an Apostle, when they desired access to Jesus, and Philip spoke to Andrew, as still more closely in our Lord's confidence, and then both came to Him, is it strange that the Mother should have power with the Son, distinct in kind from that of the purest Angel and the most triumphant Saint? If we have faith to admit the Incarnation itself, we must admit it in its fulness; why then should we start at the gracious appointments which arise out of it, or are necessary to it, or are included in it? If the Creator comes on earth in the form of a servant and a creature, why may not His Mother on the other hand rise to be the Queen of heaven, and be clothed with the sun, and have the moon under her feet?

I am not proving these doctrines to you, my brethren; the evidence of them lies in the declaration of the Church. The Church is the oracle of religious truth, and dispenses what the Apostles committed to her in every time and place. We must take her word, then, without proof, because she is sent to us from God to teach us how to please Him; and that we do so is the test whether we be really Catholics or no. I am not proving then what you already receive, but I am showing you the beauty and the harmony, as seen in one instance, of the Church's teaching; which are so well adapted, as they are divinely intended, to recommend that teaching to the inquirer and to endear it to her children. One word more, and I have done; I have shown you how full of meaning are the truths themselves which the Church teaches concerning the Most Blessed Virgin, and now consider how full of meaning also has been the Church's dispensation of them.

You will find, then, in this respect, as in Mary's preroga-tives themselves, there is the same careful reference to the glory of Him who gave them to her. You know, when first He went out to preach, she kept apart from Him; she inter-fered not with His work; and even when He was gone up on high, yet she, a woman, went not out to preach or teach, she seated not herself in the Apostolic chair, she took no part in the Priest's office; she did but humbly seek her Son in the daily Mass of those, who, though her ministers in heaven, were her superiors in the Church on earth. Nor, when she and they had left this lower scene, and she was a Queen upon her Son's right hand, not even then did she ask of Him to publish her name to the ends of the world, or to hold her up to the world's gaze, but she remained waiting for the time, when her own glory should be necessary for His. He indeed had been from the very first proclaimed by Holy Church, and enthroned in His temple, for He was God; ill had it beseemed the living Oracle of Truth to have withholden from the faithful the very object of their adoration; but it was otherwise with Mary. It became her, as a creature, a mother, and a woman, to stand aside and make way for the Creator, to minister to her Son, and to win her way into the world's homage by sweet and gracious persuasion. So when His name was dishonoured, then it was that she did Him service; when Emmanuel was denied, then the Mother of God (as it were) came forward; when heretics said that God was not incarnate, then was the time for her own honours. And then, when as much as this had been accomplished, she had done with strife; she fought not for herself. No fierce controversy, no persecuted con-fessors, no heresiarch, no anathema, marks the history of her manifestation; as she had increased day by day in grace and merit at Nazareth, while the world knew not of her, so has she raised herself aloft silently, and has grown into her place in the Church by a tranquil influence and a natural process. She was as some fair tree, stretching forth her fruitful branches and her fragrant leaves, and overshadowing the territory of the Saints. And thus the Antiphon speaks of her; "Let thy dwelling be in Jacob, and thine inheritance in Israel, and *strike thy roots* in My elect." Again, "And so in Sion was I established, and in the holy city I likewise rested, and in Jerusalem was my power. And I *took root* in an honourable people, and in the glorious company of the Saints was I *detained.* I was exalted like a cedar in Lebanus, and as a cypress in Mount Sion; I have stretched out My branches as the terebinth, and My branches are of honour and grace." Thus was she reared without hands, and gained a modest victory, and exerts a gentle sway, which she has not claimed. When dispute arose about her among her children, she hushed it; when objections were urged against her, she waived her claims and waited; till now, in this very day, should God so will, she will win at length her most radiant crown, and, without opposing voice, and amid the jubilation of the whole Church, she will be hailed as immaculate in her conception.

Such art thou, Holy Mother, in the creed and in the worship of the Church, the defence of many truths, the grace and smiling light of every devotion. In thee, O Mary, is fulfilled, as we can bear it, an original purpose of the Most High. He once had meant to come on earth in heavenly glory, but we sinned; and then He could not safely visit us, except with a shrouded radiance and a bedimmed Majesty, for He was God. So He came Himself in weakness, not in power; and He sent thee a creature, in His stead, with a creature's comeliness and lustre suited to our state. And now thy very face and form, dear Mother, speak to us of the Eternal; not like earthly beauty, dangerous to look upon, but like the morning star, which is thy emblem, bright and musical, breathing purity, telling of heaven, and infusing peace. O harbinger of day! O hope of the pilgrim! lead us still as thou hast led in the dark night, across the bleak wilderness, guide us on to our Lord Jesus, guide us home.

Maria, mater gratiæ,
Dulcis parens clementiæ,
Tu nos ab hoste protege
Et mortis horâ suscipe.

XIX

ON THE FITNESS OF THE GLORIES
OF MARY[1]

YOU MAY RECOLLECT, MY BRETHREN, our Lord's words,
when on the day of His resurrection He had joined the
two disciples on their way to Emmaus, and found them
sad and perplexed in consequence of His death. He said,
"Ought not Christ to suffer these things, and so enter into
His glory?" He appealed to the fitness and congruity which
existed between this otherwise surprising event and the other
truths which had been revealed concerning the divine purpose of saving the world. And so too, St. Paul, in speaking of
the same wonderful appointment of God; "It *became* Him," he
says, "for whom are all things, and through whom are all
things, who had brought many sons unto glory, to consummate
the Author of their salvation by suffering." Elsewhere, speaking of prophesying, or the exposition of what is latent in
divine truth, he bids his brethren exercise the gift "according
to the *analogy* or rule of faith;" that is, so that the doctrine
preached may correspond and fit into what is already received.
Thus you see, it is a great evidence of truth, in the case of
revealed teaching, that it is so consistent, that it so hangs together, that one thing springs out of another, that each part
requires and is required by the rest.

This great principle, which is exemplified so variously in
the structure and history of Catholic doctrine, which will
receive more and more illustrations the more carefully and

[1] From *Discourses to Mixed Congregations* (1849), No. 18. [Ed.]

minutely we examine the subject, is brought before us especially at this season, when we are celebrating the Assumption of our Blessed Lady, the Mother of God, into heaven. We receive it on the belief of ages; but, viewed in the light of reason, it is the *fitness* of this termination of her earthly course which so persuasively recommends it to our minds: we feel it "ought" to be; that it "becomes" her Lord and Son thus to provide for one who was so singular and special both in herself and her relations to Him. We find that it is simply in harmony with the substance and main outlines of the doctrine of the Incarnation, and that without it Catholic teaching would have a character of incompleteness, and would disappoint our pious expectations.

Let us direct our thoughts to this subject to-day, my brethren; and with a view of helping you to do so, I will first state what the Church has taught and defined from the first ages concerning the Blessed Virgin, and then you will see how naturally the devotion which her children show her, and the praises with which they honour her, follow from it.

Now, as you know, it has been held from the first, and defined from an early age, that Mary is the Mother of God. She is not merely the Mother of our Lord's manhood, or of our Lord's body, but she is to be considered the Mother of the Word Himself, the Word incarnate. God, in the person of the Word, the Second Person of the All-glorious Trinity, humbled Himself to become her Son. *Non horruisti Virginis uterum,* as the Church sings, "Thou didst not shrink from the Virgin's womb." He took the substance of His human flesh from her, and clothed in it He lay within Her; and He bore it about with Him after birth, as a sort of badge and witness that He, though God, was hers. He was nursed and tended by her; He was suckled by her; He lay in her arms. As time went on, He ministered to her, and obeyed her. He lived with her for thirty years, in one house, with an uninterrupted intercourse, and with only the saintly Joseph to share it with Him. She was the witness of His growth, of His joys, of His sorrows, of His prayers; she was blest with His smile, with the touch of His hand, with the whisper of His affection, with the expression of His thoughts and His feelings for that length of time.—Now, my brethren, what ought she to be, what is it *becoming* that she should be, who was so favoured?

Such a question was once asked by a heathen king, when he would place one of his subjects in a dignity becoming the relation in which the latter stood towards him. That subject had saved the king's life, and what was to be done to him in return? The king asked, "What should be done to the man whom the king desireth to honour?" And he received the following answer, "The man whom the king wisheth to honour ought to be clad in the king's apparel, and to be mounted on the king's saddle, and to receive the royal diadem on his head; and let the first among the king's princes and presidents hold his horse, and let him walk through the streets of the city, and say, Thus shall he be honoured, whom the king hath a mind to honour." So stands the case with Mary; she gave birth to the Creator, and what recompense shall be made her? what shall be done to her, who had this relationship to the Most High? what shall be the fit accompaniment of one whom the Almighty has deigned to make, not His servant, not His friend, not His intimate, but His superior, the source of His second being, the nurse of His helpless infancy, the teacher of His opening years? I answer, as the king was answered: Nothing is too high for her to whom God owes His human life; no exuberance of grace, no excess of glory but is becoming, but is to be expected there, where God has lodged Himself, whence God has issued. Let her "be clad in the king's apparel," that is, let the fulness of the Godhead so flow into her that she may be a figure of the incommunicable sanctity, and beauty, and glory, of God Himself: that she may be the Mirror of Justice, the Mystical Rose, the Tower of Ivory, the House of Gold, the Morning Star. Let her "receive the king's diadem upon her head," as the Queen of heaven, the Mother of all living, the Health of the weak, the Refuge of sinners, the Comforter of the afflicted. And "let the first amongst the king's princes walk before her," let Angels, and Prophets, and Apostles, and Martyrs, and all Saints kiss the hem of her garment and rejoice under the shadow of her throne. Thus is it that King Solomon has risen up to meet His Mother, and bowed Himself unto her, and caused a seat to be set for the King's Mother, and she sits on His right hand.

We should be prepared then, my brethren, to believe, that the Mother of God is full of grace and glory, from the very fitness of such a dispensation, even though we had not been taught it; and this fitness will appear still more clear and certain when we contemplate the subject more steadily. Consider then, that it has been the ordinary rule of God's dealings with us, that personal sanctity should be the attendant upon high spiritual dignity of place or work. The Angels, who, as the word imports, are God's messengers, are also perfect in holiness; "without sanctity no one shall see God;" no defiled thing can enter the courts of heaven; and the higher its inhabitants are advanced in their ministry about the throne, the holier are they, and the more absorbed in their contemplation of that Holiness upon which they wait. The Seraphim, who immediately surround the Divine Glory, cry day and night, "Holy, Holy, Holy, Lord God of Hosts." So is it also on earth; the Prophets have ordinarily not only gifts, but graces; they are not only inspired to know and to teach God's will, but inwardly converted to obey it. For surely those only can preach the truth duly, who feel it personally; those only transmit it fully from God to man, who have in the transmission made it their own.

I do not say that there are no exceptions to this rule, but they admit of an easy explanation; I do not say that it never pleases Almighty God to convey any intimation of His will through bad men; of course, for all things can be made to serve Him. By all, even the wicked, He accomplishes His purposes, and by the wicked He is glorified. Our Lord's death was brought about by His enemies, who did His will, while they thought they were gratifying their own. Caiaphas, who contrived and effected it, was made use of to predict it. Balaam prophesied good of God's people in an earlier age, by a divine compulsion, when he wished to prophesy evil. This is true; but in such cases Divine Mercy is plainly overruling the evil, and manifesting His power, without recognizing or sanctioning the instrument. And again, it is true, as He tells us Himself, that in the last day "Many shall say, Lord, Lord, have we not prophesied in Thy Name, and in Thy Name cast out devils, and done many miracles?" and that He shall answer, "I never knew you." This, I say, is undeniable; it is undeniable first, that those who have prophesied in God's Name may *afterwards* fall from God, and lose their souls. Let a man be ever so holy now, he may fall away; and, as present grace is no pledge of perseverance, much less are present gifts; but how does this show that gifts and graces do not commonly go together? Again, it is undeniable that those who have had miraculous gifts may nevertheless have *never* been in God's favour, not even when they exercised them; as I will explain presently. But I am now speaking, not of having gifts, but of being prophets. To be a prophet is something much more personal than to possess gifts. It is a sacred office, it implies a mission, and is the high distinction, not of the enemies of God, but of His friends. Such is the Scripture rule. Who was the first prophet and preacher of justice? Enoch, who walked "by faith," and "pleased God," and was taken from a rebellious world. Who was the second? "Noe," who "condemned the world, and was made heir of the justice which is through faith." Who was the next great prophet? Moses, the lawgiver of the chosen people, who was the "meekest of all men who dwell on the earth." Samuel comes next, who served the Lord from his infancy in the Temple; and then David, who, if he fell into sin, repented, and was "a man after God's heart." And in like manner Job, Elias, Isaias, Jeremias, Daniel, and above them all St. John Baptist, and then again St. Peter, St. Paul, St. John, and the rest, are all especial instances of heroic virtue, and patterns to their brethren. Judas is the exception, but this was by a particular dispensation to enhance our Lord's humiliation and suffering.

Nature itself witnesses to this connexion between sanctity and truth. It anticipates that the fountain from which pure doctrine comes should itself be pure; that the seat of divine teaching, and the oracle of faith, should be the abode of Angels; that the consecrated home, in which the word of God is elaborated, and whence it issues forth for the salvation of the many, should be holy, as that word itself is holy. Here you see the difference of the office of a prophet and a mere gift, such as that of miracles. Miracles are the simple and direct work of God; the worker of them is but an instrument or organ. And in consequence he need not be holy, because he has not, strictly speaking, a share in the work. So again the power of administering the Sacraments, which also is supernatural and miraculous, does not imply personal holiness; nor is there anything surprising in God's giving to a bad man this gift, or the gift of miracles, any more than in His giving him any natural talent or gift, strength or agility of frame, eloquence, or medical skill. It is otherwise with the office of preaching and prophesying, and to this I have been referring; for the truth first goes into the minds of the speakers, and is apprehended and fashioned there, and then comes out from them as, in one sense, its source and its parent. The divine word is begotten in them, and the offspring has their features and tells of them. They are not like "the dumb animal, speaking with man's voice," on which Balaam rode, a mere instrument of God's word, but they have "received an unction from the Holy One, and they know all things," and "where the Spirit of the Lord is, there is liberty;" and while they deliver what they have received, they enforce what they feel and know. "We have *known and believed,*" says St. John, "the charity which God hath to us."

So has it been all through the history of the Church; Moses does not write as David; nor Isaias as Jeremias; nor St. John as St. Paul. And so of the great Doctors of the Church, St. Athanasius, St. Augustine, St. Ambrose, St. Leo, St. Thomas, each has his own manner, each speaks his own words, though he speaks the while the words of God. They speak from themselves, they speak in their own persons, they speak from the heart, from their own experience, with their own arguments, with their own deductions, with their own modes of expression. Now can you fancy, my brethren, such hearts, such feelings to be unholy? how could it be so, without defiling, and thereby nullifying, the word of God? If one drop of corruption makes the purest water worthless, as the slightest savour of bitterness spoils the most delicate viands, how can it be that the word of truth and holiness can proceed profitably from impure lips and an earthly heart? No, as is the tree, so is the fruit; "beware of false prophets," says our Lord; and then He adds, "from their fruits ye shall know them. Do men gather grapes of thorns, or figs of thistles?" Is it not so, my brethren? which of you would go to ask counsel of another, however learned, however gifted, however aged, if you thought him unholy? nay, though you feel and are sure, as far as absolution goes, that a bad priest could give it as really as a holy priest, yet for advice, for comfort, for instruction, you would not go to one whom you did not respect. "Out of the abundance of the heart, the mouth speaketh;" "a good man out of the good treasure of his heart bringeth good, and an evil man out of the evil treasure bringeth forth evil."

So then is it in the case of the soul; and so is it with the body also; as the offspring of holiness is holy in the instance of spiritual births, so is it in the instance of physical. The child is like the parent. Mary was no mere instrument in God's dispensation; the Word of God did not merely come to her and go from her; He did not merely pass through her, as He may pass through us in Holy Communion; it was no heavenly body which the Eternal Son assumed, fashioned by the Angels, and brought down to this lower world: no; He imbibed, He sucked up her blood and her substance into His Divine Person; He became man of her; and received her lineaments and her features, as the appearance and character under which He should manifest Himself to the world. He was known doubtless, by His likeness to her, to be her Son. Thus she may be called the first of Prophets, for of her came the Word bodily; she is the sole oracle of Truth, for the Way, the Truth, and the Life, vouchsafed to be her Son; she is the one mould of Divine Wisdom, and in that mould it was indelibly cast. Surely then, if "the first fruit be holy, the mass also is holy; and if the root be holy, so are the branches." It was natural, it was fitting, that so it should be; it was congruous that, whatever the Omnipotent could work in the person of the finite, should be wrought in her. I say, if the Prophets must be holy, "to whom the word of God comes," what shall we say of her, who was so specially favoured, that the true and substantial Word, and not His shadow or His voice, was not merely made in her, but born of her? who was not merely the organ of God's message, but the origin of His human existence, the living fountain from which He drew His most precious blood, and the material of His most holy flesh? Was it not fitting, beseemed it not, that the Eternal Father should prepare her for this ministration by some pre-eminent sanctification? Do not earthly parents act thus by their children? do they put them out to strangers? do they commit them to any chance person to suckle them? Shall even careless parents show a certain tenderness and solicitude in this matter, and shall not God Himself show it, when He commits His Eternal Word to the custody of man? It was to be expected then that, if the Son was God, the Mother should be as worthy of Him, as creature can be worthy of Creator; that grace should have in her its "perfect work;" that, if she bore the Eternal Wisdom, she should be that created wisdom in whom "is all the grace of the Way and the Truth;" that if she was the Mother of "fair love, and fear, and knowledge, and holy hope," "she should give an odour like cinnamon and balm, and sweetness like to choice myrrh." Can we set bounds to the holiness of her who was the Mother of the Holiest?

Such, then, is the truth ever cherished in the deep heart of the Church, and witnessed by the keen apprehension of her children, that no limits but those proper to a creature, can be assigned to the sanctity of Mary. Did Abraham believe that a son should be born to him of his aged wife? then Mary's faith was greater when she accepted Gabriel's message. Did Judith consecrate her widowhood to God to the surprise of her people? much more did Mary, from her first youth, devote her virginity. Did Samuel, when a child, inhabit the Temple, secluded from the world? Mary too was by her parents lodged in the same holy precincts, at the age when children begin to choose between good and evil. Was Solomon on his birth called "dear to the Lord"? and shall not the destined Mother of God be dear to Him, from the moment she was born? But further still; St. John Baptist was sanctified by the Spirit before his birth; shall Mary be only equal to him? is it not fitting that her privilege should surpass his? is it wonderful, if grace, which anticipated his birth by three months, should in her case run up to the very first moment of her being, outstrip the imputation of sin, and be beforehand with the usurpation of Satan? Mary must surpass all the Saints; the very fact that certain privileges are known to have been theirs persuades us, almost from the necessity of the case, that she had the same and higher. Her conception then was immaculate, in order that she might surpass all Saints in the date as well as the fulness of her sanctification.

But though the grace bestowed upon her was so marvellously great, do not therefore suppose, my brethren, that it excluded her co-operation; she, as we, was on her trial; she, as we, increased in grace; she, as we, merited the increase. Here is another thought leading to the conclusion which I have been drawing. She was not like some inanimate work of the Creator, made beautiful and glorious by the law of its being; she ended, not began, with her full perfection. She had a first grace and a second grace, and she gained the second from the use of the first. She was altogether a moral agent, as others; she advanced on, as all Saints do, from strength to strength, from height to height, so that at five years old she had merited what she had not merited at her birth, and at thirteen what she had not merited at five. Well, my brethren, of what was she thought worthy, when she was thirteen? what did it seem fitting to confer on that poor child, at an age when most children have not begun to think of God or of themselves, or to use the grace He gives them at all; at an age, when many a Saint, as he is in the event, is still in the heavy slumber of sin, and is meriting, not good, but evil at the hands of his just Judge? It befitteth the sanctity with which she was by that time beautified, that she should be then raised even to the dignity of Mother of God. There is doubtless no measure between human nature and God's rewards; He allows us to merit what we cannot claim except from His allowance. He promises us heaven for our good deeds here, and under the covenant of that promise we are justly said to merit it, though heaven is an infinite good and we are but finite creatures. When, then, I say that Mary merited to be the Mother of God, I am speaking of what it was natural and becoming that God, being God, should grant to the more than angelical perfection which she by His grace had obtained. I do not say that she could simply claim, any more than she did contemplate, the reward which she received; but allowing this, still consider how heroical, how transcendental, must have been that saintliness, for which this prerogative was God's return. Enoch was taken away from among the wicked, and we therefore say, Behold a just man who was too good for the world. Noe was saved, and saved others, from the flood; and we say therefore that he earned it by his justice. How great was Abraham's faith, since it gained him the title of the friend of God! How great was the zeal of the Levites, since they merited thereby to be the sacerdotal tribe! How great the love of David, since, for his sake, the kingdom was not taken away from his son when that son fell into idolatry! How great the innocence of Daniel, since he had it revealed to him in this life that he should persevere to the end! What then the faith, the zeal, the love, the innocence of Mary, since it prepared her after so brief a period to be the Mother of God!

Hence you see, my brethren, that our Lady's glories do not rest simply on her maternity; that prerogative is rather the crown of them: unless she had been "full of grace," as the Angel speaks, unless she had been predestinated to be the Queen of Saints, unless she had merited more than all men and Angels together, she would not have fitly been exalted to her unspeakable dignity. The Feast of the Annunciation, when Gabriel came to her, the Christmas Feast, when Christ was born, is the centre, not the range of her glories; it is the noon of her day, the measure of her beginning and her ending. It recalls our thoughts to the Feast of her Conception, and then it carries them on to the Feast of the Assumption. It suggests to us how pure had been her first rising, and it anticipates for us how transcendent were to be the glories of her setting.

Come, my dear brethren, I would not weary you with argument in a festive season, when we should offer to the Blessed Virgin the homage of our love and joy, rather than of our philosophy; yet, let me finish as I have begun;—I will be brief, and bear with me if I view her bright Assumption, as I have viewed her immaculate purity, rather as a point of doctrine, than as a theme for devotion.

It was surely fitting then, it was becoming, that she should be taken up into heaven and not lie in the grave till Christ's second coming, who had passed a life of sanctity and of miracle such as hers. All the works of God are in a beautiful harmony; they are carried on to the end as they begin. This is the difficulty which men of the world find in believing miracles at all; they think these break the order and consistency of God's visible world, not knowing that they do but subserve to a higher order of things, and introduce a supernatural perfection. But at least, my brethren, when one miracle is wrought, it may be expected to draw others after it for the completion of what is begun. Miracles must be wrought for some great end; and if the course of things fell back again into a natural order before its termination, how could we but feel a disappointment? and if we were told that this certainly was to be, how could we but judge the information improbable and difficult to believe? Now this applies to the history of our Lady. I say, it would be a greater miracle, if, her life being what it was, her death was like that of other men, than if it were such as to correspond to her life. Who can conceive, my brethren, that God should so repay the debt, which He condescended to owe to His Mother, for the elements of His human Body, as to allow the flesh and blood from which It was taken to moulder in the grave? Do the sons of men thus deal with their mothers? do they not nourish and sustain them in their feebleness, and keep them in life while they are able? Or who can conceive, that that virginal frame, which never sinned, was to undergo the death of a sinner? Why should she share the curse of Adam, who had no share in his fall? "Dust thou art, and into dust thou shalt return," was the sentence upon sin; she then, who was not a sinner, fitly never saw corruption. She died then, my brethren, because even our Lord and Saviour died; she died, as she suffered, because she was in this world, because she was in a state of things in which suffering and death are the rule. She lived under their external sway; and, as she obeyed Cæsar by coming for enrolment to Bethlehem, so did she, when God willed it, yield to the tyranny of death, and was dissolved into soul and body, as well as others. But though she died as well as others, she died not as others die; for, through the merits of her Son, by whom she was what she was, by the grace of Christ which in her had anticipated sin, which had filled her with light, which had purified her flesh from all defilement, she had been saved from disease and malady, and all that weakens and decays the bodily frame. Original sin had not been found in her, by the wear of her senses, and the waste of her frame, and the decrepitude of years, propagating death. She died, but her death was a mere fact, not an effect; and, when it was over, it ceased to be. She died that she might live; she died as a matter of form or (as I may call it) a ceremony, in order to fulfil, what is called, the debt of nature,—not primarily for herself or because of sin, but to submit herself to her condition, to glorify God, to do what her Son did; not however as her Son and Saviour, with any suffering for any special end; not with a martyr's death, for her martyrdom had been in living; not as an atonement, for man could not make it, and One had made it, and made it for all; but in order to finish her course, and to receive her crown.

And therefore she died in private. It became Him, who died for the world, to die in the world's sight; it became the Great Sacrifice to be lifted up on high, as a light that could not be hid. But she, the lily of Eden, who had always dwelt out of the sight of man, fittingly did she die in the garden's shade, and amid the sweet flowers in which she had lived. Her departure made no noise in the world. The Church went about her common duties, preaching, converting, suffering; there were persecutions, there was fleeing from place to place, there were martyrs, there were triumphs; at length the rumour spread abroad that the Mother of God was no longer upon earth. Pilgrims went to and fro; they sought for her relics, but they found them not; did she die at Ephesus? or did she die at Jerusalem? reports varied; but her tomb could not be pointed out, or if it was found, it was open; and instead of her pure and fragrant body, there was a growth of lilies from the earth which she had touched. So, inquirers went home marvelling, and waiting for further light. And then it was said, how that when her dissolution was at hand, and her soul was to pass in triumph before the judgment-seat of her Son, the Apostles were suddenly gathered together in the place, even in the Holy City, to bear part in the joyful ceremonial; how that they buried her with fitting rites; how that the third day, when they came to the tomb, they found it empty, and angelic choirs with their glad voices were heard singing day and night the glories of their risen Queen. But, however we feel towards the details of this history (nor is there anything in it which will be unwelcome or difficult to piety), so much cannot be doubted, from the consent of the whole Catholic world and the revelations made to holy souls, that, as is befitting, she is, soul and body, with her Son and God in heaven, and that we are enabled to celebrate, not only her death, but her Assumption.

And now, my dear brethren, what is befitting in us, if all that I have been telling you is befitting in Mary? If the Mother of Emmanuel ought to be the first of creatures in sanctity and in beauty; if it became her to be free from all sin from the very first, and from the moment she received her first grace to begin to merit more; and if such as was her beginning, such was her end, her conception immaculate and her death an assumption; if she died, but revived, and is exalted on high; what is befitting in the children of such a Mother, but an imitation, in their measure, of her devotion, her meekness, her simplicity, her modesty, and her sweetness? Her glories are not only for the sake of her Son, they are for our sakes also. Let us copy her faith, who received God's message by the Angel without a doubt; her patience, who endured St. Joseph's surprise without a word; her obedience, who went up to Bethlehem in the winter and bore our Lord in a stable; her meditative spirit, who pondered in her heart what she saw and heard about Him: her fortitude, whose heart the sword went through; her self-surrender, who gave Him up during His ministry and consented to His death.

Above all, let us imitate her purity, who, rather than relinquish her virginity, was willing to lose Him for a Son. O

my dear children, young men and young women, what need
have you of the intercession of the Virgin-mother, of her
help, of her pattern, in this respect! What shall bring you
forward in the narrow way, if you live in the world, but the
thought and patronage of Mary? What shall seal your senses,
what shall tranquillize your heart, when sights and sounds
of danger are around you, but Mary? What shall give you
patience and endurance, when you are wearied out with the
length of the conflict with evil, with the unceasing necessity
of precautions, with the irksomeness of observing them, with
the tediousness of their repetition, with the strain upon your
mind, with your forlorn and cheerless condition, but a loving
communion with her! She will comfort you in your discourage-
ments, solace you in your fatigues, raise you after your falls,
reward you for your successes. She will show you her Son,
your God and your all. When your spirit within you is excited, or relaxed, or depressed, when it loses its balance, when
it is restless and wayward, when it is sick of what it has, and
hankers after what it has not, when your eye is solicited with
evil and your mortal frame trembles under the shadow of the
Tempter, what will bring you to yourselves, to peace and
to health, but the cool breath of the Immaculate and the
fragrance of the Rose of Sharon? It is the boast of the Catholic
Religion, that it has the gift of making the young heart chaste;
and why is this, but that it gives us Jesus Christ for our food,
and Mary for our nursing Mother? Fulfil this boast in yourselves; prove to the world that you are following no false
teaching, vindicate the glory of your Mother Mary, whom the
world blasphemes, in the very face of the world, by the
simplicity of your own deportment, and the sanctity of your
words and deeds. Go to her for the royal heart of innocence.
She is the beautiful gift of God, which outshines the fascinations of a bad world, and which no one ever sought in
sincerity and was disappointed. She is the personal type and
representative image of that spiritual life and renovation in

grace, "without which no one shall see God." "Her spirit is sweeter than honey, and her heritage than the honeycomb. They that eat her shall yet be hungry, and they that drink her shall still thirst. Whoso hearkeneth to her shall not be confounded, and they that work by her shall not sin."

X X

THE MISSION OF ST. PHILIP NERI [1]

PART I

"Et ego novissimus evigilavi, et quasi qui colligit acinos post vinde miatores. In benedictione Dei et ipse speravi, et quasi qui vindemiat, replevi torcular. Respicite quoniam non mihi soli laboravi, sed omnibus exquirentibus disciplinam." (I awaked last of all, and as one that gathereth after the grape-gatherers. In the blessing of God I also have hoped; and as one that gathereth grapes, have I filled the wine-press. See that I have not laboured for myself only, but for all that seek discipline).—Eccli., c. xxxiii. v. 16–18.

THE PICTURE OF ST. PHILIP is ever in this Chapel, and his image is ever in our minds. Not only we, who belong to his Congregation, and have devoted ourselves to his service, but you, my dear Brethren and Children, who come to worship here under his shadow, you, too, I am persuaded, carry him away with you to your homes, and find by experience the benefit of such a Patron. His commemoration is of daily wont in this neighbourhood, and the Octave of his Festival runs round the full circuit of the year. At no season is it necessary to remind you of him; nor at this particular season is there any special reason, either from ritual or from custom, which makes it suitable or dutiful to do so. And yet, in our own case it is more natural to think and speak of him at this time than at any other, for we are approaching the anniversary of his coming into England and into Birmingham, and are returning thanks to our good God in a series

[1] Preached in the Oratory, Birmingham. From *Sermons Preached on Various Occasions,* No. 12. [Ed.]

277

of devotions, for all the mercies which, through his intercession, have, in the course of two years, been poured out upon us. We are now close upon completing the second year since the first introduction [2] of the Oratory into England; close upon completing the first, since it took up its abode in this populous town,[3] to which the Apostolical Brief sent it. Our prospects, we know surely, will extend, and our successes multiply, as time goes on; and we may be enabled to furnish the elements, or to lay the rudiments of Oratories for other places; but, if the proverb be true, that "he who begins, does half the work," we had a mercy shown us this time last year, the like of which we never can have shown us again.

Nor do we at this season turn only in gratitude to our dear Saint and Father, for what he has gained for us; we also turn to him as our most necessary pattern in the acknowledgment which we must make to God for it. He who has gained for us God's mercies, he, my dear Fathers of the Oratory, must teach us to use them worthily and this leads us to think over and dwell both on him and on his history, as though it were now his yearly festival;—to enlarge upon the special traits of his character and memorable passages of his life, if not for his sake, at least for our own; if not to do him honour, at least to gain guidance for ourselves, by reason of the light which all that is recorded of him casts upon our vocation, our duties, and our work; for then only are we his true followers, when we do as he did. Moreover, although all this is a subject of thought which concerns us, the members of the Oratory, primarily, yet it must have an interest for those also who, like yourselves, my Brethren, make use of our ministrations; for, whereas there are many professions, missions, and undertakings in the length and breadth of the Catholic Church, you will, by considering it, understand more exactly

[2] February 2, 1848.
[3] Birmingham.

what it is in particular, that the Oratory proposes to do for you.

Let us, then, inquire what St. Philip's times were, and what place he holds in them; what he was raised up to do, how he did it, and how we, my Fathers of the Oratory, may make his work and his way of doing it a pattern for ourselves in this day.

1. His times were such as the Church has never seen before nor since, and such as the world must last long for her to see again; nor peculiar only in themselves, but involving a singular and most severe trial of the faith and love of her children. It was a time of sifting and peril, and of "the fall and resurrection of many in Israel." Our gracious Lord, we well know, never will forsake her; He will sustain her in all dangers, and she will last while the world lasts; but, if ever there was a time when He seemed preparing to forsake her,—it was not the time of persecution, when thousands upon thousands of her choicest were cut off, and her flock decimated; it was not in the middle age, when the ferocity of the soldier and subtlety of the sophist beleaguered her,—but it was in that dreary time, at the close and in the fulness of which St. Philip entered upon his work. A great author, one of his own sons, Cardinal Baronius, has said of the dark age, that it was a time when our Lord seemed to be asleep in Peter's boat; but there is another passage of the Gospel still more wonderful than the record of that sleep, and one which had a still more marvellous accomplishment in the period of which I have to speak. There was a time when Satan took up bodily the King of Saints, and carried Him whither he would. Then was our most Holy Saviour and Lord clasped in the arms of ambition, avarice, and impurity:—and in like manner His Church also after Him, though full of divine gifts, the Immaculate Spouse, the Oracle of Truth, the Voice of the Holy Ghost, infallible in matters of faith and morals, whether in the chair of her Su-

preme Pontiff, or in the unity of her Episcopate, nevertheless was at this time so environed, so implicated, with sin and lawlessness, as to appear in the eyes of the world to be what she was not. Never, as then, were her rulers, some in higher, some in lower degree, so near compromising what can never be compromised; never so near denying in private what they taught in public, and undoing by their lives what they professed with their mouths; never were they so mixed up with vanity, so tempted by pride, so haunted by concupiscence; never breathed they so tainted an atmosphere, or were kissed by such traitorous friends, or were subjected to such sights of shame, or were clad in such blood-stained garments, as in the centuries upon and in which St. Philip came into the world. Alas, for us, my Brethren! the scandal of deeds done in Italy then is borne by us in England now.

It was an age when the passionate wilfulness of the feudal baron was vigorous still; when civilization, powerless as yet to redress the grievances of society at large, gave to princes and to nobles as much to possess as before, and less to suffer; increased their pomp, and diminished their duties and their risks; became the cloak of vices which it did not extirpate, made revenge certain by teaching it to be treacherous, and unbelief venerable by proving it to be ancient. Such were the characteristics of St. Philip's age; and Florence, his birthplace, presented the most complete exhibition of them,— and next to Florence, Rome, the city of his adoption.

Florence was at that time the most intellectual, the most magnificent city of Italy. About a century before, one of its richest merchants and bankers [4] had become its virtual ruler, and had transmitted his power to his descendants, who still possessed it. The history of this family is intimately connected with that of the Holy See; at times they were its enemies: they ended in giving to it three or four princes of their own blood to fill it: but whether in alliance with it or at war, whether at Florence or at Rome, they exerted, at least for

[4] Cosmo de' Medici.

many years, an influence prejudicial to its real, that is, its religious well-being.

This was the time of the revival of what is called classical learning; that is, the learning of ancient Greece and Rome. Constantinople had lately been taken by the Turks, who still hold it; its scholars, with their traditions and their manuscripts, escaped to Italy, and they found a home at Florence with this powerful family. The heads of this family became the special patrons of Literature and the Arts, and leaders of the classical revival. Under their auspices, public schools were opened; the Greek language was studied; an academy was established for philosophy; a library was founded, and placed in the Dominican Convent of St. Mark. Its librarian in course of time became Pope,[5] and founded at Rome the famous Vatican Library. Books in the languages of the East, —Hebrew, Arabic, even Indian, were collected; the lost writings of Greek and Roman authors were brought to light and published.

So far, you will see, there was little which could be censured; the revival of learning was in itself a great benefit to mankind, and the labour which it involved was well bestowed. But, in this world, evil follows good as its shadow; human nature perverting and corrupting what is intrinsically innocent or praiseworthy. So, in this instance, the pursuit of the old learning became a passion. As the crumbling cloisters of the East were ransacked, and manuscripts were found and deciphered,—as the ruins of pagan edifices were excavated, mounds of earth removed, and the sculptures of classical art disinterred,—an uncontrollable excitement, an intoxication, seized upon the classes which were engaged in the work. It seized upon young and old: while one celebrated archæologist [6] spent fifty years in the discovery of ancient authors, and another's [7] hair turned white on his losing by

[5] Nicholas V.

[6] Poggio.

[7] Guarino.

shipwreck his cargo of discoveries, noble ladies became prodigies of learning, and a youth [8] of twenty exhibited himself at Rome as the master of twenty-two languages, and proposed nine hundred subjects for disputation.

The wonderful art of printing, which had been lately discovered, added to the excitement, not merely by what it actually did in that day, but by the brilliant future which it opened on the imagination, to the advance both of knowledge and of society.

Nor was this the limit of the discoveries of that remarkable age;—news came of another continent beyond the ocean; America, North and South, became known to Europe, and the extent of the earth was doubled. The strangest tales were circulated, true and false, of the riches, of the gold, silver, and gems, of the animals, of the vegetable productions, of the new hemisphere. The public mind was agitated by a thousand fancies; no one knew what was coming; anything might be expected; a new era had opened upon the world, and enormous changes, political and social, were in preparation. There was an upheaving of the gigantic intellect of man; he found he had powers and resources which he was not conscious of before, and began in anticipation to idolize their triumphs.

And, while the world was becoming so strong, the Church, on the other hand, was at the moment proportionally weak, as far as relates to the human instruments of her power. Great, indeed, was her temporal exaltation at that day; great she was then, as she will ever be, in her invisible, divine strength; but in the ordinary elements of her greatness and weapons of her success, in order and discipline, in pastoral vigilance, in the sanctity of her individual members, in these respects certainly she was taken at disadvantage. I do not like, nor would you, my Brethren, wish me, to enlarge upon a most sorrowful subject. The great Italian families intrigued and fought for her supreme rule, as if it had been a mere

[8] Pico of Mirandola.

earthly principality. And on this account, she was unable at the moment, from scarcity of champions, to cope with the vehement and enthusiastic movement which I have been describing, and which assailed her within and without. All things are good in their place: human learning and science, the works of genius, the wonders of nature, all, as I have said, have their use, when kept in subordination to the faith and worship of God; but it is nothing else but an abuse, if they are suffered to engross the mind, and if religion is made secondary to them. Yet they are so fascinating,—so enchanting,—so present, tangible, constraining, in their influence,—that, unless the watchmen of the Holy City are on the alert, they are almost sure to act to the prejudice of the highest interests of man. So it was at the time I speak of; what was beautiful was placed before what was true; or rather, the beauty of the creature was preferred to the transcendent beauty of the Creator. Nature and art, the rich material, the creative mind, were suffered to invade and oppress the Church, instead of ministering to her. The world entered her sacred precincts forcibly, and embellished them after its own fashion. It addressed itself to her rulers, who were already enervated by the homage of nations; and it attempted to persuade them to disguise the awful Bride of the Lamb in an old heathen garb, of which her very coming had long since been the destruction. More seemly by far had it been to ask her to take part in the abolished ceremonies of the Mosaic law, than to intrude classical literature upon her instead of the teaching of the Holy Fathers. It was Satan carrying her up to the high mountain, and showing her all the kingdoms of the earth and their glory, with the hope of tempting her to forget her mission.

"Eat and drink, for to-morrow we die:" so was it said of old by the heathen; so was it now said, almost in the same words, by Christians, not meaning, indeed, to deny the life to come, but hoping to inherit the future without giving up any enjoyment of the present. The artists, poets, and philosophers, who flourished under the smile of the great Florentine family, and their disciples through Italy, if they were not allowed to decorate Holy Church at their will and pleasure, at least could do as they would with the world; and fallen as it is, they made it still, by the splendour of their genius a very paradise of delight. They flung a grace over sin, and a dignity over unbelief. Life was to them one long revel; they feasted, they sported, they moulded forms and painted countenances of the most perfect human beauty; they indulged in licentious wit, they wrote immodest verses, they lightly used the words of Scripture; they quarrelled, they used the knife, they fled to sanctuary, and then they issued forth again, to go through the same round of pleasure and of sin. Festivals and Carnivals became seasons of popular licence, for dramas and masquerades; and the excesses of paganism were renewed with the refinements supplied by classical associations. Dances, processions, and songs, formed part of the entertainment. Florence especially was the scene of the pageant, and its whole population were either actors in it, or spectators. The time chosen for it was the night; the performances were carried on by torchlight; bands of women, as well as of men, had their appointed parts in them, nor were they concluded till after daybreak. On St. John Baptist's day, in the year preceding St. Philip's birth, such an exhibition, with tournaments and other celebrations, was held in that same city, his birth-place. Seven sacred princes came up incognito to attend it; two lions and a panther were sent as a present from a member of the reigning family, then seated in the Vatican; and a triumphal arch was erected, in honour of the donor, opposite to the Dominican convent of St. Mark.

All this for the people:—Their rulers, who had introduced or patronized these shows, and the immediate circle of those rulers, went further. They took heathen names; they kept the feasts of the heathen founder of Rome, and the heathen philosopher Plato; they died with heathen consolations sounding in their ears. They attempted to hold intercourse with the evil powers;—we have the record of a scene in the great Roman amphitheatre, called the Coliseum. The sorcerer is said to have possessed a sacred character; thousands of devils are described as rising at his incantation, who promised, and who kept their promise, to grant a wicked gratification to the celebrated artist [9] who consulted them. A greater sin could not have been committed by an ecclesiastic, but scandals there were worse. If even in the very opening of the Gospel, when faith was keenest and the heart purest, there was a Judas among the Apostles, and a Nicolas among the deacons, and a Simon Magus among the neophytes, we need not wonder, much as we may lament, that in the degenerate age I am speaking of, lapses should occur, far more numerous than those early ones, if not so great in enormity of crime. One of the most zealous restorers of the ancient learning, who has been already spoken of, was an ecclesiastic with a family; [10] one of the chief writers of licentious tales had on him both religious and episcopal obligations.[11] And a writer,[12] who is reckoned the vilest of his day, being patronized by one of the great Florentine family at Rome, was audacious enough to set his heart (unsuccessfully) on becoming a Cardinal of Holy Church.

Good and evil, sacred prerogatives and sinful hearts, were brought into close contact, marvellously and awfully. The Sovereign Pontiffs were familiarly dealt with, and then slandered behind their backs, by the profligate artists whom they had benefited. Holy men grew up and won their crowns, out of families on which history has set its note of shame. Two saints, contemporaries of St. Philip, will occur to you, my dear Fathers, as instances of this portent:—St. Francis Borgia, the third Father-General of the Society of Jesus, bears a name, shameful in the history of Rome; St. Mary Magdalene of the

---

[9] Cellini.
[10] Poggio.
[11] Bandello.
[12] Pietro Aretino.

Pazzi came of a Florentine stock infamous for a deed of combined sacrilege, bloodshed, and treachery perhaps without a parallel.

These are some of the traits of the times in which St. Philip was sent on earth: certainly, an Apostle was needed both for Florence and for Rome.

2. And for Florence, that Apostle seemed to have been found just before St. Philip's day. You may recollect, my Brethren, I have more than once spoken of the great Dominican convent of St. Mark. That convent, built though it was by the first prince of the rich family I have so often mentioned, was devoted to a style of art and a description of learning far different from those for which Greece or Rome was famous. Under the shadow of St. Dominic, such learning alone had place, which ministered to the most symmetrical theology, and to a philosophy in accordance; and the serene wisdom which his name recalls, had been carried out into poetry and the fine arts, by the genius of his children and his clients. That very convent of St. Mark is still adorned by the celebrated paintings executed by the Dominican artist, called, like the Dominican St. Thomas, the Angelical; and about the same time, it had been under the rule of the celebrated Dominican confessor and writer, afterwards archbishop of the city, St. Antoninus. Here, too, came about thirty years afterwards, and shortly before St. Philip's birth, that fiery Reformer, also a Dominican, of whom I am to speak as a sort of Apostle of Florence, a man certainly of commanding eloquence and extraordinary influence, full of the traditions of his order, and cherishing a fierce hatred of the reviving heathen literature and the classical taste of the day; I mention his name, on account of the affection which St. Philip felt for his memory,—Savonarola.

A true son of St. Dominic, in energy, in severity of life, in contempt of merely secular learning, a forerunner of the Dominican St. Pius in boldness, in resoluteness, in zeal for the honour of the House of God, and for the restoration of holy discipline, Savonarola felt "his spirit stirred up within him," like another Paul, when he came to that beautiful home of genius and philosophy; for he found Florence, like another Athens, "wholly given to idolatry." He groaned within him, and was troubled, and refused consolation, when he beheld a Christian court and people priding itself on its material greatness, its intellectual gifts, and its social refinement, while it abandoned itself to luxury, to feast and song and revel, to fine shows and splendid apparel, to an impure poetry, to a depraved and sensual character of art, to heathen speculations, and to forbidden, superstitious practices. His vehement spirit could not be restrained, and got the better of him, and,—unlike the Apostle, whose prudence, gentleness, love of his kind, and human accomplishments are nowhere more happily shown than in his speech to the Athenians,[13]—he burst forth into a whirlwind of indignation and invective against all that he found in Florence, and condemned the whole established system, and all who took part of it, high and low, prince or prelate, ecclesiastic or layman, with a pitiless rigour,—which for the moment certainly did a great deal more than St. Paul was able to do at the Areopagus; for St. Paul made only one or two converts there, and departed, whereas Savonarola had great immediate success, frightened and abashed the offenders, rallied round him the better disposed, and elicited and developed whatever there was of piety, whether in the multitude or in the upper class.

It was the truth of his cause, the earnestness of his convictions, the singleness of his aims, the impartiality of his censures, the intrepidity of his menaces, which constituted the secret of his success. Yet a less worthy motive lent its aid; men crowded round a pulpit, from which others were attacked as well as themselves. The humbler offender was pleased to be told that crime was a leveller of ranks, and to find that he thus was a gainer in the common demoralization. The laity

[13] Acts xvii.

bore to be denounced, when the clergy were not spared; and the rich and noble suffered a declamation which did not stop short of the sacred Chair of St. Peter.

"In the houses of great prelates and great doctors," he cried out, "nothing is thought of but poetry and rhetoric. Go and see for yourselves; you will find them with books of polite literature in their hands, pernicious writings, with Virgil, Horace, and Cicero, to prepare themselves for the cure of souls withal. Astrologers have the governance of the Church. There is not a prelate, there is not a great doctor, but is intimate with some astrologer, who predicts for him the hour and the moment for riding out, or for whatever else he does. Our preachers have already given up Holy Scripture, and are given to Philosophy, which they preach from the pulpit, and treat as their queen. As to Holy Scripture, they make it the handmaid, because to preach philosophy looks learned, whereas it should simply be an aid in the interpretation of the divine word."

"Our Church," he continued, "has outside many fine ceremonies in divine worship, fine vestments, an uncommon display of drapery, gold and silver candlesticks, so many fine chalices, quite magnificent. Those great prelates with their fine mitres on, of gold and jewels, with crosiers of silver, with their fine chasubles, and copes of brocade, there they are at the altar, singing fine vespers, fine masses, so solemnly, with so many fine ceremonies, so many organs and singers, that your head turns. And they seem to you, those men, to have great gravity and a saintly show; and you think that they cannot do wrong, but that their words and their deeds are Gospel, and claim your observance. That is how the modern Church is made. Men feed on these husks, and make themselves happy in these ceremonies, and say that the Church of Jesus Christ never was in a more flourishing state, and that divine worship never was so well carried out as at present,—as on one occasion a great prelate said, that the Church never was in such honour, and its prelates never in such repute, whereas its first prelates were but small men, because they were humble and poor, because they had not such ample bishoprics, such rich abbeys, as ours of this day, nor had they as yet such gold mitres, such chalices. Do you take me? I mean in the primitive Church, the chalices were of wood, and the prelates of gold; but now the chalices are of gold, and the prelates are wooden."

"O Italy!" he cried out in the tone of a prophet, "O rulers of Italy! O prelates of the Church! the wrath of God is over you, and your conversion alone will avert it. Do penance, while the sword is in the scabbard, and ere it is imbrued in your blood. O Italy! thou shalt be given into the hands of a fierce, a barbarous nation, whose only pleasure will be to do thee ill. And Rome shall fare worse from them than any other city; your possessions and your treasures shall be given into their hands."

Such bold language effected for the moment a revolution rather than a reform. The eloquent preacher became the political partisan; the great family was forced by political circumstances to give way, and for the better part of ten years Savonarola was ruler of Florence. Not only the populace, but courtiers, noble ladies, scholars, artists, all put themselves at his disposal, and became his disciples. He found a way to the hearts of philosophers, poets, painters, engravers, sculptors, architects, and made them renounce their heathen tastes and heathen aspirations. "Behold the sun," he said; "its beauty consists in possessing light; behold the blessed spirits, their beauty is light; and God Himself, because He is the most full of light, is beauty itself. The beauty of every creature is more perfect, the more closely it resembles God's beauty; and the body is beautiful in proportion to the beauty of the soul. Conceive what must have been the beauty of the Blessed Virgin, who possessed such sanctity, sanctity that shone from all her features. Conceive how beautiful was Christ, who was God and man. Now even Aristotle, who was a pagan, bids us not to tolerate indecent pictures, lest children, seeing them, be corrupted; but what shall I say to you, Christian painters, who execute these immodest figures? I tell you to do so no more. You who have them and destroy them, will do a work pleasing to Almighty God and the Holy Virgin. 'You have dedicated My Temple and My Churches to your God Moloch,' says the Almighty. See how they act at Florence! mothers take their unmarried daughters to the cathedral, decked out for show, till they look like nymphs. 'These are your idols, which you have placed in My Temple.' The young men say of this or that maiden, 'This is Magdalen,' 'That is St. John,' because you paint figures in the church, which resemble this woman or that. You painters act wrongly; you introduce worldly vanities into the Church. Do you believe that the Blessed Virgin was dressed as you represent her? I tell you that she was modestly dressed, and so veiled that one could scarce see her face; and St. Elizabeth too was modest and simple in her attire." [14]

Wonderful were the conversions which followed on the enunciation of truth so undeniable, so grave in import, so earnestly enforced. As to the artists, many of them became Dominicans, and the convent of St. Mark had to be enlarged to hold them. The members of another convent in the city, feeling their state of relaxation, begged to be allowed to come over to him in a body, and to take the rule of St. Dominic upon them. The population of Florence rose from their beds after midnight in winter to attend upon his sermons. There they stood in the Church, waiting, taper in hand, or singing hymns, or praying, or saying office, for three or four hours, till he began to preach. They showed the fruits of his exhortations in their homes. Women reformed their dress, youths unlearned their light songs, heads of families read the lives of the Saints to their children. At length the zealous preacher determined on having, in token of repentance, a solemn conflagration in the great square, of all the scandals and the vari-

[14] *Vide* Father Meehan's translation of Marchetti's [Marchese's?] work.

ous occasions of sin with which the city abounded. At the time of the Carnival, the special festival of the world, the flesh, and the devil, he invited the whole city to this stern act of reparation. He raised a high pyramid, with a quantity of gunpowder at its base. His innumerable penitents formed in long procession, and hither they marched with the instruments and incentives of iniquity in their hands, to be offered up in expiation of their sins. It was a costly sacrifice, ruthlessly performed. Artists brought their beautiful pictures, portraits, and figures in ivory or alabaster, and flung them upon the pyre; others brought richly worked tapestries; others, lutes, flutes, guitars, cards, dice, looking-glasses, perfumery, paint, masks, disguises; others, novels and poems. Lighted torches were then applied, and, amid the ringing of bells and the acclamations of the vast multitude, the whole was reduced to ashes. A foreigner had in vain offered 20,000 crowns to ransom them from the flames. The same impressive ceremony was repeated in the following year.

A very wonderful man, you will allow, my Brethren, was this Savonarola. I shall say nothing more of him, except what was the issue of his reforms. For years, as I have said, he had his own way; at length, his innocence, sincerity, and zeal were the ruin of his humility. He presumed; he exalted himself against a power which none can assail without misfortune. He put himself in opposition to the Holy See, and, as some say, disobeyed its injunctions. Reform is not wrought out by disobedience; this was not the way to be the Apostle either of Florence or of Rome. Then trouble came upon him, a great reaction ensued; his enemies got the upper hand; he went into extravagances himself; the people deserted him; he was put to death, strangled, hung on a gibbet, and then burned in the very square where he had set fire to the costly furniture of vanity and sin. And then the rich and powerful family returned to Florence; and things went on pretty much as before; and, on the very year preceding St. Philip's birth, took place that riotous festivity on St. John Baptist's day, over against the convent of St. Mark, of which I have already spoken.

And now I have added something more to the picture, which I have proposed to give you, of the state of things both in Florence and in Rome, when St. Philip was raised up to be an Apostle of another sort.

[*January 15, 1850.*]

PART II

FLORENCE, THEN, had her Apostle;—we have reviewed his commencement and his end:—a zealous, heroic man, but not, as far as we can judge, reaching to the level of a saint. It is not by the enthusiasm of the multitude, or by political violence,—it is not by powerful declamation, or by railing at authorities, that the foundations are laid of religious works. It is not by sudden popularity, or by strong resolves, and demonstrations, or by romantic incidents, or by immediate successes, that undertakings commence which are to last. I do not say, that to be roused, even for a moment, from the dream of sin, to repent and be absolved, even though a relapse follow it, is a slight gain; or that the brilliant, but brief, triumphs of Savonarola are to be despised. He did good in his day, though his day was a short one. Still, after all, his history brings to mind that passage in sacred history, where the Almighty displayed His presence to Elias on Mount Horeb. "The Lord was not in the wind," nor "in the earthquake," nor "in the fire;" but after the fire came "the whisper of a gentle air."

So was it with the Lord of grace Himself, when He came upon earth; so it is with His chosen servants after Him. He grew up in silence and obscurity, overlooked by the world; and then He triumphed. He was the grain cast into the earth, which, while a man "sleeps and rises, night and day, springs

up and grows whilst he knoweth not." He was the mustard
seed, "which is the least of all seeds, but, when it is grown
up, becometh a tree, and shooteth out great branches, so that
the birds of the air dwell under its shadow." He grew up "as
a tender plant, and as a root out of a thirsty land;" and "His
look was, as it were, hidden and despised, wherefore we
esteemed Him not." And, when He began to preach, He did
not "contend nor cry out, nor break the bruised reed, nor
quench the smoking flax;" and thus "He sent forth judgment
unto victory." So was it in the beginning, so has it been ever
since. After the storm, the earthquake and the fire, the calm,
soothing whisper of the fragrant air. After Savonarola, Philip.

1. Philip was born in Florence within twenty years after
him. The memory of the heroic friar was then still fresh in
the minds of men, who would be talking familiarly of him
to the younger generation,—of the scenes which their own
eyes had witnessed, and of the deeds of penance which they
had done at his bidding. Especially vivid would the recollec-
tions of him be in the Convent of St. Mark; for there was his
cell, there the garden where he walked up and down in meditation, and refused to notice the great prince of the day; [15]
there would be his crucifix, his habit, his discipline, his books,
and whatever had once been his. Now, it so happened, St.
Philip was a child of this very convent; here he received his
first religious instruction, and in after times he used to say,
"Whatever there was of good in me, when I was young, I
owed it to the Fathers of St. Mark's, in Florence." For Savonarola he retained a singular affection all through his life;
he kept his picture in his room, and about the year 1560,
when the question came before Popes Paul IV. and Pius IV.,
of the condemnation of Savonarola's teaching, he interceded
fervently and successfully in his behalf before the Blessed
Sacrament, exposed on the occasion in the Dominican church
at Rome. This was in his middle age.

To return to his youth: at the age of eighteen, he left Flor-

[15] Lorenzo de' Medici.

ence for good, first going to a town in the kingdom of Naples; then at the end of two years, to Rome, where he lived for sixty years, without once going beyond the circuit of its seven Basilicas. There he died, when he had nearly completed his eightieth year. A simple outline of a history, you will say, my Brethren, singularly deficient in incident or adventure; yet, though he made only one journey in his long life, he turned it to account; and the chances of external situation which then befell him, few as they were, were instruments in the formation of his mind and in the direction of his future course. The Florentine pupil of St. Dominic fell under the inspirations of St. Benedict in the territory of Naples, and found St. Ignatius in person, and in the flesh, when he got to Rome.

Benedict, Dominic, Ignatius:—these are the three venerable Patriarchs, whose Orders divide between them the extent of Christian history. There are many Saints besides, who have been fruitful in followers and institutions, and have multiplied themselves in Christendom, and lived on earth in their children, when they themselves were gone to heaven. But there are three who, in an especial way, have had committed to them the office of a public ministry in the affairs of the Church one after another, and who are, in some sense, her "nursing fathers," and are masters in the spiritual Israel, and ruling names in her schools and her libraries; and these are Benedict, Dominic, and Ignatius. Philip came under the teaching of all three successively.

2. It was the magnificent aim of the children of St. Dominic to form the whole matter of human knowledge into one harmonious system, to secure the alliance between religion and philosophy, and to train men to the use of the gifts of nature in the sunlight of divine grace and revealed truth. It required the dissolution and reconstruction of society to give an opportunity for so great a thought; and accordingly, the Order of Preachers flourished after the old Empire had passed away, and the chaos which followed on it had resulted in the creation of a new world. Now, in the age of St. Philip, a violent

effort was in progress, on the part of the powers of evil, to break up this sublime unity, and to set human genius, the philosopher and the poet, the artist and the musician, in opposition to religion. Accordingly, the work of the glorious Order of St. Dominic was more than ever called for, whatever might be those new methods of prosecuting it, more suitable to the times; and, if Philip was destined, as he was, to play an important part in them in the cause of God, it was therefore necessary that he should be imbued with the great idea of that Order. It was necessary that he should have deeply fixed within him, as the object of his life, that single aim of subduing this various, multiform, many-coloured world to the unity of divine service. I mean there are Saints, whose mission lies rather in separating off from each other the world and the Truth; that of other Saints lies in bringing them together. Philip's was the latter. Suitably then, and reasonably, did he receive his elementary formation of mind from the Fathers of St. Mark. And when this had been secured, then he was sent off, "not knowing whither he went, to other tutors, and towards the scene of his destined labours, to do a work like St. Dominic's work, though he was not to be a Dominican.

3. Then he came to St. Benedict. Close by the town to which his father had sent him, is the celebrated monastery of Monte Cassino, the principal seat of the Benedictine Order. The relaxation, which at that time prevailed in so many regular communities, seems not to have reached this ancient sanctuary; [16] but the judgments, which even in Savonarola's day were falling on Italy, had not fallen short of Monte Cassino. The neighbourhood had been the scene of war; and the foreign troops had pillaged the Church, and the new generation of monks had been nurtured in adversity. "Not far from San Germano," that is, the town to which Philip had been sent, says the author of his life, "there is a celebrated mountain, which, according to a very ancient and common tradition, is one of those which opened at our Saviour's death. It

[16] *Vide* Tosti's history of that abbey.

belongs to the Benedictine Fathers of Monte Cassino, who have a church there dedicated to the Most Holy Trinity. This mountain is split from top to bottom by three huge fissures; and in the middle of the three, which is the steepest, there is a little chapel on a rock, under the care of the monks, and on it is a crucifix painted, which the sailors salute with their guns as they pass by. Here Philip was in the habit of retiring for prayer and meditation on the Lord's Passion."

Observe, my dear Brethren, Philip is now in quite a new scene,—no longer amid the mediæval grandeur, but among the Saints and associations of primitive ages; it is no longer the busy, gaudy town, but the calm and pure country; no longer cloisters and paintings, but rocks and sea, leading to meditation; no longer golden mitres and jewelled copes, under high arches and painted windows, but secluded, unfurnished chapels, and rude crucifixes; no longer the vision of our Lord's Passion portrayed by sacred art, but the very rent in the solid mountain, opened in that same hour when He hung upon the Cross; no longer the holy doctrines and devotions of later piety, but the aboriginal mystery, contained in Scripture, Creed, and Baptism, and battled for in the first centuries, the dogma of the most Holy Trinity. Thus, everything about Philip threw him back into the times of simplicity, of poverty, of persecution, of martyrdom; the times of patience, of obscure and cheerful toil, of humble, unrequited service; ere Christianity had gained a literature, or theology had become a science, or any but saints had sat in Peter's chair; while the book of nature and the book of grace were the chief instruments of knowledge and of love. Such was the school of St. Benedict; nor did that dear and venerable Father let the young pilgrim go, even when his two years' sojourn in his neighbourhood was at an end. For if a direct divine summons took him to Rome, still St. Benedict, as I may say, chose out for him his lodgings there; for he sent him to those ancient basilicas, and cemeteries, and catacombs of the Holy City which spoke of the early monks and the most primitive religion, and these you know he haunted, or almost lived in them, till ten years and more had passed from the date of his leaving Florence. "Philip Neri is a great saint," said a Dominican Friar, who kept his eyes upon the youth; "and among his other wonderful things, he has dwelt for a whole ten years in the caves of St. Sebastian, by way of penance;" lodging, I say, as St. Benedict would have had him, with the old martyr Popes, and their saintly court and retinue, their deacons and chamberlains, and chaplains; with St. Callistus, and St. Sebastian, and St. Laurence; with St. Mark and St. Marcellian, with St. Agnes and St. Cecilia, with St. Nereus and St. Achilleus, with St. Papias and St. Maurus, till at length he had that marvellous visitation, when the Holy Ghost came down upon him in a ball of fire, about the time of Pentecost, and filled his heart with consolations so overwhelming that, lest he should die of ecstasy, he came up into the world of men, and set about a work to flesh and blood more endurable.

Thus was the second stage of Philip's education brought to a close; and, as from St. Dominic he gained the end he was to pursue, so from St. Benedict he learned how to pursue it. He was to pursue Savonarola's purposes, but not in Savonarola's way; rather, in the spirit and after the fashion of those early Religious, of which St. Benedict is the typical representative. Those early Religious lived in communities, which were detached from each other, not brought together under one common governance; they were settled in one place, and had no duties beyond it; vows were not a necessary element of their state; they had little or nothing to do with ecclesiastical matters or secular politics; they had no large plan of action for religious ends; they let each day do its work as it came; they lived in obscurity, and laid a special stress on prayer and meditation; they were simple in their forms of worship, and they freely admitted laymen into their fellowship. In peculiarities such as these we recognize the Oratory of St. Philip. Least thought had he of all men, of living in his works beyond his day: he could scarcely be brought to throw his disciples into the form of community, and to perpetuate that form by ecclesiastical recognition. Then he would not go and preside over them; then, when obliged to go, he would not let them call him Father Superior. Then he would not listen to their founding houses in other cities. Much less would he take dignities himself, or suffer them to do so. He would not permit any forms or observances to be the characteristics of his Congregation, besides mutual love and hard work. For the interior life he sent them back, with especial earnestness, to the Apostolic Epistles, and to the traditions of that early monk, John Cassian. In his exterior worship, he imitated, as Cardinal Baronius observes, the form furnished by St. Paul, in his first Epistle to the Corinthians. "It is by a divine counsel," says that glory of the Oratory, speaking, in his *Annals*, in the tone of an historian, "that there has been in great measure renewed in our age in Rome, after the pattern of the Apostolic assembly, the edifying practice of discoursing in sermons of the things of God. This has been the work of the Reverend Father Philip Neri, a Florentine, who, like a skilful architect, laid the foundation of it. It was arranged, that almost every day those who were desirous of Christian perfection should come to the Oratory. First, there was some length of time spent in mental prayer, then one of the brothers read a spiritual book, and during the reading the aforesaid Father commented on what was read. Sometimes he desired one of the brethren to give his opinion on some subject, and then the discourse proceeded in the form of dialogue. After this, he commanded one of them to mount a seat, and there, in a familiar, plain style, to discourse upon the lives of the Saints. To him succeeded another, on a different subject, but equally plain; lastly, a third discoursed upon ecclesiastical history. When all was finished, they sang some spiritual hymn, prayed again for a short time, and so ended. Things being thus disposed, and approved by the Pope's authority, it seemed as though the beautiful form of the Apostolical assembly had returned, as far as times admitted."

This, of course, took place long after that portion of Philip's life on which I am immediately engaged. From eight to eighteen, ten years, he was under the teaching of St. Dominic; from eighteen to twenty-eight or twenty-nine, he was with St. Benedict, and the ancient Saints of Rome. Nor even, when the end of that period was come, did he quite leave St. Benedict. During the whole sixty years that he passed at Rome, there was only one great turning-point or crisis of his life; it was when, at about the age of forty, he thought of going to the East. Now, to determine this point, he did not take the counsel of any Dominican, nor of any Jesuit, either of which courses might have seemed natural, but he went to a Benedictine of the great Basilica of St. Paul, and by him was referred to another monk of the Benedictine family, who lived on the spot of St. Paul's martyrdom; and this father, directed by St. John the Evangelist, told him that "*his* Indies were to be in Rome, where God would make much use of him." Observe this, too, my Brethren: St. John the Evangelist was the informant. Philip lives in especial intercourse with the Saints of the Apostolic ages, with St. Paul, with St. John the Evangelist. Again, St. Mary Magdalen and St. Philip and St. James were his own particular patrons; and St. John the Baptist appeared to him in vision. I do not recollect any Saints of a later date, with whom he was in such intimate communion.

4. Such was the character of the devotions, such the cast and fashion of interior life, which are proper to St. Philip; Benedictine, as I may call them. At length he came back to the world, and there he found and made acquaintance with the third great Patriarch whom I have named, St. Ignatius, who was then in Rome. That memorable Saint had taken up his abode, and established his Society there, while Philip was in his long retreat, and now he was at hand for Philip to hear and to consult, for the space of eleven years, when he

died. Now what did St. Ignatius do for him? There is a remarkable resemblance, as any one may see, in the practical
teaching of the two, and that, in matters where that teaching
is in contrast to what was more usual in and before their day.
It cannot be doubted that, while in theological traditions St.
Philip was one with St. Dominic, in the cure of souls he
was one with St. Ignatius. An earnest enforcement of interior
religion, a jealousy of formal ceremonies, an insisting on obedience rather than sacrifice, on mental discipline rather than
fasting or hair-shirt, a mortification of the reason, that illumination and freedom of spirit which comes of love; further, a
mild and tender rule for the Confessional; frequent confessions, frequent communions, special devotion towards the
Blessed Sacrament, these are peculiarities of a particular
school in the Church, and St. Ignatius and St. Philip are
Masters in it. From St. Benedict's time there had been a
broad line between the world and the Church, and it was
very hard to follow sanctity without entering into Religion.
St. Ignatius and St. Philip, on the contrary, carried out the
Church into the world, and aimed to bring under her light
yoke as many men as they could possibly reach. Both of them,
of course, acted under a divine guidance; but, as they lived
at the same time and on the same spot, it is natural to think
that, humanly speaking, one must have taken his tradition
from the other; and, as St. Philip is the younger, it is as natural
to think that he gained it from St. Ignatius. As then he learned
from Benedict *what to be*, and from Dominic *what to do*,
so let me consider that from Ignatius he learned *how he was
to do it*.

St. Philip, on one occasion, acknowledged his debt in one
particular to the elder Saint; he said to some Jesuits whom he
met, "You are children of a great Father. I am under obligations to him, for your Master, Ignatius, taught me to make
mental prayer." Nay, strange as it may appear, it would seem
that, at least at one time of his life, he wished to be admitted
among his children; at another time, perhaps, to which I have

already alluded, to join them in the East with others in his train.

5. My Brethren, I do not feel it to be any want of devotion or reverence towards our dear Father, to speak of him as looking out to be taught, or willing to be governed. It is like his most amiable, natural, and unpretending self. He was ever putting himself in the background, and never thought of taking on himself rule, or seizing on a position, in the Church, or of founding a religious body. And I seem to have Father Consolini's authority for saying that I please him more by doing towards him what he would do for himself, than by showing now a zeal in his behalf, for which he would not have thanked me when living. Father Consolini, as you recollect, was the most intimate friend of St. Philip, of all his spiritual children. The Saint "was most jealous in concealing his gifts from the eyes of the world," but "from Consolini he hid nothing." Well, then, you would think, that after Philip's death, his loving disciple would tell all that he could, as loudly and as widely as he could, in his honour. Not so; so far from it, that the author of that Father's life, whom I have just been quoting, tells us that, although he was the most devoted, as well as the best beloved of the sons of St. Philip, yet, when the Holy Father's canonization was first commenced, he did not wish it to be forwarded by the Congregation. He himself at first refused to give evidence in the Process, and, when commanded by his Superiors, he gave it with evident reluctance. How natural this is! St. Philip was too *near* him to allow of his speaking to his praise. To praise him was to praise himself and all the Fathers. Let strangers praise him, not a son of his own. And if they wish to love him, let them come and learn to love him for what he is. We too do not wish him other than he is; we love him too much for what he is, to wish him praised for what he is not.

It is further said of Father Consolini: "He was so deeply penetrated with this feeling, that, though he knew from the Saint himself the way in which he received from the Holy

Ghost that wonderful visitation of the fracture of his ribs, yet he never revealed the particulars to any living person till within a few days of his death." He recollected the Saint's words, "*Secretum meum mihi*," "My secret is my own." And again: "When he heard that some priests had united together under the invocation and institute of St. Philip, with the name of Reformed Priests, he was gravely displeased with the vanity of such a title, saying, that had Philip been living, he would have gone to the Pope to dissolve such a Congregation."

O touching and most genuine traits of our sweetest and dearest Father, and most impressive lesson to us, and remarkable contrast to the spirit of the vehement friar of St. Mark's! Philip had shown them from a boy. One of the first things told us of him in his very childhood is, that "he never spoke lightly, as boys do, of becoming a priest or a religious; he concealed the wish of his heart, and from childhood upwards, he eschewed display, of which he ever had a special hatred." Things which other saints have allowed in themselves, or rather have felt a duty, he could not abide. He did not ask to be opposed, to be maligned, to be persecuted, but simply to be overlooked, to be despised. Neglect was the badge which he desired for himself and for his own. "To despise the whole world," he said, "to despise no member of it, to despise oneself, *to despise being despised*." He took great pleasure in being undervalued and made little of, according to the Apostle's sentiment, "If any man among you seem to be wise, let him become a fool, that he may be wise." And hence you know, when he became so famous in his old age, and every one was thinking of him mysteriously, and looking at him with awe, and solemnly repeating Father Philip's words and rehearsing Father Philip's deeds, and bringing strangers to see him, it was the most cruel of penances to him, and he was ever behaving himself ridiculously on purpose, and putting them out, from his intense hatred and impatience of being turned into a show. "He was always trying," says his biographer, "either by gesture, or motions, or words, or some facetious levity, to hide his great devotion; and when he had done any virtuous action, he would do something simple to cover it."

6. This being the disposition of St. Philip, you will understand how it was, that while he wished to do the very work which Savonarola intended, he set about it, not on principle merely, but on instinctive feeling, in so different a way. Here, as in other cases, the slowest way was the surest, and the most quiet the most effectual; and he rather would not have attempted that work at all, than have sacrificed his humility and modesty to the doing of it. Accordingly he, whose mission was to Popes, Cardinals, and nobles, to philosophers, authors, and artists, began with teaching the poor who are found about the doors of the Roman Churches. This was his occupation for years; soon he added to it another undertaking of the same kind. He used to go about the squares, shops, warehouses, schools, and shop-counters, "talking with all sorts of persons in a most engaging way about spiritual things, and saying, 'Well, my brothers, when are we to set about serving God, and doing good?'" and he began to make some great conversions.

Rome was at that time in a very different state from what it was when Savonarola had discharged his threats upon it. A most heavy judgment had come upon it a few years before Philip arrived there, and that judgment had come in mercy upon the city of God's choice. The Germans and Spaniards had besieged, taken, and sacked it, with excesses and outrages so horrible, that it is thought to have suffered less from the Goths and Huns than from troops nominally Christian. Its external splendour has never been recovered down to this day; its churches were spoiled and defaced; its convents plundered; its Cardinals, Bishops, monks, and nuns, treated with the most extreme indignities, and many of them murdered; and sacrileges committed innumerable. People thought what happened was the fulfilment of the predictions of Savonarola; but, amid these miseries, the grace of God spoke, and the guilty population was softened. First St. Caietan, who was himself tortured by the ruffianly soldiers, had already begun to call to prayer and repentance; St. Ignatius followed, preaching. Then came St. Philip, but in his own quiet way, like "the whispering of a gentle air," "his speech trickling like dew, as a shower upon the herb, and as drops upon the grass."

He began, as I have said, with the poor; then he went among shopmen, warehousemen, clerks in banks, and loungers in public places. Encouraged by these successes, he addressed himself to men, not merely of careless, but of the worst kind of lives; and them also he gained for God. His charity brought him into various situations of trial; but when attempts were made upon his virtue, his zeal and devotion brought him through them. All this time he was visiting the hospitals, and attending to the necessities, both bodily and spiritual, of the sick.

This had been his life, in some degree, before he left his retreat in the basilicas and cemeteries; and it lasted altogether ten years. At the end of them he joined a small community of pious people, in number fifteen, "simple and poor," we are told, "but full of spirit and devotion," and "inflaming one another, by words and by example, with the desire of Christian perfection." Philip, though still a layman, preached: and, because he was doing an unusual thing, dissolute youths came to make game of him; but it was dangerous for such to come near him: on one occasion he converted thirty of them by a single sermon. He and his associates made it their duty to attend on the pilgrims, and on the sick who had left the hospitals, convalescent, but not recovered. Thus his work gradually extended; for these pilgrims and sick were from all countries, and many of them were Jews or heretics, whom he brought into the fold of the Church.

7. He had been fifteen years in Rome before he was ordained; and then at length, on his receiving faculties for hearing confessions, he began, at the age of thirty-five, his real mission,—that long course of ministry, which, carried on

for years three times fifteen, down almost to the hour of his death, has gained for him the title of Apostle of Rome.

You know, my brethren, what is commonly meant by an Apostle of a country. It means one who converts its heathen inhabitants to the Christian faith, such as St. Augustine of England; accordingly, his proper function is Baptism. Hence you find St. Augustine, St. Patrick, St. Boniface, or St. Francis baptizing their hundreds and thousands. This was the office to which St. Philip wished to minister in India; but it was his zeal and charity that urged him, not his mature judgment; for the fierce conflicts, and the pastoral cares, and the rude publicity of such exalted duties, were unsuited to his nature; so he was kept at home for a different work. He was kept at home, in the very heart of Christendom, not to evangelize, but to recover; and his instrument of conversion was, not Baptism, but Penance. The Confessional was the seat and seal of his peculiar Apostolate. Hence, as St. Francis Xavier baptized his tens of thousands, Philip was, every day and almost every hour, for forty-five years, restoring, teaching, encouraging, and guiding penitents along the narrow way of salvation.

We are told in his *Life*, that "he abandoned every other care, and gave himself to hearing confessions." Not content with the day, he gave up a considerable portion of the night to it also. Before dawn he had generally confessed a good number. When he retired to his room, he still confessed every one who came; though at prayers, though at meals, he broke off instantly, and attended to the call. When the church was opened at daybreak, he went down to the Confessional, and remained in it till noon, when he said Mass. When no penitents came, he remained near his Confessional; he never intermitted hearing confessions for any illness. "On the day of his death, he began to hear confessions very early in the morning;" after Mass "again he went into the Confessional;" in the afternoon, and "during the rest of the day down to supper time," he heard confessions. After supper, "he heard the confessions of those Fathers who were to say the first

Masses on the following morning," when he himself was no longer to be on earth. It was this extraordinary persevering service in so trying, so wearing a duty, for forty-five years, that enabled him to be the new Apostle of the Sacred City. Thus it was, as the lesson in his Office says, that "he bore innumerable children to Christ." He was ever suffering their miseries, and fighting with their sins, and travailing with their good resolves, year after year, whatever their state of life, their calling, their circumstances, if so be that he might bring them safe to heaven, with a superhuman, heroic patience, of which we see so few traces in the fiery preacher at Florence.

Savonarola, in spite of his personal sanctity, in spite of his protests against a mere external sanctity in Catholics, after all, began with an external reform; he burned lutes and guitars, looking-glasses and masks, books and pictures, in the public square: but Philip bore with every outside extravagance in those whom he addressed, as far as it was not directly sinful, knowing well that if the heart was once set right, the appropriate demeanour would follow. You recollect how a youth came to his Exercises one day, dressed out "in a most singular and whimsical fashion;" and how Philip did but fix his eyes on him, and proceed with the discourses and devotions of the Oratory, and how, by the time that they were at an end, the poor sinner had become quite another man; his nature was changed all at once, and he became one of the Saint's most fervent penitents. A rich ecclesiastic came to him in coloured clothes, like a layman: Philip talked with him for a fortnight, without saying a word about his dress. At the end of the time he put it off of his own accord, and made a general confession. His biographer says: "He was very much against stiffness and off-hand prohibitions about wearing fine clothes, collars, swords, and such-like things, saying that if only a little devotion gained admittance into their hearts, you might leave them to themselves." If he spoke of them, it was good-naturedly and playfully. You recollect he said to a lady, who asked if it was a sin to wear slippers with very high heels, according to an excessive fashion of the day, "Take care they do not trip you up." And to a youth, who wore one of those large, stiff frills, which we see in pictures, he remarked, "I should caress you much more, if your collar did not hurt me."

Savonarola is associated in our minds with the pulpit rather than the confessional: his vehemence converted many, but frightened or irritated more. The consequences came back upon himself and his penitents. Some of his convert artists were assassinated, others were driven into exile, others gave up their profession altogether in disgust or despair. Philip had no vocation, and little affection, for the pulpit; he was jealous of what the world calls eloquence, and he mortified his disciples when they aspired to it. One he interrupted and sent down; another he made preach his sermon six times over: he discoursed and conversed rather than preached. And "he could not endure harsh rebukes," says the writer of his life, "or anything like rigour. He allured men to the service of God so dexterously, and with such a holy, winning art, that those who saw it cried out, astonished: 'Father Philip draws souls as the magnet draws iron.' He so accommodated himself to the temper of each, as, in the words of the Apostle, to become 'all things to all men, that he might gain all.'" And his love of them individually was so tender and ardent, that, even in extreme old age, he was anxious to suffer for their sins; and "for this end he inflicted on himself severe disciplines, and he reckoned their misdeeds as his own, and wept for them as such." I do not read that Savonorola acted thus towards Pope Alexander the Sixth, whom he so violently denounced.

It is not surprising that, with this tenderness, with this prudence, and with the zeal and charity to which both were subordinate, his influence increased year by year, till he gained a place in the heart of the Roman population, which he has never lost. There are those whose greatest works are their earliest; there are others, who, at first scarcely distinguishable from a whole class who look the same, distance them in the long run, and do more and more wonderful works the longer they live. Philip was thirty-five before he was ordained; forty, before he began his exercises in his room; fifty, before he had a church; sixty before he formed his disciples into a congregation; near seventy, before he put himself at the head of it. As the Blessed Virgin's name has by a majestic growth expanded and extended itself through the Church, "taking root in an honourable people, and resting in the Holy City," so the influence of Philip was, at the end of many years, paramount in that place which he has so long dwelt in as an obscure, disregarded stranger. Sharp eyes and holy sympathies indeed had detected "Philip Neri, as a saint living in caves," when he was a youth; but it required half a century to develope this truth to the intelligence of the multitude of men. At length there was no possibility of mistaking it. Visitors to Rome discerned the presence of one who was greater than Pope and Cardinals, holy, venerable and vigilant as the rulers of the Church then were. "Among all the wonderful things which I saw in Rome," says one of them, writing when Philip was turned fifty, " I took the chief pleasure in beholding the multitude of devout and spiritual persons who frequented the Oratory. Amid the monuments of antiquity, the superb palaces and courts of so many illustrious lords, it appeared to me that the glory of this exemplar shone forth with surpassing light." "I go," says another visitor, ten years later, "to the Oratory, where they deliver every day most beautiful discourses on the gospel, or on the virtues and vices, or ecclesiastical history, or the lives of the saints. Persons of distinction go to hear them, bishops, prelates, and the like. They who deliver them are in holy orders, and of most exemplary life. Their superior is a certain Reverend Father Philip, an old man of sixty, who, they say, is an oracle, not only in Rome, but in the far-off parts of Italy, and of France and Spain, so that many come to him for counsel; indeed he is another Thomas a Kempis, or Tauler."

But it required to live in Rome to understand what his influence really was. Nothing was too high for him, nothing too low. He taught poor begging women to use mental prayer; he took out boys to play; he protected orphans; he acted as novice-master to the children of St. Dominic. He was the teacher and director of artisans, mechanics, cashiers in banks, merchants, workers in gold, artists, men of science. He was consulted by monks, canons, lawyers, physicians, courtiers; ladies of the highest rank, convicts going to execution, engaged in their turn his solicitude and prayers. Cardinals hung about his room, and Popes asked for his miraculous aid in disease, and his ministrations in death. It was his mission to save men, not from, but in, the world. To break the haughtiness of rank, and the fastidiousness of fashion, he gave his penitents public mortifications; to draw the young from the theatres, he opened his Oratory of Sacred Music; to rescue the careless from the Carnival and its excesses, he set out in pilgrimage to the Seven Basilicas. For those who loved reading, he substituted, for the works of chivalry or the hurtful novels of the day, the true romance and the celestial poetry of the Lives of the Saints. He set one of his disciples to write history against the heretics of that age; another to treat of the Notes of the Church; a third, to undertake the Martyrs and Christian Antiquities;—for, while in the discourses and devotions of the Oratory, he prescribed the simplicity of the primitive monks, he wished his children, individually and in private, to cultivate all their gifts to the full. He, however, was, after all and in all, their true model,—the humble priest, shrinking from every kind of dignity, or post, or office, and living the greater part of day and night in prayer, in his room or upon the housetop.

And when he died, a continued stream of people, says his biographer, came to see his body, during the two days that it remained in the church, kissing his bier, touching him with their rosaries or their rings, or taking away portions of his hair, or the flowers which were strewed over him; and, among the crowd, persons of every rank and condition were heard lamenting and extolling one who was so lowly, yet so great; who had been so variously endowed, and had been the pupil of so many saintly masters; who had the breadth of view of St. Dominic, the poetry of St. Benedict, the wisdom of St. Ignatius, and all recommended by an unassuming grace and a winning tenderness which were his own.

Would that we, his children of this Oratory, were able—I do not say individually, but even collectively, nor in some one generation, but even in that whole period during which it is destined to continue here—would that we were able to do a work such as his! At least we may take what he was for our pattern, whatever be the standard of our powers and the measure of our success. And certainly it is a consolation that thus much we can say in our own behalf,—that we have gone about his work in the way most likely to gain his blessing upon us, because most like his own. We have not chosen for ourselves any scene of exertion where we might make a noise, but have willingly taken that humble place of service which our Superiors chose for us. The desire of our hearts and our duty went together here. We have deliberately set ourselves down in a populous district, unknown to the great world, and have commenced, as St. Philip did, by ministering chiefly to the poor and lowly. We have gone where we could get no reward from society for our deeds, nor admiration from the acute or learned for our words. We have determined, through God's mercy, not to have the praise or the popularity that the world can give, but according to our Father's own precept, "to love to be unknown."

May this spirit ever rule us more and more! For me, my dear Fathers of the Oratory, did you ask me, and were I able, to gain some boon for you from St. Philip, which might distinguish you and your successors for the time to come, persecution I would not dare to supplicate for you, as holy men have sometimes supplicated; for the work of the Oratory is a tranquil work, and requires peace and security to do it well.

Nor would I ask for you calumny and reproach, for to be slandered is to be talked about, and to some minds notoriety itself is a gratification and a snare. But I would beg for you this privilege, that the public world might never know you for praise or for blame, that you should do a good deal of hard work in your generation, and prosecute many useful labours, and effect a number of religious purposes, and send many souls to heaven, and take men by surprise, how much you were really doing, when they happened to come near enough to see it; but that by the world you should be over-looked, that you should not be known out of your place, that you should work for God alone with a pure heart and single eye, without the distractions of human applause, and should make Him your sole hope, and His eternal heaven your sole aim, and have your reward, not partly here, but fully and entirely hereafter.

Blessed shall you and I be, my dear Fathers, if we learn to live now in the presence of Saints and Angels, who are to be our everlasting companions hereafter. Blessed are we, if we converse habitually with Jesus, Mary, and Joseph,—with the Apostles, Martyrs, and great Fathers of the early Church,— with Sebastian, Laurence, and Cecilia,—with Athanasius, Ambrose, and Augustine,—with Philip, whose children we are, —with our guardian angels and our patron saints, careless what men think about us, so that their scorn of us involves no injury to our community, and their misconception of us is no hindrance to their own conversion.

[*January 18, 1850.*]

XXI

CHRIST UPON THE WATERS [1]

PART I

"Navicula autem in medio mari jactabatur fluctibus; erat enim contrarius ventus. Quartâ autem vigiliâ noctis, venit ad eos ambulans super mare. Et videntes eum super mare ambulantem, turbati sunt dicentes: Quia phantasma est. Et præ timore clamaverunt. Statimque Jesus locutus est eis, dicens: Habete fiduciam; ego sum; nolite timere." (*The boat in the midst of the sea was tossed with the waves; for the wind was contrary. And in the fourth watch of the night He came to them, walking upon the sea. And they, seeing Him walking upon the sea, were troubled, saying: It is an apparition. And they cried out for fear. And immediately Jesus spoke to them, saying: Be of good heart; it is I; fear ye not.*)—Evang. sec. Matt., c. xiv. v. 24–27.

THE EARTH IS FULL OF THE MARVELS of divine power; "Day to day uttereth speech, and night to night showeth knowledge." The tokens of Omnipotence are all around us, in the world of matter, and the world of man; in the dispensation of nature, and in the dispensation of grace. To do impossibilities, I may say, is the prerogative of Him, who

[1] Preached in St. Chad's, Birmingham. From *Sermons Preached on Various Occasions*, No. 9. [Ed.]

The following sermon is written from the notes made previously to its delivery, with an attempt to preserve closely, as far as memory served, the course and matter of it, as actually delivered.

As it has been publicly asserted, that its author has been concerned in the great measure which occasioned it, he takes this opportunity of distinctly negativing the report. It is utterly and absolutely untrue. He denies it in every shape into which it can be cast. He never was asked, and made all things out of nothing, who foresees all events before they occur, and controls all wills without compelling them. In emblem of this His glorious attribute, He came to His disciples in the passage I have read you, walking upon the sea,—the emblem or hieroglyphic among the ancients of the impossible; to show them that what is impossible with man, is possible with God. He who could walk the waters, could also ride triumphantly upon what is still more fickle, unstable, tumultuous, treacherous—the billows of human wills, human purposes, human hearts. The bark of Peter was struggling with the waves, and made no progress; Christ came to him walking upon them; He entered the boat, and by entering it He sustained it. He did not abandon Himself to it, but He brought it near to Himself; He did not merely take refuge in it, but He made Himself the strength of it, and the pledge and cause of a successful passage. "Presently," another gospel says, "the ship was at the land, whither they were going."

Such was the power of the Son of God, the Saviour of man, manifested by visible tokens in the material world, when He came upon earth; and such, too, it has ever since signally shown itself to be, in the history of that mystical ark which He then formed to float upon the ocean of human opinion. He told His chosen servants to form an ark for the salvation of souls: He gave them directions how to construct it,—the length, breadth, and height, its cabins and its windows; and the world, as it gazed upon it, forthwith began to criticize. It pronounced it framed quite contrary to the scientific rules of shipbuilding; it prophesied, as it still prophesies, that such

---

never gave, his opinion upon it, nor had he any opinion to give. He doubts whether, even in private, and to his intimate friends, he has ever expressed any sort of opinion. It was a measure in agitation before he was a Catholic. It was one of the first subjects he heard in discussion, when he became one, five years ago, and that from the lips of persons high in authority. He believes its adoption has been simply owing to the growing and full conviction of both rulers and laity in England in its favour, unattended by any suspicion whatever of its giving offence to others.—*Advertisement to First Edition.*

a craft was not sea-worthy; that it was not water-tight; that it would not float; that it would go to pieces and founder. And why it does not, who can say, except that the Lord is in it? Who can say why so old a framework, put together eighteen hundred years ago, should have lasted, against all human calculation, even to this day; always going, and never gone; ever failing, yet ever managing to explore new seas and foreign coasts—except that He, who once said to the rowers, "It is I, be not afraid," and to the waters, "Peace," is still in His own ark which He has made, to direct and to prosper her course?

And hence so many instances are to be found in history, of the triumph of the bark of Peter amid adversity of every kind. "The floods have lifted up, the floods have lifted up their voice; the floods have lifted up their waves with the noise of many waters. Wonderful are the surges of the sea; wonderful is the Lord on high." It is the Lord from heaven, who is our light in the gloom, our confidence in the storm. There is nothing hard to Him who is almighty; nothing strange to Him who is all-manifold in operation and all-fruitful in resource. The clouds break, and the sun shines, and the sea is smooth, in its appointed season. Such, my dear Brethren, is the thought which naturally possesses the mind on a day like this,[2] when we are met together solemnly to return thanks to our merciful God for the restoration of the Catholic Hierarchy to the faithful of this land. His works are ever slow and gradual; year after year brings its silent influence and contribution in aid of the object which He may have in view; and we are unable, except artificially and for convenience, to divide into portions or stages what with Him is the continuous introduction of an integral whole. But still from time to time occur greater and more striking events, in which the past and the future are, as it were, summed up; and which, though intrinsically great, may be taken as symbols and are representatives

[2] The installation of the Right Rev. Dr. Ullathorne as first Bishop of Birmingham.

of even more than they are themselves, of the labours and the
prospects of a course of years. And such as this is the great
act which we are now commemorating: it witnesses that much
has been done; it predicts that much is to follow: it is the
authoritative recognition and seal of the successes which God
has given us, and the instrument of their consolidation. Well
then may we rejoice on this day; and happily does it fall on
the Feast of Our Lady's Patronage, for to whom, under God,
are our acknowledgments more truly due, and our expectations more securely turned, than to His all-holy and ever-
glorious Mother?

Time was, my Brethren, when the forefathers of our race
were a savage tribe, inhabiting a wild district beyond the
limits of this quarter of the earth. Whatever brought them
thither, they had no local attachments there or political
settlement; they were a restless people, and whether urged
forward by enemies or by desire of plunder, they left their
place, and passing through the defiles of the mountains on
the frontiers of Asia, they invaded Europe, setting out on a
journey towards the farther west. Generation after generation
passed away; and still this fierce and haughty race moved
forward. On, on they went; but travel availed them not; the
change of place could bring them no truth, or peace, or hope,
or stability of heart; they could not flee from themselves. They
carried with them their superstitions and their sins, their gods
of iron and of clay, their savage sacrifices, their lawless witch-
crafts, their hatred of their kind and their ignorance of their
destiny. At length they buried themselves in the deep forests
of Germany, and gave themselves up to indolent repose; but
they had not found their rest; they were still heathens, making
the fair trees, the primeval work of God, and the innocent
beasts of the chase, the objects and the instruments of their
idolatrous worship. And, last of all, they crossed over the
strait and made themselves masters of this island, and gave
their very name to it; so that, whereas it had hitherto been
called Britain, the southern part, which was their main seat,

obtained the name of England. And now they had proceeded forward nearly as far as they could go, unless they were prepared to look across the great ocean, and anticipate the discovery of the world which lies beyond it.

What, then, was to happen to this restless race, which had sought for happiness and peace across the globe, and had not found it? Was it to grow old in its place, and dwindle away, and consume in the fever of its own heart, which admitted no remedy? or was it to become great by being overcome, and to enjoy the only real life of man, and rise to his only true dignity, by being subjected to a Master's yoke? Did its Maker and Lord see any good thing in it, of which, under His divine nurture, profit might come to His elect, and glory to His Name? He looked upon it, and He saw nothing there to claim any visitation of His grace, or to merit any relaxation of the awful penalty which its lawlessness and impiety had incurred. It was a proud race, which feared neither God nor man—a race ambitious, self-willed, obstinate, and hard of belief, which would dare everything, even the eternal pit, if it was challenged to do so. I say, there was nothing there of a nature to reverse the destiny which His righteous decrees have assigned to those who sin wilfully and despise Him. But the Almighty Lover of souls looked once again; and He saw in that poor, forlorn, and ruined nature, which He had in the beginning filled with grace and light, He saw in it, not what merited His favour, not what would adequately respond to His influences, not what was a necessary instrument of His purposes, but what would illustrate and preach abroad His grace, if He took pity on it. He saw in it a natural nobleness, a simplicity, a frankness of character, a love of truth, a zeal for justice, an indignation at wrong, an admiration of purity, a reverence for law, a keen appreciation of the beautifulness and majesty of order, nay, further, a tenderness and affectionateness of heart, which He knew would become the glorious instruments of His high will, when illuminated and vivified by His supernatural gifts. And so He who, did it so please Him, could raise up children to Abraham out of the very stones of the earth, nevertheless determined in this instance in His free mercy to unite what was beautiful in nature with what was radiant in grace; and, as if those poor Anglo-Saxons had been too fair to be heathen, therefore did He rescue them from the devil's service and the devil's doom, and bring them into the house of His holiness and the mountain of His rest.

It is an old story and a familiar, and I need not go through it. I need not tell you, my Brethren, how suddenly the word of truth came to our ancestors in this island and subdued them to its gentle rule; how the grace of God fell on them, and, without compulsion, as the historian tells us, the multitude became Christian; how, when all was tempestuous, and hopeless, and dark, Christ like a vision of glory came walking to them on the waves of the sea. Then suddenly there was a great calm; a change came over the pagan people in that quarter of the country where the gospel was first preached to them; and from thence the blessed influence went forth, it was poured out over the whole land, till one and all, the Anglo-Saxon people were converted by it. In a hundred years the work was done; the idols, the sacrifices, the mummeries of paganism flitted away and were not, and the pure doctrine and heavenly worship of the Cross were found in their stead. The fair form of Christianity rose up and grew and expanded like a beautiful pageant from north to south; it was majestic, it was solemn, it was bright, it was beautiful and pleasant, it was soothing to the griefs, it was indulgent to the hopes of man; it was at once a teaching and a worship; it had a dogma, a mystery, a ritual of its own; it had an hierarchical form. A brotherhood of holy pastors, with mitre and crosier and uplifted hand walked forth and blessed and ruled a joyful people. The crucifix headed the procession, and simple monks were there with hearts in prayer, and sweet chants resounded, and the holy Latin tongue was heard, and boys came forth in white, swinging censers, and the fragrant cloud arose, and

mass was sung, and the saints were invoked; and day after
day, and in the still night, and over the woody hills and in
the quiet plains, as constantly as sun and moon and stars go
forth in heaven, so regular and solemn was the stately march
of blessed services on earth, high festival, and gorgeous
procession, and soothing dirge, and passing bell, and the
familiar evening call to prayer: till he who recollected the old
pagan time, would think it all unreal that he beheld and heard,
and would conclude he did but see a vision, so marvellously
was heaven let down upon earth, so triumphantly were chased
away the fiends of darkness to their prison below.

Such was the change which came over our forefathers;
such was the Religion bestowed upon them, bestowed on them
as a second grant, after the grant of the territory itself; nay,
it might almost have seemed as the divine guarantee or pledge
of its occupation. And you know its name; there can be no
mistake, my Brethren; you know what that Religion was called.
It was called by no modern name—for modern religions then
were not. You know, my dear Brethren, *what* religion has
priests and sacrifices, and mystical rites, and the monastic
rule, and care for the souls of the dead, and the profession of
an ancient faith, coming through all ages from the Apostles.
There is one, and only one religion such: it is known everywhere; every poor boy in the street knows the name of it;
there never was a time, since it first was, that its name was
not known, and known to the multitude. It is called *Catholicism*—a world-wide name, and incommunicable; attached to
us from the first; accorded to us by our enemies; in vain
attempted, never stolen from us, by our rivals. Such was the
worship which the English people gained when they emerged
out of paganism into gospel light. In the history of their
conversion, Christianity and Catholicity are one; they are,
as in their own nature, so in that history, convertible terms.
It was the Catholic faith which that vigorous young race
heard and embraced,—that faith which is still found the further
you trace back towards the age of the Apostles, which is still

visible in the dim distance of the earliest antiquity, and to which the witness of the Church, when investigated even in her first startings and simplest rudiments, "sayeth not the contrary." Such was the religion of the noble English; they knew not heresy; and, as time went on, the work did but sink deeper and deeper into their nature, into their social structure and their political institutions; it grew with their growth, and strengthened with their strength, till a sight was seen,—one of the most beautiful which ever has been given to man to see,—what was great in the natural order, made greater by its elevation into the supernatural. The two seemed as if made for each other; that natural temperament and that gift of grace; what was heroic, or generous, or magnanimous in nature, found its corresponding place or office in the divine kingdom. Angels in heaven rejoiced to see the divinely wrought piety and sanctity of penitent sinners: Apostles, Popes, and Bishops, long since taken to glory, threw their crowns in transport at the foot of the throne, as saints, and confessors, and martyrs, came forth before their wondering eyes out of a horde of heathen robbers; guardian spirits no longer sighed over the disparity and contrast which had so fearfully intervened between themselves and the souls given to them in a character and genius of its own; I will say a bold thing—charge. It did indeed become a peculiar, special people, with that rules, through all time, the princely line of Roman pontiffs, in its staidness, sagacity, and simplicity, more like the mind than perhaps any other Christian people whom the world has seen. And so things went on for many centuries. Generation followed generation; revolution came after revolution; great men rose and fell: there were bloody wars, and invasions, conquests, changes of dynasty, slavery, recoveries, civil dissensions, settlements; Dane and Norman overran the land; yet all along Christ was upon the waters; and if they rose in fury, yet at His word they fell again and were in calm. The bark of Peter was still the refuge of the tempest-tost, and ever solaced and recruited those whom it rescued from the deep.

But at length a change again came over the land: a thousand years had well-nigh rolled, and this great people grew tired of the heavenly stranger who sojourned among them. They had had enough of blessings and absolutions, enough of the intercession of saints, enough of the grace of the sacraments, enough of the prospect of the next life. They thought it best to secure this life in the first place, because they were in possession of it, and then to go on to the next, if time and means allowed. And they saw that to labour for the next world was possibly to lose this; whereas, to labour for this world might be, for what they knew, the way to labour for the next also. Anyhow, they would pursue a temporal end, and they would account any one their enemy who stood in the way of their pursuing it. It was a madness; but madmen are strong, and madmen are clever; so with the sword and the halter, and by mutilation and fine and imprisonment, they cut off, or frightened away from the land, as Israel did in the time of old, the ministers of the Most High, and their ministrations: they "altogether broke the yoke, and burst the bonds." "They beat one, and killed another, and another they stoned," and at length they altogether cast out the Heir from His vineyard, and killed Him, "that the inheritance might be theirs." And as for the remnant of His servants whom they left, they drove them into corners and holes of the earth, and there they bade them die out; and then they rejoiced and sent gifts either to other, and made merry, because they had rid themselves of those "who had tormented them that dwelt upon the earth." And so they turned to enjoy this world, and to gain for themselves a name among men, and it was given unto them according to their wish. They preferred the heathen virtues of their original nature, to the robe of grace which God had given them: they fell back, with closed affections, and haughty reserve, and dreariness within, upon their worldly integrity, honour, energy, prudence, and perseverance; they made the most of the natural man, and they "received their reward." Forthwith they began to rise to a station higher than the heathen Roman, and have, in three centuries, attained a wider range of sovereignty; and now they look down in contempt on what they were, and upon the Religion which reclaimed them from paganism.

Yes, my dear Brethren, such was the temptation of the evil one, such the fall of his victim, such the disposition of the Most High. The tempter said, "All these will I give thee, if, falling down, thou wilt adore me;" and their rightful Lord and Sovereign permitted the boast to be fulfilled. He permitted it for His greater glory: He might have hindered it, as He might hinder all evil; but He saw good, He saw it best, to let things take their course. He did not interfere, He kept silence, He retired from the land which would be rid of Him. And there were those at that crisis who understood not His providence, and would have interfered in His behalf with a high hand. Holy men and true they were, zealous for God, and tender towards His sheep; but they divined not His will. It was His will to leave the issue to time, and to bring things round slowly and without violence, and to conquer by means of His adversaries. He willed it that their pride should be its own correction; that they should be broken without hands, and dissolve under their own insufficiency. He who might have brought myriads of Angels to the rescue, He who might have armed and blessed the forces of Christendom against His persecutors, wrought more wondrously. He deigned not to use the carnal weapon: He bade the drawn sword return to its sheath: He refused the combinations and the armaments of earthly kings. He who sees the end from the beginning, who is "justified in His words, and overcomes when He is judged," did but wait. He waited patiently; He left the world to itself, nor avenged His Church, but stayed till the fourth watch of the night, when His faithful sons had given up hope, and thought His mercy towards them at an end. He let the winds and the waves insult Him and His own; He suffered meekly the jeers and blasphemies which rose on every side, and pronounced the downfall of His work. "All things have an

end," men said; "there is a time for all things; a time to be
born, and a time to die. All things have their course and their
term; they may last a long time, but after all, a period they
have, and not an immortality. So is it with man himself; even
Mathusala and Noe exhausted the full fountain of their being,
and the pitcher was at length crushed, and the wheel broken.
So is it with nations; they rise, and they flourish, and they
fall; there is an element in them, as in individuals, which wears
out and perishes. However great they may be in their day,
at length the moment comes, when they have attained their
greatest elevation, and accomplished their full range, and
fulfilled their scope. So is it with great ideas and their manifestations; they are realized, they prevail, and they perish.
As the constituents of the animal frame at length refuse to
hold together, so nations, philosophies, and religions one day
lose their unity and undergo the common law of decomposition.
Our nation doubtless will find its term at length, as well as
others, though not yet; but that ancient faith of ours has come
to nought already. We have nothing then to fear from the
past; the past is not, the past cannot revive; the dead tell no
tales; the grave cannot open. New adversaries we may have,
but with the Old Religion we have parted once for all."

Thus speaks the world, deeming Christ's patience to be
feebleness, and His loving affection to be enmity. And the
faithful, on the other hand, have had their own misgivings too,
whether Catholicism could ever flourish in this country again.
Has it yet happened anywhere in the history of the Church,
that a people which once lost its faith ever regained it? It is a
gift of grace, a special mercy to receive it once, and not to
be expected a second time. Many nations have never had it at
all; from some it has been taken away, apparently without
their fault, nay, in spite of their meritorious use of it. So was
it with the old Persian Church, which after enduring two
frightful persecutions, had scarcely emerged from the second,
when it was irretrievably corrupted by heresy. So was it with
the famous Church of Africa, whose great saint and doctor's

dying moments were embittered by the ravages around him of those fierce barbarians who were destined to be its ruin. What are we better than they? It is then surely against the order of Providence hitherto that the gift once given should be given again; the world and the Church bear a concordant testimony here.

And the just Judge of man made as though He would do what man anticipated. He retired, as I have said, from the field; He yielded the battle to the enemy;—but He did so that He might in the event more signally triumph. He interfered not for near three hundred years, that His enemies might try their powers of mind in forming a religion instead of His own. He gave them three hundred years' start, bidding them to do something better than He, or something at all, if so be they were able, and He put Himself to every disadvantage. He suffered the daily sacrifice to be suspended, the hierarchy to be driven out, education to be prohibited, religious houses to be plundered and suppressed, cathedrals to be desecrated, shrines to be rifled, religious rites and duties to be interdicted by the law of the land. He would owe the world nothing in that revival of the Church which was to follow. He wrought, as in the old time by His prophet Elias, who, when he was to light the sacrifice with fire from heaven, drenched the burnt-offering with water the first time, the second time, and the third time; "and the water ran round about the altar, and the trench was filled up with water." He wrought as He Himself had done in the raising of Lazarus; for when He heard that His friend was sick, "He remained in the same place two days:" on the third day He "said plainly, Lazarus is dead, and I am glad for your sake, that I was not there, that you may believe;" and then, at length, He went and raised him from the grave. So too was it in His own resurrection; He did not rise from the cross; He did not rise from His mother's arms; He rose from the grave, and on the third day.

So, my dear Brethren, is it now; "He hath taken us, and He will heal us; He will strike, and He will cure us. He will revive us after two days; on the third day He will raise us up, and we

shall live in His sight." Three ages have passed away; the bell
has tolled once, and twice, and thrice; the intercession of the
saints has had effect; the mystery of Providence is unravelled;
the destined hour is come. And, as when Christ arose, men
knew not of His rising, for He rose at midnight and in silence,
so when His mercy would do His new work among us, He
wrought secretly, and was risen ere men dreamed of it. He
sent not His Apostles and preachers, as at the first, from the
city where he has fixed His throne. His few and scattered
priests were about their own work, watching their flocks by
night, with little time to attend to the souls of the wandering
multitudes around them, and with no thoughts of the conversion of the country. But He came as a spirit upon the
waters; He walked to and fro Himself over that dark and
troubled deep; and wonderful to behold, and inexplicable to
man, hearts were stirred, and eyes were raised in hope, and
feet began to move towards the Great Mother, who had almost
given up the thought and the seeking of them. First one, and
then another, sought the rest which she alone could give. A
first, and a second, and a third, and a fourth, each in his turn,
as grace inspired him,—not altogether, as by some party understanding or political call,—but each drawn by divine power,
and against his will, for he was happy where he was, yet with
his will, for he was lovingly subdued by the sweet mysterious
influence which called him on. One by one, little noticed at
the moment, silently, swiftly, and abundantly, they drifted in
till all could see at length that surely the stone was rolled
away, and that Christ was risen and abroad. And as He rose
from the grave, strong and glorious, as if refreshed with His
sleep, so, when the prison doors were opened, the Church
came forth, not changed in aspect or in voice, as calm and
keen, as vigorous and as well furnished, as when they closed
on her. It is told in legends, my Brethren, of that great saint
and instrument of God, St. Athanasius, how that when the
apostate Julian had come to his end, and persecution with
him, the saintly confessor, who had been a wanderer over the

earth, was found to the surprise of his people in his cathedral at Alexandria, seated on his episcopal throne, and clad in the vestments of religion. So is it now; the Church is coming out of prison as collected in her teaching, as precise in her action, as when she went into it. She comes out with pallium, and cope, and chasuble, and stole, and wonder-working relics, and holy images. Her bishops are again in their chairs, and her priests sit round, and the perfect vision of a majestic hierarchy rises before our eyes.

What an awful vitality is here! What a heavenly-sustained sovereignty! What a self-evident divinity! She claims, she seeks, she desires no temporal power, no secular station; she meddles not with Cæsar or the things of Cæsar; she obeys him in his place, but she is independent of him. Her strength is in her God; her rule is over the souls of men; her glory is in their willing subjection and loving loyalty. She hopes and fears nothing from the world; it made her not, nor can it destroy her. She can benefit it largely, but she does not force herself upon it. She may be persecuted by it, but she thrives under the persecution. She may be ignored, she may be silenced and thrown into a corner, but she is thought of the more. Calumniate her, and her influence grows; ridicule her, —she does but smile upon you more awfully and persuasively. What will you do with her, ye sons of men, if you will not love her, if at least you will not endure her? Let the last three hundred years reply. Let her alone, refrain from her; for if her counsel or her work be of men, it will come to nought; but if it be of God, you cannot overthrow it, lest perhaps you be found even to fight against God.

And here I might well stop, for I have brought the line of thought which I have been pursuing to an end; but it is right to inquire how our enemies view these things, as well as how we view them ourselves; and this will lead me to ask your patient attention for a longer time.

[*October 27, 1850.*]

PART II

"Et videntes eum super mare ambulantem, turbati sunt, dicentes: Quia phantasma est. Et præ timore clamaverunt." (And they, seeing Him walking upon the sea, were troubled, saying: It is an apparition. And they cried out for fear.)—Ibid.

YES, MY DEAR BRETHREN, would I could end at the point to which I have brought you! I ought to be able to end here; it is hard I cannot end here. Surely I have set before you a character of the Church of this day remarkable enough to attach to her the prerogatives of that divinely favoured bark in which Peter rowed, and into which the Eternal Lord entered, on the lake of Genesareth. Her fortunes during eighteen centuries have more than answered to the instance of that miraculous protection which was manifested in the fisher's boat in Galilee. It is hard that I must say more, but not strange; not strange, my Brethren, for both our Saviour's own history and His express word prepare us to expect that what is in itself so miraculous would fail to subdue, nay, would harden, the hearts of those to whom it so forcibly appeals. There is, indeed, no argument so strong but the wilful ingenuity of man is able to evade or retort it; and what happens to us in this day happened to Him also, who is in all things our archetype and forerunner. There was a time when He wrought a miracle to convince the incredulous, but they had their ready explanation to destroy its cogency. "There was offered unto Him," says the Evangelist, "one possessed with the devil, both blind and dumb; and He healed him, so that he both spoke and saw. And all the multitudes were amazed, and said, Is not this the son of David? But the Pharisees hearing it, said, *This man casteth not out devils but by Beelzebub, the prince of the devils.*" So said the Pharisees; and He of whom they spoke forewarned His disciples, that both He and His adversaries would have their respective representatives in after times, both in uttering and bearing a like blasphemy. "The disciple is not above his master," He said, "nor the servant above his lord. It is enough for the disciple that he is as his master, and the servant as his lord. *If they have called the good-man of the house Beelzebub, how much more them of His household!*"

So it was, my Brethren, that our Saviour was not allowed to point to His miracles as His warrant, but was thought the worse off for it; and it cannot startle us that we too have to suffer the like in our day. The Sinless was called Beelzebub, much more His sinful servants. And what happened to Him then, is our protection as well as our warning now: for that must be a poor argument, which is available, not only against us, but against Him. For this reason, I am not called upon to enter upon any formal refutation of this charge against us; yet it will not be without profit to trace its operation, and that I shall now proceed to do.

The world, then, witnesses, scrutinizes, and confesses the marvellousness of the Church's power. It does not deny that she is special, awful, nay, supernatural in her history; that she does what unaided man cannot do. It discerns and recognizes her abidingness, her unchangeableness, her imperturbability, her ever youthful vigour, the elasticity of her movements, the consistency and harmony of her teaching, the persuasiveness of her claims. It confesses, I say, that she is a supernatural phenomenon; but it makes short work with such a confession, viewed as an argument for submitting to her, for it ascribes the miracle which it beholds, to Satan, not to God.

This being taken for granted, as an initial assumption from which the whole course of investigation is to proceed, and to which every result is to be referred,—viz., that the Church is not the spouse of Christ, but the child of the evil one, the sorceress described by St. John; and her supreme head, not the vicar of Christ, and pastor and doctor of His people, but the man of sin, and the destined deceiver and son of perdition,—

I say, this is being assumed without proof on starting, it is plain that the very evidences, which really demonstrate our divine origin, are plausibly retorted on us, as they were retorted on our Lord and Saviour, as tokens of our reprobation. Antichrist, when he comes, will be an imitative or counterfeit Christ; therefore he will *look* like Christ to the many, otherwise he would not *be* a counterfeit; but if Antichrist looks like Christ, Christ, of course, must look like Antichrist. The idolatrous sorceress, if she is to have any success in her enchantments, must feign a gravity, an authority, a sanctity, and a nobleness, which really belong to the Church of Christ alone; no wonder, then, since Satan is to be able to persuade men that she is like the Church, he is also able to persuade them that the Church is like her. Christ Himself twice was not recognized even by His disciples in the boat, who loved Him: St. Peter did not know Him after the resurrection, till St. John detected Him; and when, before this, He came walking on the sea, they at first were afraid of Him, as though He had been some evil or malignant being: "they were troubled, saying, it is an apparition, and they cried out for fear." No wonder the enemy of souls should have abundant opportunity and means of seducing the thoughtless and the headstrong, when the very Apostles, in the first years of their discipleship, were so dull in spiritual apprehension.

1. I say, the more numerous and striking are the evidences of the divinity of the Church, so much the more conclusively are they retorted against her, when men assume on starting that she comes, not from above, but from below. Does she claim to be sent from God? but Antichrist will claim it too. Do men bow before her, "and lick up the dust of her feet"? but on the other hand, it is said of the apocalyptic sorceress also, that the kings of the earth shall be made "drunk with her wine." Does the Church receive the homage of "the islands, and the ships of the sea"? The answer is ready; for it is expressly said in Scripture that the evil woman shall make "the merchants of the earth rich by the abundance of her delica-

cies." Is the Church honoured with "the gold and frankincense
of Saba, the multitude of camels, the dromedaries of Madian,
and the flocks of Cedar"? Her impious rival, too, will be
clothed "in purple and scarlet, and gilded with gold," and
enriched with "beasts, and sheep, and horses, and chariots."
Does the Church exercise a power over the soul? The en-
chantress, too, will be possessed, not only of the goods of this
world, but of "the souls of men." Was it promised to the sons
of the Church to do miracles? Antichrist is to do "lying
wonders." Do they exhibit a meekness and a firmness most
admirable, a marvellous self-denial, a fervency in prayer,
and a charity? It is answered: "This only makes them more
dangerous. Do you not know that Satan can transform himself
into an angel of light?" Are they, according to our Lord's
bidding, like sheep, defenceless and patient? This does but
fulfil a remarkable prophecy, it is retorted; for the second
beast, which came up out of the earth, "had two horns like a
lamb's, while it spoke like a dragon." Does the Church fulfil
the Scripture description of being weak and yet strong, of
conquering by yielding, of having nothing yet gaining all
things, and of exercising power without wealth or station?
This wonderful fact, which ought surely to startle the most
obstinate, is assigned, not to the power of God, but to some
political art or conspiracy. Angels walk the earth in vain; to
the gross prejudice of the multitude their coming and going
is the secret plotting, as they call it, of "monks and Jesuits."
Good forsooth it cannot, shall not be; rather believe anything
than that it comes from God; believe in a host of invisible
traitors prowling about and disseminating doctrine adverse
to your own, believe us to be liars and deceivers, men of blood,
ministers of hell, rather than turn your minds, by way of
solving the problem, to the possibility of our being what we
say we are, the children and servants of the true Church.
There never was a more successful artifice than this, which
the author of evil has devised against his Maker, that God's
work is not God's but his own. He has spread this abroad in

the world, as thieves in a crowd escape by giving the alarm; and men, in their simplicity, run away from Christ as if Christ were he, and run into his arms as if he were Christ.

2. And if Satan can so well avail himself even of the gifts and glories of the Church, it is not wonderful that he can be skilful also in his exhibition and use of those offences and scandals which are his own work in her now or in former times. My Brethren, she has scandals, she has a reproach, she has a shame; no Catholic will deny it. She has ever had the reproach and shame of being the mother of children unworthy of her. She has good children;—she has many more bad. Such is the will of God, as declared from the beginning. He might have formed a pure Church; but He has expressly predicted that the cockle, sown by the enemy, shall remain with the wheat, even to the harvest at the end of the world. He pronounced that His Church should be like a fisher's net, gathering of every kind, and not examined till the evening. Nay, more than this, He declared that the bad and imperfect should far surpass the good. "Many are called," He said, "but few are chosen;" and His Apostle speaks of "a remnant saved according to the election of grace." There is ever, then, an abundance of materials in the lives and the histories of Catholics, ready to the use of those opponents who, starting with the notion that the Holy Church is the work of the devil, wish to have some corroboration of their leading idea. Her very prerogative gives special opportunity for it; I mean, that she is the Church of all lands and of all times. If there was a Judas among the Apostles, and a Nicholas among the deacons, why should we be surprised that in the course of eighteen hundred years, there should be flagrant instances of cruelty, of unfaithfulness, of hypocrisy, or of profligacy, and that not only in the Catholic people, but in high places, in royal palaces, in bishops' households, nay, in the seat of St. Peter itself? Why need it surprise, if in barbarous ages, or in ages of luxury, there have been bishops, or abbots, or priests who have forgotten themselves and their God, and served the world or

the flesh, and have perished in that evil service? What triumph is it, though in a long line of between two and three hundred popes, amid martyrs, confessors, doctors, sage rulers, and loving fathers of their people, one, or two, or three are found who fulfil the Lord's description of the wicked servant, who began "to strike the manservants and maidservants, and to eat and drink and be drunk"? What will come of it, though we grant that at this time or that, here or there, mistakes in policy, or ill-advised measures, or timidity, or vacillation in action, or secular maxims, or inhumanity, or narrowness of mind have seemed to influence the Church's action, or her bearing towards her children? I can only say that, taking man as he is, it would be a miracle were such offences altogether absent from her history. Consider what it is to be left to oneself and one's conscience, without others' judgment on what we do, which at times is the case with all men; consider what it is to have easy opportunities of sinning; and then cast the first stone at churchmen who have abused their freedom from control or independence of criticism. My Brethren, with such considerations before me, I do not wonder that these scandals take place; which, of course, are the greater in proportion as the field on which they are found is larger and wider, and the more shocking in proportion as the profession of sanctity, under which they exhibit themselves, is more prominent. What religious body can compare with us in duration or in extent? There are crimes enough to be found in the members of all denominations: if there are passages in our history, the like of which do not occur in the annals of Wesleyanism or of Independency, or the other religions of the day, recollect there have been no Anabaptist pontiffs, no Methodist kings, no Congregational monasteries, no Quaker populations. Let the tenets of Irving or Swedenborg spread, as they never can, through the world, and we should see if, amid the wealth, and power, and station which would accrue to their holders, they would bear their faculties more meekly than Catholics have done.

Come, my Brethren, I will use a very homely illustration;

suffer it, if it be but apposite. You know what a sensation railway accidents occasion. Why? because so enormous are the physical and mechanical forces which are put in motion in that mode of travelling, that, if an accident occurs, it must be gigantic. It is horrible from the conditions under which it takes place. In consequence, it impresses the imagination beyond what the reason can warrant; so that you may fall in with persons, who, on hearing, and much more, on undergoing such a misfortune, are not slow to protest that they never will travel by a railroad again. But sober men submit the matter to a more exact investigation. They do not suffer their minds to be fastened down or carried away by the thought of one or two casualties which shock them. They consider the number of lines, the frequency of trains, the multitude of passengers; they have recourse to the returns, and they calculate the average of accidents, and determine the percentage. And then they contrast with the results thus obtained the corresponding results which coach travelling supplies, and they end, perhaps, by coming to the conclusion that, in matter of fact, the rail is safer than the road; and yet still, in spite of these undeniable facts, there are timid persons, whose imagination is more active than their reason, and who are so arrested by the exceptions, few as they are, that they cannot get themselves to contemplate the rule. In consequence they protest as steadily as before, that steam travelling is perilous and suicidal, and that they never will travel except by coach. Oh, my Brethren, there are many such alarmists in religion; they dress out in tract or pamphlet, they cut out and frame, some special story of tyranny, or fraud, or immorality in the long history of world-wide Catholicism, and that to them is simply Catholicism— that to them is nothing short of a picture, a definition of Catholicism. They shrink from the great road of travel which God has appointed, and they run, as I may say, their own private conveyance, be it Wesleyanism, or Anglicanism, or Dissent, on their own track, as safer, surer, pleasanter, than the Catholic way of passage, because that passage is not secure from danger and mishap. And if this frame of mind is possible in a matter of this life, into which prejudice, and especially religious prejudice, does not enter, much more commonly and fatally will it obtain, when men are not looking for reasons to ascertain a point, but for arguments to defend it.

3. You see, my Brethren, from what I have been saying, how it is that on the one hand, the visible prerogatives of Catholicism do but make men suspicious of it, while on the other its scandals are sure to fill them with dread and horror. But now let me pursue the matter further; let me attempt to trace out more fully how the English mind, in these last centuries, has come to think there is nothing good in that Religion, which it once thought the very teaching of the Most High. Consider, then, this: most men, by nature, dislike labour and trouble; if they labour, as they are obliged to do, they do so *because* they are obliged. They exert themselves under a stimulus or excitement, and just as long as it lasts. Thus they labour for their daily bread, for their families, or for some temporal object which they desire; but they do not take on them the trouble of doing so without some such motive cause. Hence, in religious matters, having no urgent appetite after truth, or desire to please God, or fear of the consequences of displeasing Him, or detestation of sin, they take what comes, they form their notions at random, they are moulded passively from without, and this is what is commonly meant by "private judgment." "Private judgment" commonly means passive impression. Most men in this country like opinions to be brought to them, rather than to be at the pains to go out and seek for them. They like to be waited on, they like to be consulted, for they like to be their own centre. As great men have their slaves or their body-servants for every need of the day, so, in an age like this, when every one reads and has a voice in public matters, it is indispensable that they should have persons to provide them with their ideas, the clothing of their mind, and that of the best fashion. Hence the extreme influence of periodical publications at this day, quarterly, monthly, or daily; these

teach the multitude of men what to think and what to say. And thus is it that, in this age, every one is, intellectually, a sort of absolute king, though his realm is confined to himself or to his family; for at least he can think and say, though he cannot do, what he will, and that with no trouble at all, because he has plenty of intellectual servants to wait on him. Is it to be supposed that a man is to take the trouble of finding out truth himself, when he can pay for it? So his only object is to have cheap knowledge; that he may have his views of revelation, and dogma, and policy, and conduct,—in short, of right and wrong,—ready to hand, as he has his tablecloth laid for his breakfast, and the materials provided for the meal. Thus it is, then, that the English mind grows up into its existing character. There are nations naturally so formed for speculation, that individuals, almost as they eat and drink and work, will originate doctrines and follow out ideas; they, too, of course have their own difficulties in submitting to the Church, but such is not the Englishman. He is in his own way the creature of circumstances; he is bent on action, but as to opinion he takes what comes, only he bargains not to be teased or troubled about it. He gets his opinions anyhow, some from the nursery, some at school, some from the world, and has a zeal for them, because they are his own. Other men, at least, exercise a judgment upon them, and prove them by a rule. He does not care to do so, but he takes them as he finds them, whether they fit together or not, and makes light of the incongruity, and thinks it is proof of common sense, good sense, strong shrewd sense, to do so. All he cares for is, that he should not be put to rights; of that he is jealous enough. He is satisfied to walk about, dressed just as he is. As opinions come, so they must stay with him: and, as he does not like trouble in his acquisition of them, so he resents criticism in his use.

When, then, the awful form of Catholicism, of which he has already heard so much good and so much evil—so much evil which revolts him, so much good which amazes and troubles him—when this great vision, which hitherto he has known from books and from rumour, but not by sight and hearing, presents itself before him, it finds in him a very different being from the simple Anglo-Saxon to whom it originally came. It finds in him a being, not of rude nature, but of formed habits, averse to change and resentful of interference; a being who looks hard at it, and repudiates and loathes it, first of all, because, if listened to, it would give him much trouble. He wishes to be let alone; but here is a teaching which purports to be revealed, which would mould his mind on new ideas, which he has to learn, and which, if he cannot learn thoroughly, he must borrow from strangers. The very notion of a theology or a ritual frightens and oppresses him; it is a yoke, because it makes religion difficult, not easy. There is enough of labour in learning matters of this life, without concerning oneself with the revelations of another. He does not choose to believe that the Almighty has told us so many things, and he readily listens to any person or argument maintaining the negative. And, moreover, he resents the idea of interference itself; "an Englishman's house is his castle;" a maxim most salutary in politics, most dangerous in moral conduct. He cannot bear the thought of not having a will of his own, or an opinion of his own, on any given subject of inquiry, whatever it be. It is intolerable, as he considers, not to be able, on the most awful and difficult of subjects, to think for oneself; it is an insult to be told that God has spoken and superseded investigation.

4. And, further still, consider this: strange as it may be to those who do not know him, he really believes in that accidental collection of tenets, of which I have been speaking; habit has made it all natural to him, and he takes it for granted; he thinks his own view of things as clear as day, and every other view irrational and ludicrous. In good faith and in sincerity of heart, he thinks the Englishman knows more about God's dealings with men, than any one else; and he measures all things in heaven and earth by the floating opinions

which have been drifted into his mind. And especially is he
satisfied and sure of his *principles;* he conceives them to be
the dictates of the simplest and most absolute sense, and it
does not occur to him for a moment, that objective truth claims
to be sought, and a revealed doctrine requires to be ascertained. He himself is the ultimate sanction and appellate authority of all that he holds. Putting aside, then, the indignation which, under these circumstances, he naturally feels in
being invited to go to school again, his present opinions are
an effectual bar to his ever recognizing the divine mission of
Catholicism; for he criticizes Catholicism simply by those
opinions themselves which are antagonists of it, and takes
his notes of truth and error from a source which is already
committed against it. And thus you see that frequent occurrence, of really worthy persons unable to reconcile their minds,
do what they will, to the teaching and the ways of the Catholic Church. The more they see of her members, the more their
worst suspicions are confirmed. They did not wish, they say, to
believe the popular notions of her anti-Christian character;
but, really, after what they have seen of her authorities and
her people, nothing is left to them but an hostility to her, which
they are loth to adopt. They wish to think the best of every
one; but this ecclesiastical measure, that speech, that book,
those persons, those expressions, that line of thought, those
realized results, all tend one way, and force them to unlearn
a charitableness which is as pernicious as it is illusory.
Thus, my Brethren, they speak; alas, they do not see that they
are assuming the very point in dispute; for the original question is, whether Catholics or they are right in their respective
principles and views, and to decide it merely by what is
habitual to themselves is to exercise the double office of accuser
and judge. Yet multitudes, of sober and serious minds and
well-regulated lives, look out upon the Catholic Church and
shrink back again from her presence, on no better reasons
than these. They cannot endure her; their whole being revolts
from her; she leaves, as they speak, a bad taste in their mouths;

all is so novel, so strange, so unlike what is familiar to them, so unlike the Anglican prayer-book, so unlike some favourite author of their own, so different from what they would do or say themselves, requires so much explanation, is so strained and unnatural, so unreal and extravagant, so unquiet, nay, so disingenuous, so unfeeling, that they cannot even tolerate it. The Mass is so difficult to follow, and we say prayers so very quickly, and we sit when we should stand, and we talk so freely when we should be reserved, and we keep Sunday so differently from them, and we have such notions of our own about marriage and celibacy, and we approve of vows, and we class virtues and sins on so unreasonable a standard; these and a thousand such details are, in the case of numbers, de-cisive proofs that we deserve the hard names which are heaped on us by the world.

5. Recollect, too, my Brethren, that a great part of the actions of every day, when narrowly looked into, are neither good nor bad in themselves, but only in relation to the persons who do them, and the circumstances or motives under which they are done. There are actions, indeed, which no circum-stances can alter; which, at all times, and in all places, are duties or sins. Veracity, purity, are always virtues—blasphemy, always a sin; but to speak against another, for instance, is not always detraction, and swearing is not always taking God's name in vain. What is right in one person, may be wrong in another; and hence the various opinions which are formed of public men, who, for the most part, cannot be truly judged, except with a knowledge of their principles, characters, and motives. Here is another source of misrepresenting the Church and her servants; much of what they do admits both of a good interpretation and a bad; and when the world, as I have sup-posed, starts with the hypothesis that we are hypocrites or tyrants, that we are unscrupulous, crafty, and profane, it is easy to see how the very same actions which it would extol in its friends, it will unhesitatingly condemn in the instance of the objects of its hatred or suspicion. When men live in their

own world, in their own habits and ways of thought, as I have been describing, they contract, not only a narrowness, but what may be called a one-sidedness of mind. They do not judge of us by the rules they apply to the conduct of themselves and each other; what they praise or allow in those they admire is an offence to them in us. Day by day, then, as it passes, furnishes, as a matter of course, a series of charges against us, simply because it furnishes a succession of our sayings and doings. Whatever we do, whatever we do not do, is a demonstration against us. Do we argue? men are surprised at our insolence or effrontery; are we silent? we are underhand and deep. Do we appeal to the law? it is in order to evade it; do we obey the Church? it is a sign of our disloyalty. Do we state our pretensions? we blaspheme; do we conceal them? we are liars and hypocrites. Do we display the pomp of our ceremonial, and the habits of our Religious? our presumption has become intolerable; do we put them aside and dress as others? we are ashamed of being seen, and skulk about as conspirators. Did a Catholic priest cherish doubts of his faith? it would be an interesting and touching fact, suitable for public meetings; does a Protestant minister, on the other hand, doubt of the Protestant opinions? he is but dishonestly eating the bread of the Establishment. Does a Protestant exclude Catholic books from his house? he is a good father and master; does a Catholic do the same with Protestant tracts? he is afraid of the light. Protestants may ridicule a portion of our Scriptures under the name of the Apocrypha: we may not denounce the mere Protestant translation of the Bible. Protestants are to glory in their obedience to their ecclesiastical head; we may not be faithful to ours. A Protestant layman may determine and propound all by himself the terms of salvation; we are bigots and despots, if we do but proclaim what a thousand years have sanctioned. The Catholic is insidious, when the Protestant is prudent; the Protestant frank and honest, when the Catholic is rash or profane. Not a word that we say, not a deed that we do, but is viewed in the medium of that one idea, by the light of that one prejudice, which our enemies cherish concerning us; not a word or deed but is grafted on the original assumption that we certainly come from below, and are the servants of Antichrist.

6. Now, my dear Brethren, I have not said a word of much more that might be insisted on, and of the greatest importance. I have not said a word of the unhappy interest that men have in denying a Religion so severe against the wilful sinner as ours is:—no one likes a prophet of evil. Nor have I shown you, as I might, how natural it is, that they who sit at home and judge of all things by their personal experience of what is possible, and their private notion of what is good, should, humanly speaking, be incapable of faith in religious mysteries, such as ours. They think nothing true which is strange to them; and, in consequence, they consider our very doctrines a simple refutation of our claims. Nor, again, have I spoken of the misrepresentations and slanders with which the father of lies floods the popular mind, and which are so safe to utter, because they are, as he knows, so welcome to hear. Alas! there is no calumny too gross for the credulity of our countrymen, no imputation on us so monstrous which they will not drink up greedily like water. There is a demand for such fabrications, and there is a consequent supply; our antiquity, our vastness, our strangeness, our successes, our unmoveableness, all require a solution; and the imposter is hailed as a prophet, who will extemporize against us some tale of blood, and the orator as an evangelist, who points to some real scandal of the Church, dead and gone, man or measure, as the pattern fact of Catholicism. And thus it comes to pass that we are distrusted, feared, hated, and ridiculed, whichever way we look; all parties, the most hostile to each other, are still more hostile to us, and will combine in attacking us. No one but is brave enough to spurn us; it is no cowardice to accuse us when we cannot answer, no cruelty to fasten on us what we detest. We are fair game for all comers. Other men they view and oppose in their doctrines, but us they oppose in our persons; we are thought

morally and individually corrupt, we have not even natural
goodness; we are not merely ignorant of the new birth, but
are signed and sealed as the ministers of the evil one. We have
his mark on our foreheads. That we are living beings with
human hearts and keen feelings, is not conceived; no, the best
we can expect is to be treated as shadows of the past, names
a thousand miles away, abstractions, commonplaces, historical
figures, or dramatic properties, waste ground on which any
load of abuse may be shot, the convenient conductors of a
distempered political atmosphere—who are not Englishmen,
who have not the right of citizens, nor any claim for redress,
nor any plea for indulgence, but who are well off, forsooth, if
they are allowed so much as to pollute this free soil with their
odious presence.

And thus we are thrown back on ourselves: for nothing we
can do on the stage of the world, but is turned against us as
an offence. Our most innocent actions, our attempts to please
the community, our sanguine expectations of conciliating our
foes, our expressions of love, are flung back upon us with scorn,
to our pain and disappointment. Our simplicity, inexperience
of life, ignorance of human nature, or want of tact and prudence, are put down to duplicity; and the more honest and
frank are our avowals, the more certainly it is thought that
a fraud lurks in the background. We are never so double-
dealing as when we are candid. We are never so deep as when
we have been accused and acquitted. Thus we find ourselves
quite at fault how anything we do is likely to be taken; and
at length, with wounded feelings, we determine to let it alone,
as never knowing where to find men, or how to treat them.
I have often been reminded, my Brethren, by these circumstances of ours, of the complication, not uncommon, I think,
in the fictions of a popular writer who died some twenty years
ago. He delights to represent innocent persons involved in
circumstances which plausibly convict them of guilt, and
which they are unable satisfactorily to explain. I think I
recollect a young man who is accused of treason, and who,

when fact after fact is brought forward to his disadvantage, conscious of his innocence, yet feeling the ingenuity of the allegation, and the speciousness of the evidence by which it is supported, and, moreover, the prejudice and cold suspicion of his judge, bursts into tears, buries his head in his hands, and refuses to answer any more interrogatories. "Do your worst," he seems to say, "not a word more shall you extract from me. You refuse to believe me; cease to question me. You are determined I am guilty; make the most of your persuasion." What is there represented in fiction happens to us in fact. We are innocent, we seem guilty, we despair of the vindication which we deserve; but we do not bury our faces in our hands, we raise our hands and our faces to our Redeemer. "As the eyes of servants are on the hands of their masters, and the eyes of the handmaid are on the hands of her mistress, so are our eyes unto the Lord our God, until He have mercy upon us. Have mercy on us, O Lord; have mercy on us, for we are greatly filled with contempt. We are a reproach to the rich and a contempt to the proud." To Thee do we appeal, O true Judge, for Thou seest us. We care not for man while we have Thee. We can afford to part with the creature while we have the Creator. We can endure "the snare of an unjust tongue, and the lips of them that forge lies," while we have Thy presence in our assemblies, and Thy witness and Thy approval in our hearts.

We do not, then, we cannot, rejoice in a mere worldly temper or in a political tone, on occasion of the event which we are celebrating today: no, we are too conscious both of our divine prerogatives and our high destiny, and again of the weight of that calumny and reproach which is our cross. We rejoice, not "as those who rejoice in the harvest, or as conquerors rejoice when they divide the spoils." We rejoice surely, but solemnly, religiously, courageously, as the priests of the Lord, when they were carrying into battle "the ark of the Lord, the God of the whole earth." We rejoice as those who love men's souls so well that they would go through much to save them, yet love God more, and find the full reward of all disappointments in Him; as those whose work lies with sinners, but whose portion is with the saints. We love you, O men of this generation, but we fear you not. Understand well and lay it to heart, that we will do the work of God and fulfil our mission, with your consent, if we can get it, but in spite of you, if we cannot. You cannot touch us except in a way of which you do not dream, by the arm of force; nor do we dream of asking for more than that which the Apostle claimed, freedom of speech, "an open door," which, through God's grace, will be "evident," though there be "many adversaries." We do but wish to subdue you by appeals to your reason and to your heart; give us but a fair field and due time, and we hope to gain our point. I do not say that we shall gain it in this generation; I do not say we shall gain it without our own suffering; but we look on to the future, and we do not look at ourselves. As to ourselves, the world has long ago done its worst against us; long ago has it seasoned us for this encounter. In the way of obloquy and ridicule it has exhausted upon us long since all it had to pour, and now it is resourceless. More it cannot say against us than it has said already. We have parted company with it for many years; we have long chosen our portion with the old faith once delivered to the saints, and we have intimately comprehended that a penalty is attached to the profession. No one proclaims the truth to a deceived world, but will be treated himself as a deceiver. We know our place and our fortunes: to give a witness, and to be reviled; to be cast out as evil, and to succeed. Such is the law which the Lord of all has annexed to the promulgation of the truth: its preachers suffer, but its cause prevails. Joyfully have we become a party to this bargain; and as we have resigned ourselves to the price, so we intend, by God's aid, to claim the compensation.

Fear not, therefore, dear Brethren of the household of faith,

any trouble that may come upon us, or upon you, if trouble
be God's will; trouble will but prove the simplicity of our
and your devotion to Him. When our Lord walked on the
sea, Peter went out to meet Him, and "seeing the wind strong
he was afraid." Doubt not that He, who caught the disciple
by the hand, will appear, to rescue you; doubt not that He,
who could tread the billows so securely, can self-sustained
bear any weight your weakness throws upon Him, and can
be your immovable refuge and home amid the tossing and
tumult of the storm. The waves roared round the Apostle,
they could do nothing more: they could but excite his fear;
they could but assault his faith; they could not hurt him but
by tempting him; they could not overcome him except through
himself. While he was true to himself, he was safe; when he
feared and doubted, he began to sink. So it is now: "your
adversary, the devil, as a roaring lion, goeth about:" it is all
he can do. So says the great Saint Antony, the first monk,
who lived his long life in the Egyptian desert, and had abundant experience of conflicts with the evil one. He tells his
children that bad spirits make a noise and clatter, and shout
and roar, because they have nothing else to do; it is their way
of driving us from our Saviour. Let us be true to ourselves,
and the blustering wind will drop, the furious sea will calm.
No, I fear not, my Brethren, this momentary clamour of our
foe: I fear not this great people, among whom we dwell, of
whose blood we come, and who have still, under the habits
of these later centuries, the rudiments of that faith by which,
in the beginning, they were new-born to God: who still, de-
spite the loss of heavenly gifts, retain the love of justice,
manly bearing, and tenderness of heart, which Gregory saw
in their very faces. I have no fear about our Holy Father,
whose sincerity of affection towards His ancient flock, whose
simplicity and truthfulness I know full well. I have no fear
about the zeal of the college of our bishops, the sanctity of
the body of our clergy, or the inward perfection of our Religious. One thing alone I fear. I fear the presence of sin in

the midst of us. My Brethren, the success of the Church lies not with pope, or bishops, or priests, or monks; it rests with yourselves. If the present mercies of God come to nought, it will be because sin has undone them. The drunkard, the blasphemer, the unjust dealer, the profligate liver,—these will be our ruin; the open scandal, the secret sin known only to God, these form the devil's real host. We can conquer every foe but these: corruption, hollowness, neglect of mercies, deadness of heart, worldliness,—these will be too much for us.

And, O my dear Brethren, if, through God's mercy, you are among those who are shielded from these more palpable dangers and more ordinary temptations of humanity, then go on to pray for all who are in a like state with yourselves, that we may all "forget the things that are behind, and stretch forth to those that are before;" that we may "join with faith, virtue, and with virtue, knowledge, and with knowledge, abstinence, and with abstinence, patience, and with patience, pity, and with pity, love of brotherhood, and with love of brotherhood, charity." Pray that we may not come short of that destiny to which God calls us; that we may be visited by His effectual grace, enabling us to break the bonds of lukewarmness and sloth, to command our will, to rule our actions through the day, to grow continually in devotion and fervour of spirit, and, while our natural vigour decays, to feel that keener energy which comes from heaven.

[*October 27, 1850.*]

XXII

THE SECOND SPRING [1]

"Surge, propera, amica mea, columba mea, formosa mea, et veni. Jam enim hiems transiit, imber abiit et recessit. Flores apparuerunt in terrâ nostrâ." (Arise, make haste, my love, my dove, my beautiful one, and come. For the winter is now past, the rain is over and gone. The flowers have appeared in our land).—Can., c. ii. v. 10–12.

WE HAVE FAMILIAR EXPERIENCE of the order, the constancy, the perpetual renovation of the material world which surrounds us. Frail and transitory as is every part of it, restless and migratory as are its elements, never-ceasing as are its changes, still it abides. It is bound together by a law of permanence, it is set up in unity; and, though it is ever dying, it is every coming to life again. Dissolution does but give birth to fresh modes of organization, and one death is the parent of a thousand lives. Each hour, as it comes, is but a testimony, how fleeting, yet how secure, how certain, is the great whole. It is like an image on the waters, which is ever the same, though the waters ever flow. Change upon change,—yet one change cries out to another, like the alternate Seraphim, in praise and in glory of their Maker. The sun sinks to rise again; the day is swallowed up in the gloom of night, to be born out of it, as fresh as if it had never been

[1] Preached in St. Mary's, Oscott. From *Sermons Preached on Various Occasions*, No. 10. [Ed.]

Dedication in the first Edition:—To the Fathers of the Synod at Oscott, to the Clergy who assisted at it, who, in the strength of the Most High, have begun a work which is to live after them, the following Sermon, preached under the illumination of their presence, is humbly and affectionately inscribed, by their devoted servant in Christ, the Author.

quenched. Spring passes into summer, and through summer and autumn into winter, only the more surely, by its own ultimate return, to triumph over that grave, towards which it resolutely hastened from its first hour. We mourn over the blossoms of May, because they are to wither; but we know, withal, that May is one day to have its revenge upon November, by the revolution of that solemn circle which never stops, —which teaches us in our height of hope, ever to be sober, and in our depth of desolation, never to despair.

And forcibly as this comes home to every one of us, not less forcible is the contrast which exists between this material world, so vigorous, so reproductive, amid all its changes, and the moral world, so feeble, so downward, so resourceless, amid all its aspirations. That which ought to come to nought, endures; that which promises a future, disappoints and is no more. The same sun shines in heaven from first to last, and the blue firmament, the everlasting mountains, reflect his rays; but where is there upon earth the champion, the hero, the lawgiver, the body politic, the sovereign race, which was great three hundred years ago, and is great now? Moralists and poets, often do they descant upon this innate vitality of matter, this innate perishableness of mind. Man rises to fall: he tends to dissolution from the moment he begins to be; he lives on, indeed, in his children, he lives on in his name, he lives not on in his own person. He is, as regards the manifestations of his nature here below, as a bubble that breaks, and as water poured out upon the earth. He was young, he is old, he is never young again. This is the lament over him, poured forth in verse and in prose, by Christians and by heathen. The greatest work of God's hands under the sun, he, in all the manifestations of his complex being, is born only to die.

His bodily frame first begins to feel the power of this constraining law, though it is the last to succumb to it. We look at the bloom of youth with interest, yet with pity; and the more graceful and sweet it is, with pity so much the more;

for whatever be its excellence and its glory, soon it begins
to be deformed and dishonoured by the very force of its
living on. It grows into exhaustion and collapse, till at length
it crumbles into that dust out of which it was originally
taken.

So is it, too, with our moral being, a far higher and diviner
portion of our natural constitution; it begins with life, it ends
with what is worse than the mere loss of life, with a living
death. How beautiful is the human heart, when it puts forth
its first leaves, and opens and rejoices in its spring-tide. Fair
as may be the bodily form, fairer far, in its green foliage and
bright blossoms, is natural virtue. It blooms in the young, like
some rich flower, so delicate, so fragrant, and so dazzling.
Generosity and lightness of heart and amiableness, the confiding spirit, the gentle temper, the elastic cheerfulness, the
open hand, the pure affection, the noble aspiration, the heroic
resolve, the romantic pursuit, the love in which self has no
part,—are not these beautiful? and are they not dressed up
and set forth for admiration in their best shapes, in tales and
in poems? and ah! what a prospect of good is there! who could
believe that it is to fade! and yet, as night follows upon day,
as decrepitude follows upon health, so surely are failure, and
overthrow, and annihilation, the issue of this natural virtue,
if time only be allowed to it to run its course. There are those
who are cut off in the first opening of this excellence, and then,
if we may trust their epitaphs, they have lived like angels;
but wait a while, let them live on, let the course of life proceed, let the bright soul go through the fire and water of the
world's temptations and seductions and corruptions and trans-
formations; and, alas for the insufficiency of nature! alas for
its powerlessness to persevere, its waywardness in disappointing its own promise! Wait till youth has become age; and not
more different is the miniature which we have of him when
a boy, when every feature spoke of hope, put side by side of
the large portrait painted to his honour, when he is old, when
his limbs are shrunk, his eye dim, his brow furrowed, and his

hair gray than differs the moral grace of that boyhood from the forbidding and repulsive aspect of his soul, now that he has lived to the age of man. For moroseness, and misanthropy, and selfishness, is the ordinary winter of that spring.

Such is man in his own nature, and such, too, is he in his works. The noblest efforts of his genius, the conquests he has made, the doctrines he has originated, the nations he has civilized, the states he has created, they outlive himself, they outlive him by many centuries, but they tend to an end, and that end is dissolution. Powers of the world, sovereignties, dynasties, sooner or later come to nought; they have their fatal hour. The Roman conqueror shed tears over Carthage, for in the destruction of the rival city he discerned too truly an augury of the fall of Rome; and at length, with the weight and the responsibilities, the crimes and the glories, of centuries upon centuries, the Imperial City fell.

Thus man and all his works are mortal; they die, and they have no power of renovation.

But what is it, my Fathers, my Brothers, what is it that has happened in England just at this time? Something strange is passing over this land, by the very surprise, by the very commotion, which it excites. Were we not near enough the scene of action to be able to say what is going on,—were we the inhabitants of some sister planet possessed of a more perfect mechanism than this earth has discovered for surveying the transactions of another globe,—and did we turn our eyes thence towards England just at this season, we should be arrested by a political phenomenon as wonderful as any which the astronomer notes down from his physical field of view. It would be the occurrence of a national commotion, almost without parallel, more violent than has happened here for centuries,—at least in the judgments and intentions of men, if not in act and deed. We should note it down, that soon after St. Michael's day, 1850, a storm arose in the moral world, so furious as to demand some great explanation, and to rouse in us an intense desire to gain it. We should observe it increasing from day to day, and spreading from place to place, without remission, almost without lull, up to this very hour, when perhaps it threatens worse still, or at least gives no sure prospect of alleviation. Every party in the body politic undergoes its influence,—from the Queen upon her throne, down to the little ones in the infant or day school. The ten thousands of the constituency, the sum-total of Protestant sects, the aggregate of religious societies and associations, the great body of established clergy in town and country, the bar, even the medical profession, nay, even literary and scientific circles, every class, every interest, every fireside, gives tokens of this ubiquitous storm. This would be our report of it, seeing it from the distance, and we should speculate on the cause. What is it all about? against what is it directed? what wonder has happened upon earth? what prodigious, what preternatural event is adequate to the burden of so vast an effect?

We should judge rightly in our curiosity about a phenomenon like this; it must be a portentous event, and it is. It is an innovation, a miracle, I may say, in the course of human events. The physical world revolves year by year, and begins again; but the political order of things does not renew itself, does not return; it continues, but it proceeds; there is no retrogression. This is so well understood by men of the day, that with them progress is idolized as another name for good. The past never returns—it is never good;—if we are to escape existing ills, it must be by going forward. The past is out of date; the past is dead. As well may the dead live to us, as well may the dead profit us, as the past return. *This*, then, is the cause of this national transport, this national cry, which encompasses us. The past *has* returned, the dead lives. Thrones are overturned, and are never restored; States live and die, and then are matter only for history. Babylon was great, and Tyre, and Egypt, and Nineve, and shall never be great again. The English Church was, and the English Church was not, and the English Church is once again. This is the portent, worthy of a cry. It is the coming in of a Second Spring; it is a restoration in the moral world, such as that which yearly takes place in the physical.

Three centuries ago, and the Catholic Church, that great creation of God's power, stood in this land in pride of place. It had the honours of near a thousand years upon it; it was enthroned in some twenty sees up and down the broad country; it was based in the will of a faithful people; it energized through ten thousand instruments of power and influence; and it was ennobled by a host of Saints and Martyrs. The churches, one by one, recounted and rejoiced in the line of glorified intercessors, who were the respective objects of their grateful homage. Canterbury alone numbered perhaps some sixteen, from St. Augustine to St. Dunstan and St. Elphege, from St. Anselm and St. Thomas down to St. Edmund. York had its St. Paulinus, St. John, St. Wilfrid, and St. William; London, its St. Erconwald; Durham, its St. Cuthbert; Winton, its St. Swithun. Then there were St. Aidan of Lindisfarne, and St. Hugh of Lincoln, and St. Chad of Lichfield, and St. Thomas of Hereford, and St. Oswald and St. Wulstan of Worcester, and St. Osmund of Salisbury, and St. Birinus of Dorcester, and St. Richard of Chichester. And then, too, its religious orders, its monastic establishments, its universities, its wide relations all over Europe, its high prerogatives in the temporal state, its wealth, its dependencies, its popular honours,—where was there in the whole of Christendom a more glorious hierarchy? Mixed up with the civil institutions, with king and nobles, with the people, found in every village and in every town,—it seemed destined to stand, so long as England stood, and to outlast, it might be, England's greatness.

But it was the high decree of heaven, that the majesty of that presence should be blotted out. It is a long story, my Fathers and Brothers—you know it well. I need not go through it. The vivifying principle of truth, the shadow of St. Peter, the grace of the Redeemer, left it. That old Church in its day became a corpse (a marvellous, an awful change!); and then it did but corrupt the air which once it refreshed, and cumber

the ground which once it beautified. So all seemed to be lost;
and there was a struggle for a time, and then its priests were
cast out or martyred. There were sacrileges innumerable. Its
temples were profaned or destroyed; its revenues seized by
covetous nobles, or squandered upon the ministers of a new
faith. The presence of Catholicism was at length simply removed,—its grace disowned,—its power despised,—its name,
except as a matter of history, at length almost unknown. It
took a long time to do this thoroughly; much time, much
thought, much labour, much expense; but at last it was done.
Oh, that miserable day, centuries before we were born! What
a martyrdom to live in it, and see the fair form of Truth, moral
and material, hacked piecemeal, and every limb and organ
carried off, and burned in the fire, or cast into the deep! But
at last the work was done. Truth was disposed of, and shov-
elled away, and there was a calm, a silence, a sort of peace;—
and such was about the state of things when we were born
into this weary world.

My Fathers and Brothers, *you* have seen it on one side,
and some of us on another; but one and all of us can bear
witness to the fact of the utter contempt into which Catholicism had fallen by the time that we were born. You, alas,
know it far better than I can know it; but it may not be out
of place, if by one or two tokens, as by the strokes of a pencil,
I bear witness to you from without, of what you can witness
so much more truly from within. No longer the Catholic
Church in the country; nay, no longer, I may say, a Catholic
community;—but a few adherents of the Old Religion, moving
silently and sorrowfully about, as memorials of what had been.
"The Roman Catholics;"—not a sect, not even an interest, as
men conceived of it,—not a body, however small, representative of the Great Communion abroad,—but a mere handful
of individuals, who might be counted, like the pebbles and
detritus of the great deluge, and who, forsooth, merely happened to retain a creed which, in its day indeed, was the
profession of a Church. Here a set of poor Irishmen, coming

and going at harvest time, or a colony of them lodged in a miserable quarter of the vast metropolis. There, perhaps an elderly person, seen walking in the streets, grave and solitary, and strange, though noble in bearing, and said to be of good family, and a "Roman Catholic." An old-fashioned house of gloomy appearance, closed in with high walls, with an iron gate, and yews, and the report attaching to it that "Roman Catholics" lived there; but who they were, or what they did, or what was meant by calling them Roman Catholics, no one could tell;—though it had an unpleasant sound, and told of form and superstition. And then, perhaps, as we went to and fro, looking with a boy's curious eyes through the great city, we might come to-day upon some Moravian chapel, or Quaker's meeting-house, and to-morrow on a chapel of the "Roman Catholics:" but nothing was to be gathered from it, except that there were lights burning there, and some boys in white, swinging censers; and what it all meant could only be learned from books, from Protestant Histories and Sermons; and they did not report well of "the Roman Catholics," but, on the contrary, deposed that they had once had power and had abused it. And then, again, we might, on one occasion, hear it pointedly put out by some literary man, as the result of his careful investigation, and as a recondite point of information, which few knew, that there was this difference between the Roman Catholics of England and the Roman Catholics of Ireland, that the latter had bishops, and the former were governed by four officials, called Vicars-Apostolic.

Such was about the sort of knowledge possessed of Christianity by the heathen of old time, who persecuted its adherents from the face of the earth, and then called them a *gens lucifuga,* a people who shunned the light of day. Such were Catholics in England, found in corners, and alleys, and cellars, and the housetops, or in the recesses of the country; cut off from the populous world around them, and dimly seen, as if through a mist or in twilight, as ghosts flitting to and fro, by the high Protestants, the lords of the earth. At length so feeble did they become, so utterly contemptible, that contempt gave birth to pity; and the more generous of their tyrants actually began to wish to bestow on them some favour, under the notion that their opinions were simply too absurd ever to spread again, and that they themselves, were they but raised in civil importance, would soon unlearn and be ashamed of them. And thus, out of mere kindness to us, they began to vilify our doctrines to the Protestant world, that so our very idiotcy or our secret unbelief might be our plea for mercy.

A *great* change, an *awful* contrast, between the time-honoured Church of St. Augustine and St. Thomas, and the poor remnant of their children in the beginning of the nineteenth century! It was a miracle, I might say, to have pulled down that lordly power; but there was a greater and a truer one in store. No one could have prophesied its fall, but still less would any one have ventured to prophesy its rise again. The fall was wonderful; still after all it was in the order of nature;—all things come to nought: its rise again would be a different sort of wonder, for it is in the order of grace,—and who can hope for miracles, and such a miracle as this! Has the whole course of history a like to show? I must speak cautiously and according to my knowledge, but I recollect no parallel to it. Augustine, indeed, came to the same island to which the early missionaries had come already; but they came to Britons, and he to Saxons. The Arian Goths and Lombards too, cast off their heresy in St. Augustine's age, and joined the Church; but they had never fallen away from her. The inspired word seems to imply the almost impossibility of such a grace as the renovation of those who have crucified to themselves again, and trodden underfoot, the Son of God. Who then could have dared to hope that, out of so sacrilegious a nation as this is a people would have been formed again unto their Saviour? What signs did it show that it was to be singled out from among the nations? Had it been prophesied some fifty years ago, would not the very notion have seemed preposterous and wild?

My Fathers, there was one of your own order, then in the maturity of his powers and his reputation. His name is the property of this diocese; yet is too great, too venerable, too dear to all Catholics, to be confined to any part of England, when it is rather a household word in the mouths of all of us. What would have been the feelings of that venerable man, the champion of God's ark in an evil time, could *he* have lived to see this day? It is almost presumptuous for one who knew him not, to draw pictures about him, and his thoughts, and his friends, some of whom are even here present; yet am I wrong in fancying that a day such as this, in which we stand, would have seemed to him a dream, or, if he prophesied of it, to his hearers nothing but a mockery? Say that one time, rapt in spirit, he had reached forward to the future, and that his mortal eye had wandered from that lowly chapel in the valley which had been for centuries in the possession of Catholics, to the neighbouring height, then waste and solitary. And let him say to those about him: "I see a bleak mount, looking upon an open country, over against that huge town, to whose inhabitants Catholicism is of so little account. I see the ground marked out, and an ample enclosure made; and plantations are rising there, clothing and circling in the space. And there on that high spot, far from the haunts of men, yet in the very centre of the island, a large edifice, or rather pile of edifices, appears, with many fronts and courts, and long cloisters and corridors, and story upon story. And there it rises, under the invocation of the same sweet and powerful name which has been our strength and consolation in the Valley. I look more attentively at that building, and I see it is fashioned upon that ancient style of art which brings back the past, which had seemed to be perishing from off the face of the earth, or to be preserved only as a curiosity, or to be imitated only as a fancy. I listen, and I hear the sound of voices, grave and musical, renewing the old chant, with which Augustine greeted Ethelbert in the free air upon the Kentish strand. It comes from a long procession, and it winds along the cloisters. Priests and

Religious, theologians from the schools, and canons from the Cathedral, walk in due precedence. And then there comes a vision of well nigh twelve mitred heads; and last I see a Prince of the Church, in the royal dye of empire and of martyrdom, a pledge to us from Rome of Rome's unwearied love, a token that that goodly company is firm in Apostolic faith and hope. And the shadow of the Saints is there:—St. Benedict is there, speaking to us by the voice of bishop and of priest, and counting over the long ages through which he has prayed, and studied, and laboured; there, too, is St. Dominic's white wool, which no blemish can impair, no stain can dim:—and if St. Bernard be not there, it is only that his absence may make him be remembered more. And the princely patriarch, St. Ignatius, too, the St. George of the modern world, with his chivalrous lance run through his writhing foe, he, too, sheds his blessing upon that train. And others, also, his equals or his juniors in history, whose pictures are above our altars, or soon shall be, the surest proof that the Lord's arm has not waxen short, nor His mercy failed,—they, too, are looking down from their thrones on high upon the throng. And so that high company moves on into the holy place; and there, with august rite and awful sacrifice, inaugurates the great act which brings it thither." What is that act? it is the first Synod of a new Hierarchy; it is the resurrection of the Church.

O my Fathers, my Brothers, had that revered Bishop spoken then, who that had heard him but would have said that he spoke what could not be? What! those few scattered worshippers, *the* Roman Catholics, to form a Church! Shall the past be rolled back? Shall the grave open? Shall the Saxons live again to God? Shall the shepherds, watching their poor flocks by night, be visited by a multitude of the heavenly army, and hear how their Lord has been new-born in their own city? Yes; for grace can, where nature cannot. The world grows old, but the Church is ever young. She can, in any time, at her Lord's will, "inherit the Gentiles, and inhabit the desolate cities." "Arise, Jerusalem, for thy light is come, and the glory

of the Lord is risen upon thee. Behold, darkness shall cover
the earth, and a mist the people; but the Lord shall arise
upon thee, and His glory shall be seen upon thee. Lift up thine
eyes round about, and see; all these are gathered together,
they come to thee; thy sons shall come from afar, and thy
daughters shall rise up at thy side." "Arise, make haste, my
love, my dove, my beautiful one, and come. For the winter is
now past, and the rain is over and gone. The flowers have
appeared in our land . . . the fig-tree hath put forth her green
figs; the vines in flower yield their sweet smell. Arise, my
love, my beautiful one, and come." It is the time for thy
Visitation. Arise, Mary, and go forth in thy strength into that
north country, which once was thine own, and take possession
of a land which knows thee not. Arise, Mother of God, and
with thy thrilling voice, speak to those who labour with child,
and are in pain, till the babe of grace leaps within them. Shine
on us, dear Lady, with thy bright countenance, like the sun
in his strength, *O stella matutina*, O harbinger of peace, till
our year is one perpetual May. From thy sweet eyes, from
thy pure smile, from thy majestic brow, let ten thousand
influences rain down, not to confound or overwhelm, but to
persuade, to win over thine enemies. O Mary, my hope, O
Mother undefiled, fulfil to us the promise of this Spring. A
second temple rises on the ruins of the old. Canterbury has
gone its way, and York is gone, and Durham is gone, and
Winchester is gone. It was sore to part with them. We clung
to the vision of past greatness, and would not believe it could
come to nought; but the Church in England has died, and
the Church lives again. Westminster and Nottingham, Bev-
erley and Hexham, Northampton and Shrewsbury, if the world
lasts, shall be names as musical to the ear, as stirring to the
heart, as the glories we have lost; and Saints shall rise out
of them, if God so will, and Doctors once again shall give the
law to Israel, and Preachers call to penance and to justice,
as at the beginning.

Yes, my Fathers and Brothers, and if it be God's blessed

will, not Saints alone, not Doctors only, not Preachers only, shall be ours,—but Martyrs, too, shall re-consecrate the soil of God. We know not what is before us, ere we win our own; we are engaged in a great, a joyful work, but in proportion to God's grace is the fury of His enemies. They have welcomed us as the lion greets his prey. Perhaps they may be familiarized in time with our appearance, but perhaps they may be irritated the more. To set up the Church again in England is too great an act to be done in a corner. We have had reason to expect that such a boom would not be given to us without a cross. It is not God's way that great blessings should descend without the sacrifice first of great sufferings. If the truth is to be spread to any wide extent among this people, how can we dream, how can we hope, that trial and trouble shall not accompany its going forth? And we have already, if it may be said without presumption, to commence our work withal, a large store of merits. We have no slight outfit for our opening warfare. Can we religiously suppose that the blood of our martyrs three centuries ago and since, shall never receive its recompense? Those priests, secular and regular, did they suffer for no end? or rather, for an end which is not yet accomplished? The long imprisonment, the fetid dungeon, the weary suspense, the tyrannous trial, the barbarous sentence, the savage execution, the rack, the gibbet, the knife, the caldron, the numberless tortures of those holy victims, O my God, are they to have no reward? Are Thy martyrs to cry from under Thine altar for their loving vengeance on this guilty people, and to cry in vain? Shall they lose life, and not gain a better life for the children of those who persecuted them? Is this Thy way, O my God, righteous and true? Is it according to Thy promise, O King of saints, if I may dare talk to Thee of justice? Did not Thou Thyself pray for Thine enemies upon the cross, and convert them? Did not Thy first Martyr win Thy great Apostle, then a persecutor, by his loving prayer? And in that day of trial and desolation for England, when hearts were pierced through and through with Mary's woe, at the crucifixion of Thy body mystical, was not every tear that flowed, and every drop of blood that was shed, the seeds of a future harvest, when they who sowed in sorrow were to reap in joy?

And as that suffering of the Martyrs is not yet recompensed, so, perchance, it is not yet exhausted. Something for what we know, remains to be undergone, to complete the necessary sacrifice. May God forbid it, for this poor nation's sake! But still, could we be surprised, my Fathers and my Brothers, if the winter even now should not yet be quite over? Have we any right to take it strange, if, in this English land, the spring-time of the Church should turn out to be an English spring, an uncertain, anxious time of hope and fear, of joy and suffer-ing,—of bright promise and budding hopes, yet withal, of keen blasts, and cold showers, and sudden storms?

One thing alone I know,—that according to our need, so will be our strength. One thing I am sure of, that the more the enemy rages against us, so much the more will the Saints in Heaven plead for us; the more fearful are our trials from the world, the more present to us will be our mother Mary, and our good Patrons and Angel Guardians; the more malicious are the devices of men against us, the louder cry of supplica-tion will ascend from the bosom of the whole Church to God for us. We shall not be left orphans; we shall have within us the strength of the Paraclete, promised to the Church and to every member of it. My Fathers, my Brothers in the priest-hood, I speak from my heart when I declare my conviction, that there is no one among you here present but, if God so willed, would readily become a martyr for His sake. I do not say you would wish it; I do not say that the natural will would not pray that that chalice might pass away; I do not speak of what you can do by any strength of yours;—but in the strength of God, in the grace of the Spirit, in the armour of justice, by the consolations and peace of the Church, by the blessing of the Apostles Peter and Paul, and in the Name of Christ, you would do what nature cannot do. By the intercession of the

Saints on high, by the penances and good works and the prayers of the people of God on earth, you would be forcibly borne up as upon the waves of the mighty deep, and carried on out of yourselves by the fulness of grace, whether nature wished it or no. I do not mean violently, or with unseemly struggle, but calmly, gracefully, sweetly, joyously, you would mount up and ride forth to the battle, as on the rush of Angels' wings, as your fathers did before you, and gained the prize. You, who day by day offer up the Immaculate Lamb of God, you who hold in your hands the Incarnate Word under the visible tokens which He has ordained, you who again and again drain the chalice of the Great Victim; who is to make you fear? what is to startle you? what to seduce you? who is to stop you, whether you are to suffer or to do, whether to lay the foundations of the Church in tears, or to put the crown upon the work in jubilation?

My Fathers, my Brothers, one word more. It may seem as if I were going out of my way in thus addressing you; but I have some sort of plea to urge in extenuation. When the English College at Rome was set up by the solicitude of a great Pontiff in the beginning of England's sorrows, and missionaries were trained there for confessorship and martyrdom here, who was it that saluted the fair Saxon youths as they passed by him in the streets of the great City, with the salutation, "Salvete flores martyrum"? And when the time came for each in turn to leave that peaceful home, and to go forth to the conflict, to whom did they betake themselves before leaving Rome, to receive a blessing which might nerve them for their work? They went for a Saint's blessing; they went to a calm old man, who had never seen blood, except in penance; who had longed indeed to die for Christ, what time the great St. Francis opened the way to the far East, but who had been fixed as if a sentinel in the holy city, and walked up and down for fifty years on one beat, while his brethren were in the battle. Oh! the fire of that heart, too great for its frail tenement, which tormented him to be kept at home when the whole Church was at war! and therefore came those bright-haired strangers to him, ere they set out for the scene of their passion, that the full zeal and love pent up in that burning breast might find a vent, and flow over, from him who was kept at home, upon those who were to face the foe. Therefore one by one, each in his turn, those youthful soldiers came to the old man; and one by one they persevered and gained the crown and the palm,— all but one, who had not gone, and would not go, for the salutary blessing.

My Fathers, my Brothers, that old man was my own St. Philip. Bear with me for his sake. If I have spoken too seriously, his sweet smile shall temper it. As he was with you three centuries ago in Rome, when our Temple fell, so now surely when it is rising, it is a pleasant token that he should have even set out on his travels to you; and that, as if remembering how he interceded for you at home, and recognizing the relations he then formed with you, he should now be wishing to have a name among you, and to be loved by you, and perchance to do you a service, here in your own land.

[*July 13, 1852.*]

XXIII

OMNIPOTENCE IN BONDS [1]

"Et descendit cum eis, et venit Nazareth: et erat subditus illis."
(*And He went down with them, and came to Nazareth; and was subject to them*).—Evang. sec. Luc., c. ii. v. 51.

AT THIS CHRISTMAS SEASON, when we are celebrating those joyful mysteries which ushered in the Gospel, it seems almost an officious intrusion upon our holiday to engage in any exercise of the reason, even though it be in order to enliven the devotional feelings proper to the holy tide. It is a time of religious rest and spiritual festivity, and even on the ground that discussion is a kind of labour, we seem to have a right to be protected against it. And yet, as the days go on, and thankfulness has had free current and joy has had its fill, it seems allowable too, to look back at length on what has been occupying the heart, and to reason upon it. Nay, we seem to have the highest of possible authorities for doing so; for after two of the joyful mysteries, the third and the fifth, the holy Virgin is said to have done this very thing. Upon the Nativity of our Lord and Saviour, the very feast we have been celebrating, the Evangelist tells us, "Mary kept all these words, *pondering* them in her heart;" and after she had found Him in the Temple in the midst of the Doctors, which is the subject of this day's Gospel, "His Mother," we are told, "kept all these words in her heart." Surely, then, it is permitted to me, consistently with the love and adoration due to this happy time of Christmas, to direct your minds, my Brethren, to a consid-

[1] Preached in the University Church, Dublin. From *Sermons Preached on Various Occasions*, No. 6. [Ed.]

eration which it suggests, not indeed very recondite, on the contrary, obvious to all of us, lying on the very face of the great Mystery, but adapted, I think, both to strengthen the faith and to deepen the love, with which we receive it into our hearts.

"The Word was made flesh, and dwelt among us;" this is the glorious, unsearchable, incomprehensible Truth, on which all our hopes for the future depend, and which we have now been commemorating. It is the wonderful Economy of Redemption, by which God became man, the Highest became the lowest, the Creator took His place among His own creatures, Power became weakness, and Wisdom looked to men like folly. He that was rich was made poor; the Lord of all was rejected: "He came unto His own, and His own received Him not." This, I say, is the grand mystery of the season, and this is the subject on which I now propose to make one remark.

I say then, my Brethren, consider what the Divine Being is, and what we mean, when we use His name. The very first idea of Him, if we make the Creed our guide, is Omnipotence: "I believe in God, the Father Almighty." And if you wish to enter into this idea of Omnipotence, and investigate what it is, trace it back into the further mystery of a past eternity. For ages innumerable, for infinite periods, long and long before any creature existed, He was. When there was no creature to exercise His power upon, still He was Omnipotent in His very Essence, as being not sovereign merely, but sole,—as the One Being, without any greater, less, or equal, full of all resources within, and in need of nothing, and, though infinitely one, yet being, at the same time, a whole infinite universe, as I may say, in Himself;—so much so that the breadth and depth and richness and variety and splendour of this created world which we behold, is simply nothing at all, compared to the vastness of that Ocean of perfection which lay concentrated in the intensity of His unity. A king of this world, though a sovereign, though an autocrat, depends on his subjects; but the Almighty God is absolutely and utterly free from any

necessary alliance with His creatures. He is complete in Himself, for this reason, if for no other, that He existed for
everlasting ages before any one of them was, and was able to
do without them for a past eternity, and then created them all
out of nothing. He borrows nothing from them; He owes
nothing whatever even to the highest of them; they, on the
contrary, owe it to Him that they are even able to remain
in their own proper nature, and they derive from Him, moment
by moment, every pulsation of their life and every ray of such
glory as they possess.

Such is the omnipotent, self-dependent God: fixed in His
own centre, and needing no point of motion or vantage-ground
out of Himself, whereupon to bring into action, or to use,
or to apply, His inexhaustible power. He can make, He
can unmake; He can decree and bring to pass, He can direct,
control, and resolve, absolutely according to His will. He could
create this vast material world, with all its suns and globes,
and its illimitable spaces, in a moment. All its overwhelming
multiplicity of laws, and complexity of formations, and in-
tricacy of contrivances, both to originate and to accomplish,
is with Him but the work of a moment. He could destroy it
all in all its parts in a moment; in the same one moment He
could create another universe instead of it, indefinitely more
vast, more beautiful, more marvellous, and indefinitely unlike
that universe which he was annihilating. He could bring into
existence and destroy an infinite series of such universes, each
in succession more perfect than that which immediately preceded it. He is the Creator, too, of all the intellectual natures
which exist, whether in the heavens above, or on the earth,
or in the regions under the earth. Angels in their nine multi-
tudinous orders, and men in their populous generations, good
spirits and bad, saints and souls on trial, the saved and the lost,
first, He created them and creates, each in its own time; and
next, He keeps the complete and exact tale of them all, as He
keeps the catalogue also of all the beasts, the birds, the fishes,
the reptiles, and insects, all over the earth. Not a sparrow falls

without Him; not a hair of our heads, but He has counted it in with the rest; and so, too, not a soul, but He has before Him its whole history from beginning to end, and its every thought, word, and deed, and its every motion through every day, and its relative place in the scale of merit and of sin.

And, while He thus intermingles His presence and His operations with an ineffable intimacy of union in every place, in every substance, in every act, everywhere, He is at the same time, as I have said, infinitely separated from everything, and absolutely incommunicable and unapproachable, and self-dependent in His own glorious Essence. Nothing can add to Him; no one can be His creditor, no one can claim anything of Him. He has no duties (if I may use such a term) towards the beings He has created. It is a saying about earthly possessions, that property has its duties as well as its privileges. Such words and such ideas apply not to the Self-subsisting, Everlasting God. He asks of His creatures, "Is it not lawful for Me to do what I will?" and St. Paul says of Him: "O man! who art thou that repliest against God? shall the thing formed say to Him who formed it, Why hast Thou made me thus?" If I must still use the word "duties" or obligations of Almighty God, I will say, that He has obligations towards Himself, but none towards us. What binds Him is the dictate of His own holy and perfect attributes. He is just and true, because His attributes are such; but we have no claims upon Him. Or, if we have claims, it is in consequence of His own gratuitous and express promise, by which indeed He does bind Himself; and then He is but faithful to His own word, because He is the Truth, and His obligation is still to Himself, and not to us. You know, my Brethren, we, in our turn, have no duties toward the brute creation; there is no relation of justice between them and us. Of course we are bound not to treat them ill, for cruelty is an offence against that holy Law which our Maker has written on our hearts, and is displeasing to Him. But *they* can claim nothing at our hands; into our hands they are absolutely delivered. We may use them, we may destroy them at our pleasure, not our wanton pleasure, but still for our own ends, for our own benefit or satisfaction, provided we can give a rational account of what we do. Now, I do not say that the case is the same between us and our Maker, but it is illustrated by this parallel. He has no account at all to render to us: He has no claims of ours to settle: we are bound to Him; He is not bound to us, except as He binds Himself: we have no merit in His sight, and can do Him no service, unless His promise brings these ideas into existence. I say, He is only bound by His own perfect Nature, infinitely good, and holy, and true, as it is; and in that is the creature's stay. If we accuse Him, He will prevail, according to the text, "that Thou mayest be justified in thy words, and mayest overcome when Thou art judged." And if we are utterly without claims upon Him as creatures, we are doubly destitute considered as sinners also: and thus, if even Angels are unprofitable in His sight, what are we?

In the words of Holy Scripture:[2] "Can a man be compared with God? What doth it profit God, if thou be just? or what dost thou give Him, if thy way be unspotted? Behold, even the moon doth not shine, and the stars are not pure in His sight. Behold, among His saints, none is unchangeable, and the heavens are not pure in His sight. Behold, they that serve Him are not steadfast, and in His Angels He found wickedness. How much more is man abominable and unprofitable, who drinketh iniquity like water! Behold, He taketh away, and who can hinder Him? Who will say to Him: What dost Thou? Why dost thou strive against Him? for He giveth not account of any of His matters."

Such is the Omnipotence, the Self-dependence, the Self-sufficiency, the infinite Liberty of the Eternal God, our Creator and Judge. And now, this being so, let me go on to the particular thought which I wish, my Brethren, to suggest to you for your reflection at this season.

It is, not merely that God became man, not merely that

[2] Job iv., ix., xv., xxii., xxv., xxxiii.

the All-possessing became destitute; but the point on which I shall particularly insist is, in contrast with what I have been enlarging on, that the All-powerful, the All-free, the Infinite, became and becomes, as the text says, "subject" to the creature; nay, not only a subject, but literally a captive, a prisoner, and that not once, but on many different occasions and in many different ways.

Now, observe, my Brethren, when the Eternal son of God came among us, He might have taken our nature, as Adam received it, from the earth, and have begun His human life at mature age; He might have been moulded under the immediate hand of the Creator; He need have known nothing of the feebleness of infancy or the slow growth of manhood. This might have been, had He so willed; but no: He preferred the penance of taking His place in the line of Adam, and of being born of a woman. This was the very scandal of the ancient heretics, as it has been of free-thinkers in all ages. They shrank from the notion of such a birth from Mary, as a something simply intolerable and past belief; and truly in that belief is the commencement of the wonderful captivity of the Infinite God, on which I am to dwell. Yet I will not do more than suggest so much of it to your devout meditation. I mean the long imprisonment He had, before His birth, in the womb of the Immaculate Mary. There was He in His human nature, who, as God, is everywhere; there was He, as regards His human soul, conscious from the first with a full intelligence, and feeling the extreme irksomeness of the prison-house, full of grace as it was.

At length He sees the light, and He is free; but free only in that His imprisonment is changed. The very first act of His Mother's on His birth, is both an example and a figure of His life-long captivity. "Mary brought forth her first-born Son, and wrapped Him up in swaddling clothes, and laid Him in a manger." It is the custom in those southern parts to treat the new-born babe in a way strange to this age and country. The infant is swathed around with cloths much resembling the

winding-sheet, the bandages and ligaments of the dead. You
may recollect, my Brethren, the account of Lazarus's revival;
how that, when miracle had lifted him up out of the tomb,
there he lay motionless, till his fastenings were cut off from
him. "He that had been dead came forth, bound foot and hand
with winding-bands; and Jesus said to them: Loose him, and
let him go." So was it with that wonder-working Lord Himself
in His own infancy. He submitted to the customs, as well as to
the ritual, of His nation; and, as He had lain so long in Mary's
womb, so now again He left that sacred prison, only that her
loving hands might manacle and fetter Him once more, inflict-
ing on Him the special penance which He had chosen. And so,
like some inanimate image of wood or stone, the All-powerful
lies in the manger, or on her bosom, doubly helpless, both
because His infancy is feeble, and because His bonds are
strong.

It is in this wise He was shown to the shepherds; thus He
was worshipped by the wise men; thus He was presented in
the Temple, taken up in Simeon's arms, hurried off to Egypt
by night, His tender Mother adoring the while that abject
captivity to which it was her awful duty to reduce Him. So
His first months passed; and though, as time went on, He grew
in stature, and burst His bonds, still through a slow and tedious
advance did He enter on His adolescence. And then, when
for a moment He anticipated His mission and sat down among
the Doctors in the Temple, He was quickly recalled by His
Mother's chiding, and went back again to her and Joseph,
and, in the emphatic words of the text, was "subject unto
them." It is said, He worked at His father's trade, not even
yet His own master, and confined till the age of thirty to the
limits of one city.

And when at length the hour came for His breaking
away from His humble home and quitting Nazareth, even
then this law of captivity, as I may call it, continued, and
that even with the circumstances of a frightful development. For is it not terrifying, so as even to scare the mind, that

in His infancy indeed His Mother's pure embrace had been His prison, but now, as a preparation for His public ministry, He is made over to His enemy, and undergoes the handling of the foul spirit himself! The rebel archangel, who would *not* be in subjection, who had assailed the throne of God, and had been cast out of heaven, he it is who now has got fast hold of the Eternal Word Incarnate, and is lifting Him up, and transporting Him according to His will; taking Him into the holy city, and setting Him upon the pinnacle of the Temple, and taking Him up into a very high mountain in order to seduce Him with the bribe of the unshackled lordship of the wide earth. "What concord hath Christ with Belial?" Yet the fiend is allowed the momentary possession of the Omnipotent.

But at least when He has begun to preach, He will be free. My Brethren, it is true; but even then the threatenings at least and the earnests of a renewed captivity pursue Him. As soon as He does miracles and collects followers, His brethren take the alarm, and try to capture Him. "When His friends had heard of it, they went out to lay hold of Him, for they said, He is become mad." When He preached in Nazareth, "the people rose and seized Him violently, and brought Him to the brow of the hill, to cast Him headlong." At another time He was in danger from His own hearers; they went about to take Him by force to make Him a king. At another time, "the Scribes and Pharisees sent ministers to apprehend Him." At another time, Herod was about to seize Him and put Him to death.

At length He is to die for us; but still that sacrifice of Himself was not to please Him, if imprisonment was away. He allowed Himself, in the Church's words, "manibus tradi nocentium," to be given into the hands of the violent. Now, I ask, what need of this superfluity of humiliation? He was to shed His blood and die; doubtless: but in the manifold dispositions of Providence there were many ways whereby to die, without falling into the fierce handling of jailers and hangmen. He might have taken upon Himself the mode of satisfying the Divine Decree, and have dispensed with the instrumentality of man. We read in history of kings going to death, who refused the assistance of the executioner, and submitted to their fate by their own act. And it was in order to remind us that He *need* not have undergone that profanation, that, on His enemies first approaching Him, He smote them to the ground. And again, it was in order to impress upon us that He *did* undergo it, that He touchingly asked them: "Are ye come out as to a robber, with swords and clubs, to apprehend Me? but this is your hour and the power of darkness."

Thus He spoke, and that expostulation was the immediate signal for those special indignities to begin in which He chose to invest His passion and death. He who was submitted to the wine-press in Gethsemani, and agonized with none to see Him but Apostles and attendant Angels, might surely have gone through His solemn sacrifice in solitude, as He commenced it; but He preferred the "hands of men;" He preferred the loathsome kiss of the traitor; He preferred the staves and swords of the ministers of a fallen priesthood; He preferred to die in the midst of a furious mob, haling Him to and fro; under the fists and scourges and hammers of savage lictors; now shut up in a dungeon, now dragged before the judgment-seat, now tied to a pillar, now nailed to the Cross, and then at length, when the worst was over, and His soul was fled, hurried as the best His friends could do for Him, hurried into a narrow sepulchre of stone. O marvellous dispensation, full of mystery! that the God of Nature, the Lord of the Universe, should take to Himself a body to suffer and die in; nor only so, but should not even allow Himself the birthright of man, should refuse to be master of His own limbs, and outgrow the necessity of a Mother's arms, only to present Himself to the tyrannous grasp of the heathen soldiers.

And now surely, my Brethren, we are come to the end of these wonders. He tore open the solid rock; He rose from the tomb; He ascended on high; He is far off from the earth; He is safe from profanation; and the soul and body, which

He assumed, partake of course, as far as created nature allows, of the Sovereign Freedom and the Independence of Omnipotence. It is not so: He is indeed beyond the reach of suffering; but you anticipate, my Brethren, what I have yet to say. Is He then so enamoured of the prison, that He should purpose to revisit earth again, in order that, as far as possible, He may undergo it still? Does He set such a value on subjection to His creatures, that, before He goes away, on the very eve of His betrayal, He must actually make provision, after death, for perpetuating His captivity to the end of the world? My Brethren, the great truth is daily before our eyes: He has ordained the standing miracle of His Body and Blood under visible symbols, that He may secure thereby the standing mystery of Omnipotence in bonds.

He took bread, and blessed, and made it His Body; He took wine, and gave thanks, and made it His Blood; and He gave His priests the power to do what He had done. Henceforth, He is in the hands of sinners once more. Frail, ignorant, sinful man, by the sacerdotal power given to him, compels the presence of the Highest; he lays Him up in a small tabernacle; he dispenses Him to a sinful people. Those who are only just now cleansed from mortal sin, open their lips for Him; those who are soon to return to mortal sin, receive Him into their breasts; those who are polluted with vanity and selfishness and ambition and pride, presume to make Him their guest; the frivolous, the tepid, the worldly-minded, fear not to welcome Him. Alas! alas! even those who wish to be more in earnest, entertain Him with cold and wandering thoughts, and quench that Love which would inflame them with Its own fire, did they but open to It. Such are the best of us; and then for the worst? O my Brethren, what shall we say of sacrilege? of His reception into hearts polluted with mortal unforsaken sin? of those further nameless profanations, which from time to time occur, when unbelief dares to present itself at the Holy Altar, and blasphemously gains possession of Him?

My Brethren, it is plain that, when we confess God as

Omnipotent only, we have gained but a half-knowledge of Him: His is an Omnipotence which can at the same time swathe Itself in infirmity and can become the captive of Its own creatures. He has, if I may so speak, the incomprehensible power of even making Himself weak. We must know Him by His Names, Emmanuel and Jesus, to know Him perfectly.

One word more before I conclude. Some persons may consider that a thought, such as that I have been enlarging on, is a difficulty to faith. Every one has his own trials and his own scandals: I grant it. For me, my Brethren, I can only say that its effect on myself lies just in the very opposite direction, and, awful as it is, it does but suggest an incentive, as for adoration, so for faith also. What human teacher could thus open for us an insight into the infinitude of the Divine Counsels? Eye of man hath not seen the face of God; and heart of man could never have conceived or invented so wonderful a manifestation, as the Gospel contains, of His ineffable, overwhelming Attributes. I believe the infinite condescension of the Highest to be true, because it has been imagined. Moreover, I recognize it to be true, just as I believe in the laws of this material world, according as human science elicits them; viz. because I see here the silent operation, beneath the surface, of a great principle, which is not seen till it is investigated. I adore a truth, which, though patent to all who look for it, yet, to be seen in its consistency and symmetry, *has* to be looked for. And further, I glory in it, for I see in it the most awful antagonism to the very idea and essence of sin, whether as existing in Angels or in men. For what was the sin of Lucifer, but the resolve to be his own master? What was the sin of Adam, but impatience of subjection, and a desire to be his own god? What is the sin of all his children, but the movement, not of passion merely, not of selfishness, not of unbelief, but of pride, of the heart rising against the law of God, and set on being emancipated from its trammels? What is the sin of Antichrist, but, as St. Paul says, that of being "the

Lawless One," of "opposing or being lifted up against all that is called God, or worshipped, so that he sitteth in the temple of God, showing himself as if he were God"? If, then, the very principle of sin is insubordination, is there not a stupendous meaning in the fact, that He, the Eternal, who alone is sovereign and supreme, has given us an example in His own Person of that love of subjection, which in Him alone is simply voluntary, but in all creatures is an elementary duty?

O my Brethren, let us blush at our own pride and self-will. Let us call to mind our impatience at God's providences towards us, our wayward longings after what cannot be, our headstrong efforts to reverse His just decrees, our bootless conflicts with the stern necessities which hem us in, our irritation at ignorance or suspense about His will, our fierce, passionate wilfulness when we see that will too clearly, our haughty contempt of His ordinances, our determination to do things for ourselves without Him, our preference of our own reason to His word,—the many, many shapes in which the Old Adam shows itself, and one or other of which our conscience tells us is our own; and let us pray Him who is independent of us all, yet who at this season became as though our fellow and our servant, to teach us our place in His wide universe, and to make us ambitious only of that grace here and glory hereafter, which He has purchased for us by His own humiliation.

[*January 13, 1857.*]

INDEX

[The publishers here wish to acknowledge their indebtedness to Mr. R. Lawrence Davis, who compiled the index.]

opposes the natural to the supernatural, 167 ff.; and the Church, the essential opposition of, 168 f., 181 f.; slanders the Church and ridicules its doctrines, 181 f.; cannot comprehend God's munificence and condescension, 223 f.; hates the mortifications of the Saints, 224; ascribes the miracle of the Church to Satan as it did the miracles of Christ, 327.

Zacharias, 64, 65.
Zeno, 76.
Zorobabel, 199.

$$\frac{2001s}{30°}$$